# Economic Globalisation

# Economic Globalisation

## Social Conflicts, Labour and Environmental Issues

*Edited by*

Clem Tisdell

*Professor of Economics, School of Economics, University of Queensland, Australia*

Raj Kumar Sen

*Professor of Economics, Department of Economics, Rabindra Bharati University, Kolkata, India*

**Edward Elgar**

Cheltenham, UK • Northampton, MA, USA

Published by
Edward Elgar Publishing Limited
Glensanda House
Montpellier Parade
Cheltenham
Glos GL50 1UA
UK

Edward Elgar Publishing, Inc.
136 West Street
Suite 202
Northampton
Massachusetts 01060
USA

This book has been printed on demand to keep the title in print.

A catalogue record for this book
is available from the British Library

ISBN 1 84376 315 X (cased)

# Contents

# List of Figures

# List of Tables

# List of Contributors

**Dr M. Zainul Abedin**

Dr M. Zainul Abedin is Professor of Economics at the postgraduate research organisation, Institute of Bangladesh Studies (IBS), Rajshahi University, Bangladesh. He has written several books and over fifty articles on research methodology, finance and banking, development economics and rural development.

**Dr Joseph C.H. Chai**

Dr Joseph C.H. Chai is Associate Professor in the School of Economics at The University of Queensland. He has written extensively on the Chinese economy. His recent books include *The Economic Development of Modern China* and *China: Transition to a Market Economy.*

**Professor Ruddar Datt**

Professor Ruddar Datt is a Visiting Professor of Economics at the Institute for Human Development, Delhi. He is a previous President of the Indian Economic Association and the Indian Society of Labour Economics. He is also the retired Principal of the School of Correspondence Courses, University of New Delhi.

**Dr Andrew K. Dragun**

Dr Andrew Dragun has published extensively on environmental and economic issues and has undertaken consultancies with the FAO and the World Bank in various developing countries. He holds a PhD from the University of Wisconsin and has held teaching and administrative positions at the Australian National University, University of Wollongong, La Trobe University, the Swedish University of Agricultural Sciences, and the University of New England, as well as visiting positions at Resources for the Future, The University of Queensland, and the University of Victoria. He was the founding editor of the *International Journal for Agricultural Resources, Globalisation and Ecology* in 1999, and edited it until 2003. He is now applying his experience in the private sector.

**Dr Dilip Dutta**

Dr Dilip Dutta is Director of the *Centre for South Asian Studies* at the University of Sydney and Editor of *International Journal of Development Issues*. His research interests include three distinct areas: (i) endogenous growth analysis and its links with trade liberalisation, environmental degradation, information and communication technology development in Asia and other regions; (ii) methodological foundations of socio-economic analysis, especially for the dualistic economies; and (iii) theoretical models of growth and development under conditions of structural disequilibrium in dualistic economies. Apart from his publications in journals such as *Journal of Interdisciplinary Economics, Applied Economics, International Journal of Social Economics, Economic Papers, Indian Economic Review, Journal of Contemporary Asia*, he has contributed chapters to several edited books.

**Professor B.N. Ghosh**

Professor B. N. Ghosh is a Visiting Professor of Economics at Eastern Mediterranean University, North Cyprus and the Director of the Centre of the Study of Human Development, Leeds. He held a professorial position in Malaysia for over a decade. Publishers of his work include Arnold-Heinemann, Ashgate Publishing, Macmillan, Longman and Routledge.

**Dr John Gowdy**

Dr John Gowdy is Professor of Economics at Rensselaer Polytechnic Institute and Director of the PhD Programme in Ecological Economics. His recent books include *Paradise for Sale: A Parable of Nature and Limited Wants* and *Unlimited Means: A Reader on Hunter-Gatherer Economics and the Environment.*

**Dr Colin Hunt**

Dr Colin Hunt was a Senior Research Fellow at the National Research Institute, Port Moresby. He is currently Director of Research and Consulting for Economy and Environment, Queensland. Dr Colin Hunt has been researching and providing policy advice to governments and international agencies on economics and the environment in Oceania for over 20 years. He specialises in issues of development and environment in the Pacific region, and publishes extensively on the exploitation and conservation of marine and forest resources.

**Raluca Iorgulescu**

Raluca Iorgulescu is a PhD candidate in Ecological Economics at Rensselaer Polytechnic Institute. Her areas of interest include the role of institutions in economic development and the problems of transitional economies. Her research has been strongly influenced by the work of Nicholas Georgescu-Roegen.

**Dr Kristin M. Jakobsson**

Dr Kristin Jakobsson has published papers and books on non-market valuation, biodiversity conservation, water and soil management, gender and environment, globalisation, and sustainability, and was co-editor of the *International Journal for Agricultural Resources, Globalisation and Ecology* from 2001 to 2003. She has held teaching positions at La Trobe University in Melbourne, Australia, and at the Swedish University of Agricultural Sciences, as well as visiting positions at The University of Queensland. She is currently putting economic theory into practice in private enterprise.

**Professor Amarjit Kaur**

Amarjit Kaur is Professor of Economic History at the University of New England. She has written widely on changing labour relations in Southeast Asia. Her most recent book, *Wage Labour in Southeast Asia since 1840,* and an edited book, *Women Workers in Industrializing Asia,* are published by Palgrave.

**Professor W.D. Lakshman**

W.D. Lakshman [BA (Ceylon); D.Phil. (Oxford)] is currently Senior Professor of Economics, University of Colombo, and was previously the Dean, Faculty of Graduate Studies, and the Vice Chancellor of the University of Colombo. His numerous publications include *Dilemmas of Development: Fifty Years of Economic Change in Sri Lanka* (Sri Lanka Association of Economists, 1997) and (edited jointly with Clement Tisdell) *Sri Lanka's Development since Independence: Socio-Economic Perspectives and Analyses* (Nova Science, 2000).

**Dr Laurence Lasselle**

Dr Laurence Lasselle is Lecturer at the University of St Andrews. She gained her PhD in 1996 from the University of Aix-Marseille II, France. Her research interests lie in the area of macroeconomics, especially in macroeconomic analysis involving imperfect competition. Recently, she was awarded a Jean Monnet Research Fellowship tenable at the European University Institute, Florence.

**Yanmei Lin**

Yanmei Lin is a postgraduate student in the School of Law, Fudan University, Shanghai, PR China and has a particular interest in international law, especially as it relates to environmental issues.

**Dr Steve Onyeiwu**

Dr Steve Onyeiwu is an Assistant Professor of Economics at Allegheny College, Meadville, Pennsylvania, USA. He has previously taught at the University of Port Harcourt, Nigeria, Wesleyan University, Trinity College, and Rensselaer Polytechnic Institute, all in the United States. His research interests include development economics, political economy, and industrial organisation.

**Dr U. Sankar**

Dr U. Sankar is Honorary Professor and Member Secretary, Centre of Excellence in Environmental Economics in the Madras School of Economics, India. He is at present a National Fellow of the Indian Council of Social Science Research. He was President of the Indian Econometric Society, 1993-94.

**Professor Raj Kumar Sen**

Raj Kumar Sen is Professor of Economics and Head of Department of Economics at the Rabindra Bharati University, Kolkata, India. He is also President of the Indian Economic Association and President of the Bengal Economic Association. He has many publications to his credit.

**Dr Serge Svizzero**

Dr Serge Svizzero is Professor of Economics in the Faculté de Droit et des Sciences Economiques at Université de la Réunion, France. He is Director of CERESUR and Vice-President of the Scientific Council of the University of La Reunion. He has published academic articles dealing with unemployment and with globalisation issues in journals such as *Oxford Economic Papers*, *Journal of Economic Surveys* and *Intereconomics: Review of European Economic Policy*.

**Professor Clem Tisdell**

Clem Tisdell is Professor of Economics at The University of Queensland. He has published widely on social, economic and environmental issues. He was a joint recipient (with Serge Svizzero) of a FEAST-France Award in 2002-2003 for collaborative EU-Australian research on economic globalisation. His recent books include *Ecological and Environmental Economics* and *Economics and Ecology in Agriculture and Marine Production*.

**Dr Mariel Tisdell**

Since her retirement from the position of Senior Lecturer, Dr Mariel Tisdell has been an Honorary Research Adviser to the School of Languages and Cross Cultural Studies at The University of Queensland. She has published widely in the areas of language policies, second language acquisition and curriculum studies. Currently she is also a consultant and occasional writer in Curriculum Strategies with the State Department of Education in Brisbane, Queensland.

**Dr Dayuan Xue**

Dr Dayuan Xue is Professor at the Nature Conservation Division at the Nanjing Institute of Environmental Sciences, State Environmental Protection Administration, China. For two years, he was a Postdoctoral Research Fellow in Economics at The University of Queensland. He is author or editor of several books and has many journal articles to his credit.

# Preface

A rapid increase in international interdependence, a phenomenon often described as increased globalisation, has occurred in recent decades. Globalisation is a complex multidimensional process – increased international economic interdependence is just one aspect of it. This book concentrates on its economic dimensions but in doing so does not ignore other dimensions, such as cultural and social ones, because all of its dimensions are interdependent.

This book was originally conceived in 2000 when issues involving economic globalisation were at the centre of the world political stage. Clem Tisdell met with Raj Kumar Sen during one of his visits to India. They discussed the idea of editing a book on economic globalisation that would include contributors from developing countries, as well as from higher income nations, and give particular attention to social conflicts, labour and environmental issues. The resulting product is this book.

At the turn of the twentieth century and in the early twenty-first century, public concern (especially in higher-income countries) about the possible social, environmental and economic consequences of globalisation reached a crescendo. This is highlighted by demonstrations in many cities in Europe and in the USA. The demonstrations that accompanied the WTO Millennium Meeting in Seattle, some of which were violent, underline the depth of public feeling at the time.

Currently (2003), the so-called 'war on terrorism' may have moved questions about economic globalisation from the centre of the world political stage. Yet, even today's terrorism is international and appears to be linked with globalisation processes. For example, the deep involvement of some nations, such as the USA, in globalisation processes make them vulnerable to terrorist attacks. Furthermore, some terrorist organisations struggling against major centre countries may gain support from the perception that these countries, especially the USA, are using globalisation to their own advantage and foisting their culture on less powerful nations.

Nevertheless, issues involving globalisation are not going to disappear in the foreseeable future, as is perhaps highlighted by the public demonstrations that accompanied the G8 Summit in France in June 2003. Furthermore, the failure of the WTO meeting in Cancun, Mexico, in September 2003 does not mean that processes of globalisation have finished. However, it may proceed more now by means of regional agreements, aspects of which are addressed in Chapter 4 of this book. The agenda of official international organisations, such as the WTO, IMF and World Bank, still favour the extension of market systems, that is, the continuing implementation of structural adjustment policies involving substantial economic liberalisation. There is no indication of any major deviation from this agenda. No plans exist to roll back the degree of globalisation already experienced and further increases in the extent of economic globalisation seem probable. We need to know more about the economic, social, cultural and environmental consequences that stem from economic globalisation. We need to explore both its possible pleasant and unpleasant aspects. Contributions to this book help to fill this need.

We would like to thank all those who have contributed chapters to this book. Its production has been in itself a major exercise in international cooperation. Furthermore, we would like to thank everyone who helped in reviewing manuscripts. Apart from those contributors who reviewed the manuscripts of other contributors, reviewers included Mohammad Alauddin, Gareth Leeves, Tony Makin, Maxine Pitt, Jackie Robinson and Clevo Wilson.

We are grateful for the permission given by Peter Nicholson, of *The Australian* to Andrew Dragun and Kristin Jacobsson to reproduce the cartoons included in Chapter 10, each of which is given the following credit: 'Cartoon by Nicholson of *The Australian*: http://www.nicholsoncartoons.com.au/'. Also, we are grateful to John Wiley & Sons Limited for permission granted to Dr J.C.H. Chai, to reproduce materials in Chapter 8 of this book which originally appeared in J.C.H. Chai, 'Trade and environment: evidence from China's manufacturing sector', *Sustainable Development*, **10**(1), 2002 ©John Wiley & Sons Limited. This material is produced with permission.

Alison Mohr and Genevieve Larsen assisted with the copy-editing and formatting of manuscripts and Dr Glyn Edwards kindly helped with checking the final proofs. We wish to thank them sincerely for their efforts. The typescript was finalised in the School of Economics at The University of Queensland and we appreciate the support provided by it. Finally, we thank Edward Elgar for agreeing to publish this book and our families for their patience while we were editing it.

*Clem Tisdell*
*Brisbane, Australia*

*Raj Kumar Sen*
*Kolkata, India*

# PART I

# BACKGROUND

# 1. An Overview of Economic Globalisation: Its Momentum and its Consequences Examined

**Clem Tisdell and Raj Kumar Sen**

## 1.1 INTRODUCTION

The general pattern of human development during recent centuries has been for communities/nations throughout the world to become more closely interconnected in economic, social and other dimensions. Furthermore, there is a widespread perception that processes of globalisation have accelerated in recent decades. For example, in the economic sphere since about the mid-1970s, sustained efforts have been made to reduce barriers to international commerce, such as tariff and non-tariff barriers to trade.

GATT (General Agreement on Tariffs and Trade) and its successor, the WTO (World Trade Organisation) have played a leading role in fostering policies to reduce barriers to international commerce. Other international bodies, such as the IMF (International Monetary Fund) and the World Bank, have fulfilled an important complementary role by favouring structural adjustment policies designed to promote small government sectors and encourage substantial reliance on free market mechanisms for economic decision-making. This preference for free markets extends to international trade in goods and services, foreign currency exchange and international movements of capital, for instance involving foreign direct investments.

The long-term tendency has been for the degree of economic integration of the different regions of the world to increase, although this process has not been a steady one, nor always in the same direction and has not been even geographically. After World War II from around 1945 to about the mid-1970s, inward-looking economic policies dominated the global economic climate and restricted economic globalisation. These policies favoured protection for local industries, particularly manufacturing industries. But a political swing against protectionism gathered momentum from the early 1970s onward. This, coupled with continuing reductions in transport and communication costs, contributed greatly to growing economic globalisation. This process is likely to continue, even if it is not always at the rapid pace experienced during the last two to three decades of the twentieth century. Furthermore, temporary setbacks in the direction of economic globalisation are bound to be experienced from time to time.

The processes of growing globalisation, economic and otherwise, create new economic adjustments and political challenges for us all. The ability of national governments to act independently on economic and social policies is reduced by growing global economic interdependence. Given the reduced ability of national governments to regulate economic, social, environmental and cultural change, there is likely to be a growing need for internationally coordinated global political action to deal with any undesirable changes in these variables as a result of growing globalisation and international interdependence. However, the economic, social, environmental and cultural consequences of economic globalisation still remain uncertain. This is partly reflected in the social conflict that often surrounds policy measures to promote greater economic globalisation and in hostility of some groups towards international bodies, such as the WTO, seen by many member of the public as champions of economic globalisation (see Tisdell, Chapter 6 in this book).

In the short to medium term, not all social groups, and possibly not every nation, gains from processes of economic globalisation and this creates considerable social conflict and tension. The main purpose of this book is to explore economic, social and environmental conflicts arising from economic globalisation. Contributions are intended to identify the economic changes (and to some extent, broader social changes) that have, or might occur, as globalisation proceeds, especially in relation to labour markets and environmental matters. Particular attention is given to the sources of social conflicts generated by globalisation within nations, and between nations, especially between less developed and higher income nations, and the possibilities for resolving these conflicts. Nevertheless, some contributors (for example, Abedin) also stress the benefits of economic globalisation and the relative absence of social conflict for some nations (for example, Bangladesh) or observe that in the subject area of their study (for example, the food sector in West Bengal), economic globalisation has as yet had comparatively little impact. Worldwide the economic and social impacts of globalisation remain quite uneven between regions and views about its consequences differ considerably. As pointed out by Mittleman (2000, p. 922), 'globalisation involves a series of interactions among the economic, political and cultural spheres of life. It also appears in diverse sizes and shapes in different regions'.

The coverage of this book is divided into four parts.

1. Socioeconomic conflicts arising from economic globalisation: overview and general issues.
2. Differing perspectives of developing and higher income countries about globalisation
3. Labour issues and distributional conflicts arising from globalisation
4. Environmental impacts of globalisation

This chapter belongs to Part I and is developed by first presenting empirical data to highlight changes in the extent of globalisation that have occurred in recent decades. Then follows an overview of the contributions arranged in accordance with the parts just listed, followed by concluding observations.

## 1.2 THE GROWING IMPORTANCE OF ECONOMIC GLOBALISATION IN RECENT TIMES – EMPIRICAL EVIDENCE

Although economic globalisation has many dimensions, measurement of most indicate that the overall extent of economic globalisation has increased considerably since the early to mid-1970s. Here, world exports of goods and services as a percentage of global GDP, and foreign direct investment as a percentage of GDP are mainly used to indicate the extent of economic globalisation.

Figure 1.1 sets out the general pattern of variations in the extent of globalisation as measured by world exports (of goods and services) as a percentage of GDP for the period 1950-2004. The graph is based on the observations specified in Table 1.1. After remaining relatively stationary in the period 1958 to 1972 in the range 11 to a little over 12 per cent, this indicator suddenly shot up in 1973 and 1974 and from then on, continued an upward trend with fluctuations. By 2002, this indicator stood at almost 25 per cent. Consequently, world exports of goods and services accounted for almost a quarter of world GDP whereas prior to 1973 these exports accounted for a much lower proportion of global GDP, namely an eighth or less of world GDP.

It is worthwhile noting that beginning in about the mid-1970s, economic inequality in incomes within rich countries began to increase markedly and this inequality has risen as economic globalisation has proceeded. The extent to which this growing inequality is a result of growing economic globalisation is one of the issues discussed in this book (see also, Svizzero and Tisdell 2002; Tisdell and Svizzero 2003).

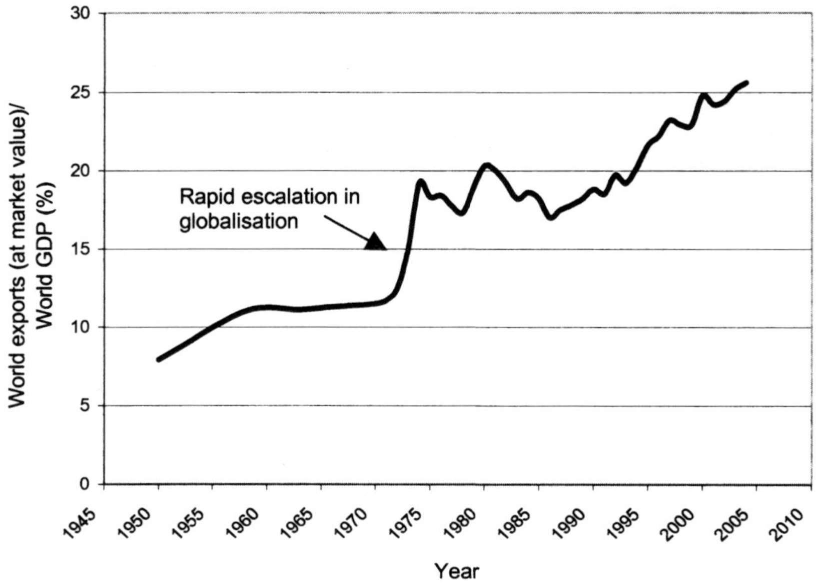


*Source*: Based on Table 1.1.

*Figure 1.1 Generalised graph of world exports (goods plus services) as a percentage of world GDP, 1950-2004, based on IMF, WTO and United Nations statistics. The figures for 2003 and 2004 are estimates*

A second possible indicator of the growing importance of globalisation is the trend in world foreign direct investment as a percentage of world GDP. This is graphed in Figure 1.2 for the period 1970 to 1998 on the basis of Table 1.2. This indicator shows an upward exponential-like trend since 1970. Whereas foreign direct investment amounted to less than a quarter of a per cent of global GDP in 1970 by 1998 it was about ten times larger in relation to global GDP. This is a further indication of the momentum of economic globalisation in recent years.

In addition, there has been considerable expansion in international short-term financial flows in recent decades. While the role of these is not a focus of this book, there has been considerable speculation that such large movements of flows can destabilise the world economy (Eatwell and Taylor 2000). Such large international monetary flows can have destabilising consequences not only for money markets but also for aggregate levels of economic production and employment.

*Table 1.1 World exports (goods plus services) as a percentage of global GDP, 1950-2004*

| Year | % | Year | % |
|---|---|---|---|
| 1950 | 7.9 | 1986 | 17.0 |
| 1958 | 11.0 | 1987 | 17.5 |
| 1963 | 11.1 | 1988 | 17.8 |
| 1966 | 11.3 | 1989 | 18.2 |
| 1970 | 11.5 | 1990 | 18.8 |
| 1971 | 11.7 | 1991 | 18.5 |
| 1972 | 12.5 | 1992 | 19.7 |
| 1973 | 15.1 | 1993 | 19.2 |
| 1974 | 19.2 | 1994 | 20.2 |
| 1975 | 18.3 | 1995 | 21.6 |
| 1976 | 18.4 | 1996 | 22.2 |
| 1977 | 17.7 | 1997 | 23.2 |
| 1978 | 17.3 | 1998 | 22.9 |
| 1979 | 18.9 | 1999 | 22.9 |
| 1980 | 20.3 | 2000 | 24.8 |
| 1981 | 20.0 | 2001 | 24.2 |
| 1982 | 19.2 | 2002 | 24.4 |
| 1983 | 18.2 | 2003 | 25.2* |
| 1984 | 18.6 | 2004 | 25.6* |
| 1985 | 18.2 | | |

*Note*: * Estimates.

*Source*: IMF, *World Economic Outlook* Database April 2003; United Nations, *Statistical Year Book*; WTO, *Doho WTO Ministerial 2001 Briefing Notes*.

The upsurge in international monetary flows was stimulated by the replacement of the Bretton Woods relatively fixed international exchange system by a flexible exchange rate system largely market determined. Eatwell (1993) points out that in 1971, just before the collapse of the 'fixed' foreign exchange system, about 90 per cent of all foreign exchange transactions financed trade and long-term investment, and only about 10 per cent were short-term, primarily speculative, capital movements (compare Hogan, 1995). By the early 1990s, these percentages were reversed, with short-term money flows accounting for 90 per cent of daily foreign exchange turnover. Such daily ('speculative') flows exceeded the combined foreign exchange reserves of all the world's major economies.

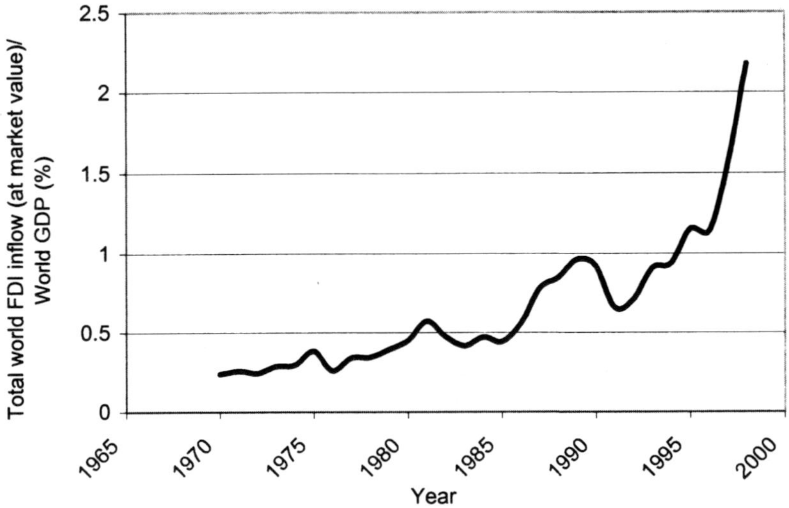


*Source*: Based on Table 1.2.

*Figure 1.2 Generalised graph of total world FDI inflows as a percentage of world GDP, 1970-1998, based on IMF and World Bank statistics*

In fact, speculative short-term money flows in relation to world trade continued to grow rapidly with liberalisation of international monetary markets. Eatwell and Taylor (2000, p. 4) report that average daily foreign exchange trading in 1995 in relation to world exports reached a ratio of nearly 70 to 1. In their view, the sheer speed and scale of short-term international monetary movements have produced a succession of major financial crises. They find that the relatively privatised international financial system is highly volatile and susceptible to contagion (Eatwell and Taylor 2000, p. 5). It places all nations at increasing economic risk in their view.

A large quantity of the short-term monetary funds flowing internationally is managed by professional funds managers. They move finance internationally to exploit anticipated profitable opportunities, such as expected exchange rate variations, and abandon stock markets thought to be likely to move in an unfavourable direction. International money markets therefore become increasingly subject to speculation from a growing wall of finance. Individual governments have little power to control the financial gyrations that can emerge. Nevertheless, international financial markets can play a useful role in directing and expanding economic activity if participants act on the basis of economic fundamentals. But they can become destabilising, disrupt and distort global economic activity if they are driven mainly by speculative motives.

*Table 1.2 Aggregate world FDI inflows as a percentage of world GDP, 1970-1998*

| Year | % | Year | % |
|---|---|---|---|
| 1970 | 0.24 | 1985 | 0.44 |
| 1971 | 0.26 | 1986 | 0.56 |
| 1972 | 0.24 | 1987 | 0.78 |
| 1973 | 0.29 | 1988 | 0.85 |
| 1974 | 0.30 | 1989 | 0.96 |
| 1975 | 0.38 | 1990 | 0.92 |
| 1976 | 0.26 | 1991 | 0.66 |
| 1977 | 0.34 | 1992 | 0.71 |
| 1978 | 0.34 | 1993 | 0.91 |
| 1979 | 0.39 | 1994 | 0.94 |
| 1980 | 0.45 | 1995 | 1.15 |
| 1981 | 0.57 | 1996 | 1.14 |
| 1982 | 0.47 | 1997 | 1.56 |
| 1983 | 0.41 | 1998 | 2.18 |
| 1984 | 0.47 | | |

*Sources*: IMF, *World Economic Outlook Database* April 2003; IMF and World Bank, Country Status Reports (various).

Thus this brief background indicates that there was comparatively little increase in economic globalisation from the beginning of the 1950s to the early 1970s. However, from the early 1970s onwards, economic globalisation accelerated. This is reflected in the upsurge in global international exports as a percentage of global GDP in the first half of the 1970s, the burgeoning of short-term international financial flows starting at a similar time, as well as commencement of exponential growth in global FDI as a percentage of world GDP. The pattern of growth in FDI indicates that at first, in the 1970s, its expansion was relatively slow but accelerated after the mid-1980s. This pattern may reflect lags in the policies of many nations in reducing their restrictions on FDI and the timing of economic transition of Communist and former Communist countries into the market system, and their increased integration with the world economy.

Given this broad background about the momentum of economic globalisation in recent times, consider now the economic globalisation issues raised by individual contributors to this book.

## 1.3 GENERAL ISSUES INVOLVING GLOBALISATION COVERED IN THE REMAINDER OF PART I

General background issues posed by globalisation are covered in the three remaining contributions in this part of this book. W.D. Lakshman debates the question of whether globalisation is inevitable and whether there are acceptable alternatives to it. Cultural and linguistic inequalities arise as a result of the processes of globalisation. Mariel Tisdell identifies these types of inequalities and considers ways in which cultural and linguistic inequalities arising from globalisation can be addressed. Economic regionalism (the formation of economic and political blocs of countries) may be an alternative to, or a step towards, greater economic globalisation. Furthermore, economic regionalism along with greater economic globalisation developed significantly in the last half of the twentieth century. Svizzero, Lasselle and Tisdell discuss whether involvement in regionalism is a viable alternative for nations to their greater involvement in the global economy, and whether or not regionalism is a response to insufficient or excessive globalisation. Consider now each of the contributions in a little more detail.

In Chapter 2, Professor Lakshman focuses on whether economic globalisation combined with liberal economic policies constitutes the ideal strategy for increasing the wealth of nations and the welfare of their peoples. He argues that many advocates of globalisation have oversold such a strategy as an ideal one for economic development, whereas many critics of globalisation have made wild allegations about its ill effects. In his view, a stark economic liberalisation-globalisation policy is not the most effective development strategy nor a highly desirable one. Therefore, there is a need to search for alternatives. Two different approaches are, in fact, being explored, One group of thinkers, for example some socialists and activists, want to reject globalisation altogether, or virtually do so. They are seeking alternatives to globalisation. The second group accepts globalisation but believes that it should be combined with appropriate state (and global institutional) intervention. They, therefore, reject the ultra-liberal economic platform of the liberalisation-globalisation strategy. Lakshman pursues this approach and suggests that it provides the best prospect for the economic development of some less developed countries. In his view, an ultra-liberal globalised economy favours more developed countries relative to less developed ones, and could hamper the potential economic development of some less developed countries. This view has some similarities to that of Stiglitz (2002). Basically, however, Lakshman's contribution is a plea for open-mindedness and alternative thinking about this matter in view of the fact that global thought seems to have become locked into the desirability/inevitability of the economic liberalism-globalisation strategy.

Increasing globalisation has been accompanied by growing international migration, despite restrictions on immigration in most countries. Consequently, the presence of cultural and linguistic minority groups in higher income economies has become more widespread. Such minority groups frequently suffer from cultural and linguistic deprivation, and economic and social disadvantage. While international human movements are not new, they are now occurring at a speed and on a scale that makes it difficult for governments to address such issues. Furthermore, if international income inequality continues to exist or grow in magnitude (discussed in Chapter 5), economic motives for international migration will remain strong or intensify.

Mariel Tisdell provides a historical background to such language and cultural issues in Chapter 3 and outlines the language policies that governments have adopted to address these matters. The matters are complex. They arise from migration across existing national boundaries and from the creation of more permeable national boundaries allowing migration within an economic union, such as occurs within the confederate-like structure of the EU. Mariel Tisdell gives particular attention to the language policies of the EU and considers to what extent these may be a model for other countries to emulate. The EU has both to address language needs arising from the diversity of established languages within the EU and consider what to do about language policies for its immigrants speaking languages other than those established in the EU.

In Chapter 4, Svizzero, Lasselle and Tisdell provide historical background on the development of multilateralism and regionalism. They note that the United States began to push politically for multilateralism in the second part of the twentieth century in order to gain access to foreign markets, many of which were protected before World War II under colonial arrangements. However, subsequently the United States shifted to a two-pronged approach. On the one hand, it favoured multilateralism but also entered into preferential trade agreements with particular nations or groups of nations when these seemed advantageous to it. This appears to be present policy of the United States.

They also consider whether regionalism is a useful stepping stone to further globalisation, an alternative, or an impediment to it. They conclude that regional (sub-global) integration allows economic integration to proceed and at the same time limits problems arising from lack of world political integration. It, therefore, can be considered to be a second-best strategy. The development of global economic interdependence is occurring at a faster rate than global political integration. Lack of global political integration is highlighted by the inability of the United Nations to prevent the 2003 military attack on Iraq led by the United States.

It might also be observed that much of the upsurge in world international trade and FDI in relation to global GDP can be attributed to the growth of regionalism rather than multilateralism itself. Figures 1.1 and 1.2 should also be considered in this light.

## 1.4 GAINS OF DEVELOPING COUNTRIES AND HIGHER INCOME COUNTRIES FROM ECONOMIC GLOBALISATION: THE DIFFERENT PERSPECTIVES IN PART II

There are six different contributions in Part II and the broad coverage of each is as follows. Tisdell, Lasselle and Svizzero in the first contribution consider whether or not growing globalisation can be expected to increase or decrease economic inequality between nations. This is an important issue because growing inequality in the wealth of nations can be a major source of international tension and conflict. Next, Tisdell discusses conflicts that have arisen between developing and higher income countries about labour and environmental standards, as highlighted as the Millennium Meeting of the WTO, and examines the case for such standards. Ruddar Datt concentrates on globalisation from an Indian and developing country perspective and concentrates on India's experience. However, even within India, economic globalisation has been very uneven. This is confirmed by the study of Raj Kumar Sen of the food sector in West Bengal. He finds that this sector has been little influenced so far by economic globalisation. Gowdy, Iorgulescu and Onyeiwu report on a comparative study of two villages in Nigeria; a new one that is directly dependent on and connected to the global economy, and another established one that acts as a 'feeder' for the new one. They observe significant differences in the social fabric of these two villages and in their economic conditions. For instance, the 'feeder' village has experienced disintegration of its institutions and significant social problems, some as a result of growing income inequality. Jakobsson and Dragun concentrate on international inequalities that can arise from trade liberalisation, particularly given the persistence of agricultural subsidies in rich countries, and the implications of this for poverty in developing countries.

Consider now these contributions in slightly more depth.

Chapter 5, by Tisdell, Lasselle and Svizzero briefly review different theories and opinions about whether globalisation is likely to result in greater economic equality or inequality between nations. These authors see restrictions on international labour movements as barriers to the creation of greater equality of personal income between nations. World Bank data indicates that income inequality between nations has risen in recent years despite growing globalisation. The World Bank suggests that this has occurred because countries that have opened up to the outside world have benefited from the globalisation process whereas those that have been tardy in doing so have denied themselves the economic fruits of being involved in the globalisation process. However, this explanation seems too facile. Deep-seated structural reasons may explain why some economies have failed to achieve much economic interdependence with the global economic system. Not all countries wishing to become highly integrated with the global economy are able to do so. Doubts are also expressed about the ability of globalisation to stimulate economic growth in the long term and the ability of free international markets to bring about a Kaldor-Hicks optimum globally. It is easy to be overly euphoric about the economic benefits of economic globalisation.

Disagreements have arisen between several higher income countries and most developing countries as to whether labour and environmental standards are desirable. These disagreements were highlighted at the WTO Millennium Meeting. In Chapter 6, Tisdell discusses the desirability of international labour and environmental standards. In doing so, he points out that labour standards are just a part of social standards. He expresses concern that international fiscal competition, sharpened by economic globalisation may reduce social entitlements and disadvantage the poor everywhere. As a result of increased fiscal competition generated by growing economic globalisation, all nations may experience a Paretian welfare loss (see also Tisdell and Svizzero 2003). At present there are no effective global government institutions to deal with such issues.

In Chapter 7, Ruddar Datt expresses concerns from a developing country perspective about possible global labour and environmental standards. He also critically assesses the impacts on India of globalisation and the WTO. After providing some historical background on export-led growth and globalisation, Datt considers the apparent impact of economic globalisation on India's international trade and on foreign investment on India. He is concerned that India's recent globalisation strategies have lowered the rate at which it has been reducing its incidence of poverty and is decreasing the growth in its employment opportunities. He also identifies unwelcome effects on Indian industry. He is critical of what he sees as the double standards of rich countries in relation to free trade, labour and agriculture. In his view, the main gains from globalisation processes and WTO policies have gone to higher income countries with little economic benefit to developing countries, such as India. Consequently, he warns of the erosion of faith in globalisation as the new 'mantra' for stimulating development in India.

However, not all regions and sectors of the Indian economy have been significantly affected by globalisation.

In Chapter 8, Raj Kumar Sen explores the impact of economic globalisation on the supply of food items and the consequences of this for human welfare in a less developed area, namely the state of West Bengal in India. West Bengal is a major food producing state in India and appears to have a comparative advantage in food production. It was thought likely that economic liberalisation/globalisation would stimulate its production of food, increase its exports of food products and encourage foreign direct investment in its agro-processing sector. While Sen finds that West Bengal's agricultural production has risen, there is no conclusive evidence to suggest that liberalisation is the reason for this. Its agricultural exports as a percentage of total exports have fallen and foreign direct investment in West Bengal's agricultural processing sector has been minimal. Many investors attribute lack of this investment to poor infrastructure in West Bengal. Furthermore, while greater freedom of international trade has resulted in some increase in imports of food, two-thirds of West Bengalis consume no foreign brands of food, and those that do purchase foreign brands of food, consume very little of such food. Overall, it seems that as yet globalisation has had little effect on food production in West Bengal, on foreign direct investment in its food-processing sector, and has not significantly affected the food consumption patterns of West Bengalis. Therefore, West Bengal has not yet reaped the reputed economic benefits of economic globalisation as far as its food sector is concerned. Possibly, to a large extent, West Bengal is being bypassed by the process of economic globalisation. As pointed out in Chapter 5, some regions and commodities escape significant involvement in the globalisation process.

In Chapter 9, Gowdy, Iorgulescu and Onyeiwu provide an interesting case study of how economic globalisation can erode social capital, and generate poverty and inequality at the village level. Two Nigerian villages are the basis of this case study. One, Obigbo, has developed in response to the global economic demand for Nigerian oil, whereas the other, Umuluwe, is a traditional rural village. The latter has experienced a decline in population and worsening social and economic conditions with the advent of structural adjustment policies and economic globalisation, partly as result of outward migration of many of its villagers to Obigbo. Demographic and other imbalances have arisen in both villages. The authors argue that the socioeconomic and institutional problems that have arisen in Umuluwe are compounded by urban bias. Burdensome taxes imposed on villagers greatly exceed the social benefits they receive and the main beneficiaries are believed to be city dwellers. Current economic policies are eroding the social and economic fabric of Umuluwe and could well be a recipe for social and political instability. It is an open question whether economic gains at Obigbo justify the near social and economic collapse of Umuluwe. However, there is no doubt that considerable social conflict has been generated by the globalisation process.

In Chapter 10, Kristin Jakobsson and Andrew Dragun argue that international trade liberalisation is likely to increase the occurrence of poverty in less developed countries mainly because of high levels of subsidisation of agriculture by rich countries. Furthermore, there appear to be other market distortions that principally benefit rich countries, such as higher than average non-tariff and tariff barriers imposed by rich countries on competitive agricultural imports from developing countries, of which sugar is an example. In addition, market power in relation to the supply of manufactured agricultural inputs, such as pesticides and chemical fertilisers, appears to be increasingly in the hands of fewer companies with their headquarters in rich countries. In some industries, a few Western-owned companies are the principal purchasers of agricultural produce, such as coffee beans, from less developed countries. Hence, a monopsony-like position exists for purchases of some agricultural imports from poor countries. Oxfam has expressed its concern about this situation. Market distortions in favour of rich countries in the supply of agricultural imports to developing countries can be expected to grow as international regimes protecting intellectual property rights are strengthened, such as through the WTO agreement on Trade-Related Aspects of Intellectual Property Rights (TRIPS).

In general, these authors lend support to the view expressed by Oxfam (2002) that given current market distortions, emanating mainly from rich countries, trade liberalisation in developing countries is likely to increase the incidence of poverty in developing countries. In particular, rural poverty could become more marked as a result of trade liberalisation.

## 1.5 LABOUR ISSUES AND DISTRIBUTIONAL CONFLICTS: THE COVERAGE OF PART III

The question is not yet resolved of whether and to what extent economic globalisation has added to problems of maintaining full employment and contributed to growing income inequalities within nations. Dilip Dutta considers whether globalisation has added to employment problems and poverty in a dualistic economy, namely India, In particular, he explores the impact of economic globalisation on the size of India's informal sector. Lasselle, Svizzero and Tisdell examine the influence of globalisation on the nature of employment in higher income countries. B.N. Ghosh finds that income inequalities in most East Asian economies have risen as economic globalisation has gathered ground. Rising income inequality has not been confined to OECD countries. On the other hand, M. Zainul Abedin suggests that structural adjustment programmes in Bangladesh have mostly had favourable economic consequences and have been associated with increased public funding of the social sector. While economic globalisation has been associated with reduced international restrictions on most commodity markets, capital and money markets, there have not been concomitant reductions on restrictions on international labour movements. Nevertheless, the developing global economy has stimulated substantial international labour flows. This aspect is explored by Amarjit Kaur in relation to labour migration in Southeast Asia.

Consider each of these contributions a little further.

Dilip Dutta suggests in Chapter 11 that while it is too early yet to evaluate the long-run socioeconomic effects of economic liberalisation and privatisation, along with globalisation generally, on a dualistic economy such as India's, there are already reasons to feel uneasy. He examines the often raised concerns that these economic changes have led to erosion of the living standards of the Indian poor; increased India's regional economic and industrial disparity, resulted in sluggish employment generation and a greater casualisation of India's workforce as well as increased feminisation and deskilling of its workforce. He also comments on the consequences of growing economic uncertainty and identifies hidden hardships associated with India's economic reforms and with its greater opening up to the outside economic world. Particular attention is given to the flow-on effects on economic conditions and the size of the unorganised sector of the Indian economy. The unorganised sector of India's economy accounts for a major part of its agricultural sector as well as its rural non-agricultural and urban informal sector.

Problems have also arisen from globalisation and economic liberalisation for employment, working conditions and wage rate inequality in higher income countries. Lasselle, Svizzero and Tisdell observe in Chapter 12 that with market deregulation and growing international economic integration, most OECD countries have experienced high and persistent levels of unemployment. It is argued that a consequence of globalisation has been to reinforce all the different causes of unemployment as identified in Classical, Ricardian and Keynesian theories, namely frictional/disequilibrium-type unemployment, technological unemployment, and unemployment arising from a deficiency in aggregate demand. It is also noted that wage inequality and income inequality has risen in most OECD countries since the mid-1990s, that is following a rapid increase in global economic integration. Undoubtedly, a rise in levels of persistent aggregate unemployment income in recent times compared to those prior to the mid-1970s has contributed to growing income inequality in higher income countries. In the concluding portion of this chapter, international labour movements (legal and illegal) are considered as possible contributors to unemployment and wage inequality in higher income countries.

While rising income inequality in higher income countries since the mid-1970s is well documented, less attention has been given to changes in income inequality in developing countries associated with their increased economic liberalisation and integration into the world economy. In Chapter 13, B.N. Ghosh provides evidence of growing income inequalities in East Asian economies since the mid-1970s.

From the study by B.N. Ghosh (Chapter 13), it can be seen that economic growth in east Asian economies is associated, in the 1960s and in the early 1970s, with falling income inequality. However, starting in the mid-1970s, for some East Asian nations, for example South Korea, and for most at some time during the last two decades of the twentieth century, this pattern was reversed, with their further economic growth being associated with rising income inequality. This pattern is inconsistent with that suggested by the Kuznets inverted 'U' hypothesis. In fact, it is similar to a pattern that has been observed in more developed countries (Tisdell and Svizzero 2003). But, on the whole, this has occurred in some less developed countries later than in higher income ones.

This increasing income inequality may, as suggested by Ghosh, be partly a consequence of the greater integration of Asian economies with the global economy, and the structural changes in these economies arising from this. As Ghosh points out, there are, however, multiple influences and limitations to his available data. Therefore, some caution is needed in interpreting his results. Nonetheless, it seems that gaps in incomes between those of skilled and unskilled labourers have widened greatly in East Asia in recent decades. As in more developed countries, this has been a significant contributor to growing income inequality (compare Ryscavage 1999).

M. Zainul Abedin examines the origin, implementation and economic effects of Bangladesh's structural adjustment programmes in Chapter 14. He points out that they really only approached full implementation in the 1990s, as in India's case. In general he presents a positive view of their effects on Bangladesh. He argues that they have been partially successful in removing Bangladesh's serious balance of payments problem, keeping its rate of inflation at reasonable levels, reducing the size of its budget deficits and in promoting its economic growth. He also is of the view that effects on the social sector are positive and encouraging. He claims, however, that the benefits would have been even greater if Bangladesh had greater political stability and less corruption.

His positive view of the impacts of economic globalisation on Bangladesh contrast with the more circumspect views of Datt and Dutta about its socioeconomic consequences for India. Nevertheless, it is far from clear that Bangladesh's globalisation path is strewn with roses. For instance, inequality of income in Bangladesh has risen in recent times and rural poverty has remained persistently high (Tisdell and Alauddin 2003; Tisdell 2003). Furthermore, Bangladesh's growing specialisation in exports, especially in exports of garments, seems to increase its vulnerability to changes in external demand. In addition, more research may be needed to find out whether increased public support for the social sector in Bangladesh translates into greater support for less well-off Bangladeshis.

Globalisation tends to encourage international labour migration. Bangladesh, for example, has received considerable receipts of foreign currency from short-term labour migration. Readers in higher income countries will be aware of public debate and concern about immigration to their country from countries with lower incomes, especially when this migration is illegal. This debate is often sharpened when there are marked language and cultural differences between immigrants and citizens of the country receiving them (see Chapter 3). At the same time, significant migration takes place between countries in developing regions as globalisation gathers momentum. However, international migration involving other than centre countries is often overlooked in the more developed world in examinations of labour migration.

The contribution by Amarjit Kaur in Chapter 15 helps to rectify this bias. She discusses international labour migration in the Southeast Asian region, concentrating on Malaysia as a prime case. Malaysia is a major recipient of labour (mostly unskilled or of low skill) within the Southeast Asian region. Migrants from different countries are employed often in unlike sectors of the Malaysian economy, and gender composition of migrants from source countries can differ significantly. A degree of specialisation in supply of different types of labour exists between countries that are a source of migrants to Malaysia. While Southeast Asia has long been subjected to international migration, as in its European-centred colonial past, new arrangements have arisen in recent years involving official recruitment agencies and private enterprises charging fees to migrants or would-be migrants for their services. Kaur makes the point that this type of 'institutionalisation of the migration process, particularly for unskilled labour, serves to create both a black market in migration and conditions conducive to human trafficking and exploitation'.

International labour migration remains a source of social tension within countries and between countries. Many higher income countries have regulations designed in particular to restrict immigration of unskilled workers, mostly from developing countries. However, as income inequality between nations increases so does the incentive for residents from low-income countries to migrate to higher income ones.

## 1.6 ENVIRONMENTAL ISSUES AND IMPACTS: AN OUTLINE OF THE COVERAGE OF PART IV

Different opinions exist about the likely impact of economic globalisation on the global state of the environment. Some believe that by stimulating economic growth, globalisation will eventually improve the state of the environment globally. The environmental Kuznets curve is frequently used to underpin this view. Possibly most orthodox economists share this prognosis. However, there are those with worries about this optimistic view. This is first indicated in Chapter 6 in discussing the possible role of the WTO and environmental standards. Neo-Malthusians reject the optimistic environmental view. They believe that strong restrictions must be imposed on resource-depletion and environmental use if sustainable global economic growth is to be achieved. They believe that continuing global economic growth may breach the environmental requirements for maintaining economic growth, with catastrophic global consequences. Tisdell (2001) discusses these alternative points of view, and they are, therefore, not covered here again.

In Part IV, Tisdell outlines deficiencies in biodiversity conservation that arise from global market failures. This is followed by a series of country-based or regional case studies of the environmental effects of economic liberalisation and globalisation. Sankar considers the environmental consequences of globalisation for India, and Chai those for China. Xue, Lin and Tisdell concentrate on international conflicts arising from global trade and exchange in genetically modified organisms (GMOS), giving particular attention to China's situation. In the last contribution in this book, Colin Hunt explores the consequences of economic globalisation for environments and natural resource depletion in Pacific Island countries. He finds that economic globalisation is associated with the unsustainable use of natural resources in the Pacific Islands. Several small nations in the Pacific have adopted resource-utilisation policies that involve very high user-costs.

Consider each of these contributions further.

Chapter 16 by Tisdell is based on the view that non-use values lead to significant market failures in biodiversity conservation. It is argued that these failures are more marked in developing countries and that their significance increases with greater globalisation. A case is presented that higher income countries should help finance nature conservation in less developed countries. Furthermore, it is contended that policies designed to foster market-making are incapable of overcoming the failures identified. These include national property rights in endemic genetic materials. Serious limits are identified to the possible effectiveness of property-rights solutions, such as are possible under the International Convention on Biological Diversity or as have been foreshadowed by the Cancun Declaration (see also Chapter 19). Furthermore, it is argued that the development of ecotourism or nature-based tourism can, at best, only provide a partial (and a biased) remedy to this problem. The basic problem is that market-based solutions fail to account for the non-use values of nature and these can be substantial, even in developing countries (see Bandara and Tisdell 2003, for example).

Professor Sankar believes that unless India reforms its system of environmental management, it will experience substantial environmental degradation as it becomes more closely integrated with the world economy. He emphasises in Chapter 17 that India essentially has a command-and-control system of environmental management and is reluctant to adopt systems of environmental control that involve the use of economic instruments. He argues that these command-and-control systems are not very efficient means for pollution control and for environmental conservation. This is partly because of the way environmental regulations are formulated in India, irregularities in their enforcement, and lack of available finance for monitoring compliance and ensuring enforcement.

India plans to achieve a compound annual growth rate of GDP of 8 per cent as a result of its growing liberalisation of markets and its opening up to the outside world, that is, its growing involvement in the global economy. Sankar contends that unless reforms to India's system of environmental management keep pace with its adoption of policies for its market liberalisation and globalisation, India will experience growing environmental degradation. This is inevitable in the absence of changed environmental policies given the high economic growth rates predicted for India as a result of its market reforms and its pro-globalisation policies.

While Sankar accepts that India should efficiently enforce environmental standards, he objects to global or external determination of such standards. His objection also extends to external interference in setting social standards, such as those relating to the use of child labour.

He argues that greater foreign investment in India as a result of India's economic reforms will not encourage 'dirty industries' to relocate to India. In that regard, his views are similar to those of Chai, who finds, on the basis of empirical evidence, that foreign investment in China has not been associated with any growth of environmentally 'dirty' industries in China.

At the same time, Sankar is keen for India to play a more proactive role in international forums concerned with the establishment of global environmental rules, and rules governing property rights, such as those relating to property rights in local unique species.

Joseph Chai's contribution (Chapter 18) examines the impact of China's opening up to the outside work on its pollution intensities. He decomposes these effects into an industrial composition effect, a technological change effect and a scale effect. He concludes that although increasing involvement of the Chinese economy in the global economic system has reduced pollution intensities in China, aggregate levels of pollution in China have risen, because of the expanding scale of China's international trade and production. Furthermore, he finds that China has not become a haven for foreign investment in dirty industries. In fact, he discovers that trade liberalisation has enabled China to transfer many of the environmental costs of its economic expansion to other countries by importing dirty industrial products rather than producing these domestically.

China also features in Chapter 19. The development of genetically modified organisms (GMOs), the creation of property rights in these, held in most cases by large transnational corporations, and moves to increase international trade and exchange in GMOs have been contentious, continue to be contentious, and have been a source of significant social and international tension. This is amplified by the contribution of Xue, Lin and Tisdell in Chapter 19. This chapter examines the general issues involved and illustrates these by Chinese case studies giving particular attention to genetically modified soybeans and cotton. The USA (the major source of GMOs) has by its exports to China of GM soybeans created economic problems for many Chinese farmers. Also, China is concerned that patent protection for GM soybeans could limit its future options for developing new types of soybeans, and it has serious environmental concerns about the import of GM soybeans to China. China, as are several developing countries, is also uneasy about the possible consequences of GM seed monopolisation. This is illustrated in this case by Monsanto's Bt cotton strategy and the possibility of a soybean monopoly by Monsanto. The relevance of the Cartegena Biosafety Protocol to the Convention on Biological Diversity and various WTO Treaties are given particular attention.

In Chapter 20, Colin Hunt points out that the world's largest ocean, the Pacific Ocean, contains many island countries that are vulnerable to environmental changes resulting from economic globalisation. He gives particular attention to the effects of the exports of these countries on their natural capital stocks. In several cases, these stocks are being exploited unsustainably. This is so for forests, especially in the Solomon Islands, and possibly for harvesting of tuna for the world market, particularly big eye (*Thunnus obesus*).

Environmental problems have also emerged from agricultural production intended for sales to world markets and from production of minerals for export. Furthermore, many Pacific islands will suffer complete or severe inundation if the greenhouse effect results in sea level rises. Most of the small island countries of the Pacific have not escaped from impacts of economic globalisation.

## 1.7 CONCLUDING OBSERVATIONS

Even though it is difficult to measure globalisation, there can be little doubt that there has been a substantial upsurge in economic and social interdependence between nations since the early 1970s. This chapter provides evidence to support this observation. The book begins by considering some basic issues involved in globalisation. Is it inevitable? Are there alternatives to economic globalisation? What types of impacts is globalisation having on cultures and languages? To what extent are regionalism and globalisation (multilateralism) compatible or in conflict? The latter is an important issue given the rapid expansion in regional economic integration (beginning with the Treaty of Rome) that occurred in the second half of the twentieth century, and still continues.

Coverage then shifts to an examination of possible differences in the gains of nations from globalisation and to a consideration of the views of some groups, especially in higher income countries, that increasing economic globalisation calls for global labour and environmental standards. In general, developing countries oppose the introduction of such 'norms'. Experiences and perspectives on globalisation from India follow and then a case study is reported of consequences for rural villages in Nigeria of their links with the global economy. Part II concludes with a discussion of how globalisation (and particularly partial globalisation) of agricultural trade can adversely impact on poor countries.

Growing economic globalisation has been associated with growing income inequality and rising persistent unemployment in higher income countries. The increased level of persistent unemployment is, for example, documented by Eatwell and Taylor (2000, p. 158) for the G7 countries. Labour issues and income distribution changes associated with growing globalisation are the focus of Part III. Increasing globalisation has important environmental consequences and raises serious questions about global environmental policy. Part IV addresses such matters. Both parts include, as does Part II, contributions providing general analysis as well as illustrative country and regional case studies.

Thus, while this book does not cover every aspect of globalisation, it considers many of its major consequences and policy implications. This provides a critical perspective and a basis for further analysis and research.

# REFERENCES


Bandara, R. and C. Tisdell (2003), 'Use and non-use values of wild Asian elephants: a total economic valuation approach', *Economics, Ecology and the Environment*, Working Paper No. 80, School of Economics, The University of Queensland, Brisbane.

Eatwell, J. (1993), 'The global money trap', *American Prospect*, Winter, p. 118.

Eatwell, J. and L. Taylor (2000), *Global Finance at Risk: The Case for International Regulation*, Cambridge UK: Polity Press.

Hogan, W. P. (1995), 'Foreign debt and foreign exchange markets', The Fifth Colin Clark Memorial Lecture, *Working Paper* No. 177, Department of Economics, The University of Queensland, Brisbane.

Mittleman, J. H. (2000), 'Globalization: captives and captors', *Third World Quarterly*, **21** (6), 917-29.

Oxfam (2002), *Rigged Rules and Double Standards. Trade, Globalisation and the Fight against Poverty,* Oxford: Oxfam. www.maketradefair.com

Ryscavage, P. (1999), *Income Inequality in America: An Analysis of Trends*, New York: M. E. Sharpe.

Stiglitz, J. (2002) *Globalization and its Discontents*, London: Penguin Books.

Svizzero, S. and C. A. Tisdell (2002), 'Growing income inequalities and remedial policies', *Intereconomics: Review of European Economic Policy*, **37**, 162-71.

Tisdell, C.A. (2001), 'Globalisation and sustainability: environmental Kuznets curve and the WTO', *Ecological Economics*, **39**, 185-96.

Tisdell, C.A. (2003), 'Economic globalisation, liberalization and Bangladesh: poverty, labour norms and the environment', *South Asia*, (forthcoming).

Tisdell, C.A. and M. Alauddin (2003), 'Market-oriented reforms and poverty in Bangladesh', in K. Sharma (ed.), *Trade Policy, Growth and Poverty in Asian Developing Countries*, London and New York: Routledge, pp.189-201.

Tisdell, C.A. and S. Svizzero (2003), 'Globalization, social welfare and market inequalities', *Economic Theory, Applications and Issues*, Working Paper No.20, School of Economics, The University of Queensland, Brisbane.

# 2. Globalisation as Development Strategy: In Search of Alternatives

**W. D. Lakshman**

## 2.1 INTRODUCTION

Globalisation refers to a complex and wide-ranging process of socio-cultural and politico-economic transformation taking place at both national and global levels. Though decomposing globalisation into its economic, social, political and cultural aspects is a difficult exercise, the focus of this chapter has been deliberately restricted to economic globalisation. The expansion in the following forms of inter-country interaction constitutes the objective process through which global integration is taking place among countries and peoples:

- Trade in goods and services,
- Capital flows,
- Cross-border relocation of production facilities,
- Transfer of knowledge and technology, and
- Migration of people.

These exchanges and transfers constitute the core processes of globalisation. These core processes were in fact taking place in the world over a long period of time, particularly so since the nineteenth century (see, for example, Hirst and Thompson 1996, p. 2). However, in the minds of many, globalisation is substantially more than the sum of these core processes of international exchange and transfer. They were taking place in the nineteenth century but no one talks of globalisation in regard to that period. In the current process of globalisation, the integration of countries and peoples in the world is taking place at an enormously greater intensity and speed. Furthermore, today's globalisation incorporates significant qualitative changes in the world we are living in.

Different countries and peoples have achieved successful integration with the global economy under different policy regimes. Countries like South

Korea, Singapore, Malaysia and China, to name a few, have moved into globalisation and are getting more and more globally integrated within strongly state-guided policy frameworks. Yet when used to indicate a development strategy for developing countries, the term globalisation would generally exclude such strongly state-guided policy frameworks. In such contexts, globalisation usually means global integration within 'market friendly' or 'neo-liberal' policies. To make things clearer, the expression 'liberalisation-globalisation' process is occasionally used in this chapter to indicate this concept of globalisation. The term internationalisation can be used to indicate merely the core processes of globalisation, namely inter-country exchange and trade in goods and services, and capital and technology.

The process of globalisation can be reviewed from a number of different perspectives. The examination in this chapter uses the perspective of 'globalisation as development strategy'. After the present introductory comments, Section 2.2 examines the arguments in favour of and against globalisation as a development strategy. Section 2.3 reviews the progress of ideas among critics of globalisation, which gradually produced a move towards the development of alternatives. Section 2.4 discusses some important elements of alternatives within globalisation rather that alternatives to globalisation, which can be implemented in individual developing countries without drastic changes in the basic structure of the state and society. Since the focus in the chapter is on globalisation as development strategy, various proposals for the reform of the present global economic and financial system are not at all discussed. The chapter concludes with a brief section summarising its main arguments.

## 2.2 GLOBALISATION: ADVOCACY AND CRITIQUE

Ardent advocates of globalisation consider the process to be the pinnacle of human achievement as well as the guaranteed cure for most (if not all) economic and social ills. It has become for many economists and most management gurus 'the mantra that promises prosperity and development' (Tujan Jr. 1998). The pro-globalisation argument often proceeds by claiming that, by promoting foreign direct investments, globalisation enables developing countries to obtain needed capital without getting into indebtedness. Furthermore, globalisation enables developing countries also to obtain essential knowledge and technology easily and at low cost without having to reinvent the wheel. Faster diffusion of knowledge raises the standards of production technology and the level of productivity on a worldwide basis. Furthermore, through globalisation, the producers in developing countries gain access to required markets for growth of production, without being constrained by the small size of their domestic markets. Globalisation is associated with lower transport costs and reduced tariffs. Consumers too are, therefore, supposed to benefit from globalisation as a result of price reductions and the increase in the variety of consumer goods available for their consumption. Globalisation is thus equated with growth, technological advancement, social modernisation and broad-based development, including poverty reduction.

Empirical evidence shows quite clearly that benefits of globalisation, as presented in the foregoing paragraph, are greatly exaggerated. Globalisation has indeed been oversold. In the relatively early years of the globalisation era, the bulk of the world community concerned with issues of development was overwhelmed by the forceful conceptualisation presented in its favour. With the gradual accumulation of evidence regarding the developmental impacts of the process, critics of globalisation have gradually begun to be quite vociferous, in some instances, also exaggerating their case. Many contemporary developments in the world, undesirable and objectionable from social and human points of view, are being attributed to globalisation. Very long indeed would be the list of ill effects of globalisation, as presented by its critics. The following paragraphs present a selective summary of the major arguments of the critics of globalisation.

First, various factors – socio-economic structural changes and policy adjustments – accompanying globalisation have contributed to widen the gaps between the rich and the poor within nations and between the rich and poor countries in the world. [1] Globalisation, brought about through sweeping measures of liberalisation without proper sequencing, implemented in conditions of unpreparedness on the part of the people, has rarely been neutral in its effects on different income groups. Population groups that can be described as the excluded, the powerless and the vulnerable are found to suffer from extensive policy-induced social hardships. This growing inequality has its corollary in the extreme concentration of wealth and power in the hands of a few super-rich persons. [2]

Second, globalisation has failed to make any significant dent in the incidence of poverty in the world. This is perhaps the least controversial way of expressing the poverty implications of globalisation, in the midst of extensive claims and counter-claims about poverty effects of globalisation (Cobham 2001; Stiglitz 2002, p. 248; Chossudovsky 1997; Mohan et al. 2000; UNCTAD, 2002). [3] Increasing commoditisation of public services like education and health care, as a corollary of neo-liberal policies, exacerbate the adverse effects of globalisation on absolute poverty in the world. Less labour-absorbing activities of trade and services have come to occupy more central roles than agricultural and manufacturing pursuits. Even the latter activities are becoming capital-intensive and labour-replacing as a result of revolutionary changes in science and technology. Globalisation and growth under the control of multinationals has ushered in, according to some critics, a pattern of 'jobless growth' (Pendse 1998). There have been growing displacement and dislocation of lives in general, and intensification of landlessness, unemployment and poverty in rural areas in particular. An important point in this connection is the increased exploitation of women and children in labour markets under globalisation. Economic crises (see next paragraph), which came in quick succession during the last two decades in different parts of the world, have exacerbated poverty implications of globalisation.

Third, judged by relevant empirical data for the recent past, globalisation has enhanced the extent of economic instability and the frequency of crises in the world. [4] Changes in the structure of world trade and finance in the era of globalisation have caused this heightened global instability. The turnover of foreign exchange transactions in the world today per period of time is many times larger than the turnover of trade in goods and services.[5] Capital account liberalisation is being widely promoted in the world. Coupled with the inherent instability of hot money flows across countries and the volatility in exchange rates, this has made today's global economy extremely crisis-prone. Frequent crashes and bailouts punctuate the current process of financial liberalisation.

Fourth, globalisation has been accompanied by continued and accelerated degradation of the world's natural environment (Khor 2002).[6] The overwhelmingly high priority placed on economic growth in the process of globalisation, without proper safeguards, regulatory policies or controls, has led to very rapid increases in global energy use, bringing with it increased greenhouse gas emissions from fossil fuel use and projected increase in global warming. Consumption of water has increased rapidly and its shortages are projected to become one of the most pressing resource issues of this century. Rapid industrial development has led to high levels of air, water and waste pollution in many countries. Deforestation and urbanisation and even agricultural growth, heavily dependent on green revolution technologies, are adding to this problem. Hazardous technologies are being transferred from the advanced to the developing countries, causing widespread problems of environmental abuse and health deterioration. Economic growth of the style pushed forward by globalisation has outstripped both the absorption capacity of the environment and the speed with which policies and institutions can be developed to address the environmental challenges so heightened.

Fifth, having led to increasing centralisation of decision-making processes, globalisation has created difficulties in representative government

(Scholte 2000, Ch. 11).[7] Decision-making powers have moved to points further and further away from citizens (Klein 2001, pp. 86-7). The past gains of social movements have been eroded and there has been a general regression in democratic practices. Trade union movements have been brought under control in order to keep the investment climate attractive to multinationals. Enhancing already excessive socio-economic inequalities, governments in many of the countries in the process of globalisation are seen to be using their powers with impunity to promote 'crony capitalism'. Huge profit opportunities are opening up through privatisation of 'natural monopoly' types of public enterprises. Powerful multinationals are in strong competition to acquire these highly profitable state-owned enterprises, which are being privatised. These conditions have often exacerbated problems of large-scale bribery and corruption in society. While the rich classes are getting richer, barriers operate against upward social mobility of people, particularly the young, in lower social classes. This is particularly so in societies divided also through various ethnic, religious, social and cultural differences. All these developments create ideal breeding grounds for dissidence, social alienation and protest. It is not surprising that globalisation has been associated with intensifying violence and increasing militarisation, along with worsening conditions of human rights violations in developing societies. The result has been the further weakening of democratic governance.

Sixth, it is highlighted that globalisation destroys the capacity of nation states to manage economic processes within their territories without creating in its place an authority with such capacity (Bienefeld 1994, p. 120). The governments are becoming increasingly weak in dealing with domestic fiscal problems and external obligations, and guiding the country's economic activities according to the wishes of the people. Furthermore, these governments are rendered incapable of satisfactorily meeting their social responsibilities and maintaining internal political stability for growth and development.

Seventh, the strongest positive claim made in favour of the liberalisation-globalisation process is that it promotes economic growth and productive efficiency more successfully than policies of state intervention. This pro-globalisation view concerning its economic growth effects is also coming increasingly under criticism. Even some writers believing in economic orthodoxy are expressing doubts as to whether the evidence is firm enough about the liberalisation-globalisation package being pro-growth. As Tony Killick, a writer sympathetic to the liberal cause, has argued: 'Neither the IMF nor the World Bank has been able to demonstrate a convincing connection, in either direction, between SAPs[8] and economic growth; most independent research similarly does not find a systematic connection'

(Killick 1999, p. 2).

Studies like Weisbrot et al. (2001) are more forthright in arguing that in the era of globalisation the countries of the world have achieved lower rates of growth than during the preceding period of state intervention. Furthermore, there is independent evidence from many developing countries to show regressive growth effects of the globalisation-liberalisation policy package.[9]

In the anti-globalisation literature, one comes across wild allegations attributing to globalisation all manner of undesirable things. Exaggeration is the rule in this part of the literature, as much as in the pro-globalisation part of it. Clearly globalisation generates both positive and negative effects. The core processes of internationalisation, without the neo-liberal paraphernalia of globalisation,[10] have indeed helped some developing countries to achieve sustainable development by making more capital, technology, information, markets, better management systems and so on available to them. The liberalisation-globalisation process has not, however, helped the bulk of the developing world to achieve material and human development. In actual practice, the liberalisation-globalisation process appears to have been harmful to many developing societies participating in that process. Countries integrating with the process without conducive initial conditions have become further marginalised.

## 2.3 ALTERNATIVES TO AND WITHIN GLOBALISATION

Despite the evidence of its extensive ill effects on the bulk of mankind, globalisation is advocated as the most effective development strategy for developing countries. More often than not, the ruling classes and elite groups in these countries accept this advocacy for purposes of selfish class/ group interests. Many developing countries invite multinationals through various fiscal and other incentives provided for accumulation/acquisition of capital, modern technology, world markets and access. Liberal economic policies are considered an essential precondition for attracting multinationals. As there is excessive competition among developing countries to attract multinational corporations (MNCs), there is indeed a competitive abandonment of the state's regulatory powers by these countries. Powerful multinationals, supported by advanced country regimes, often render independent policy action of developing country governments ineffective by changing their global investment and production strategies. That powers of the nation state are withering away and the concept of national sovereignty has become anachronistic in this era of globalisation is a widespread viewpoint. Globalisation is highlighted as a process making independent national strategies infeasible.

At the same time, globalisation is being widely hailed as an inevitable and irreversible process. The business and social elites and political leaders in positions of power spread the viewpoint that, for developing societies, 'there is no alternative'[11] but to accommodate globalisation. Once leaders take the position that 'there are no alternatives', many other groups in society too, would, in herd-like fashion convert themselves to that position. After the collapse of socialist regimes in Russia and Eastern Europe, even the socialist and/or working class groups in developing countries initially lost their commitment to search and fight for more desirable alternatives to liberalisation-globalisation. Another factor, which helped in this 'no alternative' propaganda, was the ability of socialist countries like China and Vietnam to selectively use policies of globalisation with a great deal of national economic success.

An increasing awareness about negative effects of globalisation however, is now being created. The relevant information and analyses are increasing in volume and spreading extensively in the world. The plight of the millions of people in the world who have suffered in the process of globalisation has gradually been brought to light through research and publications, including the Internet and mass media, and also strong protest movements. How increasing numbers of people have lost their jobs, homes, communities and livelihoods in the liberalisation-globalisation process and have been pushed to poverty and starvation is being revealed in research and propagandist literature. Increasing media coverage of the widespread human suffering due to economic crises in various countries in the recent past has helped in this awareness creation. The Internet has turned out to be a rather effective instrument in spreading the message of ill effects of globalisation and organising like-minded people in different parts of the world against its further spread in the same form. The nature of collaboration, explicit or implicit, that operates among multinational corporations, multilateral financial organisations and developing country elites and governments is gradually being exposed. Having remained initially confused and disillusioned, socialist thinkers and activists are now quite vigorously active in the search for alternatives.

There are two modes in which the search for alternatives can be carried out. One mode is to search for alternatives to globalisation. This is what socialist thinkers and activists are working towards. The other mode is to search for alternatives within globalisation (see, for example, Mohan et al. 2000, p. 119). In this mode, globalisation is viewed as a complex process, which has, 'as development strategy', both good and bad elements. The 'alternatives' in this second mode try to identify the good elements of globalisation for further strengthening, and the bad elements for conscious avoidance. In either mode, the search for alternatives would imply a belief that the societies and states in developing countries could selectively intervene in the process of globalisation. The capacity of the state of a developing country to determine the development strategy for that country has, no doubt, weakened but the state is looked upon as a pivotal institution in this sort of thinking. Among many things the state is still capable of doing is to regulate market forces to promote 'national' goals, without breaking down the market mechanism and also without violating the conditions of international agreements and charters the country had opted to sign.

The contribution of this chapter falls mainly into the second one of the two modes of search of globalisation alternatives. There is rather strong historical evidence from a great variety of countries in support of economic policies of selective interventionism. Yet whenever it is advocated for development in today's developing world, there is a commonly heard neo-liberal argument that most developing countries do not have the necessary state structures and institutions, including the bureaucracy, to produce desired results from interventionism (World Bank 1993). Careful reading of history would show that every country which had made good use of selective interventionism in an early historical phase of development had suffered from these state structural and institutional weaknesses. There is a virtuous cycle here to be exploited. The normal historical tendency is for different components of development – economic, social, technological, institutional and so on – to move hand in hand.

## 2.4 SOME CONCRETE THOUGHTS ON ALTERNATIVES

There are many proposals today about how to change the existing system. These proposals are developed in response to observed failures of globalisation as well as to challenges various elements of the globalisation process continue to throw up. Some of these proposals are about how to change the international institutional structures or the international financial architecture, including the methods of their operations (Bello et al. 2000, pp. 16-21). This chapter is not concerned with these proposals about reform of international institutional structures. In this section, some development strategy alternatives within the globalisation framework will be briefly looked at.[12] Proposals about alternatives to globalisation as a development model, discussed in both published and Internet literature, vary greatly in terms of the extent of idealism/pragmatism. The discussion here is of a few very pragmatic ideas.

History would help a great deal in developing alternative policy packages within globalisation that can be implemented at single developing country level without drastic structural changes in state and society. Working out such alternatives requires correct conceptualisation of various key relationships among different variables affecting growth and development. However well formulated, implementation success in respect of any alternative policy package will nevertheless depend on pro-development changes in the thinking and commitment at the level of political and administrative leadership. What is most important is for these leaders to be able to rise above sectarian interests and work with the participation of important segments of society. In multi-ethnic, multi-religious and multi-caste societies, their ability to rise above such social divisions would be of particular relevance and significance. There is no gainsaying however, that leaderships of this quality are indeed very rare in developing societies.

The tendency to view every attempt to develop alternatives to or within the liberalisation-globalisation package as a move to abandon internationalism, turning back to autarky, would not at all be helpful in this type of policy dialogue. [13] That globalisation has a desirable core is a point worth repeating here. The following could be some common features of the kind of alternative development strategy we are looking for. [14]

First, it is necessary to acknowledge that the state will have a significant positive role to play in development policy. The 'state-market divide or conflict' is a bogeyman created by neo-liberal policy stances. Historically the state and the market have been partners rather than antagonists. There is much that can be learnt in this respect from the 'developmental state' theory. Whenever needed, the state might be allowed to go beyond the role of 'private sector facilitation'. The state-owned enterprise (SoE) may be called upon to play the role of pioneering industries in promising fields, to be later handed over to private enterprise. Infrastructure provision would continue to be the function primarily of the state, although private sector participation in this sphere might be allowed wherever it is forthcoming. The policy priority in respect of existing SoEs ought to be efficiency improvement. There are enough empirical cases to dispel the misconception that efficiency is a monopoly of the private enterprise. [15] In this conceptualisation, the state is entrusted with a wider and more critical role than under neo-liberal policies, but it will not encroach into economic activity areas where private enterprise can do better (Panitch 1994).

Second, the emphasis in economic policy has to shift from the excessive focus on the external, as under globalisation, to a balanced focus on the internal and external economic processes. The almost fanatical hostility to protectionism, found in stabilisation-globalisation strategy, may be replaced in the alternative development strategy by a more pragmatic approach in which infant industry protection regains its due developmental role.[16] The deepening of the home market in this alternative framework, however, should not amount to making the country autarkic. External linkage is of crucial significance because it provides developing countries with easy access to the vast accumulated world knowledge, without those countries having to go through the rigorous and time-consuming early stages of creation of that knowledge (Petras 1998). Through openness to the rest of the world, developing countries can produce for a market larger in size than the domestic market, thereby gaining benefits of larger-scale production. The important point in the policy alternative is that the external exchanges do not substitute for local markets and local centres of knowledge creation. In addition, linkages among various domestic economic sectors would be strengthened in the alternative policy package. Most importantly, the alternative development strategy works on the firm belief that a developing country can maintain the necessary external links through a strategy of selectivity in opening the country to global influences.

Third, history clearly recommends the abandonment of the sector-neutral approach to development advocated in the liberalisation-globalisation model. Specific reference may be made here to the needs of two sectors of a developing economy – the sector producing basic foods and the industrial sector. There is the argument in the liberalisation-globalisation model that markets be permitted to import the basic food items available at lower prices in the world market, encouraging the transfer of resources used in their domestic production to other activities in which the country concerned is more efficient. The alternative development model, however, would be developed on the recognition of growth and poverty alleviating benefits of a basic food production strategy. Policy action to raise productivity in this sector would ensure adequate food supplies for mass consumption at affordable prices, while also providing liveable incomes for rural producers. The alternative policy package will, simultaneously with its agricultural modernisation policies, proactively promote agro-industrial complexes and related activities for the creation of off-farm occupations.

In addition to providing basic food production sectors with promotional incentives, the alternative strategy would provide similar encouragement to manufacturing industry. The importance of industrial growth in general, and the growth of export-oriented manufacturing industry (EOI) in particular is highlighted. A successful programme of EOI is indeed the *sine qua non* of an effective strategy of employment creation and poverty alleviation. The important point is that liberalisation-globalisation strategy as widely practised does not automatically lead to EOI. Recent histories of successful cases of economic growth offer many guidelines as to how an effective EOI strategy could be evolved through intelligent systems of state interventionism.

Fourth, there is widespread criticism of globalisation that it is more concerned about profits than about people (MacEvan 1994, pp. 138-39).

These are often profits made in financial markets. Profits and their growth in production sectors, no doubt, are crucial for investment growth as they provide incentives and funding sources for investment. The alternative development strategy, while recognising this, would work out incentive systems to ensure greater distributive justice, which has been almost totally absent among the guiding principles of globalisation-liberalisation package. If the alternative development strategy promotes a 'job-creating' growth, providing productive employment to unused or under-used labour, then the level and the rate of expansion of profits are unlikely to raise too many objections. Productive utilisation of unused or under-used labour will be the hallmark. For export strategies under globalisation, labour is viewed basically as a cost item, but the alternative policy package would treat it also as a source of consumer demand. This will provide a different basis of looking at remuneration packages for workers. Under liberalisation-globalisation, low wages are paid for the purpose of maintaining high profits and international competitiveness in overseas markets. The alternative policy package would consider people as more important than profits, and wages may therefore be raised to enable workers to maintain more comfortable lives than under the 'sweatshop' syndrome of globalisation. The beneficial effects of this would include a rise in domestic aggregate demand, reduction of relative inequality in society, improvement of work incentives and the spread among workers of perceptions of partnership with management.

Fifth, the alternative development strategy would make productive activities participatory as much as possible. While globalisation packages ignore this,[17] the alternative would deliberately promote it. A structural adjustment programme 'from below' must replace the IMF-World Bank programme, which usually falls on developing societies 'from above', if policy priorities were to change as suggested above. Such changes of priorities are absolutely needed to facilitate investment of larger volumes of qualitatively better resources in education, research, health and productivity for the achievement of balanced and sustained development. Guided by enlightened self-interest, developing country leaders ought to introduce effective systems of people's participation gradually, along with the improvement in other spheres of human development, including incomes, education and awareness of civil rights.

The foregoing paragraphs have highlighted only a few important elements that need incorporation into the conceptualisation of an alternative development strategy. These elements have also been considered in their basic outline. Prevalent conditions – both domestic and global – will influence the detailed conceptualisation of this alternative development strategy. Different countries and their societies have their unique and distinct characteristics. With different cultures, economic development paths will also have to be different. People's attitudes to work, consumption and saving and their value systems vary according to historical and cultural distinctiveness of each society. This is an important factor that has to be taken into account in the conceptualisation of development strategies.

## 2.5 CONCLUSIONS

Internationalisation in the sense of expanding international exchange of capital, goods and services, and various production inputs has gone on for a long period of time. Different countries have used international links as an mechanism of development under different degrees and patterns of state intervention in markets. In almost every such country, once a competitive level of productivity growth was achieved, there has been the practice of 'kicking away the ladder' by which it climbed up. Such countries, '... in order to deprive others of the means of climbing up ...' (Friedrich List, as quoted by Chang 2002, p. 4), would campaign against the use of the systems of protection and state interventionism which helped them to climb up. When globalisation is recommended as a development strategy nowadays, it is a strategy with two components – internationalisation and liberalisation. Often the measures of liberalisation so recommended go even beyond the level of liberalisation found in today's advanced countries.

The spread of globalisation, in its dual sense above, has gone on with relatively few obstacles[18] for quite some time now. Its shortcomings, both as management system for international economic relations and as a development strategy for developing countries, are being critiqued with increasing vehemence. Some major weaknesses of globalisation as a development model have been highlighted in this chapter.

One can identify in the current international discourse on alternative development strategies, alternatives *to* globalisation and alternatives *within* globalisation. This chapter explores, in rather broad outline, some principal issues raised in the discussion of the latter type of alternatives. Two main issues may be highlighted in the concluding section. First, people in developing societies have to be able to enjoy the development benefits of the internationalised world they live in through attainment of conditions of sustainable growth of production and productivity. Second, any alternative development strategy within globalisation must be able to generate a well diffused and 'inclusive' process of development that benefits the teeming millions of ordinary people. The strongest critique of the on-going process of globalisation-liberalisation is that, in today's highly unequal world and in contexts of uneven development, it has produced significant social exclusion. Globalisation is like a huge flow of water. Under social control and guidance, it could be lifeblood to mankind. But uncontrolled and unguided, it could become a viciously devastating floodwater.

## NOTES

1. One does not need great insight to understand how the liberalisation-globalisation process works in the interests of advanced countries. It is also evident that the work of international economic institutions like the IMF, the World Bank and the World Trade Organisation too favours these countries, which indeed control these institutions (compare Stiglitz 2002).
2. Critical research into the subject reveals excessive and indeed obscene forms of wealth concentration. The Washington-based Institute for Policy Studies shows that there were 497 billionaires in the world in 2001. Their combined wealth was $1.54 trillion – an amount greater than the combined GNP of all nations in sub-Saharan Africa and the combined incomes of the poorer half of humanity (see the Institute's website at http://www.ips-dc.org).
3. The argument of the economic orthodoxy about effects of the liberalisation-globalisation process on poverty generally rests on the claim that growth reduces poverty and that liberalisation-globalisation is the best known strategy for economic growth. The seventh point below deals with this argument.
4. As Soros (2000, p. 196) argued: 'Almost against my better judgement – not everything should be interpreted as a boom-bust phenomenon – I can identify the making of a boom-bust pattern: a prevailing trend – namely, international competition for capital; and a prevailing bias – namely, an excessive belief in the market mechanism.'
5. As argued in Bello et al. (2000, pp. 4-5),

   > The globalisation of finance meant that, increasingly, its dynamics serve as the engine of the global capitalist system. The increasingly unbalanced relationship of the financial sector to trade was captured in the fact, that by the mid-1990s, the volume of transactions … in foreign exchange markets came to over $1.2 trillion per day. This is equal to the value of world trade in goods and services in an entire quarter.

6. For a brief discussion of the damage to the natural environment during the last several decades see UNU/IAS (2002). See the article on 'TNCs and Globalisation: Prime Sources of Worsening Ecological Crisis' on the website of the Third World Network for a very strong version of the argument that globalisation produced this worsening of global environment (http://www.twnside.org.sg/title/pri-cn.htm).
7. It is not difficult to find circumstantial evidence in a number of developing countries (for example, Nepal, Sri Lanka) to show that violent domestic conflicts have intensified during an era of liberalisation-globalisation.
8. This widely used abbreviation refers to the Structural Adjustment Policies of the IMF-WB group.
9. If globalisation pushes up investment and technological advancement, it may promote economic efficiency and productivity improvement. Globalisation is also known to be enhancing conditions of instability and uncertainty, increasingly undermining productivity growth. The net effect of globalisation on economic efficiency, therefore, is at best unclear.
10. The significance of the interventionist role of the state in economic growth in the historical development of capitalism in general (see for example, Dowd 2000; Chang 2002) and in the more recent history of 'newly industrialising countries' in particular (see for example, Wade 1990; Hart-Landsberg 1993) is fairly well documented.
11. Margaret Thatcher, justifying her policy reform programme in the UK, is known to have used the acronym TINA to refer to the idea 'There Is No Alternative'.
12. Using the expression adopted in Bello et al. (2000, p. 19), proposals in this group fall into the 'it's the development model, stupid' school of reform proposals.

13. After a devastating critique of the liberalisation-globalisation model of development, Stiglitz writes on the question of alternatives: 'To some, there is an easy answer: Abandon globalisation. That is neither feasible nor desirable' (Stiglitz 2002, p. 214). Globalisation, according to Stiglitz, is '... the closer integration of the countries and peoples of the world which has been brought about by the enormous reduction of costs of transportation and communication, and the breaking down of artificial barriers to the flows of goods, services, capital, knowledge, and (to a lesser extent) people across borders' (Stiglitz 2002, p. 9).
14. There is no discussion here of prioritisation among different characteristics noted below and how they should be combined to form the overall development strategy. This will vary from one developing country to another. The alternative measures discussed below would fall into a structuralist frame of thinking.
15. Post-privatisation experiences of many countries are increasingly underlining the validity of this statement, particularly in respect of enterprises in utilities. Rail transport systems in Britain and the Netherlands, water companies in Britain and Bolivia, energy sector enterprises in the US (Enron), Brazil and Turkey are some widely discussed cases of efficiency loss after privatisation. As a country Singapore is extensively cited for some of its efficiently run public enterprises like its airport authority and national airlines.
16. The use of protective policies in the present era of globalisation gives rise to complex problems. Yet cautious, selective, critical and time-bound use of protectionist approaches will have a crucial role to play in infant industry promotion in the context of uneven world development. What is most needed is a strong government, which could retain a reasonable degree of autonomy from pressures emanating from industrialist lobbies.
17. Only in peripheral projects to the main policy package, like the 'integrated rural development programmes', would some element of people's participation be seen in the neo-liberal policy framework. Many instances are known where the government and donors concerned had come to realise how project designs could have been improved had the people been consulted in advance.
18. Even the serious global crises during the era of globalisation have not been able to change the fundamental contours of the process.

# REFERENCES


Bello, Walden, Nicola Bullard and Kamal Malhotra (eds) (2000), *Global Finance: New Thinking on Regulating Speculative Capital Markets*, Dhaka: The University Press and London and New York: Zed Books.

Bienefeld, Manfred (1994), 'Capitalism and the Nation State in the Dog Days of the Twentieth Century', in Ralph Miliband and Leo Panitch (eds), *Between Globalism and Nationalism: 30th Issue of Socialist Register*, pp. 94-129.

Chang, Ha-Joon (2002), *Kicking Away the Ladder: Development Strategy in Historical Perspective*, London: Anthem Press.

Chossudovsky, Michel (1997), *The Globalisation of Poverty: Impacts of IMF and World Bank Reforms*, Penang (Malaysia): Third World Network.

Cobham, Alexander (2001), *Capital Account Liberalisation and Poverty*, QEH Working Paper 70, Oxford.

Dowd, Douglas (2000), *Capitalism and its Economics: A Critical History*, London: Pluto Press.

Hart-Landsberg, Martin (1993), *The Rush to Development: Economic Change and Political Struggle in South* Korea, New York: Monthly Review Press.

Hirst, P. and G. Thompson (1996), *Globalization in Question: The International Economy and the Possibilities of Governance*, Cambridge: Polity Press.

Khor, Martin (2002), *Effects of Globalisation on Sustainable Development after UNCED*, Third World Network website: www.twnside.org.sg/title/rio-cn.htm.

Killick, Tony (1999), 'Making Adjustment Work for the Poor', *ODI Poverty Briefing* 5, May.

Klein, Naomi (2001), 'Reclaiming the Commons', *New Left Review*, May-June, 81-9.

MacEvan, Arthur (1994), 'Globalisation and Stagnation', in Ralph Miliband and Leo Panitch (eds), *Between Globalism and Nationalism: 30th Issue of Socialist Register*, pp. 130-43.

Mohan, Giles, Ed Brown, Bob Milward and Alfred B. Zack-Williams (2000), *Structural Adjustment: Theory, Practice and Impacts*, London and New York: Routledge.

Panitch, Leo (1994), 'Globalisation and the State' in Ralph Miliband and Leo Panitch (eds), *Between Globalism and Nationalism: 30th Issue of Socialist Register*, pp. 60-93.

Pendse, Sandeep (1998), 'Critique of Globalization and the Challenge for Alternatives', paper read at International Conference on Alternatives to Globalization (Nov. 7-9), Tagaytay City, Philippines, from the Internet – www.info.com.ph/~globalzn/speeches.htm.

Petras, James (1998), 'Globalization: A Socialist Persective', paper read at International Conference on Alternatives to Globalization (Nov. 7-9), Tagaytay City, Philippines, from the Internet – www.info.com.ph/~globalzn/speeches.htm.

Scholte, Jan Aart (2000), *Globalization: A Critical Introduction*, London: Macmillan.

Soros, George (2000), *Open Society: Reforming Global Capitalism*, London: Little, Brown and Company.

Stiglitz, Joseph E. (2002), *Globalization and its Discontents*, New York and London: W.W. Norton & Company.

Tujan Jr., Antonio (1998), 'Crisis and Globalization', paper read at International Conference on Alternatives to Globalization (Nov. 7-9), Tagaytay City, Philippines, from the Internet – www.info.com.ph/~globalzn/speeches.htm.

UNCTAD (2002), *Globalisation and Liberalisation: Effects of International Economic Relations on Poverty*, UNCTAD website: www.unctad.org.

UNU/IAS (2002), *The Sustainable Future of Global System: Endeavours from Rio to Johannesburg,* Tokyo: UN University.

Wade, Robert (1990), *Governing the Market: Economic Theory and the Role of Government in East Asian Industrialization,* Princeton: Princeton University Press.

Weisbrot, Mark, Dean Baker, Egor Kraev and Judy Chen (2001), 'The Scorecard on Globalization: Twenty Years of Diminished Progress', Washington Centre for Economic and Policy Research website: www.cepr.net/globalization/scorecard_on_globalization.htm.

World Bank (1993), *The East Asian Miracle: Economic Growth and Public Policy*, Oxford University Press for the World Bank.

# 3. Cultural and Linguistic Inequities: A Downside of Economic Globalisation

**Mariel Tisdell**

## 3.1 INTRODUCTION

This chapter presents some of the cultural, linguistic and, therefore, economic disadvantages resulting from the process of economic globalisation in the twentieth and twenty-first centuries. It also discusses government policies which attempt, but rarely succeed, in addressing cultural and linguistic inequities experienced by minority groups in a majority economy. It is suggested that traditional prejudice combined with the scale and the speed of global movement of people are responsible for this failure. The chapter concludes with a critical evaluation of the language policies of the European Union and their relevance to other countries within the global economy.

## 3.2 BRIEF HISTORICAL OVERVIEW

Many of the attributes of economic globalisation in the twentieth and twenty-first centuries are neither new nor recent. They have had their forerunners, albeit on a more moderate scale, throughout the development of human societies and are the result of interactions between socio-economic, cultural and political groups.

I refer to early trade in goods and commodities which used the ancient Silk Route, the shipping routes of Arabic, European and South Pacific traders, the trading practices of the Hanseatic League in the Middle Ages, the establishment of European trading posts and companies such as the Dutch East India Company and the British East India Company in the seventeenth and eighteenth centuries.

The demand for skills and expertise and the migration resulting from the demand for these specialised skills is not recent either but can be found throughout history.

Catherine the Great of Russia recruited German farmers into her empire for their proven expertise. Frederick the Great of Prussia had his royal residence in Potsdam built by Dutch craftsmen because he could not find similar levels of skills among his own people.

During the Mogul invasion in 1220/21 AD, hundreds of craftsmen were deported from the commercial centre of Samarkand because their skills were sought after by the Moguls (Rogers 1976, p. 19).

In the same region, in 750 AD, Muslim invaders captured and abducted Chinese craftsmen because of, among other things, their knowledge of how to produce paper, a skill that they subsequently made available to their Islamic masters (Rogers 1976, p. 25).

There are many more examples which show that international trade, exchange of skills and labour and the dominance of economic and political systems over other, less powerful economies are not recent developments. They predate both the European colonisation of Africa, India and the Americas and the much more recent global economic developments.

However, compared to these developments in the past, current processes of globalisation differ in the *scale* and the *speed* in which they are being established and in the way they are spreading. They also differ in the manner in which societies and governments have responded to the presence of and competition from newcomers.

The speed and scale of economic developments in our times surpass the scale of the economic effects brought about by the Roman Empire, the economic dominance of the European colonial powers, indeed of any previous economic and socio-political dominance at any time in the development of human society.

In recent decades the volumes of the production of goods and commodities and international trade have increased dramatically with drastic effects on minority economies, both on their markets and with respect to their labour force. People have moved or have been moved in search of work and in response to the demand for labour and skills in polarised areas of production. The steamroller effect created by the speed of production and marketing of goods produced by the most powerful economies has constituted a threat not only to local economies but, more importantly, to local cultures and societies by reducing, often eliminating, local production and by threatening culturally determined consumption patterns.

Inequalities in the status and the economic opportunities of political, economic and cultural minorities have been brought about principally by two factors, which in turn have been exacerbated by the current globalisation.

First, the movement of people into new work situations, the long-term separation from their home culture and home language have resulted in dislocation, isolation and social, economic and political disadvantage. Secondly, the dominance of major cultures and their economic power over established, traditional minority societies *within* the majority economy have produced inequities similar to those experienced by recent immigrant workers and their families.

In both situations the effect of globalisation has produced culturally, linguistically and educationally disadvantaged minorities within economically and politically dominant societies.

Unless governments of majority societies or the minority groups themselves have taken measures to provide access to educational facilities for workers and their families, enabling them to be integrated into mainstream society without being absorbed in the mainstream, minority groups have tended to remain disadvantaged.

The cultural and linguistic diversity of minority societies and groups has been preserved when majority governments have conferred recognition and secure status on the languages and cultures of existing minority groups and have acknowledged their diversity as a *resource* rather than as a *threatening agent*.

Such positive, inclusive policies are required both towards recently emerging minority groups such as the Turkish foreign workers in Germany, the Bangladeshi labour force in Brunei and the North African workers in France and towards indigenous groups and societies which are threatened in their own countries by dominant, exclusive economic and political practices.

Examples of historically disadvantaged minority groups can be found throughout history. I refer to the Australian Aborigines, the North American Indians, the Canadian Inuits, the Indian tribes in South America, the tribal groups in China, Bangladesh and India.

Their inequitable position within mainstream society continues to be exacerbated by global economic development.

There are now few countries that do not need to face up to the responsibilities of formulating and implementing policies which enable disadvantaged minority groups to share in the political and economic advantages of a global economy without having to give up their cultural diversity and individuality.

## 3.3 MINORITY GROUPS – CREATED FOR AND BECAUSE OF ECONOMIC DEVELOPMENTS

The movement of people in search for work and a higher standard of living as a result of demand for labour first assumed global proportions as a result of and during European colonialism.

Colonies were used to provide primary products and cheap labour. When needed, labourers were transported from one colony to another. The establishment of societies containing cultural and linguistic minorities were the result of colonial economic measures with global effects.

One of the less known but typical examples of the effects on the composition of population due to colonialism is the present population of Trinidad-Tobago. A sugar-growing agricultural area off the Venezuelan coast, this former colony was first a Spanish then a Portuguese possession. During its time as a colony, Trinidad-Tobago received slaves and indentured labourers from Madeira and Portugal and labourers from India. Recent census figures show that 40 per cent of the population are African descended and 40 per cent are Indian descended. Significant European, Chinese and Middle Eastern communities account for the rest. English (official), Hindi, Urdu, French and Spanish are Trinidad-Tobago's major languages (Ferguson 1998, p. 36).

Jamaica, situated in the Caribbean, had a similar colonial history involving the importation of people. It now has a population 90 per cent of which are African descended. English is its official language but Patois is widely spoken (Ferguson 2001, p. 36).

The smallest African nation, São Tomé & Principe, boasts a truly global labour force as a result of its amazing history. Its current population comprises the Angolares, reportedly descended from survivors of a slave ship wrecked in the 1540s, the Forros, descendents of the first Portuguese settlers and freed slaves, the Servisçais who were contract labourers from Cape Verde, Angola and Mozambique, and the Tongas who are descendents of the Servisçais. Its official language is Portuguese (Fazaeli 1999, p. 36). Madagascar's population provides an example of how, as a result of French colonial policy, Malayo-Polynesian, Arabic and African ethnic groups were transported, at times very long distances, to meet the demand for labour in this former French colony. Countries such as Brazil, the United States and many of the Pacific Islands have large multicultural, often multilingual populations as a consequence of former colonial labour and economic policies.

Dutch colonial plantation management in the nineteenth century was responsible for bringing legions of indentured workers from India, Indonesia, China and South Africa to the then Dutch colony of Suriname in the northern part of the South American continent. Guiana, the neighbour of Suriname, was subjected to a similar import of indentured labour from India, under British rule.

Indentured labourers, like the slaves who preceded them, were commodities within political and economic structures. They were victims of national and territorial ambitions that treated people as goods and assets that could be moved when and where they were considered to be most useful in providing cheap labour for the production of rubber, tea, coffee, cotton, cane sugar, minerals and precious stones.

In the nineteenth and twentieth centuries the major causes of the movements of people on an international, even global scale was migration. At times war, religious and political oppression or natural disasters resulting in famine, forced people to emigrate. Other causes for migration were the demand for specific skills, opportunities for expansion, development and investment combined with a spirit of adventure and a desire for a more independent lifestyle.[1]

Migration and the movement of people in the twentieth and twenty-first centuries have been due largely to the effects of war, persecution, famine, natural disasters and economic hardships resulting from these crises. At the end of the twentieth century one person in every 284 people on earth was a refugee looking for a new beginning. The number of foreign workers in industrialised countries continues to rise. In Germany, the number of asylum seekers doubled in the space of two years from 250,000 in 1990 to 450,000 in 1992. The following figures give some indication of the volume of people who have been on the move in search for a new home and existence. In 1998, 30 million people were forced to move within their own countries. Sixty million people are predicted to be landless and homeless by 2000 due to environmental destruction, 80 million migrants live in cities and another one and half million move there each year. In all, there are more than 100 million migrants and 20 million refugees (Ride 1998, pp. 18-19). These figures give some indication of the challenges faced by governments and societies when they attempt to meet the needs of these emerging groups in addition to those of already established multilingual and multicultural groups.

As a result of global economic development, the dominance of Western industrialised economies and their values has led to the establishment of a hierarchy of desirable and less desirable skills and levels of education. One such desirable skill is competence in the majority language and compliance with mainstream values as prerequisites to access education and training for and within the global economy.

## 3.4 THE RESPONSE FROM GOVERNMENTS

Governments of multilingual and multicultural societies face the challenge of ensuring equal rights as well as economic and social equity for all groups within their jurisdiction. The response of governments is one factor in determining the status of minority groups. The attitude of minorities themselves towards their languages and cultures is another. The third factor is the attitude of the majority society towards minority groups, which in turn influences government policies.

The need for national policies to ensure the rights of newcomers within established communities has been exacerbated by the volume of people movement throughout the world in the past decades. As mentioned above, in 1998, 100 million migrants and 20 million refugees were on the move. In more recent years, the numbers of refugees and migrants have increased even further.

Once placed in a new country or area, these people need to find work and means to earn their livelihood. Large cities attract most immigrants and refugees. Consequently our cities have grown even larger and more difficult to administer, yet they need to provide the infrastructure for large and diverse populations. Forty per cent of the population of Los Angeles consists of immigrants; comparable percentages of immigrants are 42 per cent in Toronto, 35 per cent in Vancouver, 34 per cent in Sydney and 33 per cent in Perth (Ride 1998 p. 19).

Most governments, minority and majority groups regard *language skills* in the majority language as the key to successful integration based on employment and acceptance within the majority society. However, because language and culture are crucial also to the retention of personal identity, self-worth and social fabric, speakers of minority languages call for the protection and secure status of their languages *alongside* access to the majority language. Governments need to accommodate both; the demands of minority and of majority groups in society.

In the formulation of national and regional language policies, governments may need to decide which language is to be the official language and whether there is to be more than one official language. The status of any other languages in the country needs to be clarified. Funds for the provision of language education in both the majority and the minority languages need to be allocated. Language policies can be a political hotbed. Some voters see a language and competence in the majority language as a symbol of dominance over speakers of other languages. Other voters interpret too much protection of minority languages and cultures as a threat to national identity and unity. The negation of language rights has led to violent conflict in defence of the right to speak, write and teach home languages. I refer to the war of independence in Bangladesh (involving Bengali in preference to Urdu), the riots in Belgium (involving French and Flemish), the bloody protests in Spain (demanding the protection of Catalan) and the conflict between English and French in Canada, which led to the establishment of two official languages.

Language constitutes the link to history and cultural identity. In times of crisis the language of one's community becomes the constant in an upheaval affecting every other aspect of life of displaced, moved and resettled migrants and refugees. It is, therefore, little wonder that they hold on to their home language, that they defend it and that they try to establish its value and relevance against the pressure exerted by the majority language and by linguistic globalisation through English.

While most countries have one official language, governments in other countries have established two, three or more official languages. Examples are countries like South Africa (English, Afrikaans, nine local languages), Singapore (Chinese, Malay, Tamil, English), New Zealand (English, Maori), Belgium (French, Flemish), Canada (English, French), India (Hindi, English, regional languages), Eire (Irish, English) and Switzerland (French, German, Italian, Romansch). In the United States, there are strong moves to establish Spanish as the second official language at least in the state of California.

Many of the multilingual and multicultural former colonies in Africa, Central and South America have adopted as their official language that of their former colonial rulers. For economic reasons and in order to bypass any local linguistic rivalry, a European language has been retained as the official language of communication, education and administration. In Rwanda the official language is French, in Zambia and Zimbabwe it is English. The official language of Argentina, Colombia, Guatemala and Mexico is Spanish, of Brazil it is Portuguese. In some countries indigenous languages have attained official language status alongside the European language. Kenya, Tanzania and Uganda use Swahili and English. Swaziland uses Swati and English, Peru and Bolivia include Quechua as a second language. The challenges to governments lie in the provision of education and training for speakers of all languages. In most cases, this means the establishment of classes and schools where minority language speakers learn to use the official language as a second language to a level of competence comparable to that of citizens whose first language is the official language.

Not all governments have insisted that minority groups become proficient in the majority/official language. Until recently, the governments in Sweden and Germany have left it to individuals as to whether and to what degree they became proficient in Swedish and German. This has now changed. Attendance at language classes has been made compulsory. Despite the inevitable additional costs, the governments in both countries have decided that ignorance of the official language has hindered the integration of minority groups. It has placed minority group employees at a disadvantage from which many could not, or would not, free themselves.

Predictably, the compulsion to achieve adequate proficiency levels in the official (often majority) language has met with some resistance among minority groups. They object to having to learn and use the majority language because of loyalty to and in defence of their own home language. Almost invariably such an attitude has meant that they have remained at the bottom of the economic ladder. They are excluded from mainstream education and training. Their access to school and post-secondary curricula is limited. They are at a disadvantage also when it comes to examinations and assessments, job applications, interviews and promotion at the workplace, all of which are conducted in the majority/official language

A review in 1986 of OECD policies showed that most governments had developed policies which treated minority languages and their speakers as a problem rather than as a resource (Fettes 1997, p. 17). This finding is confirmed when examining the policies of industrialised countries today, many of which have English as their majority and their official language.

The United States, Canada, New Zealand and Australia provide indigenous minority groups with bilingual schools. They encourage the teaching of minority languages and teaching of curriculum areas in the minority languages but only in the first three or four years of primary school. The funding for these programmes is often disputed. It is subject to cutbacks and to annual reviews. Long-term planning is hampered by the fact that funding for bilingual schools is tied to the budgets of respective governments. This makes the position of bilingual programmes vulnerable. Even in the best of situations, the early bilingual programmes are replaced in middle and upper primary by schooling in the majority language alone. Early bilingual education is rarely recognised as a means of retaining linguistic resources. Instead, it constitutes a first, transitionary stage towards monolingual education.

Programmes that try to overcome linguistic and cultural barriers and which rectify disadvantages created by the inability to use majority languages competently require considerable financial commitment on the part of governments. Often such commitment is considered to be outside the limits of what governments can afford. The inclusion of majority groups in mainstream education and the simultaneous support for the teaching of minority languages is considered by most governments and by most speakers of majority languages to be a luxury not a right, a privilege not an entitlement. In Britain, the provision of early bilingual education is restricted to the speakers of Welsh and Gaelic. It does not extend to the languages spoken by immigrants from former British colonies nor to recent refugee groups.

In Australia *The National Policy on Languages* (NPL) was launched in 1987 (Lo Bianco 1987). It consists of a range of recommendations, which acknowledge the cultural, social, economic and intellectual advantages, that arise from the fact that Australia has a multicultural and multilingual population. The NPL also states the right of all members of Australian society to receive instruction in order to acquire proficiency in the majority and official English language (Lo Bianco 1987, pp. 193-5).

However, despite its name the NPL never became law. It remained a set of recommendations upon which different state and federal governments acted in a variety of ways. Its effectiveness, therefore has been limited (Tisdell 2002, pp. 256-67).

Currently, the Australian state education systems provide and finance bridging programmes enabling adults and learners who have been accepted as migrants, or who have been granted refugee status, to acquire levels of English at no or at minimal cost to the learners. These programmes are based on triennial funding but can be subjected to annual reviews and sudden cutbacks. The Australian federal government provides some funding to minority groups so that they can provide for the teaching of their individual languages using teachers and facilities from within their own communities. This funding is also subject to conditions being met and is reviewed annually.

The success of programmes such as these is dependent not only on adequate government funding but on the attitude within the mainstream community. Australian prejudice towards monolingualism remains. The conviction expressed in the recommendations of the NPL that multilingualism in Australian society is a national resource (Lo Bianco 1987, pp. 15-18, 54-6) is not yet shared by the majority of Australians (Tisdell 2002).

The United States, too, is an example of how a society grows through immigration and how respective governments have failed to establish effective and equitable language policies and practices. Within its borders the United States has groups of indigenous people who, not unlike the Australian Aborigines, have been severely disadvantaged by a lack of policies and funding which safeguard their cultural and linguistic identity. From the beginning of European settlement, native American languages and cultures were stigmatised. Government policies at the beginning of the nineteenth century set about separating North American Indians, particularly their children, from their indigenous languages and cultures. English was the only language of instruction in all public schools.[2]

Today the teaching of heritage languages is allowed and provided for in the *Native American Language Act of 1990.* However, as mentioned earlier, the heritage language teaching is limited to bilingual programmes during the first three years of primary schooling. After that, native students join the 32 million Americans who speak a language other than English at home, are second language learners of the majority language and who need to find employment and social acceptance in a society which communicates in English and in particular, mainstream English at that. As in Britain and in Australia, schools in the United States focus on the teaching of mainstream English. They disallow African American English, Caribbean English and Indian English, for example. The volume of learners of mainstream English as a second language therefore increases dramatically with far reaching financial and economic implications for language policy planners.

Few countries have been able to achieve a balance between the rights and concerns of minority groups, their languages and cultures and the indisputable and perhaps unavoidable dominance and privileges of majority groups and their majority, often official language. Social and economic inequities have been the result, often leading to unrest and conflict both on a regional and on a global scale. There is no simple and generally applicable solution to the problems arising from the inability and/or unwillingness to allow for and to support linguistic and cultural diversity. Any solution requires substantial funding, long-term planning and – most importantly – a change of attitude at all levels of society. The measures that have been undertaken by the European Union over the past thirty years may provide a pattern and an example for other nations to adopt.

## 3.5 LANGUAGE POLICIES IN THE EUROPEAN UNION

The European Union (EU), its economy and its emerging European society mirror the problems and advantages of a global society and economy. The EU with its fifteen member countries and a population of 374 million is the world's largest trading power. Its population increases annually by two to three million asylum seekers from other parts of Europe and from across the world. In 2004, the EU is to be joined by a further ten new member countries.

Current and future member countries differ from one another in their history, culture, population size, living standards and economic output. They share the same currency and mostly they abide by the same economic rules and practices. The EU constitutes a response to centuries of war and self-destruction. All its members are unanimous in their desire to improve living and working conditions for all of their citizens. They accept the Charter of Human Rights and share parliamentary, democratic forms of government. Each of its members follows self-imposed regulations about providing minimum education and health services.

Given the presence of so many diverse cultures and languages, it is not surprising that the status of the eleven different languages is of significance to the EU. The EU has developed explicit policies safeguarding the languages of all member states. While English and French are two official languages in the EU, all information, all statements, every law and resolution, recommendation and any other written document must be issued and recorded in each of the languages of the member countries.

The European Council of Cultural Cooperation (ECCC) was founded in 1971. Since then it has been working towards achieving the following educational and political aims which impact directly and indirectly on the economic equity of EU citizens. These are some of the ECCC objectives:

- To build up mutual understanding – with respect to individual, local regional and national identities developing a common European intercultural identity by unforced mutual influence.
- To promote the personal development of the individual – as an active agent in a participatory, pluralist and democratic society.
- To provide a framework for close and effective international cooperation in the organisation of language learning (Trim 1996, pp. 81-5).

The ECCC policies have resulted in education initiatives ensuring that students in Europe become proficient in at least two languages other than their home language. This is a massive undertaking as the demand for proficient users of two and three European languages cannot wait for or solely rely on school systems to train such speakers over a lengthy period of time. The ECCC pushes for language learning at all levels of training and education including vocational training, university courses, the public service and adult education. Exchange programmes between schools and universities, 'year abroad' working programmes for apprentices and tradespeople, exchange possibilities for employees in banks, the public service and free enterprise establishments are commonplace. The implementation of such programmes has been successful because of the acceptance of and compliance with cultural and linguistic diversity by all EU members.

In 1998, the following recommendations were adopted by the Committee of EU Ministers concerning the position of modern languages. The governments of member countries are to:

- Pursue education policies that enable all Europeans to communicate with speakers of other tongues.
- Develop learners' respect for an intercultural world through direct links and exchanges.
- Promote widespread pluralingualism by encouraging all Europeans to achieve a degree of communicative ability in a number of languages
- Give appropriate recognition to language courses in national qualification systems, in particular public examinations
- Offer all young people in vocational training language courses so as to widen their access to information, equip them to participate in international projects, prepare them for taking up an occupation and increase their vocational mobility
- To enable adults to maintain and further develop their language skills and to encourage those with little or no previous language learning experience to acquire the ability to use a foreign language for communication purposes. (*Language Teaching* 1998, pp. 210-14)

Minimum proficiency packages have been developed for all EU majority and minority languages and for languages of countries that border the EU but are not members of it such as Norway. Language classes start at primary level and continue to the end of secondary and/or vocational training. The concept of a 'language passport' or 'language portfolio' has been developed which would assure any employer that applicants are competent in written and spoken communication in the target language. Such a portfolio also testifies to the ability and motivation of the applicant to improve existing language skills. It also testifies to the fact that applicants have developed knowledge, respect and sensitivity towards cultures other than their own as part of their training (Byram and Zarata 1996, pp. 239-43).

The implementation of these adopted recommendations will require time and will depend on the commitment of the governments of member countries to apply the recommendations within their own education systems. As we have seen in the case of Britain, some EU countries face a more difficult and a more complex task than others. Nevertheless, the EU has set itself clear goals in recognition that EU member countries need to equip their citizens in terms of linguistic skills and cultural attitudes so that they can be competitive and successful in the EU economy.

Although neither English nor French are majority languages in the EU (with 80 million speakers, German is the majority language) their status as official languages is undisputed. Most EU countries teach English and/or French as first and/or second foreign languages. Because of the secure status of their own minority languages within the European Union, speakers of minority languages do not feel that the acquisition of one or both official languages will endanger the status of their home languages. In practice, language learning in the EU countries extends beyond the learning of the two official languages. Competence in English is taken for granted and is so commonplace that it has almost ceased to put an employee at an advantage. It is the fact that a candidate is competent in *more* than 'just English' which makes a difference and gives applicants the edge.

The EU faces many economic, social and political challenges which are likely to increase, or at least re-emerge, as the number of new EU members grows and as the pressure from other countries to join the EU increases. However, the problems of economic disadvantages due to *linguistic and cultural differences* have been identified. They are being addressed by comprehensive, unambiguous and realistic policies in language planning and teaching. It is the systematic, progressive implementation of EU language policies by its member countries which could serve as a model for other countries in acknowledging and attacking the economic and social inequities arising from linguistic and cultural diversity in the context of a global economy.

## 3.6 CONCLUSION

This chapter has presented some of the causes responsible for economic inequities among linguistic and cultural minority groups within majority economies. It was noted that most governments have attempted to formulate policies to address education inequities based on linguistic and cultural diversity. It was seen, however, that governments have been reluctant to make *lasting* commitments to language laws. Instead, they have opted for 'wait and see' and 'survival of the fittest' attitudes, which leave minority groups at a permanent social and economic disadvantage. Such attitudes also deprive the majority society of valuable linguistic resources and fail to recognise the economic advantages created by cultural and linguistic diversity.

While the EU has established comprehensive language policies and while its member countries are in the process of implementing appropriate practices designed to minimise economic disadvantages arising from diverse linguistic and cultural backgrounds, the EU has yet to address the linguistic disadvantages of migrants and asylum seekers from non-member countries.

Increasing economic globalisation continues to exacerbate existing economic inequalities based on monolinguistic and monocultural prejudice. This increases the need for language policies and programmes within each country and on a global scale. Any government responses need to make long-term financial commitments to education. They need to acknowledge the scale and the speed of people movement as a consequence of global economic development and they need to accept their role in addressing arising inequities within their national economies. The acceptance of cultural and linguistic diversity and the understanding of the benefits that this diversity can produce in mainstream society needs to grow at all strata of society before the global economy can produce and accommodate the global citizen.

## NOTES

1. The migration patterns of the nineteenth century had their forerunners in the Middle Ages when examples of economically motivated voluntary emigration can be found particularly in Central and Eastern Europe. The Hungarian king Geza II invited migrants from southern Germany to settle in his kingdom for the explicit purpose of working in the mines and securing the eastern borders of the kingdom. In return and clearly as an incentive to migration the immigrants received a number of privileges from the Hungarian king. Immigrants were able to retain their own, independent lifestyle, keep their culture and language and to prosper within their settlements. Similar provisions were made for immigrants from central Europe in Russia, Rumania, and Bulgaria during the eighteenth

century. Many of the well-established ethnic enclaves in Eastern Europe owe their existence to such voluntary migration based on economic incentives.
2. The obsession with English went so far in Nebraska that in 1923 the teaching of *any* language other than English, including other European languages, was forbidden. This law was repealed by the US Supreme Court in 1927. However, the fact that such a law existed at all is indicative of the monolinguistic phobia, which prevailed at the time (Ricento 1997, p. 138).

# REFERENCES

Byram, M. and G. Zarata (1996), 'Defining and assessing intercultural competence: some principles and proposals for the European context', *Language Teaching*, October, **29**, 239-43.
Fazaeli, Z. (1999), 'Country in profile: São Tomé & Principe', *New Internationalist*, November, 36.
Ferguson, J. (1998), 'Country in profile: Trinidad & Tobago', *New Internationalist*, September, 36.
Ferguson, J. (2001), 'Country in profile: Jamaica', *New Internationalist*, April, 36.
Fettes, M. (1997), 'Language planning and education', in R. Wodak and D. Corson (eds), *Encyclopedia of Language and Education*, Vol. I, Dordrecht: Kluwer Academic Publishers, pp. 13-22.
*Language Teaching* (1998), European Union, Recommendation No R (98) 6 of the Committee of Ministers to member states concerning modern languages – adopted by the Council of Ministers on 17 March 1998 at the 623rd meeting of the Ministers' Deputies, Cambridge University Press, October, pp. 210-14.
Lo Bianco, J. (1987), *The National Policy on Languages,* Canberra: Commonwealth Department of Education.
Ride, A. (ed.) (1998), 'Migration – the facts', *New Internationalist*, **305**, September, pp. 18-19.
Ricento, T.R. (1997), 'Language policy and education in the United States', in R. Wodak and D. Corson (eds), *Encyclopedia of Language and Education,* Vol. 1, Dordrecht: Kluwer Academic Publishers, pp. 137-48.
Rogers, M. (1976), *The Spread of Islam*, Oxford: Elsevier/Phaidon.
Tisdell, M. (2002), 'Socio-economic aspects of language policies: an Australian perspective', in D.M. Lamberton (ed.), *The Economics of Language*, Cheltenham: Edward Elgar, pp. 256-67.
Trim, J. (1996), 'Modern languages in the Council of Europe', *Language Teaching*, April, **29**, 81-5.

# 4. Is Regionalism the Outcome of Insufficient or Excessive Globalisation?[1]

**Serge Svizzero, Laurence Lasselle and Clem Tisdell**

## 4.1 INTRODUCTION

It is widely agreed that during the last two decades the process of economic globalisation has been strengthened and extended to almost all countries and all economic activities. This has been a result of technological change that has reduced the real cost of communication and transport, and of institutional changes, such as the lowering of tariff barriers, designed to reduce social restrictions on international trade. The movement towards laissez-faire market systems is globally supported by bodies such as the International Monetary Fund (IMF) and the World Bank. Furthermore, after it came into existence after World War II, the General Agreement on Tariffs and Trade (GATT), and subsequently the World Trade Organisation (WTO) have played a central role in the economic globalisation process. Through its 'most favoured nation' (MFN) clause,[2] GATT promoted multilateralism. This was designed to rule out preference for one or a group of nations in international trade access to a particular country. Consequently, the aim was to make international trade access non-discriminatory thereby encouraging multilateralism with the ultimate goal of achieving global free trade.

Though economic globalisation has spread, GATT's objectives for multilateralism have encountered new barriers, partly because of the simultaneous evolution of regionalism. The Uruguay Round of GATT negotiations that commenced in 1986 and after several extensions, ended in Marrakech in 1994, were intended to extend multilateralism. Despite final agreement at Marrakech, not all nations were satisfied with the outcome and no agreement was reached on rules covering foreign direct investment. Moreover, many developing countries have found it difficult to implement the agreement and feel that it unfairly treated international trade in agricultural products, textiles and clothing (compare McCulloch et al. 2001).

As multilateral trade agreements are more and more difficult to negotiate, trade agreements have progressively taken a new form, namely regionalism. Broadly speaking, regionalism can be defined as any policy designed to reduce trade barriers between a subset of countries. Contrary to multilateralism, regionalism is intrinsically discriminatory. It is now widely developed. There are currently more than one hundred preferential trading agreements[3] (PTAs) all around the world. In theory there exist four main types of PTA: a free trade agreement, a customs union, a common market and an economic union.[4] A free trade agreement (FTA) is a PTA among members under which tariffs are lowered to other members but maintained against non-members. Contrary to the customs union, in which there is free trade among members and a common external tariff on trade with non-members, any member of an FTA may impose its own tariffs to non-members. It is probably this feature which explains why PTAs concluded in recent years consisted almost entirely of FTAs.

Two phenomena can be pointed out concerning trade agreements.

On the one hand, the WTO policies encouraging economic globalisation and based on multilateralism are in crisis. Violent protests took place at the Millennium Meeting held in Seattle in November 1999. Actions against the WTO were sustained by the widening gap between rich and poor countries and the growing number of people living on less than $2 per day (compare Tisdell et al. 2004 for a discussion about the inequality of nations). On the other hand, there has been an increasing number of PTAs.

In this article, we first outline the decline in multilateralism and the rise of regionalism and consider whether the two trends are connected (Section 4.2). We then pose the question of whether regionalism is currently an appropriate and reliable stepping-stone towards international free trade and multilateralism (Section 4.3). Authors such as Bergsten (1997) and Ethier (1998) claim strongly that it is. However, Viner's analysis (Viner 1950) suggests the need to be more cautious. Viner highlights several economic disadvantages of regionalism compared to multilateralism (Section 4.4). In view of these disadvantages, it seems possible that regionalism is a response to problems of political integration arising from intense economic globalisation rather than an economic ideal (Section 4.5).

## 4.2 REGIONALISM AND MULTILATERALISM: DEFINITION AND HISTORICAL TRENDS

Regionalism can be defined as a tendency towards some form of PTAs between a finite number of countries belonging possibly to a particular region. Such arrangements are not new. They were prevalent in the eighteenth and nineteenth centuries. These PTAs between sovereign states[5] were a means to obtain better access to markets and therefore sustained economic growth based on exports. Their purposes were also political. They were designed to build either colonial empires or a sovereign state.[6] These arrangements were also 'preferential'. Countries that did not belong to a particular regional arrangement were discriminated against.

Such intrinsic features explain the recurrent controversy regarding the desirability of regionalism. They also explain why during World War II the shift towards multilateralism[7] occurred. First, multilateralism was a means to avoid the formation of regional blocs since the latter, and more specifically, their discriminatory nature, had been partly responsible for the Second World War.[8] Second, it was also a means to avoid a massive shift back to protectionism that had transformed the 1930s economic crisis into a 'great depression'. Finally, it was a means for the powerful US economy to get access to foreign markets since most of these were protected until World War II by different PTAs derived from colonialism.

In 1947, the International Trade Organisation became the GATT. The GATT's Articles were the basis for the international trading system. Broadly speaking, GATT's goal was to promote free trade, that is, to liberalise trade at the world level. For that purpose, gradual liberalisation was negotiated among countries. The negotiations were multilateral and they dealt with the instruments of protection, namely tariffs. The two pillars of the GATT system were reciprocity and non-discrimination (Bagwell and Staiger 1998, pp. 1171-76).

The reciprocity pillar is not specific to multilateralism.[9] It simply states that the negotiated agreements feature the mutual exchange of concessions.[10] The non-discrimination pillar is the cornerstone of multilateralism. It states that each country is the MFN of every other country. The MFN clause in Article 1 of GATT forbids countries from pursuing discriminatory trade policies against one another. Indeed, '...any advantage, favour, privilege or immunity granted by any contracting party to any product originating in or destined for any other country shall be accorded immediately and unconditionally to the like product originating in or destined for the territories of all other contracting parties' (GATT 1994, p. 486). As pointed out by Krueger (1999, p. 105), the MFN existed before GATT. Indeed, except for the USA (until 1923), European countries were using such a clause in their bilateral agreements (since the nineteenth century) because in its absence, bilateral trade agreements were costly and their members were gaining little.[11] In other words, multilateralism – and its MFN clause – can be considered as a simple extension of regionalism, given the intrinsic problems of the latter.

From the late 1940s to the early 1980s, the GATT system was successful. There was a general trend towards multilateral free trade. PTAs were the exception rather than the rule. Seven major multilateral trade agreements were concluded, each a so-called 'Round'. The first five rounds were 'parallel' bilateral negotiations, the remaining two were multilateral negotiations. One major exception has been the European Union (EU). From the Treaty of Rome in 1957 to the current Union, it has probably been the most successful customs union. Of course, its creation was initially motivated by geopolitical goals. The purpose was, on the one hand to avoid a third world war due to intra-European conflicts, and on the other hand to form a bloc against the Soviet Union and the East European economic bloc.[12] Although the European customs union was a case of pure regionalism, it was considered consistent with multilateral trade liberalisation. Indeed, it appeared during the post-war period that the EU was lowering its tariffs and expanding trade with the rest of the world at a very rapid rate.

In fact, regionalism – as illustrated by the EU – is not excluded by GATT and its multilateral approach. Article 24 of the GATT[13] – and the now WTO[14] – accommodates PTAs within the multilateral trading system provided they meet three criteria. First, they must cover 'substantially all' trade of members. Second, they must avoid raising new barriers to non-members. Third, they must achieve free trade among members by a certain date.[15]

Despite the example of the EU and the opportunities provided by GATT's Article 24, PTAs were not well accepted until the early-1980s. Most trade agreements were based on multilateralism. Attitudes were in fact largely influenced by the USA which had emerged after World War II as the champion of a non-discriminatory global trade regime grounded firmly in the MFN principle.

All this changed in 1982 when the launch of a new round of multilateral trade negotiations was quickly aborted.[16] Multilateralism was then more or less abandoned in favour of regionalism (or PTAs). As the Europeans blocked the initiation of this round, the USA began efforts to start it by adopting a 'two-track' approach. On the one hand, they continued to seek multilateral liberalisation under GATT. On the other hand, they decided to abandon their opposition to regional arrangements. Thereafter, they concluded several PTAs with various partners such as the Caribbean countries,[17] Israel in 1985, Canada[18] in 1989. PTAs were also signed between other developed and developing[19] countries.[20] At the end of 1998, the WTO listed 98 PTAs in force (Krueger 1999, p. 110). Since 1994 (see Table 4.1), over 60 per cent of world trade has taken place within regional arrangements that have either achieved free trade or have pledged to do so.

In fact, the share of world trade resulting from PTAs has increased faster than world trade, the latter having itself grown[21] at an average annual rate of 6.5 per cent while world GDP grew at an average annual rate of 2 per cent. But, in parallel, the process of economic globalisation has been reinforced year after year. This emergence of regionalism leads to the following questions: is regionalism the best way under which the globalisation process can be pursued? In other words, is regionalism a stepping-stone towards further trade liberalisation and economic globalisation? If not, can regionalism be considered as a means to solve problems that have emerged from excessive globalisation?

*Table 4.1 Regional free trade arrangements (share of world trade, 1994) (%)*

| | |
|---|---|
| EU | 22.8 |
| EUROMED | 2.3 |
| NAFTA | 7.9 |
| MERCOSUR | 0.3 |
| Free trade Area of the Americas (in addition to its sub-regionals) | 2.6 |
| AFTA | 1.3 |
| Australia-New Zealand | 0.1 |
| APEC (in addition to its sub-regionals) | 23.7 |
| **Total** | **61.0** |

## 4.3 BEYOND MULTILATERALISM: FURTHER GLOBALISATION THROUGH REGIONALISM

Considering regionalism as a means to liberalise trade further than the level possible under multilateralism was the argument enunciated by US officials in the early 1980s. When negotiations on further multilateral liberalisation are blocked, like in the aborted 1982 round, a PTA allows member countries to go further, that is, to liberalise beyond the extent that takes place multilaterally. Therefore PTAs promote freer trade and multilateralism. Indeed, it is often claimed, using Viner's (1950) terminology[22] and also empirical evidence, that PTAs are predominantly 'trade creating'. Let us recall that when a country enters into a customs union, its trade is going to be affected twofold. This country can 'create' trade with its new economic partners, but it can also 'lose' trade if the trade within the customs union simply replaces trade with countries outside the union, that is, the so-called trade diversion effect.[23] Generally, one expects the former effect to dominate the latter effect. Therefore PTAs provide support for further multilateral liberalisation. This result comes from several rationales. For instance, in an FTA the producers of different members face different external tariffs. Then, competition among these producers tends to put pressure on external tariffs until harmonisation is reached as in a customs union. Of course, the implied tariffs reduction encourages trade creation.

Furthermore, regionalism promotes multilateralism since it has important demonstration effects. When countries use a PTA to go further, they provide a demonstration of the benefits of regionalism. This may in turn induce other countries to soften their resistance to multilateral liberalisation. For officials as well as for voters of countries who are reluctant to open their markets, their participation in a regional initiative can provide some 'learning by doing' and this may facilitate the adoption of further trade liberalisation. Similarly, an agreement on a thorny topic that seems impossible to be reached under multilateralism can be negotiated much faster under regionalism. Regional initiatives can often be subsequently generalised in the multilateral system.[24]

Several arguments derived from a political economy analysis also show that deepening integration in a trade bloc can trigger the expansion of the bloc, leading the world one step closer to multilateral free trade.

First, regional arrangements favour global liberalisation especially when they include developing countries and/or when they consist of a large country linking with other small countries. Indeed, under such circumstances, the regional agreement is a means for the countries to 'lock-in' their domestic reforms,[25] that is, to prevent following governments from reversing them. Such commitment, when it is credible, is synonymous with stability and usually induces an increase of trade and investment flows from large countries.

Secondly, when a country, especially if it is small and developing, participates in a regional agreement, its own interests can be better defended at the international level. For instance, small countries with similar interests can combine (CARICOM, Caribbean Community) and their mutual co-operation can be effective within their bloc but also at the world level. One can also claim that multilateral negotiations between big trade blocs are simpler than between a multitude of countries. Indeed, on the one hand, there are fewer negotiators around the table, and on the other hand, a PTA can be used as a bargaining threat to encourage multilateral trade agreements.[26] However, it is possible that fewer players at the negotiation table can also mean tougher and more radical positions.

Thirdly, regionalism offers a device to create links between countries that were previously antagonists.[27] Economic integration is often a stepping-stone to a deeper political integration.

The economic and political arguments mentioned above help to ensure that regional agreements are in practice building blocs for further liberalisation rather than stumbling blocs that deter such progress (Ethier 1998). This concept of regionalism and of PTAs is often defined as 'open regionalism' (Bergsten 1997). It contrasts sharply with the closed, import-substituting regionalism of the 1950s and the 1960s. Let us emphasise that open regionalism has only been adopted by one PTA as a fundamental principle, namely by APEC. It refers to plurilateral agreements that are non-exclusive and open to new members. The main features of open regionalism are the following ones (US Council of Economic Advisors 1995). First, members are allowed to liberalise further unilaterally or with non-members on a reciprocal basis. Therefore, customs unions are excluded while FTAs are not. Secondly, the plurilateral initiatives must be fully consistent with Article 24 of the GATT. Thirdly and more importantly, regionalism is 'open', that is, there is open membership and even positive encouragement to non-members to join. In other words, a PTA based on this 'open regionalism doctrine' can encompass the entire world and thus lead to multilateral free trade.

Regionalism, especially when it is consistent with the 'open regionalism' criteria, can be considered as a device that accelerates progress towards global liberalisation. However, that device needs to be tempered, as we shall discuss in the next section.

## 4.4 THE LIMITED BENEFITS OF REGIONALISM

Until Viner's (1950) seminal work, it was commonly acknowledged that any move towards free trade, through multilateralism or regionalism, was necessarily welfare improving. Indeed, at a first sight, a PTA increased the welfare of members while it remained neutral with respect to the welfare of non-members.

Following the end of the Second World War and pledges to create an European common market, the Carnegie Endowment commissioned Jacob Viner to study the 'Customs Union Issue'. Viner (1950) and his followers, such as Meade (1955) and Lipsey (1960), elaborated the economics of what is now called 'First Regionalism'.[28] This approach examines the static welfare effects of PTAs, specifically of customs unions. Viner reached a counter-intuitive conclusion: although regional integration arrangements may be trade-creating, they may also be trade-diverting. The entry of country A into a customs union has two effects for A. Country A can create trade with its new economic partners, but it can also 'lose' trade if the trade within the customs union simply replaces trade with countries outside the union. Therefore the net impact of the customs union on trade, and therefore on economic welfare of its members, is questionable. The net impact on trade is positive if the trade creation effect outweighs the trade diversion effect. Contrary to the intuitive pre-Vinerian belief, the welfare impact of regionalism critically depends on the circumstances surrounding each arrangement.[29] Such a conclusion is consistent with the second-best theory. While the (first-best) global trade liberalisation is necessarily welfare-improving, the (second-best) intra-regional trade liberalisation may have positive as well as negative impacts on welfare.

The effect of trade diversion needs to be closely watched. It has often been considered as a negligible phenomenon (for example, by Summers 1991). However, as reported by Bhagwati et al. (1998), an increasing number of empirical studies begin to show that trade diversion is important in current PTAs.[30]

Hence, the welfare of a country member of a PTA may decrease when trade diversion dominates since the latter involves shifting imports from lower to higher cost suppliers.[31] The trade diversion effect may be important since tariffs, which are mostly very low, remain very high for particular economic activities. For instance, several tariff peaks exist in agriculture, making PTAs quite dangerous for the countries involved. In manufacturing industry, a customs union member can displace a more efficient outside supplier by taking advantage of the tariff preference it enjoys in a partner country.[32] Buyers in the customs union then have to buy some expensive goods produced within the customs union rather than those produced outside the union. The agreement clearly improves intra-regional trade, but at the expense of buyers.

Moreover, even if all tariffs are low, other means, such as an anti-dumping policy, may be used to discriminate against non-members. Note that such instruments are elastic and selective, that is, they permit discrimination against specific countries and even specific firms within those countries. In addition to trade diversion, a country's welfare may decrease with a PTA, depending on arrangements for redistribution of tariff revenues among the members (see for instance Panagariya 1996).

Some economists may have neglected trade diversion because they were only considering PTAs as involving 'natural trading partners'. They studied countries that already traded a lot with each other and that were geographically proximate. The notion of 'natural trading partners', apparently quite intuitive, is in fact very controversial. Following Krugman (1991) and Summers (1991) who used it to explain the presumed beneficial effects of regionalism, this notion has been criticised, for instance, by Bhagwati, (1995). Natural trading partners can be defined using two criteria: a high volume of trade among partners and a low distance between them. Both criteria are dubious. For the latter, since transport costs are not different from any other cost, they do not deserve special attention.[33] Concerning the former criterion, it is not the volume of trade but the elasticities of substitution among products that are much more important in assessing the trade diversion effect.

Consequently, current theory does not provide a clear guide to the total welfare effect of regionalism. Furthermore, difficulties are encountered by regionalism in practice. Indeed, PTAs that are mainly FTAs necessarily include preferential rules of origin and regional content requirements. Recall that in an FTA, each member retains its own outside tariffs. Therefore and in the absence of rules, a product from outside will enter into the FTA through a unique country, that is, through the lowest-tariff member country. To avoid this possibility, FTAs are supplemented by rules of origin that stipulate the conditions under which goods entering a member country will be 'deemed' to have 'origin' in the partner country.

However, rules of origin lead to a significant controversy (Krueger 1999). Indeed, they necessitate determination, for a given good, of the percentage of its inputs or of its added-value that originates in the partner country. This gives rise to disputes among members. The enforcement of such rules and their implementation impose high costs on members.[34] Moreover, when a given country belongs to several FTAs, each FTA including several countries, the rules of origin overlap, leading to what Bhagwati (1995) called the 'Spaghetti Bowl' phenomenon. Rules of origin, an inherent part of FTAs, constitute in practice a hindrance to the success of regionalism.[35]

In addition to the previously mentioned shortcomings, regionalism is claimed to lead to 'attention' diversion. In other words, when a country actively engages in regional arrangements, it becomes uninterested in participating in the multilateral system. This criticism, mainly emphasized by the USA, also explains why regionalism and multilateralism can be in conflict. Furthermore the formation of strong and quite independent trade blocs, such as these existing between the First and the Second World Wars, have negative geopolitical impacts: any disagreement may transform peaceful economic blocs into aggressive political blocs.

For all the reasons previously mentioned in this section, regionalism is not a panacea, that is, it is not necessarily a stepping-stone towards freer trade and liberalisation. This rather pessimistic conclusion is in fact shared by many economists (Bagwell and Staiger 1998; Bhagwati et al. 1998; Krueger 1999) and by a growing number of officials and policy-makers. Indeed, since the late 1990s, several planned regional initiatives have been abandoned. The number of FTAs, increasing until the mid-1990s, is now stationary. For instance, the inclusion of Eastern Europe into the EU was frozen until last October. Likewise the US desire to turn APEC into an FTA has been rejected by its Asian members. The latter consider that any trade liberalisation under APEC should be on a MFN basis.[36]

## 4.5 REGIONALISM AS A REACTION TO MULTILATERAL-BASED GLOBALISATION

During the last three decades, globalisation has contributed to economic growth mainly by reducing trade barriers and increasing trade and investment flows. However economic globalisation is at the heart of several economic disequilibria and inequalities. This is so not only within countries, but also between countries and groups of countries. It is often claimed that the rise of unemployment rates observed since the mid-1970s in northern countries can be partly explained by globalisation (Lasselle et al. 2004). There has indeed been greater competition from the south and an acceleration of skill-based technological change as a result of growing globalisation (Svizzero and Tisdell 2002). The strong process of economic globalisation, encouraged by international organisations, has led in some cases to convergence but also in some other cases to increasing income inequalities between nations (Tisdell et al. 2004).

As the economic globalisation process expands rapidly, competitive pressure sharply increases and implies more structural adjustment of the national markets. In such a context, regionalism can be interpreted as a strategy to soften the negative social impacts of globalisation. In a political economy approach, trade policy – especially when it leads to regionalism – can be viewed as determined by lobbying either concentrated interest groups or sovereign states. Let us consider both influences on the choice of trade policy.

The interest group which seems to be decisive in determining trade policy consists of domestic firms. This group can promote some regional arrangements as a means to protect themselves from the rise of foreign competition.[37] Indeed, if producers are protectionist, they may accept a PTA in order to avoid further multilateral liberalisation. However, even if they are not protectionist, they may prefer regionalism to multilateralism, especially if the former is associated with a large trade-diversion effect (Krishna 1998). Assume for instance that two countries are engaged in a bilateral arrangement. If there is little trade diversion, any firm of each country gains preferential access to the market of the partner's country. But since no trade is diverted from external firms, the arrangement looks like a zero-sum game.[38] Nevertheless, if trade is diverted away from the rest of the world's firms, the producers of both countries gain more and are therefore more likely to support the arrangement. This is a well-known result in economic literature (see, for example, Krueger 1999; Winters 1996). In the presence of lobbies, trade diversion is good politics even if it is bad economics.

Beyond the fact that trade-diverting PTAs are more likely to be supported politically, they could critically change domestic incentives, so multilateral liberalisation, which was initially feasible, could be rendered infeasible by a PTA. In other words, sector-specific lobbies are a danger if regionalism is permitted since they tend to stop blocs from moving all the way to global free trade. Such an implication is illustrated for instance by MacLaren (2002). Indeed, when countries are negotiating about a future PTA, the firms of these countries are urged to make sector-specific sunk investments in order to produce accordingly to the pledged PTA. The expected regionalism leads each member country to specialise its economy in order to gain more within its regional bloc. Once the PTA is concluded, any move towards multilateral free trade that was possible before is henceforth almost impossible. After the PTA, firms within the bloc incur sunk costs as a result of their investment specific to their bloc, On the other hand, while member countries are more specialised towards each other, bloc and non-bloc countries are mutually less specialised. The expected supply of regionalism has generated its own demand since when regionalism is effective, the ex-post demand for multilateral free trade diminishes.

Besides the producers' strategy, regionalism can also be viewed as the result of decisions by states. Indeed, with growing economic globalisation, several governments have seen their policy activities curtailed to a considerable extent. Economic globalisation is making it increasingly difficult for nation states to control their own economic affairs independently of the rest of the world (Tisdell 2001). This reduction of governance possibilities is clearly illustrated by capital mobility and fiscal competitiveness. Indeed, in a world of capital mobility, governments' capacity to tax capital is eroded as jurisdictions are pitted against another. Therefore, embracing regionalism has been for states a means for recovering their governance capacity, that is, the control of the public management of the economy. This strategy can be considered as the outcome of three independent influences.

First, most large trading corporations and multinational companies are nowadays strongly in favour of economic globalisation. The decisions they take, especially about their location, have major economic influences, notably on employment opportunities. Therefore, this can result in harmful competition between countries desiring to attract these firms. Likewise, any multinational company may try to take advantage of fiscal and tariff differentials existing between the countries in which its production process is to be segmented (Eden 1998; Clausing 2001). Indeed, when a firm's production is segmented internationally, this gives rise to intra-firm trade. Such trade is realised 'out of the market' and at a price often called the 'transfer price' or the 'shadow price'. Many multinational companies manipulate their transfer pricing in order to minimise their fiscal burden. This leads to revenue losses for governments unless there exist some arrangements between countries to avoid such practices. Thus, under regionalism, nations are more able to countervail against multinational companies, that is, to maintain their revenues through the harmonisation of tariffs, fiscal policies, standards (and so on).

Secondly, northern countries have faced increasing competition for specific products from southern countries since the mid-1970s. Besides this, competition among northern countries has increased in the supply of goods such as agricultural products[39] and cars.[40] In both cases, regionalism has permitted concerned countries to protect their economy from external competition and to keep their governance capacity. For many people, notably voters, the last point is important. Indeed, the public management of the economy is regarded by many as a good thing in helping to stabilise and to regulate economic activity. It also provides some degree of social insurance to citizens.

Thirdly, it is highly probable that regionalism implies regionalism, that is, that the strategy of some countries has much more to do with herd behaviour than with rational economic choices. It is well known that at the national level or at the international level (Knickerbocker 1973) a firm mainly makes its decision in reaction to the strategies adopted by its main competitors. For nations, the same logic prevails, at least partially. Baldwin (1995, 1997) has tried to evaluate 'domino regionalism'. Countries that do not belong to a trade bloc try either to join it or to create a new bloc. As noted by Bourguignon et al. (2002, p.26), in analysing this domino effect, 'one act of regional integration may stimulate the next because, the larger a bloc, the greater the costs to excluded countries of not belonging to it'. This domino process has happened, but it has probably not led to freer trade. Indeed, as there are fewer players in a round, the players can be more sensitive to the negotiation issues and the gains can be low.

## 4.6 CONCLUDING COMMENTS

Are PTAs building blocs or rather stumbling blocs to further multilateral liberalisation? As Winters (1996) said, 'we don't know yet'. Theory, as well as practice, provides no definite answer. The theoretical models are too far from reality. Empirical studies are not able to insulate the effects of PTAs from what is happening in the world economy. Let us add that, as many PTAs are quite recent, there is not enough data for satisfactory econometric studies. However, as the number of PTAs is growing, trade is becoming more concentrated in PTAs. This does not prove anything about the extent of trade diversion or trade creation nor does it help us in our debate about 'regionalism *vs.* multilateralism'.

To our question 'Is regionalism the outcome of insufficient or of excessive globalisation?'; we can now say that it has no clear answer. According to several authors (Rodrik 2001; Summers 1999), international economic integration has not yet gone too far. Globalisation remains remarkably limited, for instance by national borders and jurisdictions. Consequently, there still remain economic, as well as political, benefits to be obtained from further economic integration.

The main hindrance faced by the globalisation process is the absence of political or institutional underpinnings for integration. Even if economics is becoming more and more integrated, politics remains highly national. One can argue that there is possibly a need for a 'world government', but there is no tendency towards such an outcome. Political integration is already far more difficult than economic integration at the regional level (the EU is a perfect example). Furthermore, the absence of the former implies the standstill of the latter. While in theory, economic integration seems to be more beneficial and, therefore, easier when national economies are quite different, the converse is true in practice for political integration.[41]

Although economic integration can be beneficial, its management is much more difficult to implement. Whereas governments of almost all developed countries are democratically elected, the election of a world democratic government is currently impossible. Such difficulties are often summarised via the existence of an 'integration trilemma'. In this trilemma, three features are impossible to conciliate: international economic integration, governance and national sovereignty (Rodrik 2001; Summers 1999). Facing such a trilemma, regionalism appears to be a compromise solution. Pursuing integration at sub-global levels allows economic integration and trade liberalisation to proceed and also limits problems arising from lack of political integration.

## NOTES

1. Collaboration of Serge Svizzero and Clem Tisdell in contributing to this chapter was assisted by their 2002-2003 award from FEAST-France. They are grateful for this award. The usual caveat applies.
2. See GATT, Article 1.
3. Nations establish PTAs under which the tariffs they apply to each other's products are lower than the rates on the same goods coming from other countries (Krugman and Obstfeld 2000, p. 241).
4. A common market is a customs union which also allows free movements of factors of production. An economic union is a common market with common economic laws such as standards across members.
5. For instance, the 1860 Franco-British free trade agreement.
6. See the German customs union called the 'Zollverein' which led to the formation of the German state.

7. The establishment of three multilateral economic institutions was considered. These were the International Monetary Fund, the International Bank for Reconstruction and Development and the International Trade Organisation.
8. See the UK's imperial preferences (later Commonwealth) and the closed economic zone created in Central Europe by Nazi Germany in the 1930s.
9. It is allowed under regionalism. Only unilateralism excludes reciprocity.
10. See GATT, Articles 28 and 28 bis.
11. For instance, without the MFN clause, bilateral agreements implied that the same imported commodity was often subject to varying tariff rates, depending on its country of origin.
12. Namely the COMECON (Council for Mutual Economic Co-operation).
13. Article 5 of GATS (General Agreement on Trade in Services), adopted in Marrakech (1994), extends to services the coverage of GATT Article 24.
14. The Uruguay Round (1994) created a new institution, the WTO, to replace the secretariat of the GATT.
15. Normally not to exceed 10 years from the start date of the regional agreement.
16. The eighth round (the so-called Uruguay Round) finally started in 1986 in Punta del Este and was completed in 1994.
17. Under the Caribbean Basin Initiative.
18. While the USA-Canada Auto-Pact was concluded in 1965.
19. For example, ASEAN (Association of Southeast Asian Nations), MERCOSUR (Southern Common Market Agreement also known as the Treaty of Asunción).
20. The only region which has so far remained firmly committed to multilateralism – and implicitly to the MFN clause – is East Asia.
21. Over the period 1990 to 1997.
22. See Section 4.4.
23. See Section 4.4 for a more detailed analysis.
24. WTO rules about investment are, for instance, largely derived from the ones adopted formerly in PTAs, namely by NAFTA (North American Free Trade Agreement) and by the Australia-New Zealand Closer External Relations Agreement.
25. Especially trade reforms.
26. Some people claim that the creation of APEC (Asia Pacific Economic Co-operation) in 1989 was a means for the US to reach agreements during the Uruguay Round (started in 1986) on topics (such as agriculture) for which there was a deep conflict with the EU.
27. See France and Germany, or Japan, China and East Asia.
28. Following Bhagwati's (1991) terminology.
29. These circumstances determine the magnitudes of the trade-creation and the trade-diversion effects.
30. This is especially true for countries (Argentina, Brazil, Paraguay, Uruguay) belonging to MERCOSUR. For an empirical study on MERCOSUR, see Yates (1996).
31. The welfare reduction also comes from the loss of tariff revenues incurred by members.
32. On the contrary, trade creation is a beneficial effect that arises from a union partner undermining another union member's less efficient industry.
33. If high transport costs prevent trade opportunities, they are not reduced by the formation of any PTA.
34. Herin (1986) estimated that the cost to EFTA (European Free Trade Agreement) members of documenting origin to receive duty-free entry into the EU averaged 3 to 5 per cent of the price.
35. This conclusion must be lessened since rules of origin also have the advantage for members of constituting an efficient instrument of protectionism.
36. Therefore, they confirm their wish to belong to any form of regionalism only if it is 'open regionalism'.
37. Firms might also want regionalism in order to create a standard of their products and capture a larger share of the market. In a longer run and if the PTA is strengthened, their products could become the world standard.
38. Of course, if the competitiveness of firms of both countries is not too different.

39. See the recurrent conflict between the USA and the EU and the Common Agricultural Policy adopted by the latter from its first days.
40. See the conflict between the EU and Japan and the Voluntary Exports Restraint (VER) adopted by the latter.
41. See for instance the difficulties encountered by the EU for the accession of Eastern Europe countries or of Turkey which are the most different from existing members.

## REFERENCES


Baldwin, R.E. (1995), 'A domino theory of regionalism', in R.E. Baldwin, P. Haaparanta and J. Kiander (eds), *Expanding Membership in the European Union*, Cambridge, UK: Cambridge University Press, pp.25-48.

Baldwin, R.E. (1997), 'The causes of regionalism', *The World Economy*, **20**, 865-88.

Bagwell, K. and R.W. Staiger (1998), 'Will preferential agreements undermine the Multilateral Trading System?', *Economic Journal*, **108** (449), 1162-82.

Bergsten, C.F. (1997), *Open Regionalism*, Working Paper 97-3, Washington: Institute for International Economics.

Bhagwati, J. (1991), *The World Trading System at Risk*, Princeton: Princeton University Press.

Bhagwati, J. (1995), 'U.S. trade policy: the infatuation with free trade areas', in J. Bhagwati and A.O. Krueger (eds), *The Dangerous Drift to Preferential Trade Agreements*, Washington DC: American Enterprise Institute, pp. 1-18.

Bhagwati, J., D. Greenaway and A. Panagariya (1998), 'Trading preferentially: theory and policy', *Economic Journal,* **108** (449), 1128-48.

Bourguignon, F., D. Coyle, R. Fernandez, F. Giavazzi, D. Marin, K. O'Rourke, R. Portes, P. Seabright, A.J. Venables, T. Verdier and L.A. Winters (2002) *Making Sense of Globalisation: A Guide to the Economic Issues*, CEPR Policy Paper #8, London: CEPR.

Clausing, K.A. (2001), *The Behaviour of Intra-Firm Trade Prices in US International Price Data*, BLS Working Paper #333, Washington: Bureau of Labor Statistics.

Eden, L. (1998), *Taxing Multinationals: Transfer Pricing and Corporate Income Taxation in North America*, Toronto: University of Toronto Press.

Ethier, W.J. (1998), 'The new regionalism', *Economic Journal*, **108** (449), 1149-61.

GATT (1994), *The Results of the Uruguay Round of Multilateral Trade Negotiations – The Legal Texts*, Geneva: GATT Secretariat.

Herin, J. (1986), *Rules of Origin and Differences between Tariff Levels in EFTA and in the EC*, EFTA Occasional Paper No. 13, February, Geneva: European Free Trade Association.

Knickerbocker, F.T. (1973), *Oligopolistic Reaction and Multinational Enterprise*. Harvard: Harvard University Press.

Krishna, P. (1998), 'Regionalism and multilateralism: a political economy approach', *Quarterly Journal of Economics*, **113** (1), 227-51.

Krueger, A.O. (1999), 'Are preferential trading arrangements trade-liberalizing or protectionist?', *Journal of Economic Perspectives,* **13** (4), 105-24.

Krugman, P. (1991), 'The Move to Free Trade Zones. Federal Reserve Bank of Kansas City', *Policy Implications of Trade and Currency Zones*, Proceedings of the Federal Reserve Bank of Kansas City, Kansas City, USA.

Krugman, P and M. Obstfeld (2000), *International Economics, Theory and Policy*, 5th edition, Reading, MA: Addison-Wesley.

Lasselle, L., S. Svizzero and C. Tisdell (2004), 'Globalisation and the nature of unemployment', in C. Tisdell and R. K. Sen (eds), *Economic Globalisation: Social Conflicts, Labour and Environmental Issues*, Cheltenham, UK and Northampton, MA, USA: Edward Elgar.
Lipsey, R.G. (1960), 'The theory of customs unions: a general survey', *Economic Journal*, **70**, 496-513.
MacLaren, J. (2002), 'A theory of insidious regionalism', *Quarterly Journal of Economics*, **117** (2), 571-608.
McCulloch, N., L.A. Winters and X. Cirera (2001), *Trade Liberalization and Poverty: a Handbook*, London: CEPR.
Meade, J. (1955), *The Theory of Customs Unions*, Amsterdam: North Holland.
Panagariya, A. (1996), 'The free trade of the Americas: good for Latin America?', *The World Economy,* **19** (5), 485-515.
Rodrik, D. (2001), 'How far will international economic integration go?', *Journal of Economic Perspectives,* **14** (1), 177-86.
Summers, L.H. (1991), Regionalism and the world trading system, in *Policy Implications of Trade and Currency Zones*, Proceedings of the Federal Reserve Bank of Kansas City, Kansas City, USA.
Summers, L.H. (1999), 'Reflections on managing global integration', *Journal of Economic Perspectives,* **13** (2), 3-18.
Svizzero, S. and C. Tisdell (2002), 'Reconciling globalisation and technological change: growing income inequalities and remedial policies', *Intereconomics. Review of European Economic Policy,* **37** (3), 162-71.
Tisdell, C. (2001), 'The political economy of globalisation: processes involving the role of markets, institutions and governance', *Economic Theory, Applications and Issues*, Working Paper N° 7, School of Economics, University of Queensland.
Tisdell, C., S. Svizzero and L. Lasselle (2004), 'Unequal economic gains of nations from globalisation', in C. Tisdell and R.K. Sen (eds), *Economic Globalisation: Social Conflicts, Labour and Environmental Issues*, Cheltenham, UK and Northampton, MA, USA: Edward Elgar.
U.S. Council of Economic Advisors (1995), *Economic Report of the President*, Council of Economic Advisors: Washington D.C.
Viner, J. (1950), *The Customs Union Issue.*, New York: Carnegie Endowment for the International Peace.
Winters, L.A. (1996), *Regionalism versus Multilateralism*, World Bank Working Paper No.1687, Washington DC: World Bank.
Yates, A.J. (1996), 'Does MERCOSUR raise concerns about the effects of regional trade arrangements?', *World Bank Economic Review*, L2:1, 1-28.

# PART II

# RICH AND POOR NATIONS AND GLOBALISATION: DIFFERENT ATTITUDES, PERSPECTIVES AND BENEFITS

# 5. Unequal Economic Gains of Nations from Globalisation[1]

**Clem Tisdell, Serge Svizzero and Laurence Lasselle**

## 5.1 INTRODUCTION

This chapter briefly reviews conflicting views about whether globalisation promotes economic equality or inequality of nations. It notes that the extent of globalisation of markets differs. Labour markets seem internationally more restricted than most other markets. Restrictions on the international mobility of labour seem to be a major reason for inequality of incomes persisting between nations and actually widening. In fact, as economic globalisation has proceeded, income inequality between nations has risen. Combined with restrictions on international labour movements, this inequality may arise, to a substantial extent, because some nations are unable or barely able to participate in economic globalisation for structural reasons. Even though some nations may be very willing to engage in international trade and accept foreign direct investment, little such trade and investment may emerge for them, whereas the opposite may be so for other nations. Such a dichotomy will add to income inequality between nations. However, a fully liberalised world economy with free labour movements may not be conducive to long-term economic growth and is unlikely to promote resource allocation globally that is economically optimal. Given current worldwide institutional arrangements, it seems that the higher income countries are the major economic beneficiaries from globalisation. This is a source of resentment by low-income countries. This resentment is intensified because higher-income countries on the whole have, as they have become richer, reduced their aid to developing countries and increased the conditionality of such aid.

There is no widely accepted definition of globalisation but basically, it is the process of connecting all parts of the Earth into one entity. Economic globalisation is the process of extending and integrating markets and economies so they are no longer confined to a single region or nation but form part of an international global economic system. The World Bank

(2000a, p. 1) suggests that the core sense of economic globalisation refers to the observation that 'in recent years a quickly rising share of economic activity in the world seems to be taking place between people who live in different countries'. This view is widely accepted.

Views differ, however, about the extent to which different nations benefit from globalisation. Mainstream economists mostly believe that all nations participating in economic globalisation realise net economic benefits and many go further and suggest that the process is a strong force for equalising per capita incomes between nations. Therefore, as globalisation proceeds, one might expect to observe convergence in per capita income between nations.

On the other hand, those economists, such as Myrdal (1956) and Frank (1978), with a strong interest in centre-periphery theories of development, take a more critical view. They argue that economic gains from globalisation will be concentrated in centre countries (mostly established high-income countries) and that few economic benefits may be received by peripheral countries, mostly low-income developing countries. Many of these low-income countries may, according to this view, suffer economic retardation and some may even become worse off economically than if not linked with economic globalisation. According to the centre-periphery view, globalisation can be expected to cause per capita national incomes to diverge, and income per head may even fall for some peripheral nations or be lower than might have been the case if they had been less strongly enmeshed in globalisation.

Given these different points of view and theories, much effort has been devoted to determining whether processes of market integration involving growing globalisation are associated with convergence or divergence of the per capita income of nations, and in some cases, regions. As we shall see, resolving the matter is extremely difficult. In considering this matter, it is useful first to discuss different types of markets that may be globalised or become more open. The extension of all markets rarely proceeds at the same rate and today some important markets remain globally restricted, such as labour markets. Furthermore, even when nations open their markets, for instance for capital for foreign direct investment, not all receive major inflows of such capital. Secondly, we identify conditions that may result in a nation making an economic gain or loss from opening different types of markets. Thirdly, recent data relating to changes in income differences between nations is presented and discussed. Finally, the possibility is raised that a high degree of openness involving intense competition could reduce global economic growth in the long term, and furthermore, that given spillovers and processes of cumulative causation, and scale economies, such as those identified by Myrdal (1956), Romer (1986) and others, resources may be globally allocated to regions in an economically inferior fashion.

Thus, an open system may result in allocation of resources that significantly fails to maximise global benefits from resources used for economic activity.

Note that in this chapter, we are not concerned about the impact of economic globalisation on income inequality, or on the incidence of poverty within nations. While these are important subjects, they are addressed to some extent elsewhere in this book. However, it may be mentioned here that despite the view of Dollar and Kraay (2001) that globalisation leads to faster growth and poverty reduction in poor countries, the evidence is indeed mixed, especially as far as the incidence of rural poverty is concerned.

The following hypotheses will be discussed.

1. The possibility that relative lack of globalisation of some markets, particularly labour markets, contributes to persistent inequalities in average per capita income levels between nations. In fact, this might help to explain widening gaps if technical progress is more rapid in high income countries than lower income ones, as seems probable. This would cause the marginal productivity curve of labour (see Figure 5.1 below) in higher income countries to rise relative to that in lower income countries.
2. The World Bank argues that income inequality between nations has risen in recent decades. But the relative economic losers, in its view, are those economies that have failed to open up. However, it is argued here that the bulk of the economies that failed to open up or have not become very open may have deep-seated reasons why opening up is not a favourable economic growth option for them. It is possible that the extent of opening up reflects internal conditions conducive to economic growth, rather than vice versa. It is easy to confuse cause and effect. This may have happened in this case. Timing in opening up may also be important in influencing gains from it.
3. The ability of globalisation to promote economic growth in the long term might be limited.
4. Globalisation cannot be expected to result in a Kaldor-Hicks optimal allocation of resources internationally.

Let us consider these matters in turn.

## 5.2 DIFFERENCES IN NATIONAL ECONOMIC BENEFITS FROM OPENING UP MARKETS FOR DIFFERENT COMMODITY AND RESOURCE TYPES

First, not all types of commodities and resources participate equally in economic globalisation because of their nature (for example, some involve high market transaction costs) and secondly, there appears to be a greater political reluctance to open the market for some commodities and factors of production, such as labour, than for others. Thus, both 'natural' and political factors help to explain differences in the degree of participation of commodities in economic globalisation. National net benefits are liable to vary with the category of commodities or resources subject to a global market and the extent to which global markets cover the full range of commodities/resources.

Consider the following categories of commodities including resources:

1. Products and services.
2. Capital, especially foreign direct investment.
3. Labour.
4. Natural resources.
5. Knowledge, especially technical and managerial know-how.
6. Entrepreneurship.

Since 1950, markets for tradable products and services and natural resources have become more open globally, and so too have capital markets (Lindert and Williamson 2003). In particular, many countries have adopted measures to open their economies to foreign direct investment. This in turn adds to the international mobility of technical and managerial know-how. On the other hand, many nations have resisted pressures for increased migration. Although illegal migration probably has increased in recent years and although there is considerable international movement of labour, global labour markets remain restricted. Yet, if a major aim of economic globalisation is to reduce international inequality, relatively easy migration could be a powerful force in bringing about such a reduction.

It could be argued that if economic globalisation is adding to income inequality between nations, this is because the opening up process is incomplete and in particular, does not include labour to a sufficient extent. If migration was not restricted, then presumably there would be a tendency for labour from low income countries to migrate to high income countries until incomes between countries became equalised on average.

Neoclassical arguments that market integration for tradeable products and services benefits all participants are well known, and include analyses based on comparative advantage in production and differences in tastes. Therefore, as a country opens up this category of markets, we might expect it at least initially to enjoy significant economic growth and rising per capita incomes. However, there has been controversy about whether specialisation by initial comparative advantage will benefit the nation in the long run. Singer (1950) and Prebisch (1950) argue that nations with an initial advantage in agricultural or primary production may become locked into these industries by engaging in free trade. Historical evidence (it is claimed) indicates that the trend in the terms of trade is against primary exports. Therefore, primary exporting countries as a whole experience falling income from exports. While an individual or a few primary exporters might increase or maintain their export revenue by expanding the value of their primary exports, this is not a viable strategy for the whole group because the price effect will reduce their total export revenue given that the elasticity of demand for primary products is relatively low. To avoid being trapped in such a situation, it is suggested that countries with an initial comparative advantage in primary production should foster the development of some secondary or tertiary industry with government support or protection.

Much depends on how strong the lock-in effect is and whether the tendency of the terms of trade to move against agricultural exporters is a longer-term one. Lindert and Williamson (2003) argue that it is not a long-term trend. Furthermore, while a lock-in effect is probably present, it is not true that all countries that initially specialised in agricultural exports continue to do so today under open trade conditions. The United States is an example. Lock-in is not, therefore, absolute but it can be substantial.

A related argument is the infant industry argument of List (1966) that selected industries may require government protection initially in order to develop them to a stage where they can become internationally competitive. The early start of other nations in industrial development and the advanced stage of their learning-by-doing, may be the main reason for their competitive advantage in an industry. As a result of protection, a late developing nation may be able to overcome this barrier and develop an industry that is even more competitive by world standards. While this argument is valid, the main problem is to select such industries accurately, if indeed the nation concerned has any such industries.

Trading in products and services, however, is not the only relevant aspect of globalisation. International movements in factors of production are also important. Movements of capital, especially those involving foreign direct investment, have been given prominence in the globalisation debate. Just as the proportion of world GDP entering international trade has risen in the modern era, so too have international capital movements.

While short-term international capital movements might add to monetary instability, in general, economists have taken a more favourable view of capital movements involving foreign direct investment. Most argue that it can be expected to benefit both the host nation and the foreign investor. Such direct investment often brings not only capital to capital-poor countries but new technologies and know-how. It can act as a catalyst for the development of complementary domestic businesses and even in the longer run, competing domestic businesses. It often provides international market access for products that could not enter this market merely on the basis of domestic effort. Initial exports achieved from production by multinationals and joint ventures in a host country may pave the way for a country to establish itself in foreign markets and eventually gain acceptance for products produced by its own firms. This is likely to happen, for example, in China's case.

These are some possible positive benefits of foreign direct investment. However, centre-periphery theorists, and others, also warn of possible drawbacks. For example, a less developed country could become locked into technological, market and even managerial dependence for its export industries because of foreign direct investment, for instance, by multinationals. Unless special effort is taken by the host, such lock-in could become relatively permanent, and may not maximise its economic advantage. While some small or least developed nations will inevitably remain in a situation of high technological dependence, it is not inevitable for large nations, such as China and India. While foreign direct investment can be expected to accelerate their development, it will probably be most beneficial to such large countries to reduce their degree of dependence on it in the long term. While this may happen naturally, it may require some government intervention. Although foreign direct investment can bring immediate economic benefits for the host country, it may not be an unmixed long-term blessing. In the long term, it may retard the economic growth of the host nation if the host is passive. But some nations have few prospects for development on their own and could obtain most by following a process of continuing economic dependence on foreign direct investment.

Markets for natural resources that are reasonably transportable now appear to be relatively open globally. However, common access to some natural resources of an environmental nature is creating problems as the global economy expands. Emission of greenhouse gases is one such problem. If it does trigger sea-level rises, the economic gains and losses from this will be very uneven between nations.

It is probably true that international movements of knowledge, especially technical and managerial know-how and entrepreneurship, have been facilitated in recent years. For one thing, increasing foreign direct investment makes their transfer easier. Nevertheless, technological gaps between more developed countries and less developed ones can be a persistent (and even a growing source) of international income inequality, as suggested by neo-technology theories of international trade and investment and the 'monopoly-profit' thesis of gains from international trade as developed by authors such as Posner (1961), Hufbauer (1966), Gruber et al. (1967), Wells (1969), Hirsch (1972), Lowinger (1975) and Teubal (1975) and as discussed, for example, by Tisdell (1981, Ch. 2). If more developed nations increase their technological lead and increase their ability to enforce their rights in intellectual knowledge as globalisation proceeds, this can be a strong force for increasing their incomes relative to those in developing countries. This could be a major contributor to increasing inequality between nations. Krugman and Venables (1995) have explored a related core-periphery theory but in their model, inequality between nations at first increases and subsequently declines. However, there is no reason to believe that this is a general case and it is unknown how long reversal will take in reality.

Also, highly-skilled persons find it is easier to migrate as globalisation occurs because their skills are in international demand. However, for most individuals, the possibilities of international migration are still highly restricted. The UNDP (1999, p. 31) observes: 'The collapse of space, time and borders may be creating a global village, but not everyone can be a citizen. The global professional elite faces low borders, but billions of others find borders as high as ever.' While significant international movements of labour do occur, globalisation of labour markets seems to lag considerably behind globalisation of markets for the other factors of production, as mentioned above.

This may be for political and cultural reasons. If migration or labour movements were not restricted internationally, a movement of labour from low-income to high-income countries might be expected with a tendency for wages to be equalised everywhere, if diminishing labour productivity is the rule in all countries. In a competitive static setting, wages in high-income countries would fall and they would rise in low-income countries.

This can be illustrated for a simple Ricardian-type case. Assume two countries: A, a higher income country and B, a low-income country, with no trade between the countries. Suppose also only two sets of factors of production. Labour is the sole variable factor and the other factors are fixed in supply and specific to the countries concerned. Furthermore, for simplicity, assume a single internationally untraded product, X, a static situation and diminishing marginal productivity of labour.

Given this set of assumptions, the production possibilities of these two countries can be illustrated by Figure 5.1. The line CDKE represents the marginal productivity of labour in country A and line FHG that in country B. Suppose initially that the amount of labour (population) in country A is $\hat{L}_A$ and in country B is $\hat{L}_B$ and this corresponds to the supply of labour in each. Consequently, wage levels are $w_B$ in the low-income country and $w_A$ in the high-income country. At the same time, note that the marginal productivity of labour is higher in country A than in country B so global production is not at a maximum for the initial labour allocation.

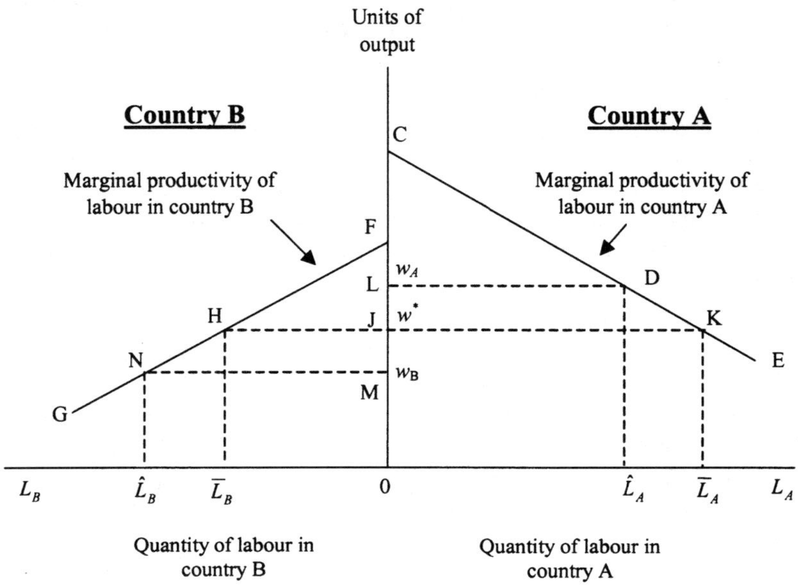


*Figure 5.1 A case in which international labour migration equalises wage-income between nations, raises global production and makes a global Kaldor-Hicks optimum possible*

If, as a result of globalising tendencies, free global migration becomes possible and if there are no barriers to labour movements, labour will move from the low-income country to the high-income one. This process will continue until wage rates equalise, in this case at $w^*$. The migration process in this case will therefore stop when population equals $\overline{L}_B$ in country B and $\overline{L}_A$ in country A. An amount of labour $\hat{L}_B - \overline{L}_B = \overline{L}_A - \hat{L}_A$ migrates from the low-income country to the high-income one.

As a result, the incomes of labourers initially in country A, the high-income country, fall whereas the wages rise of those who remain in country B or migrate. The income of those who own or possess fixed factors of production in the high-income country rises whereas rentiers in the initially lower-income country have a reduction in their income. Thus, globalisation in this case benefits some economic groups and disadvantages others. Nevertheless, a Kaldor-Hicks improvement results.

As pointed out in the Stolper-Samuelson theorem, in the absence of labour movements, free trade in products may have similar (but not identical) consequences to freedom of labour movements, as outlined above.

It should, however, be borne in mind that the above model is rather particular. It takes no account of market failures such as externalities associated with population increase in a particular country, scale and agglomeration economies and so on. In fact, when such failures are taken into account, free labour movements may not result in a global Kaldor-Hicks gain (see Tisdell 1990, Ch. 9).

It should also be noted that in more realistic models even if greater globalisation of labour tends to equalise wage rates on average between nations, it may increase income inequality within nations, for example, differences in the income of the skilled and the unskilled. If greater labour mobility internationally is associated with a general increase in intensity of market competition, it may have adverse impacts from a Schumpetarian viewpoint, on economic growth. Particular economic problems may arise for countries and regions that become heavily depopulated (see for example, Tisdell 1990, Ch. 9).

Despite this, one would expect residents of low-income countries to benefit most (on the whole) from free mobility of labour (compare Tisdell 1990, Ch. 10). It could be argued, therefore, that if there is a tendency for income *inequality* between nations to rise with globalisation, it is mainly because the economic globalisation process is incomplete since labour markets are excluded to a large extent. As long as globalisation remains partial in this way, it may be difficult to eliminate major income differences between nations. Nevertheless, given the extent of globalisation that has occurred, does the available evidence indicate that incomes per capita of nations are converging or diverging? If regular empirical relationships do exist between globalisation and income inequality of nations, how might these be explained? Let us consider both matters.

## 5.3 EVIDENCE ON THE IMPACT OF GLOBALISATION ON INCOME INEQUALITY BETWEEN NATIONS AND REASONS FOR OBSERVED RELATIONSHIPS

Evidence about whether economic globalisation has increased or decreased income inequality between nations is mixed. However, the World Bank (2000c, p. 2) reports:

> The distribution of per-capita income between countries has become more unequal in recent decades. For example, in 1960 the average per capita GDP in the richest 20 countries in the world was 15 times that of the poorest 20. Today this gap has widened to 30 times, since rich countries have on average grown faster than poor ones. Indeed, per capita incomes in the poorest countries have hardly changed since 1960, and have fallen in several.

Despite this, the World Bank is not inclined to attribute this growing international inequality to globalisation per se. Rather it suggests that those less developed nations more open to trade (those that are more globalised) have in the period 1960-1995 grown at a slightly faster rate on average than the world's rich countries, and that it is the poor *closed* economies that have grown at a very slow rate or even in some cases, experienced negative growth (World Bank 2000c, p. 2). The World Bank (2000b) cites evidence that more trade in relation to GDP (greater trade openness) promotes economic growth. The World Bank refers to Ades and Glaeser (1999) and Frankel and Romer (1999) in support of its case. The latter suggest, on the basis of empirical evidence that a rise of 10 per cent in the trade to GDP ratio of a nation raises per capita income by 5 per cent. However, the fit of their linear regression is relatively poor.

Furthermore, we need to bear in mind that a positive association between trade openness and economic growth does not imply causality. In particular, it cannot be concluded that if some currently lagging countries were able to increase their trade to GDP ratios, they would automatically experience greater economic growth. As discussed later, they may face serious natural or social barriers to increasing their trade to GDP ratio. Further, several countries that have had high trade to GDP ratios have not been engaged in free trade. China is an example and its performance influences the conclusion of the World Bank to a considerable extent – it has had a very high growth rate and it has a high proportion of trade to GDP in recent decades. Now (2001) that China has joined the World Trade Organisation, it should move towards a more liberal trade regime. In addition, there are also queries about whether the data are for a long enough period and whether the growth results will be sustained.

It is noticeable also that several rich countries are oil-exporting countries. Their high incomes do depend on exports and they have a high ratio of trade to GDP. However, in the long term their income from non-renewable resource exploitation is likely to be unsustainable. One does not suggest that they do not trade but their trade may not result in a permanent sustained stream of income for them (compare Tisdell 1998; Tisdell and Fairbairn 1984).

This all indicates that both rich and poor countries having a high degree of trade openness can be very diverse. Therefore, considerable caution needs to be exercised in interpreting the type of regression results reported by Frankel and Romer (1999).

Again, trade to GDP ratios are just one indicator of the globalisation process. For example, foreign direct investment is another significant component. Whether it is closely and positively associated with trade openness is unclear, but it may be. However, its results may be long term rather than short term and difficult to evaluate empirically using aggregated empirical data. In the final analysis, the economic results from foreign direct investments may depend upon the science and technology policies of the host, its capacity to assimilate new technologies and eventually to use these, to some extent, independently and to its own advantage. Not all countries have equal ability to benefit in this way. Furthermore, not all countries will be equally attractive to foreign direct investors. Some less developed nations have poor social and physical infrastructure, relatively unproductive resources, physical barriers to trade and commerce, or socio-cultural and political problems that deter foreign direct investment.

The fact of the matter seems to be that not all countries are able to gain from economic globalisation. If economic growth is limited to the group of those nations that can gain from globalisation, inequality in per capita incomes between nations can be expected to rise as globalisation proceeds. It is easy to suggest that those nations that do not join the globalisation bandwagon do so of their own volition. However, it seems to us that this would be a gross distortion of reality.

Nations with few resources in global demand and too remote to engage in world trade because of physical trade barriers, as are some small Pacific island nations, can hardly be blamed for their predicament or for failing to attract much foreign direct investment. Furthermore, even the socio-cultural and political impediments to investment in some countries are often beyond the individual control of small groups of nationals in the countries concerned. They are more like exogenous factors than controlled variables. Furthermore, these impediments usually take a long time to change.

Therefore, the fact that some nations do not receive much foreign direct investment and do not have high trade to GDP ratios can be a result of fundamental circumstances which they do not control. Such factors are often signs of structural or basic resource and social impediments that relegate nations to comparative poverty. They are a *result* rather than a *cause* of the poverty and lack of growth of many less developed nations. While this may not be true in every case, it seems to be so for a considerable number of poor countries described by the World Bank as poor and closed. Many of these countries would be able to gain most from the globalisation process if their residents were able to work abroad or migrate. Openness, to some extent at least, is a function of the economic growth potential within a country. Openness may largely be the result of factors conducive to economic growth within a country rather than the major impetus to such growth. Nevertheless, mutual causality is likely to be present.

Lindert and Williamson (2003) suggest that the gains which a nation obtains from globalisation depend on when it begins to participate in the process, that is, on timing. For example, Taiwan, Singapore and Hong Kong had an outward-looking economic policy at a time when most other lower-income countries did not. Therefore, they did not have so many competitors and could increase their income substantially by their outward policies. The fact that China opened up economically more quickly than India might also favour China. On the other hand, some countries might open up to foreign direct investment too quickly. For example, the governance of some may be so defective that little of the natural resource rent from the exploitation of natural resources by foreign direct investment may be captured by the host country because of corruption. Furthermore, the captured rent may not be used for investment or be used effectively for this purpose. This, for instance, has happened in the Solomon Islands in the past in relation to the exploitation of its forests (Tisdell 2000, pp. 171-2).

The plight of many of the world's poorest countries is of concern because even if economic globalisation is a panacea for economic growth (which is by no means certain), they are unable to share in the benefits of it to any considerable extent because of their particular circumstances.

Broadly speaking, nations *might* be divided into four groups on the basis of their total economic gains from economic globalisation: (A) Those able to achieve significant economic gains, such as more developed countries producing 'leading edge' technologies, and some less developed countries; (B) those countries able to achieve only moderate economic gains; (C) those making no economic gain or negligible economic gain, such as those that are too remote or which for institutional reasons are unable to open up to any great extent, such as possibly some remote Pacific island countries; and (D) countries that lose by the economic globalisation process, at least initially. This last group may include several central Asian economies in transition. It may, however, be possible for nations to shift categories with the passage of time. The value of the above framework is that it allows for the possibility of unequal gains from globalisation. While optimists may believe that sets (C) and (D) are empty, there is no reason a priori to believe that this is so.

## 5.4 WILL GLOBALISATION CONTINUE TO PROMOTE ECONOMIC GROWTH? WILL IT PROMOTE A COMPARATIVELY IDEAL ALLOCATION OF RESOURCES GLOBALLY?

If globalisation is now a major force promoting economic growth, will it continue to be so? Possibly economic globalisation might only be a strong growth force in its initial stages when considerable economic inequality exists between those nations able to participate effectively in globalisation.

Once this inequality is reduced, globalisation could become a less effective contributor to economic growth. In the mature globalisation phase, opportunities for earning high returns from making 'catching up' foreign direct investments in developing countries may well have disappeared. Furthermore, if the convergence theory is correct, low wages will no longer provide an incentive for investing in those developing countries able to participate in the globalisation processes because their wage levels will have converged to those in high-income countries.

In the mature globalisation phase, economic growth may depend heavily on the ability of firms to innovate. But there are at least three possible reasons why that might falter in the long term in a globalised world:

1. If a few dominant industries become heavily concentrated as a result of global competition, such concentration may reduce the rate of innovation for reasons mentioned by Schumpeter (1942).
2. Global competition may reduce business diversity. If such competition is fierce, firms may have to adopt the current 'best practices' to survive. This may reduce the scope for experimentation and diversity both of which can, up to a point, favour innovation and technological progress (Tisdell 1999).
3. Intense economic globalisation leads to the loss of economic niches. So businesses are deprived of some market protected areas to use as a base for innovation (Tisdell and Seidl, forthcoming) which slows innovation. This is a similar point to the main hypothesis of Schumpeter (1942).

In a world globalised but not intensely globalised, greater technical progress and innovation may occur than would be the case in a highly globalised competitive world. Furthermore, in an innovating business world, the lion's share of economic gains is likely to go to those countries able to maintain a steady rate of innovations provided that their intellectual property rights can be protected. Nevertheless, despite this inequality, the whole globe may, in the long run, be better off as a result of such innovation than would be the case in its absence.

There is, in addition, no guarantee that globalisation will promote a Pareto optimal allocation of resources globally, even if free population movements are allowed. Significant externalities seem to be associated with the creation of new knowledge and its application and, up to a point, external economies from agglomeration are present (compare Romer 1986). This gives rise to time path-dependence as does learning-by-doing. Thus, countries that become part of the economic centre early are liable to persist in the centre and attract resources. But because both timing and externalities are important influences on resource allocation, adjustments do not promote a global optimum. Lock-in effects are present (compare Tisdell 1990, Ch. 9). The importance of such effects was stressed by Myrdal (1956).

It is probably too much to expect economic globalisation to promote a global Pareto optimum, and it is not clear how distorted resource allocation would be in a completely globalised economic system. Nevertheless, economic globalisation is not the ultimate solution to promoting efficiency of resource use (a dubious ultimate goal in any case) and there is no guarantee that it is going to be a strong force ultimately in promoting economic growth. Strong economic growth in the long run may require some moderation of market competition.

## 5.5 CONCLUDING COMMENTS

Although economic globalisation has proceeded rapidly since 1960, mainly due to reduced man-made barriers to trade, such as reduced tariffs, it does not seem to have been very effective in reducing income inequality between nations taken as a whole. While some less developed nations have gained by their increased openness and will continue to do so, others have been less fortunate. China is probably an example of one of the major gainers, and it seems to have the capacity in the long term to become a centre country.

Although the World Bank makes much of the fact that in the period 1960-95, poor open countries grew at a slightly faster rate than rich countries, the difference is extremely slight. Furthermore, considering that the base per capita incomes of these countries were already very divergent in 1960, absolute per capita income differences have grown substantially. Thus, the absolute gap in per capita incomes between rich and poor open economies has grown. This seems to suggest that rich countries have made relatively greater economic gains during the initial globalisation phase so far than poor open countries, on average. If global power and income are correlated positively, the relative power of the rich countries globally has increased since 1960. Naturally, the disparity between rich countries and poor relatively closed countries has become even more marked.

It is highly probable that the residents of most poor countries resent this situation and that it is a source of international social conflict. This may be especially so because several poor countries have relatively closed economies as a result of their circumstances rather than by choice. The income gap between such countries and rich countries has increased markedly.

A further source of resentment on the part of poor countries stems from the fact that as incomes in rich countries have increased with the process of globalisation, they have reduced their per capita aid to poor countries, and have tended to replace grants by concessional loans (compare Bhattacharya and Rahman 2001). Such countries are also often advised by more developed countries to participate more fully in economic globalisation. But this is ineffective advice for backwater less developed countries unable to do so due to endogenous impediment to economic growth and development. Thus, the fruits of globalisation are not shared to any great extent by rich nations with those poor nations unable to benefit from globalisation. This adds to growing intranational income inequality and ought to be a matter for serious international social concern.

## NOTE

1. Collaboration of Serge Svizzero and Clem Tisdell in contributing to this chapter was assisted by their 2002-2003 award from FEAST-France. They are grateful for this award. The usual caveat applies.

## REFERENCES

Ades, A.F. and E.L. Glaeser (1999), 'Evidence on growth increasing returns and the extent of the market', *Quarterly Journal of Economics*, **114**, 1025-46.

Bhattacharya, D. and M. Rahman (2001), 'Third UN conference on the LDCs: making it work for Bangladesh', Dhaka: Centre for Policy Dialogue.

Dollar, D. and A. Kraay (2001), 'Trade growth, and poverty', Development and Research Group, The World Bank, http://econ.worldbank.org/files/2207_wps2615.pdf.

Frank, A.G. (1978), *Dependent Accumulation and Underdevelopment*, London: Macmillan.

Frankel, J.A. and D. Romer (1999), 'Does trade growth cause growth?', *American Economic Review*, **89**, 379-99.

Gruber, W., D. Mehta and R. Vernon, (1967), 'The R&D factor in international trade and international investment of United States industries', *Journal of Political Economy*, **75**, 20-37.

Hirsch, S. (1972), 'The United States electronics industry in international trade', in L.T. Wells (ed.), *The Product Life Cycle and International Trade*, Boston: Harvard University Press, pp. 39-52.

Hufbauer, G.C. (1966), *Synthetic Materials and the Theory of International Trade*, London: Duckworth.

Krugman, P. and A.J. Venables (1995), 'Globalization and inequality of nations', *Quarterly Journal of Economics*, **110**, 857-80.

Lindert, R.H. and Williamson, J.G. (2003), 'Does globalisation make the world more unequal?', in M.D. Bordo, A.M. Taylor and J.G. Williamson (eds), *Globalization in Historical Perspective*, Chicago: The University of Chicago Press.

List, G. F. (1966), *The National System of Political Economy (Das Nationale System der Politischen Okonomie)*, New York: A. M. Kelley. Originally published in German in 1840.

Lowinger, T. (1975), 'The technology factor and the export performance of U.S. manufacturing industries', *Economic Enquiry*, **13**, 221-36.
Myrdal, G. (1956), *On International Economy: Problems and Prospects*, London: Routledge and Kegan Paul.
Posner, M. V. (1961), 'International trade and technical change', *Oxford Economic Papers*, **13**, 323-41.
Prebisch, R. (1950), *The Economic Development of Latin America and its Principal Problems*, Lake Success, New York: United Nations.
Romer, P. M. (1986), 'Increasing returns and long-run growth', *Journal of Political Economy*, **94**, 1002-37.
Schumpeter, J.A. (1942), *Capitalism, Socialism and Democracy*, 2nd edition, New York: Harper Brothers.
Singer, H.W. (1950), 'The distribution of the gains from trade between investing and borrowing countries', *American Economic Review*, **40**, 473-85.
Teubal, M. (1975), 'Toward a neotechnology theory of comparative costs', *Quarterly Journal of Economics*, **89**, 414-31.
Tisdell, C.A. (1981), *Science and Technology Policy: Priorities of Governments*, London: Chapman and Hall.
Tisdell, C.A. (1990), *Natural Resources, Growth and Development*, New York: Praeger.
Tisdell, C.A. (1998), 'Brunei's quest for sustainable development: diversification and other strategies', *Journal of Asia Pacific Economy*, **3** (3), 388-409.
Tisdell, C.A. (1999), 'Diversity and economic evolution: failure of competitive economic systems', *Contemporary Economic Policy*, **17**, 156-65.
Tisdell, C. A. (2000), 'Implementation of the programme of action in the least developed countries in the Pacific region', in ESCAP, *Review of Implementation of the Programme of Action for the Least Developed Countries for the 1990s: Subregional Studies*, New York: United Nations, ESCAP Least Developed Countries Series No. 5, pp. 150-255.
Tisdell, C.A. and T.I. Fairbairn, (1984), 'Subsistence economies, unsustainable development and trade: some simple theory', *Journal of Development Studies*, **20**, 227-41.
Tisdell, C.A. and I. Seidl (forthcoming), 'Niches and economic competition: implications for economic efficiency growth and diversity', *Structural Change and Economic Dynamics*.
UNDP (1999), *Human Development Report*, Oxford, UK: Oxford University Press.
Wells, G.C. (1969), 'Test of a product cycle model of international trade: US exports of consumer durables', *Quarterly Journal of Economics*, **83**, 152-62.
World Bank (2000a), 'Assessing globalisation: what is globalisation?', *Briefing Paper 1*, April, http://www/worldbank.org/html/extdr/pb/globalisation/paper1.htm.
World Bank (2000b), 'Assessing globalisation: does more international trade openness increase world poverty?', *Briefing Paper 2*, http://www.worldbank.org/html/extdr/pb/globalisation/paper2.htm.
World Bank (2000c), 'Assessing globalisation: does more international trade openness worsen inequality?', *Briefing Paper 3*, http://www.worldbank.org/html/extdr/pb/globalisation/paper3/htm.

# 6. The WTO, Labour and Environmental Standards: Globalisation with Reference to India

**Clem Tisdell**

## 6.1 INTRODUCTION

This chapter considers and examines the contrasting attitudes of developing and higher-income countries, as well as the WTO, to the proposition that the failure of a country to meet core labour or social standards should constitute allowable grounds for international trade discrimination against it. Similarly, the parallel proposition for failure of a country to satisfy globally 'acceptable' environmental standards is examined. It is emphasised that social standards are much wider than social norms. Furthermore, international fiscal competition, easily fostered by globalisation, can result in a lowering of social standards in all countries and a global economic welfare loss.

Reductions of environmental standards by competing nations can have similar adverse consequences. Although, as demonstrated analytically, a case exists for lower standards in developing countries than in higher-income countries, this does not mean that developing countries should have no standards. It is argued that the development of global governance has failed to keep pace with growing international economic and environmental interdependence. This should be a matter for widespread concern.

While processes favouring economic globalisation have been evolving for centuries (compare Held et al. 1999, Ch. 3), they accelerated in the last few decades of the twentieth century. This acceleration was the result of several forces:

1. Continuing improvements in communication and transport systems which significantly reduced physical barriers or transaction costs involved in trade.
2. Many countries, such as India, turned from supporting inward-looking economic policies involving protectionism to more open policies

favouring free markets and international trade.
3. Developing countries, in particular, were put under increasing pressure by the IMF, the World Bank and similar international organisations, to adopt structural adjustment policies involving a small government sector and maximum use of free markets, including greater freedom of international trade.
4. GATT and subsequently the WTO began to exert increasing pressure on its members to adopt less restrictive trade policies following the Uruguay Round.

In addition to all these factors, the world, commencing in the 1970s, became increasingly aware of global environmental problems resulting from growing economic activity, such as the build up of greenhouse gases, for example $CO_2$. There was also greater awareness and sensitivity to biodiversity loss and growing concern that economic growth or development might prove to be unsustainable. In fact, Nehru was one of the first national leaders to express concern that the development of less developed nations might prove to be unsustainable. At the United Nations Stockholm Conference of 1972, he called on the developed countries to adopt policies designed not just to promote temporary economic growth in developing countries but to support their sustainable development.

While Nehru is not noted as an environmental conservationist, and although his policies in India seemed to be designed to be pro-growth with little consideration of the environment, his views expressed in Stockholm eventually led to the formation of the World Commission on Environment and Development (WCED) and its 1987 report. WCED searched for policies designed to ensure sustainable development on a worldwide scale. It was especially interested in discovering policies that would enable economic development to be combined with environmental conservation, because it was of the view that sustainable development could not be achieved without an appropriate degree of environmental conservation. However, WCED (1987) and the subsequent 1992 United Nations Rio de Janeiro Conference on Sustainable Development failed to resolve controversy about the appropriate way to reconcile economic policies with economic growth and environmental conservation. Possible conflict between these goals remains a contentious economic issue as, for example, underlined by the protests and demonstrations at the WTO Millennium Meeting in Seattle towards the end of 1999.

At this WTO meeting, labour issues were also a major bone of contention. Many protesters wanted the WTO to take an active role in protecting labour and environmental standards. In this regard, there appears to have been support from the 'central' more developed countries, that is the industrialised countries as represented by the G-8 governments. The main opposition came from developing countries, of which India was probably the most vocal. Also Australia, a second-tier relatively high-income country but one not belonging to a significant regional free-trade association, remained strenuously opposed to the WTO's becoming involved in enforcing labour and environmental norms. Presumably, all governments were looking to their own political interests, if not their own national self-interest.

In this chapter, particular attention will be given to assessing the role of labour standards in relation to globalisation, and the importance of taking a wider view that takes account of social service standards and international fiscal competition. Similarly, attention will be given to environmental standards. The role and position of the WTO in relation to these matters will be given particular attention. The political position of India will be highlighted and possible implications for West Bengal will be touched on. Consider each of these matters in turn.

## 6.2 INTERNATIONAL LABOUR STANDARDS

Concern about international labour standards and trade is by no means new. As early as 1919, the International Labour Organisation (ILO) accepted the view that trade should not be based on exploitation of labour. Several ILO Conventions have been developed that have implications for international trade. But not all ILO Conventions are adopted by all countries, and some countries have ratified none. However, a group of ILO Conventions are regarded as constituting core international labour standards. These include freedom of association of workers, for example, the right of workers to join trade unions, their right to bargain collectively, non-discrimination in employment, such as on the basis of race or social origin, and the prohibition of forced labour. However, according to Mah (1998) 'there is no ILO Convention that directly addresses the issue of child labour exploitation as such'.

While ILO Conventions bind countries that adopt them, mechanisms for enforcing compliance do not seem to be very strong. The ILO, in practice, does not impose sanctions on countries that do not comply with its conventions but relies mainly on social pressures, in some cases reinforced by the option of a Commission of Inquiry, to encourage compliance (Mah 1998).

Scherrer (1996, p. 9) observes that the ILO's 'method of setting voluntary conventions is increasingly considered to be inadequate, as the ILO is finding it ever more difficult to enforce conventions. Furthermore, the process of adopting and implementing ILO conventions has slowed down significantly in the last decade. The International Confederation of Free Trade Unions has therefore demanded that workers' fundamental rights be written into trade agreements as social clauses.' The social clauses in question are the core labour standards mentioned above plus the prohibition of child labour.

However, the ILO's administration has resisted attempts to involve it in supporting international trade sanctions as a means to enforce core labour standards or social clauses. For example, the Director-General of ILO in 1996 said 'The ILO's role is not to put right distortions in international competition that may arise from different levels of social protection that countries offer their workers. This problem, if such it is, is more the domain of the WTO' (Hansanne 1996). On the other hand, the WTO washes its hands of such involvement. At the 1997 WTO Singapore meeting, the Trade Ministers declared that the ILO is the competent body to deal with such standards. The WTO has made it clear that it does not want to become involved in trade sanctions to enforce the full range of core labour standards. Nevertheless, GATT does permit trade protection measures against products produced by forced labour.

Most developing countries have expressed opposition to moves by the more industrialised counties, such as members of the G-8 and especially the USA, to allow trade sanctions to be imposed on countries not adopting core labour standards. India has been particularly vocal in it opposition. For example, India was represented at the Seattle WTO meeting in 1999 by its Commerce Minister, Murosoli Maron. The *Times of India* reported that India was opposed to attempts to bring labour and environmental concerns into the trade debate on the basis that it was a protectionist objective to deny market access to products from developing countries. India was said to be firmly opposed to linking trade and non-trade issues, and Maron was quoted as saying, 'We will not accept anything which dilutes our cost advantage in international trade.' However, it is pertinent to note that what is and what is not a trade issue is not straightforward.

The South Asian position in relation to the Millennium Round of the WTO (Seattle Meeting) seems to be summarised by the South Asian Association for Regional Cooperation, SAARC. It states: 'There is a move to further overload the WTO agenda with "new issues" such as social clauses, environment, governance, labour standards etc. Since these are not trade related, they should be kept out of the multilateral trading system. There is a need to deepen and broaden concessions already provided under the Special Differential (SAD) clauses in favour of developing and least-developed countries' (SAARC 2001, p. 2). Furthermore, ASEAN (Association of South East Asian Nations) members have been firmly opposed to proposals to link social clauses with allowable trade sanctions (Mah 1998).

According to Scherrer (1996, p. 11):

> The debate about international social standards revolves primarily around the introduction and raising of standards in developing countries . . .. Opponents of social standards . . . argue that better living and working conditions cannot be legislated but would be the natural outcome of industrialisation. Economic development would be best promoted by ensuring that the trading system was as free as possible.

While some proponents of improved labour standards in developing countries believe that these may raise living standards, most opponents in developing countries see such standards as a way to help protect the jobs and incomes of unskilled or low-skilled workers in more developed countries. Theoretical argument in such cases often revolves around the application of the Samuelson-Stolper theorem (compare Svizzero and Tisdell 2001). Since unskilled and low-skilled labour is in relatively abundant supply in less developed countries but in short supply in high-income countries, it is theoretically possible that working conditions of this group of labourers in higher-income countries will be undermined by globalisation, at least initially, even if not permanently. This aspect involves international conflict about the distribution of income.

It is also sometimes suggested that the lack of core labour standards in developing countries results in unfair international trade. Supporters of this view argue that the absence of such standards acts as an implicit subsidy to exporters in developing countries. Given higher labour standards in most higher-income countries, second-best efficiency arguments suggest that lower standards in less developed countries might add to global economic inefficiency. It would, however, be incumbent on supporters of this point of view to show that the efficiency loss is significant. Yet economic efficiency is not an absolute value above all other values. Such factors as social justice in the distribution of income and economic opportunity must also be taken into account in policy-making.

## 6.3 SOCIAL STANDARDS, ENTITLEMENTS AND FISCAL COMPETITION

Amartya Sen (1981a) has emphasised the importance of entitlements in determining the economic well-being of individuals. While working conditions constitute a part of social entitlements, in most cases they are only a part of the entitlements of working people and the disadvantaged. As noted by Sen (1981b) social entitlements also include access to social services or welfare assistance provided by or arranged by the state, for example, old-age pensions, unemployment benefits, state-provided or financed educational services and healthcare. While the provision of state support for individuals is generally much less in lower-income countries than in high-income countries, even in less developed countries the role of the state in providing educational and health services can be very significant in influencing the effective distribution of income and the pattern of economic opportunity.

Following World War II, several Western countries, for example Sweden, the UK and West Germany, developed welfare states. But in recent times both the ideal of a welfare state and policies to support it have been eroded. This erosion is not confined to more developed countries. Even in China, individuals are increasingly required to pay for education and for healthcare.

This erosion can be attributed to a number of factors. As argued by Gray (1998) and as considered further later, economic globalisation tends to undermine the welfare state. Nevertheless, authors such as Hirst and Thompson (1999, p. 190) suggest that higher-income countries have considerable scope still for providing welfare services despite growing globalisation. In part, the erosion of the welfare state may reflect changing social values in high-income countries. Possibly both factors have an influence. Secondly, the world seems to have gone through, or could still be in, a phase where economic efficiency is regarded by most of its leaders as mighty above all other things, including distributional justice. Associated with this has been the emphasis of international institutions, such as the IMF and the World Bank, on the desirability of structural adjustment policies emphasizing as ideals small government, minimal government intervention in economies, free markets and international trade. Thus, there have been pressures to return to laissez-faire policies that were treated with a degree of scepticism in the 1950s and 1960s and into the early 1970s. How much further the world will proceed down the path of laissez-faire remains to be seen.

From the above, it can be seen that labour standards only constitute a part of potentially desirable social norms. A wider view of social conditions affecting labour must be taken that includes not only labour conditions but also social entitlements provided for by the intervention of the state and also by individuals or groups of individuals as a result of social custom. Indeed, this wider view was a basis for the formation of the British Labour Party and the Australian Labor Party. Therefore, it is stressed that ILO core labour standards, sometimes referred to as social clauses or even social standards, for example, by Scherrer (1996, p. 11), are in fact, incomplete indicators of social standards.

Because of their overall economic condition, low-income countries are unable to maintain as high a level of state-initiated welfare and social support as higher-income countries and usually are unable to meet the same labour standards as in high-income countries. There seems little alternative but to adjust 'acceptable' labour and social standards to the stage of economic development and the economic situation of individual nations.

While Scherrer (1996, p. 11) suggests that many in higher-income countries want social standards to be raised in lower-income countries to prevent what they see as unfair international competition from such countries, the main problem in this regard may arise from differences in standards of countries at a similar stage of economic development. While international competition does exist to some extent between developed and less developed countries, the intensity of economic competition is likely to be greatest between countries with similar factor proportions and at a similar stage of development. Thus, one might expect greater intensity of economic competition between less developed countries than between less developed countries and higher-income nations. A similar situation may exist for high-income countries. In these circumstances, differences in social standards between less developed and higher-income countries may be of secondary importance in their influence on international competition and the pattern of international trade and investment, as far as these two groups of nations are concerned. Of much greater significance are differences in social standards with each of these groups. A nation with lower social standards within its group may obtain an international competitive economic advantage, at least in the short run.

However, the competitive advantage is at the expense of near competing countries and they may retaliate also by lowering social standards. As a result, all countries in the group may become worse off. Fiscal competitiveness provides an example.

A country may attract foreign direct investment by reducing taxes on income from such investment and relaxing fiscal obligations on employers, as Ireland has done. Provided competing countries do not do likewise, the nation initiating such fiscal competitiveness may gain. However, if competing nations, or many of them, follow suit, all may suffer a reduction in welfare.

As a result of counter-responses of all nations in the competing group, government receipts are likely to fall with subsequent reduction in welfare support and lowered provision of education, and healthcare and so on by governments. This is assuming that long-term budget deficits are ruled out, as is the case in the European Union. Consequently all nations in the competing group may be made worse off by fiscal competition. The same applies, in many cases, to deliberate reduction of social standards in order to attract globally mobile capital.

Competition of the above nature can generate a prisoner's dilemma-type problem. This can be illustrated by the game theory matrix shown as Table

6.1. There player 1 is a country contemplating the adoption of a competitive strategy involving fiscal competition or lowering of employer obligations. Player 2 represents all competing countries. Furthermore, $\alpha_1$ represents a strategy in which country 1 maintains its fiscal requirements whereas $\alpha_2$ represents a situation in which these requirements are lowered. Similarly, $\beta_1$ represents a situation in which competing nations maintain their fiscal requirements and $\beta_2$ a situation in which they lower these requirements. The numbers in the matrix represent the corresponding levels of economic welfare achieved within the nations concerned. They need not be cardinal values.

*Table 6.1 A case in which international fiscal competition lowers the welfare of all competing nations*

| Strategies of player 1 (nation 1) | | Strategies of player 2 (competing nations): $\beta_1$ | $\beta_2$ |
|---|---|---|---|
| | $\alpha_1$ | (2, 3) | (0, 5) |
| | $\alpha_2$ | (4, 1) | (1, 2) |

Suppose that the game shown in Table 6.1 is replicated and initially strategies ($\alpha_1, \beta_1$) are adopted. The outcome is Pareto optimal. Suppose, however, that nation 1 decides to engage in international fiscal competition and adopts strategy $\alpha_2$. If the other competing nations maintain previous standards, nation 1 is better off but its competitors are worse off. If however, competitors react by also lowering fiscal requirements, the payoffs corresponding to ($\alpha_2$, $\beta_2$) prevail. All the nations involved are now worse off than if they had not engaged in fiscal competition. Furthermore, the combination of strategies ($\alpha_2$, $\beta_2$) results in a Nash equilibrium. This stable equilibrium will persist in the absence of collective action to break the cycle involved.

Clearly in a globalising world, fiscal competition between nations can undermine national policies designed to provide collective or national benefits. The matters involved are beyond the mandate of the WTO. In fact, there are no global institutions to govern such matters. In fact, global economic interdependence has proceeded in such cases well beyond the development of global institutions for its governance.

The type of situation illustrated in Table 6.1 is likely to be associated with increasing inequality of entitlements in society. The entitlements of the disadvantaged and their offspring are likely to be reduced whereas those of the better off may actually increase. Furthermore, the unskilled and disadvantaged may have an increasing tax burden, assuming that they have little outward mobility from higher-income countries. International fiscal competitiveness is liable to result in reduced taxes on internationally mobile resources and relatively higher taxes on less mobile resources.

## 6.4 THE ENVIRONMENT, GLOBALISATION AND THE WTO

Globalisation and the environment are interconnected in several ways. As economic globalisation has proceeded, global gross product has risen, and vice versa. Possibly mutual causation or circular causation occurs. Expanding global production has now resulted in globally significant changes to the state of the natural environment and threatens the sustainability of economic growth and development. Emissions of greenhouse gases associated with increased burning of fossil fuels provides an example. Biodiversity loss, particularly in cultivars and domesticated animals, may also imperil global economic development. No workable global solution to these problems has been agreed to so far. Furthermore, transformation of natural resources or environmental capital into man-made capital and other commodities continues at a rapid rate. In many cases, renewable resources, such as some capture fisheries are being exploited beyond their sustainable levels, and possibly non-renewable resources are being depleted at an excessive rate. In addition, the balance between natural environmental capital and man-made capital may become lopsided with the ratio of the former to the latter becoming too low to sustain economic production.

Apart from the fact that actual impacts of economic activity on the environment have become globally more important, international perceptions of environmental damage have been made more vivid and accessible as a result of globalisation of communications and of the media. Westerners, therefore, may, in particular, become more sensitive to environmental conditions not only in their own countries but also elsewhere.

For many, however, economic growth is seen as the key to eventual environmental improvement. They argue that the Environmental Kuznets Curve (EKC) demonstrates that with sufficient growth of economic output and income, pollution intensity (pollution levels in relation to GDP) eventually falls, and point out that such intensities tend to be lower in higher-income countries, such as most OECD countries, than in lower-income countries, such as India and China. According to EKC-analysis, pollution intensity as a function of a country's GDP per capita tends to conform to an inverted U-relationship. This means that if a less developed country experiences maintained economic growth, at first its pollution intensity rises but once higher incomes are achieved, this intensity begins to fall.

However, as pointed out in Tisdell (2001), the situation is not as simple as EKC-analysis might suggest. Even if EKC is of a reversed-U shape, economic growth could still cause total pollution levels to rise to thresholds that trigger catastrophic global environmental change, such as may occur as a result of the accumulation of greenhouse gases. Secondly, even though the pollution intensity in a country may fall, its total level of pollution emissions can continue to rise. For example, although the United States' total emission of $CO_2$ per unit of its GDP falls, its total level of emissions of $CO_2$ have continued to rise.

Furthermore, trends in the levels of different types of emissions are likely to differ. There appears to be a tendency once incomes in a country rise sufficiently to control first pollutants that have significant local impact, such as emissions of particulate matter. Then follows control of those pollutants less evident locally but having significant adverse consequences within national borders, such as in some cases emissions fostering acid rains or water pollution. Those pollutants that largely affect other countries or add generally to global pollution seem to be the last to be controlled, if they are controlled at all, because their effects are largely external to each nation creating the pollution.

The world is still searching for effective and acceptable policy mechanisms to control global environmental pollution. Once again, in this respect, economic systems have expanded globally beyond the present capacity of the world community to govern these. Given the conflicting interests of nations, it is for example proving difficult to develop effective global regulation of greenhouse gas emissions.

As in the case of labour standards, the WTO is, on the whole, opposed to the use of trade sanctions as a means to enforce environmental standards. The reasons are probably complex (compare Stewart 1998). In many cases, it may fear that such sanctions could be based on weak grounds and be used mainly as a back-door means to trade protection. Secondly, it feels that is more appropriate that these matters be the subject of separate international agreements and conventions. However, the possibility of trade sanctions may be necessary to enforce some multilateral environmental agreements as stressed by Brack (1999, p. 296). Possibly it takes this view because it feels that if its mission is widened to include broad environmental conditions, its mission will become too wide in relation to its capacities for it to function effectively in its determinations. Yet phytosanitory requirements can be a basis for allowable trade restrictions under the rules of the WTO. Basically this means that the environmental effects of production of a commodity in an exporting country cannot be used as a reason to restrict its international trade unless there is something inherent in the commodity that threatens health, safety or the environment in the importing country, and this can be substantiated on the basis of scientific evidence. Furthermore, the decision to exclude the commodity must be based on appropriate assessment of 'The risks for human animal or plant life or health'. This allows use to be made of the precautionary principle (Charnovitz 1999).

Nevertheless, several higher-income countries such as EU nations, Japan and the United States have been pressing for international environmental norms. It is believed that countries imposing low environmental standards in relation to economic production are providing a hidden subsidy to producers and this results in unfair international trade competition and unfair international competition for foreign direct investment. On the other hand, less developed countries, of which India is one of the more vocal, see this as a strategy of higher-income countries to discriminate against less developed countries in international competition. The situation is, however, complex.

It is possible for competitive reduction in environmental standards to give rise to a situation similar to that illustrated above in the case of fiscal competitiveness. A prisoner's dilemma type problem may arise that results in a Paretian inferior Nash equilibrium for all nations, or for groups of nations in close competition with one another. The argument is similar to that given above, and it applies even if the environmental spillovers are purely confined to the nation lowering environmental standards.

On the other hand, it is questionable whether environmental norms in developing countries should be as high as in more developed countries. Somewhat lower norms or standards in developing countries seem defensible from an economic viewpoint. This, however, does not mean that no environmental standards should apply in developing countries. This can be elucidated by considering a suggestion of the International Institute for Sustainable Development (IISD).

The IISD suggests that the polluter-pays principle should be applied by all countries so as to internalise all environmental externalities. To do this would make the environmental hidden subsidy explicit in the case of marketed commodities. It would help promote sustainable development and create a relatively level playing field as far as the environment and international competition are concerned. However, such policies are more easily proposed than implemented. This is partly because environmental externalities are difficult to measure in monetary terms and considerable government agency costs may be incurred in forcing polluters to pay.

If, however, these matters are put to one side, the economic costs of the same environmental spillover in a developing country may be rated as lower than in a higher income country. Thus it can be economically rational for less developed countries to tolerate a higher level of pollution than high income countries. Consequently, the same standards should not apply in both cases.

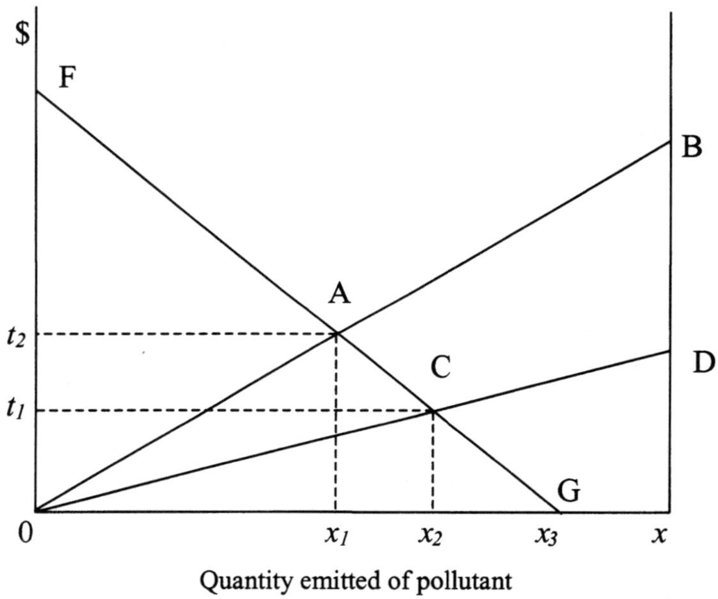


*Figure 6.1 The economically optimal level of charges for the same amount of pollution in a developing country is likely to be lower than in a more developed country given Pigou's welfare framework*

This can be illustrated by Figure 6.1. In Figure 6.1, $x$ represents the level of pollution from an economic activity. Assume that the marginal economic benefits to polluters from this activity are indicated by line FACG whether it is carried out in a higher-income country or a less developed one. The marginal external costs in a higher-income country from these emissions might be as shown by line 0AB and in a less developed country, be as shown by 0CD. If a polluter-pays approach is adopted, the appropriate tax per unit of emission in the high-income country is $t_2$ and in the low-income country $t_1$. *Assuming that environmental spillovers are intra-national,* a lower environmental standard and higher level of emissions in a less developed country is economically rational. However, in this case, it would not be rational for the less developed country not to moderate its pollution emission. If it were to do this, $x_3$ units of the pollutant would be emitted and the less developed country would suffer a deadweight social loss. Furthermore if high-income countries were charging a per unit tax of $t_2$ on emissions, they would have grounds to claim that the less developed country is engaging in 'unfair' competition.

Observe that sometimes countries not only fail to tax economic activities giving rise to unfavourable externalities but actually subsidise these. An example is the large subsidy and degree of protection for the sugar industry in the United States. This is reducing the size of the Everglades in Florida and has unfavourable consequences for nature conservation in the United States. The protection of the sugar industry in the US restricts sugar exports of other countries to the US including some countries with significantly lower levels of income than the US, for example, Brazil.

The model illustrated by Figure 6.1 assumes the environmental spillover caused by an economic activity in a country does not extend in its economic impact beyond the borders of the country concerned. If it extends beyond national borders, this complicates the welfare economics of its control. Environmental impacts extending beyond national borders may be of two types:

1. Purely psychological or subjective. For example, concern of Westerners because of destruction of marine turtles in the developing world.
2. Objective or real, as in the case of acid rains having their source in China and falling in Japan. Other examples include reduced water quality and quantity in transboundary river systems due to changed activity in their headwaters in neighbouring countries, for example, in the Brahmaputra River or the Mekong as a result of altered use of their headwaters in China. In principle also greenhouse gas emissions belong to the real or objective category.

In what manner one should deal with subjective externalities is probably contentious. They arise out of empathy. Nevertheless if we were to follow the logic of Robbins (1937), they would count in the global welfare calculus.

The presence of transnational environmental spillovers complicates the control of externalities, especially if the polluter-pays principle is adopted. If this principle is adopted, not only should the polluter pay for the environmental spillovers imposed upon those in the country where the polluter is located but also for unfavourable externalities generated in other countries. The situation can be illustrated by Figure 6.2.

In Figure 6.2, $x$ represents the quantity of emission of a pollutant by a nation. Line GCH represents the marginal benefits to polluters (within the nation) of being able to pollute and line 0AB the marginal environmental externality costs generated within the nation. Line 0CF indicates total marginal spillover costs (those imposed on the nation as well as other nations), and the difference between line 0AB and 0CF represents the marginal spillover costs imposed on other nations.

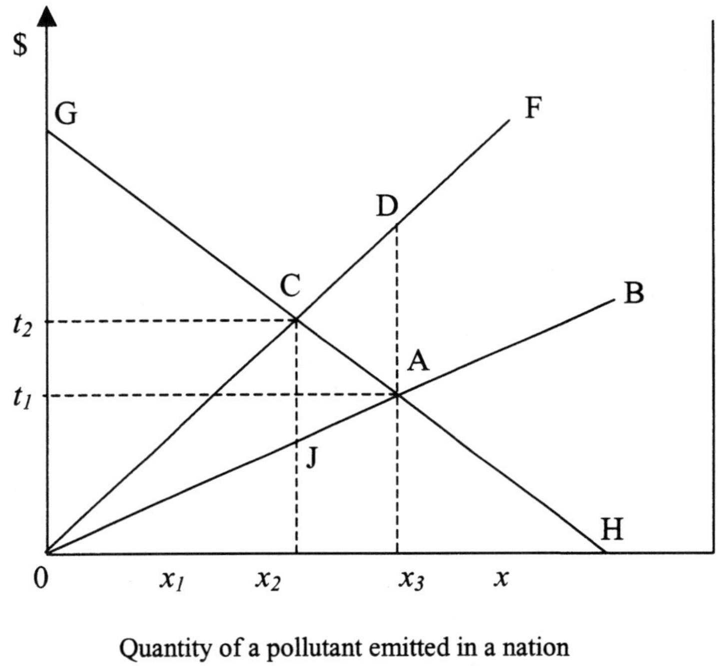


*Figure 6.2 Transnational environmental spillovers complicate their control politically*

In the absence of any control of its pollution, the polluting nation illustrated emits $x_3$ of pollutants per period of time. It suffers a deadweight source loss due to the impact of the pollutant on its own population, and the global deadweight loss is even larger. On the other hand, if the polluting nation imposes a tax of $t_1$ on each unit emitted of the pollutant, it will eliminate its national deadweight loss. From a national point of view, its situation will be optimal on the basis of the Kaldor-Hicks criterion. However, given the international spillovers, a global deadweight loss equivalent to the area of triangle CDA will occur. A tax of $t_2$ per unit of emissions would be needed to bring about a global Kaldor-Hicks optimum. But if such a tax is imposed by the polluting country, it experiences a reduction in its 'real' income equivalent to the area of triangle CJA.

In such cases, where the polluting nation is a poor nation and the beneficiaries of additional control of its spillovers are richer nations, the poor nation may argue that the richer nations should compensate it for extra control of its pollutants. Thus it may wish to reject the polluter-pays principle on income distributional grounds. Bargaining is inevitably involved and this can result in political stalemate. Once again current global mechanisms of governance are likely to prove inadequate to rectify transboundary environmental spillovers in a socially optimal away. This provides another example of the expansion of global interdependence beyond the limits of mechanisms for its adequate global governance.

## 6.5 INDIA'S POSITION IN RELATION TO GLOBALISATION AND THE WTO, AND WEST BENGAL'S SITUATION WITHIN THIS CONTEXT

In recent years, India has consistently and strongly opposed attempts that would permit trade restrictions to be imposed on international exchange with nations not maintaining 'acceptable' labour norms and environmental standards. In this respect, India has the support of most developing countries. For example, the *Telegraph India* reporting on the demonstration at the WTO meeting in Seattle in 1999 stated: 'Several trade ministers, particularly those from developing countries, felt that demonstration was stage managed by Clinton to press his demand to include labour standards and environmental protection in the WTO agenda. Developing countries have been opposing this, fearing this would legitimise protection' (*Telegraph India*, 1 December 1999, p. 1).

India is concerned that it will be economically disadvantaged by any restriction on trade designed to enforce labour and environmental standards. It fears that not all the standards likely to be proposed will be appropriate to its stage of economic development. India, and many other developing countries, point out that today's higher-income countries had low or non-existent standards of this type during their early stages of economic development. They therefore, suggest that to impose labour environmental standards on developing countries would not be just given their early stage of development. It would imply unequal treatment of nations in a similar situation.

It is feared that such measures may retard the economic growth of less developed nations. It is argued that the imposition of such standards is likely to be counterproductive since rising environmental and labour standards are a by-product of economic growth and economic development. Economic growth according to this view provides the best prospect for raising labour and environmental standards.

In addition, there is the fear that more developed countries may indiscriminately impose trade protection based on supposed failure of a developing country to maintain 'acceptable' environmental and labour norms. Thus, attempts to introduce these considerations into WTO rules are seen as a Trojan horse: a presentation seen as harbouring ulterior motives.

Nevertheless, there are also counter-arguments to consider. It can be claimed that the situation of today's developing nations differs from that of higher-income countries in their earliest stages of development. This is because the world is now much more interdependent than in those earlier times both from an economic and environmental point of view, and depletion of the world's natural resource/environmental stock is now much more advanced. Past practices may, therefore, be irrational given the current global situation. Moreover, it is possible that the past actions of today's higher-income countries were not socially optimal in their time, both from national and global viewpoints. Therefore, although the opposition of developing countries to environmental norms may have a sound political basis, absolute opposition to all such standards may not have a rational basis.

Nevertheless, very high standards are likely to be socially inappropriate for developing countries, including their regional areas, such as West Bengal. In Calcutta, for example, particulate airborne matter is well in excess of health standards set by the World Health Organisation. Possibly, they are even beyond locally optimal levels given the less developed situation of West Bengal. There may, therefore, be a case for tightening controls on emissions even if it is unrealistic for Calcutta to try to meet WHO standards for air quality in the near future.

Again, there is considerable use of child labour in India, including West Bengal, and in some neighbouring countries, for example, Bangladesh. While there is no ILO convention that specifically bans child labour, the EU has attempted to make use of child labour a violation of labour norms and thereby a basis for trade discrimination against industries in countries using such labour. But such measures are unlikely to assist families in poverty forced to employ their children as child labour to make ends meet. Any measures of this nature could be detrimental to West Bengal. At the same time, however, governments need to take measures to stamp out patent abuse of child labourers.

In practice, there may be little competition between products produced with child labour in developing countries and products produced in higher-income countries. Hence, strong feelings about the use of child labour expressed in higher-income countries may be for the most part emotionally based.

## 6.6 CONCLUDING OBSERVATIONS AND COMMENTS

The world is divided on the desirability, or otherwise, of whether the WTO should make greater allowances for environmental and labour norms in its trade policies. A large group of higher-income nations have suggested that international trade discrimination should be permitted in relation to the exports of countries that fail to achieve 'appropriate' environmental norms. In general, this proposal has been opposed by less developed countries. India has been in the forefront of the opposition.

*Table 6.2 Summary of views of pressure groups about whether the WTO should make greater allowance for environmental norms, labour norms and LDCs in its policies*

| Group | Environment norms | Labour norms | Concessions for LDCs |
|---|---|---|---|
| **Labour bodies** | | | |
| ICFTU (International Confederation of Free Trade Unions) | 4 | 4 | 4 |
| AFL-CIO (USA) | 4 | 4 | (?) |
| **Business organisations** | | | |
| Business Council of Australia | 8 | 8 | ?(8) |
| Federation of German Industries | 4 | (?)8 | (?)8 |
| **Farmers groups** | | | |
| Non-Cairns minus USA | 4 | (?)8 | ? |
| Cairns plus USA | 8 | 8 | 8 |
| **Environmentalists** | | | |
| Most | 4 | 4(?) | 4 |
| **LDCs** | | | |
| India | 8 | 8 | 4 |
| **Industrialised countries** | | | |
| G-8 Governments | 4 | 4 | ? |

*Note*: This table is purely indicative and cannot capture fully differences in views and their complexities.

*Source*: Tisdell (2000, p. 18).

Using Internet sites and other data sources, I have constructed Table 6.2 which summarises the position of the major world's pressure groups as at the end of the twentieth century about whether environmental and labour norms should be taken into account in trade policy. From this it can be seen that the major industrialised countries want environmental and labour norms to count but not developing countries. The position of the United States was somewhat ambivalent but basically favoured norms, as can be seen from Table 6.2. As part of the G-8, it supported norms. But in conjunction with the Cairns group of exporting countries (such as Australia and Brazil) mainly exporting primary products, it did not favour such norms. Indeed, some critics of the US believe that it is selective in its attitude to trade protection depending on what is most workable politically within the US itself. Hence, the position of the US is considered by some critics to be hypocritical. Table 6.2 also indicates whether the groups considered favoured economic concessions for less developed countries.

Although India and most developing countries oppose the possibility of WTO rules being altered to allow trade discrimination to enforce labour and environmental standards, most industrialised countries favour this possibility. Nevertheless, not all higher-income countries support the latter position. Australia and other members of the Cairns groups oppose it.

This chapter indicates, however, that while these positions may be appropriate political stances for the nations concerned, failure to maintain some environmental and social standards can reduce global welfare. This is not to say that the same standards are appropriate for developing and higher-income countries. Far from it. It is also debatable whether the WTO would have the capacity to deal effectively with such issues, even though their significance is apparent from this article. In fact, the world seems to face a very serious problem: its mechanisms for global governance of environmental and social standards are not adequate to take account of the degree of global interdependence that has evolved. In other words, global environmental and economic interdependence has outpaced global government, and no easy solution appears to be in sight.

## REFERENCES

Brack, D. (1999), 'Environmental treaties and trade: multilateral environmental agreements and the multilateral trading system', in G.P. Sampson and W.B. Chambers (eds), *Trade, Environment and the Millennium*, Tokyo: United Nations University, pp. 271–98.

Charnovitz, S. (1999), 'Improving the agreement on sanitary and phytosanitary standards', in G.P. Sampson and W.B. Chambers (eds), *Trade, Environment and the Millennium*, Tokyo: United Nations University, pp. 171–94.

Gray, J. (1998), *False Dawn: The Delusions of Global Capitalism*, London: Granta.

Hansanne, M. (1996), 'International trade and labour standards', paper presented at the Conference on Liberalizing World Trade, 1996.

Held, D., A. McGrew, D. Goldblatt and J. Perreton (1999), *Global Transformation: Politics, Economics and Culture*, Oxford, UK: Polity Press.

Hirst, P. and G. Thompson (1999), *Globalisation in Question: The International Economy and the Possibilities of Governance*, 2nd edn, Cambridge, UK: Polity Press.

Mah, Jai Sheen (1998), 'ASEAN, labour standards and international trade', *ASEAN Economic Bulletin*, **14** (3), 292–302.

Robbins, L. (1937), *An Essay on the Nature and Significance of Economic Science*, London: Macmillan.

SAARC (2001), *SAARCSCAN*, **7** (47).

Scherrer, C. (1996), 'The economic and political arguments for and against social clauses', *Intereconomics*, January/February, **31** (1), 9–20.

Sen, A.K. (1981a), *Poverty and Famines: An Essay on Entitlement and Deprivation*, Oxford: Clarendon Press.

Sen, A.K. (1981b), 'Public action and the quality of life in developing countries', *Oxford Bulletin of Economics and Statistics*, **24**, 267–317.

Stewart, T. (1998), 'The United States' embargo on shrimp imports: legal and economic consideration', *Environment and Development Economics*, **3**, 197–219.

Svizzero, S and C. Tisdell (2001), 'Reconciling globalisation and technological change: growing income inequalities and remedial policies', *Economic Theory, Applications and Issues*, Working Paper No. 10, The University of Queensland, Brisbane 4072.

Tisdell, C. (2000), 'Globalisation and the WTO: attitudes expressed by pressure groups and by less developed countries', *Economics, Ecology and the Environment*, Working Paper No. 40, The University of Queensland, Brisbane 4072.

Tisdell, C. (2001), 'Globalisation and sustainability: environmental Kuznets curves and the WTO', *Ecological Economics*, **39**, 185–96.

World Commission for Environment and Development (WCED) (1987), *Our Common Future*, New York: Oxford University Press.

# 7. Globalisation, the WTO and its Impact on India: A Developing Country Perspective

**Ruddar Datt**

## 7.1 AN INTRODUCTION: GLOBALISATION AND EXPORT-LED GROWTH STRATEGY

Globalisation is the process of integrating all economies of the world so that there is free movement of goods, services, technology, capital and even labour across national boundaries. The term globalisation has four parameters: (i) reduction of trade barriers to permit free flow of goods across national frontiers; (ii) creation of an environment in which free flow of capital can take place among nation states; (iii) creation of an environment permitting free flow of technology; and (iv) last but not least, from the point of view of developing countries, creation of an environment in which free movement of labour can take place in different countries of the world.

Globalisation is now frequently associated with the desire to integrate nation states within the overall economic framework of the WTO. It is a modern version of the 'Theory of Comparative Cost Advantage' propagated by the classical economists. It provided a theoretical foundation for the unrestricted flow of goods from Great Britain to other less developed countries – at that time colonies. It was argued that international specialisation benefits all countries that enter into trade relations. From this, it follows that this is not the first time that the world has experienced globalisation. The nineteenth century witnessed an enormous increase in world trade. Maddison (1995) estimated that in 1820, British trade stood at 3 per cent of GDP but, by 1870, it had reached 12 per cent of GDP. The new technologies of steam power, telegraph and telephone helped the process of globalisation by enlarging trade and the movement of people all over the world. However, when a large number of colonies achieved independence in the middle of the twentieth century, they followed inward-looking policies of import-substitution intended to achieve the objective of economic growth and self-reliance. They did permit the import of foreign technology, but only in such areas as helped to enlarge the productive capacity of the economy. Initially development of heavy industries was the basic aim to attain freedom from excessive dependence on developed economies for the import of capital and technology.

During the last two decades, the developed nations, more especially the USA and the European Union countries have again emphasised globalisation as the new 'mantra' for world development. The globalisers want us to believe that they are now sincere and as a result of the policies of globalisation, developing countries can improve their competitive strength and usher in a period of rapid economic growth. Consequently, the developing countries are cajoled both by soft and hard pressures to fall into line. India commenced the process of dismantling trade barriers in 1991 and subsequently, every year the government has been announcing reductions in custom duties and removing quantitative restrictions. For a developing country like India, economic liberalisation and globalisation opens access to new markets and new technology. Thus, India's import-substitution strategy has been replaced by export-led growth during the 1990s. The recent developments in information and communication technologies have further facilitated and accelerated the pace of globalisation. International financial markets, transborder production networks and acceleration in capital flows across national frontiers have been the driving forces leading to greater global integration. Ul Haq (2002, p. 1) in his report on *Human Development in South Asia* rightly asserted: 'Globalisation is no longer an option, it is a fact.'

## 7.2 THE IMPACT OF GLOBALISATION ON THE INDIAN ECONOMY

### India's Share in World Exports of Goods and Services

According to the data provided by the World Bank (2001), India's share in world exports rose from 0.54 per cent in 1990 to 0.67 per cent in 1999. Whereas world exports rose by about 64 per cent during 1990 to 1999 (that is, from $3,328 billion in 1990 to $5,442 billion in 1999), Indian exports rose by 103 per cent during the same period (that is, from $17.97 billion in 1990 to $36.56 billion in 1999). See Table 7.1.

Although the Indian government has taken pride in India's export performance, when compared to China, South Korea and Mexico, the Indian achievement is much less significant. China's share in world exports rose from 1.86 per cent to 3.59 per cent during 1990-99. Similarly, South Korea's share improved from 1.95 per cent to 2.66 per cent and even Mexico showed a big jump in her share from 1.22 per cent to 2.51 per cent during 1990-99. The annual average increase in exports was 8.2 per cent for India for the period 1990-99. In comparison, China demonstrated an annual increase of 13.6 per cent and Mexico of the order of 14.4 per cent during the 1990s – a creditable achievement.

*Table 7.1 Merchandise exports of selected countries*

| Country | Exports (US$ million) | | World exports (% of total) | | Percentage increase in 1999 over 1990 | Annual average growth rate (%) 1990-99 |
|---|---|---|---|---|---|---|
| | 1990 | 1999 | 1990 | 1999 | | |
| India | 17,975 | 36,560 | 0.54 | 0.67 | 103.4 | 8.2 |
| China | 62,091 | 195,150 | 1.86 | 3.59 | 214.3 | 13.6 |
| S. Korea | 65,016 | 144,745 | 1.95 | 2.66 | 122.6 | 9.3 |
| Mexico | 40,711 | 136,703 | 1.22 | 2.51 | 235.8 | 14.4 |
| World | 3,328,357 | 5,442,226 | 100 | 100 | 63.5 | 5.6 |

*Source*: Compiled and computed from the data provided in World Bank, *World Development Indicators* (2001).

*Table 7.2 Service exports of selected countries*

| Country | Exports (US$ million) | | World exports of services (% of total) | | Percentag e increase in 1999 over 1990 | Annual average growth rate (%) 1990-99 |
|---|---|---|---|---|---|---|
| | 1990 | 1999 | 1990 | 1999 | | |
| India | 4,609 | 13,940 | 0.60 | 1.1 | 202.5 | 13.1 |
| China | 1,786 | 3,701 | 0.23 | 0.29 | 107.2 | 8.4 |
| S. Korea | 9,155 | 24,822 | 1.19 | 1.95 | 171.1 | 11.7 |
| Mexico | 7,222 | 11,829 | 0.94 | 0.93 | 163.8 | 5.6 |
| World | 766,353 | 1,271,417 | 100 | 100 | 65.9 | 5.8 |

*Source*: Compiled and computed from the data provided in World Bank, *World Development Indicators* (2001).

It is also desirable to consider changes in the export of services. India's share in world service export was 0.60 per cent in 1990 and it rose to 1.1 per cent in 1999, indicating a significant improvement. In absolute terms, service exports rose from $4.6 billion in 1990 to $13.94 billion in 1999, nearly three times their level in 1990. The annual average increase in service exports works out at 13.1 per cent for India, compared to 8.4 per cent for China and 5.6 per cent for Mexico. Indian performance in service exports is influenced by a sharp increase in its exports of software services. See Table 7.2.

Pooling merchandise and service exports, it becomes evident that Indian exports of goods and services increased from $22.4 billion in 1990 to $50.5 billion in 1999. As a consequence, India's share in world exports of goods and services improved from 0.55 per cent in 1990 to 0.75 per cent in 1999. As against this, China's share in world exports rose from 1.56 per cent to 2.96 per cent and that of Mexico improved from 1.17 per cent to 2.21 per cent during the same period. Globalisation did not help India to the same extent as it helped China and Mexico. The average annual growth rate of export of goods and services increased by 8.9 per cent during 1990 and 1999 for India, but the increase was much higher for Mexico (13.4 per cent) and China (13.5 per cent). See Table 7.3.

*Table 7.3 Exports of merchandise and services of selected countries of the world*

| Country | Exports (US$ million) | | World exports of merchandise & services (% of total) | | Percentage increase in 1999 over 1990 | Annual average growth rate (%) 1990-99 |
|---|---|---|---|---|---|---|
| | 1990 | 1999 | 1990 | 1999 | | |
| India | 22,404 | 50,500 | 0.55 | 0.75 | 125.4 | 8.9 |
| China | 63,877 | 198,851 | 1.56 | 2.96 | 211.3 | 13.5 |
| S. Korea | 74,171 | 169,567 | 1.81 | 2.52 | 118.6 | 9.1 |
| Mexico | 47,933 | 148,532 | 1.17 | 2.21 | 209.8 | 13.4 |
| World | 4,094,710 | 6,713,643 | 100 | 100 | 63.9 | 5.6 |

*Source*: Compiled and computed from the data provided in World Bank, *World Development Indicators* (2001).

## Foreign Investment Flows to India

It is often claimed that globalisation leads to a greater inflow of foreign investment, which should help to increase the productive capacity of the recipient economy. It is worthwhile considering this for India.

Foreign investment takes two forms – foreign direct investment (FDI) and foreign portfolio investment (FPI). Foreign direct investment helps to increase the productive capacity of the economy, while foreign portfolio investment is of a more speculative nature and is thus very volatile. A careful perusal of the data on foreign investment flows during the 1990s reveals that during the period 1990-91 to 1994-95 the share of FDI in total investment inflow was only 24.2 per cent and that of FPI was 75.8 per cent. In other words, only a quarter of the total foreign investment was directly available for increasing productive capacity while about three-quarters was very volatile. For the six-year period (1995-96 to 2000-2001), the proportion of FDI in total investment improved to 53 per cent. However, the share of portfolio investment was still high at about 47 per cent. Furthermore, the total average inflow of foreign investment during the six-year period (1995-96 to 2000-2001) was $4.85 billion, just half the $10 billion level targeted by the government. India has not benefited from FDI to the extent to which the globalisers had led us to believe. See Table 7.4.

*Table 7.4 Foreign investment inflows to India by different categories, US$ million*

| | Foreign direct investment | Portfolio investment | Total |
|---|---|---|---|
| 1990-91 | 97 | 6 | 103 |
| 1991-92 | 129 | 4 | 133 |
| 1992-93 | 315 | 244 | 559 |
| 1993-94 | 586 | 3,567 | 4,153 |
| 1994-95 | 1,314 | 3,824 | 5,138 |
| 1995-96 | 2,144 | 2,748 | 4,892 |
| 1996-97 | 2,821 | 3,312 | 6,133 |
| 1997-98 | 3,557 | 1,828 | 5,385 |
| 1998-99 | 2,462 | -61 | 2,401 |
| 1999-2000 | 2,155 | 3,026 | 5,181 |
| 2000-2001 | 2,339 | 2,760 | 5,099 |
| 2001-2002* | 2,365 | 1,315 | 3,680 |
| **1990-91 to 1994-95** | **2,441** | **7,645** | **10,086** |
| | **(24.2)** | **(75.8)** | **(100.0)** |
| **1995-96 to 2000-2001** | **15,478** | **13,613** | **29,091** |
| | **(53.2)** | **(46.8)** | **100.0** |

*Note*: * Up to April-November.

*Source*: Compiled and computed from Government of India, *Economic Survey (2001-2002)* p. 154.

## The Gap between Foreign Investment Approved and Actual Inflows

Table 7.5 provides information about foreign technology agreements (FTAs) and foreign direct investment (FDI) approvals. It also provides information about the amount of investment approved and actual inflows. In terms of FTAs, the number of technology agreements after reaching a peak of 982 in 1995 declined thereafter. In comparison, the number of FDI agreements have been increasing and reached a maximum of 1,726 in 2000.

*Table 7.5 Total Foreign Technology Agreements (FTAs) and Foreign Direct Investment (FDI) approvals and actual inflows, India*

| **Year** | **No. of FTAs approved** | **No. of FDI approved** | **Amount approved (Rs crores)** | **Actual inflow of FDI (Rs crores)** | **(4) as % of (3)** |
|---|---|---|---|---|---|
| | (1) | (2) | (3) | (4) | (5) |
| 1991 | 661 | 289 | 534 | 351 | 65.7 |
| 1992 | 828 | 692 | 3,888 | 675 | 17.4 |
| 1993 | 691 | 785 | 8,859 | 1,787 | 20.2 |
| 1994 | 792 | 1,062 | 14,187 | 3,289 | 23.3 |
| 1995 | 982 | 1,355 | 32,072 | 6,820 | 21.3 |
| 1996 | 744 | 1,559 | 36,147 | 10,389 | 28.7 |
| 1997 | 660 | 1,665 | 54,891 | 16,425 | 29.9 |
| 1998 | 595 | 1,191 | 30,814 | 13,340 | 43.3 |
| 1999 | 498 | 1,726 | 28,367 | 16,868 | 59.5 |
| 2000 | 418 | 1,726 | 37,039 | 19,342 | 52.2 |
| 2001* | 247 | 1,590 | 23,266 | 16,127 | 69.3 |
| **1991-1995** | **3,954** | **4,183** | **59,540** | **12,922** | **21.7** |
| **1996-2000** | **2,915** | **7,867** | **187,258** | **76,364** | **40.8** |

*Note*: * January-October.

*Source*: Compiled and computed from Government of India, *Economic Survey (2001-2002)*, p. 167.

But there is a considerable gap between the level of investment approved and actual flows. No doubt, some time lag between the approvals and actual inflows of investment is inevitable. Although the proportion of actual inflow to approved investment has shown an increase as can be seen in Table 7.5, still realisations are far below the approved investment. In other words, as far as foreign investment is concerned, there is still a wide gap between promise and realisation.

**Increase of Imports is Far Greater than Increase of Exports**

Globalisers advocated the acceptance of India's new strategy on the basis that India will be able to access foreign markets more effectively. It is of interest to examine this claim using Table 7.6. Exports rose from 7.3 per cent of GDP in 1991-92 to 9.1 per cent of GDP in 1995-96. Thereafter, they experienced a gradual decline, until they were 8.4 per cent of GDP in 1999-2000. However, they reached a record level of 9.8 per cent in 2000-2001. But if we examine the trend of imports, they increased from 8.3 per cent of GDP in 1991-92 to a level of 12.3 per cent in 1995-96. Even thereafter, when exports fell in 1996-97 and 1997-98, imports continued their forward march. During 2000-2001, when exports grew to a level of 9.8 per cent of GDP, imports jumped to a level of 13.0 per cent of GDP. As a consequence, India's balance of trade deficit during 1996-97 to 2000-2001 ranged between 3.1 to 4.0 per cent of GDP.

*Table 7.6 The external sector and globalisation of the Indian economy as percentage of GDP at market prices*

| | Exports | Imports | Trade balance | Net invisibles | Current account balance | External debt | Debt service payments |
|---|---|---|---|---|---|---|---|
| 1990-91 | 5.8 | 8.8 | - 3.0 | - 0.1 | - 3.1 | 28.7 | 2.8 |
| 1991-92 | 7.3 | 8.3 | - 1.1 | 0.7 | - 0.4 | 41.0 | 3.3 |
| 1992-93 | 7.8 | 10.2 | - 2.4 | 0.6 | - 1.8 | 39.8 | 3.3 |
| 1993-94 | 8.3 | 9.8 | - 1.5 | 1.1 | - 0.4 | 33.8 | 3.1 |
| 1994-95 | 8.3 | 11.1 | - 2.8 | 1.8 | - 1.0 | 30.8 | 3.4 |
| 1995-96 | 9.1 | 12.3 | - 3.2 | 1.6 | - 1.7 | 27.0 | 3.4 |
| 1996-97 | 8.9 | 12.7 | - 3.8 | 2.7 | - 1.2 | 24.5 | 3.2 |
| 1997-98 | 8.7 | 12.5 | - 3.8 | 2.4 | - 1.4 | 24.3 | 2.7 |
| 1998-99 | 8.3 | 11.5 | - 3.2 | 2.2 | - 1.0 | 23.6 | 2.6 |
| 1999-2000 | 8.4 | 12.4 | - 4.0 | 3.0 | - 1.1 | 22.2 | 2.5 |
| 2000-2001 | 9.8 | 13.0 | - 3.1 | 2.6 | - 0.5 | 22.3 | 2.9 |

*Source*: Compiled from Government of India, *Economic Survey* (1997-98), (1999-2000) and (2001-2002).

This underlines the hard reality that foreigners have been able to penetrate the Indian market more effectively than Indians have been able to access the foreign markets.

**Growth Rates of GDP in the 1980s and the 1990s**

The advocates of globalisation argue that export-led growth leads to a sharp increase in GDP growth. Data given in Table 7.7 reveals that there is no doubt that India's growth rate picked up during the 3-year period 1994-95 to 1996-97 to more than 7 per cent, but thereafter, it has slowed down. Annual average growth rate of GDP for the decade 1980-81 to 1990-91 was 5.63 per cent and for the decade of the 1990s (1990-91 to 1999-2000) was 5.8 per cent – a shade better than the achievement of the 1980s. This implies that the high growth rate of GDP attained in the period 1994-95 to 1996-97 could not be sustained in the subsequent period. It has been argued that India's sluggish growth in 2000-2001 and 2001-2002 is due to international factors. Nevertheless, it has to be realised that globalisation increases the dependence of the Indian economy on the world economy and thus reduces its ability to withstand adverse international factors due to its strategy of export-led growth.

*Table 7.7 GDP growth in the Indian economy at 1993-94 prices (Rs crores)*

| Period | GDP at factor cost | Growth rate over the previous year |
|---|---|---|
| 1980-81 | 401,128 | |
| | | |
| 1990-91 | 692,871 | |
| 1991-92 | 701,863 | 1.3 |
| 1992-93 | 737,792 | 5.1 |
| 1993-94 | 781,345 | 5.9 |
| 1994-95 | 838,031 | 7.3 |
| | | |
| 1995-96 | 899,563 | 7.3 |
| 1996-97 | 970,083 | 7.8 |
| 1997-98 | 1,016,399 | 4.8 |
| 1998-99 | 1,082,472 | 6.5 |
| 1999-2000 | 1,148,500 | 6.1 |
| | | |
| 2000-2001* | 1,193,922 | 4.0 |
| **Growth rate (average annual)** | | |
| 1980-81 to 1990-91 | 5.63 | |
| 1990-91 to 1999-2000 | 5.80 | |

* Quick estimates.

*Source*: Computed and compiled from Government of India, *Economic Survey* (2001-2002).

## Slowing Down of the Process of Poverty Reduction in the Post-Globalisation Period

Based on the consumer expenditure data of the 55th Round of National Sample Survey, poverty ratio on a 30-day recall basis has been calculated for 1999-2000 as 27.1 per cent in rural areas, 23.6 per cent in urban areas and 26.1 per cent for the country as a whole. The corresponding figures from the 7-day recall period are 24.0 per cent in rural areas, 21.6 per cent in urban areas and 23.3 per cent for the country as a whole. Since the National Sample Survey Governing Council has not yet decided to switch from the 30-day basis for food items to the 7-day basis; for the present, the 30-day estimates are being used by the Planning Commission as the appropriate estimate of poverty. See Table 7.8.

*Table 7.8 Incidence of poverty in India*

| Poverty ratio | Rural | Urban | Total |
|---|---|---|---|
| 1987-88 | 39.1 | 38.2 | 38.9 |
| 1993-94 | 37.3 | 32.4 | 36.0 |
| 1999-00 | | | |
| (30-day recall) | 27.1 | 23.6 | 26.1 |
| (7-day recall) | 24.0 | 21.6 | 23.3 |

*Source*: National Sample Survey.

Gaurav Datt, Valerie Kozel and Martin Ravallion of the World Bank in their paper 'A model-based assessment of India's progress in reducing poverty in the 1990s' suggest that the key determinants of the rate of poverty reduction at the state level are agricultural yields, growth of the non-farm sector (depending on the state's initial conditions), development spending and inflation. This model has given the following findings:

1. The rate of average annual poverty reduction in the 1990s was slightly lower than that in the 1980s.
2. National: 0.8 percentage points against 1 percentage points
3. Rural: 0.9 percentage points against 0.7 percentage points
4. Poverty reduction in the 1990s is also slower than expected from historical (pre-reform) national elasticity of poverty with respect to mean consumption growth, that is, 0.8 percentage points in the 1990s as against 1.6 percentage points in earlier period.

The main reason for the slow decline in poverty is the geographical pattern of growth promoted following the policies of liberalisation, privatisation and globalisation. Policies of globalisation have helped the already industrialised states much more than the less industrialised states and this combined with agriculture has been responsible for the geographically skewed pattern of economic growth in the post-reform period.

## Higher GDP Growth Accompanied by a Decline in Employment Growth

A major consequence of India's policies of globalisation is the decline in the growth rate of employment in India. During the period 1983-94, the annual average growth rate of employment was 2.04 per cent, but it came down to 0.98 per cent during 1994-2000. Consequently, India's unemployment rate rose from 6.03 per cent in 1993-94 to 7.32 per cent in 1999-2000. This was despite the fact that the rate of growth of its labour force declined to 1.3 per cent per annum on average during the period 1993-94 to 1999-00. This was largely the result of deceleration in employment in agriculture and community and personal services. These two sectors account for nearly 70 per cent of total employment, but they recorded virtually no growth in employment. See Table 7.9.

*Table 7.9 Growth of employment by sectors in India*

| **Sectors** | **1983-94** | **1994-2000** |
|---|---|---|
| Agriculture | 1.51 | -0.34 |
| Mining & quarrying | 4.16 | -2.85 |
| Manufacturing | 2.14 | 2.05 |
| Electricity, gas & water supply | 4.50 | -0.88 |
| Construction | 5.32 | 7.09 |
| Trade | 3.57 | 5.04 |
| Transport, storage & communication | 3.24 | 6.04 |
| Financial services | 7.18 | 6.20 |
| Community & personal services | 2.90 | 0.55 |
| **Total** | **2.04** | **0.98** |

*Source*: Government of India Planning Commission (2001), *Report of the Task Force on Employment Opportunities*, Table 3.2.

Thus it is evident that in the decade or so since India adopted its economic liberalisation policies its reforms have failed to deliver intended benefits in terms of: GDP growth, poverty reduction, employment generation, a boost to investment, and increased export of merchandise.

This raises a number of questions: Who is responsible for this state of affairs? To what extent are international factors, namely policies adopted by developed countries responsible for this and to what extent are domestic policies responsible for the present situation?

## 7.3 THE IMPACT OF THE WTO ON VARIOUS ASPECTS OF THE INDIAN ECONOMY

India, a founding member of the WTO, has been following the WTO policy decisions. Consider some of the consequences.

**Effects on Indian Industry**

The WTO has been urging India to lower import duties, remove controls on consumer goods imports and reduce quantitative restrictions on imports. Under the Uruguay Round Agreement, India offered to reduce tariffs on capital goods, components, intermediate goods and industrial raw materials to 40 per cent in case our tariffs were above that percentage; to 25 per cent in case tariffs were between 25 to 40 per cent and to bind the tariff ceiling at 25 per cent in case of tariffs below that percentage. This reduction in tariffs was to be achieved by the end of 2000.

Since India scrupulously followed the agreement, its tariffs have been reduced year after year to conform to the WTO provisions. As the protection afforded by import duties gradually disappeared, Indian industry had to face increasing competition from foreign goods. The Confederation of Indian Industry (CII), the industrial apex body, expressed its disapproval of low duties on capital goods imports. As a result, CII estimated that indigenous capital goods industry, on a conservative estimate, lost orders worth Rs5,000 crores from foreign countries. Instead of ensuring a level playing field, indigenous industry has to pay excise duty, sales tax, octroi, and turnover tax while imported goods are allowed duty-free access to our market. Not only the entire manufacturing industry is faced with a crisis, even the machine tools industry, gensets (generator sets) and boiler producers are put at a serious disadvantage. Consequently, imports of finished products are displacing indigenously produced products. As a result, many industrial units are being closed and cheap imports have become an important cause of recession in Indian industry.

India was maintaining quantitative restrictions in the form of quotas, import and export licences on 2,700 agricultural commodities, textile and industrial products. The United States along with Australia, New Zealand, Switzerland, the European Economic Community and Canada complained to the WTO Dispute Settlement Machinery that these restrictions were inconsistent with WTO norms. The dispute settlement panel gave its verdict against India. India appealed, but the WTO panel on 23 August 1999 rejected India's appeal against its quantitative import restrictions.

As a result, although India could continue quantitative restrictions until March 2003, the process was hastened. This has opened the floodgates for foreign consumer goods to enter the Indian market, thereby seriously damaging Indian industry.

**Impact of import of second-hand cars in India**

The Government of India has allowed the import of second-hand cars. This policy has seriously affected the Indian automobile industry. Rahul Bajaj described this as an 'anti-national and anti-India Act'. In fact, experience the world over has shown that wherever second-hand imported cars are allowed, they seriously damage domestic industry. Japanese used cars virtually destroyed the New Zealand car industry. Even Phil Spender, Managing Director, Ford India reacting to the policy of permitting used cars said: 'If the government asks us what to do (about the used cars), I'll be the first to volunteer ways to keep used cars imports out of India.' Even other CEOs of MNCs who have invested in the Indian automobile market expressed similar sentiments. Richard Swano, Managing Director of General Motors is of the opinion that the import tariff on used cars should be 100 per cent and not 40-50 per cent.

Similarly, if India allows the import of used machine tools, it is likely to have serious repercussions on capital equipment manufactures.

**Import of Chinese goods**

In recent years, Chinese goods have flooded the Indian markets. They include battery cells, cigarette lighters, locks, car stereos, energy saving lamps, VCD players, wristwatches, toys, fans, electric ovens and a large variety of consumer articles. Since China has become a member of the WTO, this is going to create another problem because action against Chinese dumping of goods can be taken only within WTO provisions. Furthermore, Chinese goods are coming through normal channels of trade; they are also being smuggled via Nepal at zero duty. A very porous border from Nepal has increased clandestine imports from China. Both regular and clandestine imports from China are making serious forays into the Indian markets, thus damaging quite a large range of consumer goods industries. It is difficult to prepare an anti-dumping case against China, since it is virtually impossible to obtain information required from Chinese sources due to the non-transparent nature of the Chinese economy. Dr B.R. Sabade (2001, p. 41) states, 'It is extremely difficult to make a case about dumping of Chinese goods. Government can impose a preliminary duty, introduce a trigger price mechanism or declare China as a non-market economy.'

## Impact of WTO on Small-Sized Industrial Units

WTO agreements do not discriminate on the basis of size of industries or enterprises. In the WTO regime, reservations may have to be withdrawn, preferential purchase and other support measures may not be available and thus small-scale enterprises have to compete not only with the large units within the country, but also with cheap imported products. SSIs are thus losing their markets to cheap imported products. Consequently, a very large number of SSI units are becoming sick or have closed down. Thus, the SSI sector, which accounts for 40 per cent of manufacturing output, 50 per cent of employment and over 33 per cent of exports is in jeopardy. Next to agriculture, this sector is the principal source of employment accommodating 18 million persons. The rule of survival of the fittest is being applied to this sector and in their game, only a few will be able to survive. Dumping of Chinese goods has seriously affected the SSI sector. The real difficulty with the SSI sector is that it does not have adequate resources to prepare the case for anti-dumping duties in view of the prohibitive costs of anti-dumping investigation. The SSIs cannot collect detailed information on individual products required by the anti-dumping directorate to establish a complete case. Consequently, small industries continue to suffer due to such dumping policy.

Not only that, the entry of multinationals in ordinary consumer goods like ice cream, agarbatti (incense-sticks) manufacture, food processing, mineral water and so on is also adversely affecting the SSI sector since these were the traditional areas of this sector. In soft drinks, the entry of the powerful Coca Cola and Pepsi have practically eliminated all small units engaged in the manufacture of aerated water. MNCs are not interested in hi-tech products. Rather they prefer low technology, quick profit yielding and large volume products with regular demand throughout the year. In the name of consumer interests, MNCs continue to swallow SSIs and eliminate them from the market.

## Double Standards of Developed Countries

Developed countries demand so many concessions and reduction of tariffs from the developing countries, but are they encouraging free flow of trade, capital and technology across states; or are they using globalisation to their own advantage?

### Unfair game in agreements on textiles

India is quite competitive in textiles. But developed countries through various protectionist measures deny access to cost efficient textile producers. These measures take the form of anti-dumping duties, unilateral changes in the rules of origin and unjustifiable foisting of environmental issues. All these measures are taken to protect domestic industry in developed countries and thus, these measures hamper free flow of Indian textile exports.

Developed countries have proposed ten years to reduce quotas in their domestic textile industries, but they pressurise developing countries to reduce their tariffs, remove quantitative restrictions, introduce Intellectual Property Rights (IPRs) and so on immediately. Developed countries play an unfair game as far as textile agreements are concerned.

The United States has signed WTO agreements with the proviso that all such agreements have to be passed by the US Congress, being a sovereign body. There is another assurance given by the US President to the Congress. In the case that the decisions of Dispute Settlement Machinery of WTO go against the United States, they will be reviewed by US justices. If they find the decisions unfair, the US has unilaterally reserved for itself the right to walk out of the WTO.

Many of the US laws like Section 301 of US Trade Act clearly violate the WTO agreement. Sixteen countries, including India, Argentina, Egypt, Greece, Poland, Korea and Russia petitioned the WTO in relation to the United States' alleged violation. This matter was considered by the Dispute Settlement Panel of WTO which gave its verdict that those laws are WTO compliant. This has emboldened the US to continue to use unilateral action against countries that are not considered by the US administration as compliant with US trading interests. It passes one's comprehension how the US Congress should be considered as a super-body over the WTO, while the parliaments of other members of the WTO, especially the developing countries, are denied this right. Though patently unjustified, Section 107 of the Uruguay Round Agreement 'provides that nothing in the Uruguay Round Agreement shall be construed to limit any authority conferred under any law of the United States including sections 301-310 of the Trade Act of 1974' (Sabade 2001, pp. 52-3).

**Child labour**

When imports from developing countries hurt the interests of the United States, a number of environmental and human rights issues are raised by the US with the objective of imposing a ban on imports. The United States banned imports of several products from India on the basis of child labour being used. This has affected Indian exports of carpets, chemicals, handicrafts and ready-made garments. But the hypocrisy of the US attitude has been illustrated by Sabade when he writes: 'Many American Companies have shifted their factories to remote areas in Mexico, Indonesia and some other countries. Children are employed in these factories in large numbers and they have to work for more than 12 hours. Recently, a study conducted by Rutgers University has revealed that 290,200 child workers are sweating in shopping malls, factories and farms in the United States.' With such double standards, the US uses the child labour stick to punish India.

**US Anti-Dumping Act and Copyright Act against WTO principles**

Recently, Japan complained that the US Anti-Dumping Act violates WTO principles. A series of investigations carried out regarding Japan's steel exports to the United States revealed that the US Anti-Dumping Act was inconsistent with WTO principles. The decision of the WTO favouring Japan was delivered on 29th May 2000.

Similarly, the European Economic Community complained against the US Copyright Act since it militated against the WTO principles as provided for under the Berne Convention for the protection of literacy and artistic works. The WTO decision delivered on 15th June 2000 also went against the United States.

**Agreement on Agriculture**

The Agreement on Agriculture has only, in theory, favoured agriculture in developing countries. In practice, its implementation has adversely affected agriculture in developing countries. According to the Agreement, developed countries agreed to reduce their subsidies by 20 per cent over six years and developing countries by 13 per cent over 10 years. However, developed countries under Green Box and Blue Box subsidies continue to support agriculture on a large scale.

**Green Box subsidies**

Green Box subsidies include amounts spent on government services such as research, disease control, infrastructure and food security. They also include payments made directly to farmers that do not stimulate production, such as certain forms of direct income support, assistance to help farmers restructure agriculture, and direct payments under environmental and regular assistance programmes. This definition is very wide and includes all types of government subsidies.

**Blue Box subsidies**

Blue Box subsidies are certain direct payments made to farmers where the farmers limit production. They include certain government assistance programmes to encourage agriculture and rural development in developing countries, and other support on a small scale when compared with the total value of the products supported. This 'small-scale' support is namely 15 per cent or less in the case of developed countries and 10 per cent or less for developing countries.

As with domestic support subsidies, developing countries are not allowed to increase their negligible level of export subsidies while developed countries are allowed to maintain 64 per cent of their subsidy outlays on the base level. Consequently, agricultural imports from developed countries are available at far below the market price in the domestic economy. *Human Development Report* (UNDP 1997) reviewing this problem observes:

> According to the OECD, the per capita transfer to US farmers amounted to $29,000 in 1995. In the main maize producing areas of Mindanao and Cagayan Valley, the average per capita incomes amount to less than $300. So each US farmer receives in subsidies roughly 100 times the income of a maize farmer in the Philippines.
>
> In the real world, as distinct from imaginary or [one] inhabited by free traders, survival in agricultural markets depends less on comparative cost advantage than on comparative access to subsidies. Liberalising local food markets in the face of unequal competition is not a prescription for improving efficiency, but a recipe for the destruction of livelihood.
>
> Implementation of the Uruguay Round agriculture agreement over the next five years will not materially change the picture...Agriculture remains the only area of international trade in which export dumping is accepted as a legitimate trade practice.

Earlier, Indian agricultural prices were mostly lower than international prices. But as a result of heavy subsidisation of agricultural exports by developed countries, the situation is fast changing. Since international agricultural prices have become lower than Indian agricultural prices, Indian farmers have been put at a serious disadvantage. The phenomenon of farmers' suicides and growing unrest in several states because of the distress of farmers specialising in agricultural commodities and their exports is a severe human problem. Some economists have, therefore, drawn the attention of the Indian government to the sad plight of Indian farmers due to India's WTO obligations.

## 7.4 DEVELOPING COUNTRIES AT THE DOHA MINISTERIAL CONFERENCE (2001)

Because of pressure from the developing nations, the USA and the European Union accepted a number of issues for the agenda at the Doha Ministerial Conference (2001) that were strong irritants for developing nations.

First, it was agreed that developing countries need not source their essential medicines and drugs at high cost from Western multinational companies holding patents. South Asian, African and Caribbean countries will benefit from this decision. Since China, India and Brazil possess the capacity and technology to manufacture these drugs, they will be entitled to export these medicines without having to secure compulsory licences from licence-holders. Second, the poor countries will be able to take care of their food security concerns. This would become possible with the start of negotiations on reduction of domestic support and elimination of export subsidies being provided by the US and European Union to their farmers. Third, with regard to services and the related removal of restrictions on the natural movement of people, developed countries will be required to negotiate. The real argument put forth in this regard was that flexibility may be left to different members to establish bilateral agreements. In this way, it is hoped that India would gain by increasing access for banking, insurance and other companies and increasing opportunities for people to work in other countries. Fourth, reduction and elimination of tariffs on non-agricultural goods and other barriers, particularly on products that are important to developing countries, is another major gain for developing countries. Last, the US agreed to review anti-dumping rules, but there is a fear that this may not be achieved unless the developing countries put strong pressure on the US to do so.

## 7.5 CONCLUSION

A survey of the globalisation policies followed in India and in other parts of the world reveals that the promised benefits of globalisation in the form of a sharp increase in GDP and exports, foreign direct investment, reduction of poverty and deceleration of unemployment was not be realised by India during the 1990s. Globalisation has adversely affected Indian industry. It has enabled the developed countries to push their exports to India at a much faster rate, but did not facilitate the process of access to international markets; small-scale industry has suffered due to the policy of dumping practised by developed countries, more especially in consumer goods. The most distressing part of the story is the double standards practised by the developed countries. These manifest themselves in the form of unfair agreement on textiles; a policy marked by a bias in favour of the farmers of developed countries as against the poor farmers in India. Developed countries brought forth spurious environmental and social issues to prevent the exports from India of commodities in which India possesses comparative advantage. As Vyas (2002, p.1111) rightly points out: 'The international agreements, particularly under World Trade Organisation (WTO) have not helped the developing countries as was professed at the time of the establishment of WTO.' All these factors have resulted in an erosion of faith in globalisation as the new 'mantra' for stimulating development in India.

## REFERENCES

Datt, Gaurav, Valerie Kozel and Martin Ravallion (2003), 'A model-based assessment of India's progress in reducing poverty in the 1990s', *Economic and Political Weekly*, **38** (4), 355-361.

Government of India (1998), *Economic Survey 1997-1998*, New Delhi: Ministry of Finance, Government of India. Available: http://www.finmin.nic.in/es.htm.

Government of India (2000), *Economic Survey 1999-2000*, New Delhi: Ministry of Finance, Government of India. Available: http://www.finmin.nic.in/es.htm.

Government of India (2002), *Economic Survey 2001-2002*, New Delhi: Ministry of Finance, Government of India. Available: http://indiabudget.nic.in/es200102/welcome.html.

Government of India Planning Commission (2001), *Report of the Task Force on Employment Opportunities*, New Delhi: Government of India.

Haq, M. ul (2002), *Human Development in South Asia 2001: Globalisation and Human Development*, Oxford: Oxford University Press.

Maddison, Angus (1995), *Monitoring the World Economy 1820-1922*, OECD: Paris.

Sabade, B.R. (2001), *WTO – A Threat or an Opportunity*, Centre for Business and Industry, Akshay Society: Pune, India.

UNDP (1997), *Human Development Report*, New York: Oxford University Press.

Vyas, V.S. (2002), 'Globalisation: hopes, realities and coping strategy', *Economic and Political Weekly*, **37** (12), March 23-29: http://www.epw.org.in.

World Bank (2001), *World Development Indicators*, Washington DC: The World Bank.

# 8. Globalisation of Food Items, FDI, and Human Welfare: A Case Study for West Bengal (India)

**Raj Kumar Sen**

## 8.1 INTRODUCTION

The last two decades of the twentieth century were marked by immense changes in the world economy. The new phase of the unipolar world economic order, technological revolution and internationalisation of capital flows have changed the patterns of economic performance, and this has also affected the Indian economy. As a part of revolutionary changes in the world economy, India has gone for globalisation of its economy. This has lead to an increased inflow of foreign direct investment (FDI) and the adoption of an outward-looking export-led strategy of growth since 1991. In this chapter, the discussion is limited to the effects of globalisation and FDI on the economy of West Bengal (a state of India) during this period through trade in selected food items.

In West Bengal, agriculture plays a pivotal role in the state's economy and nearly three out of four persons in the state are directly or indirectly dependent on agriculture. The trade in selected food items (for example, basmati rice, potato, cashew, orange and other fruits, prawn/lobster, chicken and so on) is used to examine the impact of globalisation and FDI with special reference to West Bengal. The rationale behind the choice of these food items is that these are the basic food products mainly produced and traded in West Bengal. The main objectives of this chapter are to compare the pre- and post-liberalisation scenarios of trade and FDI in these selected food items in West Bengal and to study the impact of economic reforms and globalisation on them during the post-liberalisation decade. The trade of these food items has been chosen here, as human welfare is primarily dependent on quantity and quality of food consumption. No distinction is made however between FDI by multinational corporations and FDI by others.

This chapter tries to test the following hypotheses: (a) The quantity and quality of production of these food items in West Bengal vis-á-vis India have significantly increased due to the globalisation process in 2000 to 2001 compared with 1990-91; (b) The quantity and quality of international trade in these food items in West Bengal have significantly increased in 2001 compared with 1991 due to globalisation; (c) The quantity and quality of FDI in the trade of these selected food items in West Bengal vis-á-vis India have significantly increased in 2001 compared with 1991 due to liberalisation policy under India's economic reforms. It was also felt that human welfare in terms of food consumption should register a significant uplift provided all these three hypotheses are found to be acceptable.

## 8.2 GLOBALISATION AND AGRICULTURAL PERFORMANCE: WEST BENGAL VIS-Á-VIS INDIA

India's agricultural sector, which contributes nearly 30 per cent of its GDP and provides employment to 65 per cent of population, remains the backbone of the Indian economy (Government of India, 1999). The present green fields of West Bengal bear testimony to the great changes that have taken place in agriculture. This has been the result of progressive and systematic planning and implementation of various development programmes launched by the state, the dedication of the people engaged in agriculture and the application of advanced crop production technology in the field.

Out of the gross cropped area of 6539 thousand hectares (1998-99) in West Bengal, food grains occupy 71 per cent.[1] Rice, the main staple food of the State, accounts for about 90 per cent of the area under food grains and contributes about 92 per cent of total food grains production. The production of food grains, both cereals and pulses together reached a level of 13.1 million tonnes during the Eighth Plan, up from 4 million tonnes at the time of independence in 1947.[2] There has been a steady increase in the production of total food grains in recent years, made possible by increased rice production and to some extent, greater production of fruits and vegetables.

In spite of the rapid progress made in the production of food grains in the recent past, it has become difficult to keep pace with the increasing demand of the growing population of West Bengal. Agricultural production of some major items has increased in West Bengal vis-á-vis India compared to its pre-globalisation situation (Table 8.1). India's food grain production was 108.4 million tonnes in 1970-71 and 129.6 million tonnes in 1980-81; but it increased to 176.4 million tonnes in 1990-91 and 208.9 million tonnes in 1999-2000 for India. For West Bengal also, total foodgrain production increased to 14.8 million tonnes in 1999-2000 from 11.27 million tonnes in 1990-91 and 8.28 million tonnes in 1980-81. In the case of potatoes, other vegetables and fruits, marine products and farm production of chicken, the level of production is now far higher than in the pre-reform stages in West Bengal and for India also. Table 8.1 gives details about the current situation of agricultural and allied production for West Bengal as well as for India.

*Table 8.1 Production of food items in West Bengal and India ('000 tonnes)*

| Year | Rice | | Potatoes | | Fruits | | Fish & Fish Preparations | | Total Foodgrains | |
|---|---|---|---|---|---|---|---|---|---|---|
| | W.B. | India | W.B. | India | W.B. | India | W.B. | India | W.B. | India. |
| 1980-81 | 7465.6 | 53631.4 | 1971.8 | 9667.5 | - | - | 370.0 | 2444.0 | 8282.0 | 129588.5 |
| 1990-91 | 10436.5 | 74291.4 | 4481.8 | 15205.6 | 973.64 | 30000 | 680.1 | 3836.0 | 11270.1 | 176390.3 |
| 2000-2001 | 14836.2 | 89500.0 | 6796.0 | 17652.3 | 1536.5 | N.A. | 1100.0 | 5140.0 | 14846.0 | 208878.3 |
| 2001-2002* | 15597.0 | - | 7012.0 | - | 1480.0 | - | 1160.3 | - | - | - |

*Note*: *Estimated.

*Sources*: Directorate of Agriculture, Government of West Bengal.
Government of India, *Economic Survey, 2000-2001.*
Government of India (1999) *Ninth Five-Year Plan, 1997-2002.*
Government of West Bengal, *Economic Review, 2000-2001.*
Department of Food Processing Industries & Horticulture, Government of West Bengal.

Decennial percentage changes in production of food items in West Bengal and India are shown in Table 8.2. These indicate a decline in the percentage growth rates of production of most food items. Concern with how to increase the agricultural surplus has led agricultural economists to enquire about investments that increase productivity. Johnston and Mellor (1961) have drawn attention to the opportunities that exist for greatly increased productivity in agriculture by moderate injections of capital, being complementary to existing resources of land and labour.

Forty thousand hectares of land, suffering from salinity, are now producing lobster and prawn in West Bengal. The main production areas of prawn and lobster are in North 24 Parganas and Medinipur districts in West Bengal. [3]

The idea that agricultural productivity is a policy variable that can be manipulated has long been integrated within the framework of development thinking. The performance of the West Bengal economy is crucially dependent on agricultural productivity. There are links between agriculture and the rest of the economy in the product and factor markets. West Bengal has achieved some progress in the development of agriculture and allied activities in this globalisation era (Dasgupta 1998). However, it appears from the experience of the 1990s that the lack of public investment and effort has been responsible for its failure to benefit from trade liberalisation by stepping up and diversifying agricultural output in a cost-effective way.

*Table 8.2 Decennial changes (%) in production of food items in West Bengal and India*

| Decade | Rice | | Potatoes | | Fruits | | Fish & Fish Preparations | | Total Foodgrains | |
|---|---|---|---|---|---|---|---|---|---|---|
| | W.B. | India | W.B. | India | W.B. | India | W.B. | India | W.B. | India. |
| 1980-90 | 3.98 | 3.85 | 12.73 | 5.73 | - | - | 8.38 | 5.70 | 3.61 | 3.61 |
| 1990-2000 | 4.21 | 2.05 | 5.16 | 1.16 | 5.78 | - | 6.18 | 3.40 | 3.17 | 1.84 |

*Source*: Derived from Table 8.1.

West Bengal is not only the highest producer of rice, jute and fish but also a large producer of tea, fruits and vegetables in India (Government of India, 1999). As a result the state has become one of the major Indian destinations for agro-processing and the food processing industry. Its progressive land reforms in its last two decades have enabled West Bengal to achieve sustained economic development, especially in its rural areas. Thus while the observations support the first hypothesis about enhanced production levels, no certain conclusions can be drawn about the causative factors.

## 8.3 GLOBALISATION AND AGRICULTURAL TRADE IN WEST BENGAL AND INDIA

Foreign trade policies in the Ninth Five-Year Plan have been tailored to the objective of accelerating growth in an environment in which the world is becoming increasingly integrated and globalised. The process of globalisation is a reality which cannot be denied and also should not be avoided. However, it needs to be managed properly so that India can derive maximum advantage from world markets. Proponents of structural adjustment programmes expect agricultural products to play an important role in the field of export of developing countries. This is largely because a poor country's comparative advantage is seen to be in agriculture. Agricultural exports are expected to be the mainstay of Indian exports, earning enough to cover increasing import costs.

Among the new export items, three stand out. First, is the export of fish, mainly shrimps, for which there exists a heavy demand in the markets of Japan and United States. Second is high quality, long grain, Basmati rice. Third, of course, consists of various spices for which India and West Bengal are well known.

To grow faster, special emphasis must be given to the agricultural sector to enhance the agricultural exports (Rao 2001). So special export-oriented units and export-processing zones were developed in India. Units engaged in the export of farm products could obtain the benefits of duty-free imports under the export-processing zones scheme even if only 50 per cent of their production was exported and the remaining 50 per cent was sold in the domestic tariff area.

From Tables 8.3 and 8.4 it is clear that there has been a decline in the share of agriculture in total exports of both India and West Bengal. Agricultural exports declined from 30.7 per cent in 1980-81 to 13.5 per cent in 2000-2001,in India, quite the opposite of what was expected to happen (Table 8.3). Among the items, fish and fish preparations account for about 20 per cent of total agricultural exports, the lion's share being due to shrimps produced in coastal areas. In case of West Bengal also the percentage of agricultural export relative to the total exports of the state declined sharply from 71.4 per cent to 6.1 per cent (Table 8.4). Here the deceleration is sharper. Not only that, in case of fish and fish preparations, the period 1991-99 to 1999-2000 displayed a trend in West Bengal quite opposite to that of India. Though the percentage of agricultural export declined in the case of both India and West Bengal, in recent years there has been a tremendous increase in exports of rice (specially basmati), fruits (especially oranges) and fish (especially prawn and lobster). Even though there has been an increase in West Bengal's export of these items, it accounts for a very small proportion of India's exports.

From Table 8.5 it is clear that in 1990-91, India's imports of these food items listed, were negligible. In the case of basmati rice, cashew, potato, fish and cornflakes imports are insignificant in relation to the total domestic production of these items. Recently, however, India's imports of edible oil, pepper, milk and cream increased noticeably. Furthermore, the value of its imports of fruits and vegetables was Rs 45.7 million in 1990-91 and this increased to Rs 339.1 million in 1999-2000. There are apprehensions in certain quarters that the prices of some agricultural products have declined significantly on account of a surge in imports. Whereas prices are mainly a function of demand and supply, the demand for a particular product depends to a great extent on consumer preferences. An analysis of the import data reveals that there has been no significant surge in the import of these items. It would be incorrect, in general, to attribute the present decline in the domestic prices of such commodities, except fruits, to import surges or to India's WTO commitments for the domestic sector (Mukherjee 1994). Hence, the second hypothesis also does not turn out to be acceptable.

*Table 8.3 Export of some agricultural and allied commodities (India) in Rs million*

| Year | Rice | Fruits & Vegetables | Cashew Kernels | Fish & Fish Preparations | Total Agricultural Exports | Total Exports | Agricultural Exports as a Percentage of Total Exports |
|---|---|---|---|---|---|---|---|
| 1980 -81 | 2240 | 800 | 1400 | 2170 | 20570 | 67110 | 30.7 |
| 1990 -91 | 4620 | 2160 | 4470 | 9600 | 63170 | 325530 | 19.4 |
| 1999-2000 | - | 12120 | 24610 | 51140 | 255760 | 1629250 | 15.4 |
| 2000 - 2001 | 31050 | - | 18830 | - | 274230 | 2025100 | 13.5 |

*Note*: * Estimated.

*Sources*: Government of India, *Economic Survey, 2000-2001.*
*Statistical Outline of India, 2000-2001*, TATA Services Ltd, Mumbai.
Government of India, DGCI & S. Kolkata.

*Table 8.4 Export of some agricultural and allied commodities (West Bengal) in tonnes*

| Year | Rice | Cashew | Fish & Fish Preparations | Fruits | Total Agricultural Exports (Rs. Million) | Total Exports (Rs Million) | Agricultural Exports as a Percentage of Total Exports |
|---|---|---|---|---|---|---|---|
| 1980-81 | 7207 | - | - | 8 | 7837.6 | 10977.4 | 71.4 |
| 1990-91 | 30072 | 676 | 1443 | 9 | 8288.2 | 19875.7 | 41.7 |
| 1999-2000 | 16143 | 1391 | 450 | - | - | 85615.4 | - |
| 2000-2001 | - | - | - | - | 6520.3 | 106890.9 | 6.1 |

Note: * Provisional.

Sources: Government of West Bengal, *Statistical Handbook, 2000.*
Government of India, DGCI & S. Kolkata.
Government of West Bengal, *Statistical Abstract 1997-98.*
Government of West Bengal, *Economic Review, Statistical Appendix, 2000-01.*

*Table 8.5 Imports of some selected food items (India) in Rs million*

| Year | Rice | Basmati Rice | Cashew Nuts (Unprocessed) | Potato Seed | Cornflakes | Prawn/ Lobster | Fruits & Vegetables |
|---|---|---|---|---|---|---|---|
| 1990-91 | nil | nil | 1340 | nil | nil | nil | 45.7 |
| 1995-96 | 2.21 | nil | 3760 | 0.112 | nil | nil | 8.7 |
| 1999-2000 | 12.8 | nil | n.a. | 0.06 | 1.345 | 11.22 | 339.1 |

*Sources*: Indian Institute of Public Administration, New Delhi
Directorate General, 'Survey Data', *Commercial Intelligence and Statistics*, New Delhi: Government of India.

As a result of India's liberalisation measures and free market moves, a distinct change in the marketing of fruits and vegetables in the form of discernible strategies for development and new techniques of marketing have emerged (Sen and Pan 2003). What is important now is to take advantage of the new wave of globalisation. Its essence is to redefine goals, choose new market-oriented strategies and to absorb new technologies. The government hopes to boost the production and export of fruits and vegetables through further liberalisation by way of eliminating all unnecessary restraints on the farmer. Now farmers will be increasingly free to export. A good performance on the export front is, therefore, being sought for the benefit of the farmer and for stimulating private investment in the agricultural sector. Under the changing scenario, it has become imperative to develop our marketing strategy in a global perspective (Vyas 1998).

The agricultural sector was brought into the mainstream of GATT only in the Uruguay Round. However, it is not a new inclusion. The original GATT applied to agriculture also. But the application was ineffective, as there were various exceptions to the rules regarding the use of non-tariff measures and subsidies. The high protection and support granted to this sector by different countries in the form of domestic support, export subsidies and other non-tariff measures made agro-trade, mainly exports, a highly distorted one.

The Agreement on Agriculture (AoA) established a number of generally applicable rules with regard to agricultural trade-related measures. The rules are in the areas of border/import access measures, domestic support and export subsidies. These rules relate to country-specific commitments to improve market access and reduce trade-distorting subsidies. In this current climate of globalisation if India wants to do better in agricultural exports then she has to follow these rules (Raikhy and Nanda 2001).

## 8.4 THE ROLE OF FDI IN AGRICULTURAL PRODUCTION AND TRADE

Though foreign direct investment (FDI) is recognised to be playing an important role in channelling new projects in agricultural products, the Government of India's success in encouraging FDI in agricultural processing has been insignificant. It has been able to attract only a miniscule percentage of foreign investment into India – and that too mainly in the less preferred Foreign Institutional Investment sector. The West Bengal State Government has given due importance to the monitoring of foreign direct investment proposals. Since 1991, a considerable number of FDI approvals for agricultural processing have been issued for projects in West Bengal (Government of West Bengal, 2001).[4]

*Table 8.6 Status of food processing units involving FDI in West Bengal*

| Year | FDI | Items | Amount (Rs million) | Investors | Current Position |
|---|---|---|---|---|---|
| 1990-1993 | 2 | Marine products, Potato flakes | 85.174 | Singapore, NRI | Under implementation – 2 |
| 1994-1997 | 15 | Pineapple juice, Mushrooms, Potato, Seeds, Snacks, Canned vegetables, Potato flakes, Packet tea, Coffee, Yeast, Chocolates, Processed shrimp | 5170.110 | Australia, UK, USA, GDR, Ireland, NRI, Netherlands | Dropped – 9<br>Implemented – 2<br>Under implementation – 4 |
| 1998-2001 | 4 | Processed foods, Yeast, Tea, Fish, Wines & spirits, Fruit juice. | 54.325 | UK, USA, NRI, British Virginia, Mauritius | Under implementation – 4 |

*Sources*: Dept. of Commerce & Industries, Government of West Bengal.
Government of West Bengal, *Statistical Abstracts* 1997-98.
Government of West Bengal (1999a) *Ninth Five-Year Plan 1997-2002.*

During the period from August 1991 to November 2000, 326 approvals have been received for units in West Bengal, involving foreign equity participation of Rs 89141.2 million. Of these, 102 FDI approvals involving foreign equity participation or Rs 31463 million have already been implemented and 17 projects involving foreign equity participation of Rs 23938.6 million are in different stages of implementation. Table 8.6 gives details about the status of food processing units involving FDI in West Bengal. Those details clearly indicate the non-acceptability of the last hypothesis. In fact, little FDI has been undertaken in food processing in West Bengal following India's policies promoting economic liberalisation.

To ascertain the actual situation regarding these food items, a pilot survey (Sen and Pan 2003) followed by a major survey were conducted on altogether 651 consumers, 28 producers, 26 traders, 7 government officials and 7 investors; a total of 719 persons. These surveys covered a wide range of regions of West Bengal representing production and/or trading centres of these products as far as possible. On the basis of interviews through structured questionnaires prepared separately for these five groups of people, it was observed that while the impact of globalisation was felt on production methods of food items to some extent, expected impacts are not observed for foreign investment, consumers and traders. FDI entry into the food trade has been very low and consequently the impact on the consumers and especially on their welfare in terms of food consumption have been negligible. The fear of cheap food imports was not long lasting and such imports did not have any major impact on the standard of living of the people. While the percentage of consumers interviewed using any kind of foreign brand for any one of the food items considered increased from 17.5 in 1990-91 to 33.5 in 2000-2001, results show that two-thirds of the consumers are still left outside the influence of globalisation even after ten years of experience with the new economic policies. Only 16.8 per cent of the consumers surveyed stated that their standard of living had increased while 36.0 per cent said it had declined. Another 6 per cent were unsure about the changes in their standard of living during the globalisation decade, 41.3 per cent felt that there has been no change in this period. Only 44.5 per cent of the consumers are aware of the presence of an FDI component in the trade and production of food items.

On the basis of the information received from investors, it was observed that FDI in West Bengal (for food items) has occurred in (a) production of potato flakes, (b) production and trade in prawns/lobsters, (c) trade in basmati rice, (d) trade in fruit, (e) preparation of wines, (f) preparation of mushrooms, (g) preparation and trade in canned vegetables, although the percentage of such investment is very low. Lack of adequate infrastructure was said by most investors to be the reason for little foreign investment in West Bengal.

A recent article in the *Asian Wall Street Journal* (Esserman 2001) said that investing in India may have become easier with new government regulations being passed in May 2001, but foreign companies perhaps have lost interest in West Bengal. In a little over ten years, between January 1991 and February

2001, India has received an actual FDI inflow of just $24.47 billion. Its performance in attracting FDI to the agricultural processing sector is still poor. India's failure in attracting FDI is glaring when compared with the performance of countries such as China, which reportedly attracts more FDI inflow in a single year than India received in the last ten years (World Bank 2000). Realising its failure, India is now concentrating on attracting FDI for food processing. Table 8.7 gives details about such investment.

*Table 8.7 FDI in food products in India in Rs million*

| Year | Fruits | Fish & Fish Preparations | Mushrooms | Milk and Milk Processing | Sugar |
|---|---|---|---|---|---|
| 1992 | 50.0 | 859.0 | - | 13.1 | 75.6 |
| 1995 | 9121.3 | 424.6 | 51794.0 | - | 707.0 |
| 2000 | 7662.6 | 4276.0 | 161.8 | - | 1395.0 |
| 2001 (Till May) | 121.7 | 6.1 | - | - | - |

*Source*: 'Survey Data', New Delhi: Indian Institute of Public Administration.

## 8.5 CONCLUDING REMARKS

Though the WTO regime holds inherent dangers for West Bengal vis-á-vis India's agricultural sector, globalisation has had both good and bad impacts on Indian agriculture. As globalisation continues to spread throughout the world, the benefits accruing to those who participate in this process are expected to increase. This chapter has examined agricultural production, export and FDI in West Bengal, as well as India, during the globalisation decade, 1991-2001.

From this survey, it is observed that production and trade of these food items have increased during this globalisation era. It is not only because of the globalisation factor. Some strategic decisions of the state government also helped it. Nevertheless, it can be safely said that food consumption in West Bengal did not increase significantly. There has been little increase in the consumption of foreign brands of food items in West Bengal. The impact of the economic reforms on the food sector in West Bengal is negligible still after the first globalisation decade.

In West Bengal, there is need for producing quality products not only for export, but also for local consumption. Traditionally certain high quality products had sufficient internal demand to make their production quite viable. The study reveals that agricultural and allied exports have fallen as a percentage of total exports. The bulk of West Bengal's agricultural exports still consist of traditional items. West Bengal's share in India's exports of meat and meat preparations, fish and fish preparations and vegetables and fruits is very small.

To boost West Bengal's production and exports of agricultural and allied commodities (fruits and vegetables, basmati rice, marine products, cashew and so on) there is need for agricultural research, as agriculture is becoming a more capital-intensive, knowledge- and skill-based activity in this globalisation era. West Bengal's agro-food processing industry needs improved raw materials, packing and sanitary conditions to compete with other nations. Nevertheless, this study reveals that to date the impact of globalisation in West Bengal rural economy remains negligible.

## ACKNOWLEDGEMENT

This paper is part of a major research project sponsored by the University Grants Commission, New Delhi. The author is thankful to Subhransu Pan for his assistance with the preparation of this paper.

## NOTES

1. Government of West Bengal, *Statistical Handbook 2000*, Kolkata: Bureau of Applied Economics & Statistics, Government of West Bengal, pp. 68-9.
2. See Government of West Bengal (1999a) *Ninth Five-Year Plan 1997-2002*.
3. An article published in 'Bartaman Newspaper' dated 09.09.2000 published from Kolkata.
4. Government of West Bengal (2001-02) *Budget Speech of Minister of Commerce and Industries Department*.

## REFERENCES

Dasgupta, Biplab (1998), *Structural Adjustment, Global Trade and The New Political Economy of Development*, Delhi: Sea-Vistaar and London: Zed Books.

Esserman, Susan (2001), 'The WTO on Trial', *The Asian Wall Street Journal*, **25**, September.

Government of India (1999), *Ninth Five-Year Plan 1997-2002,* vol. I, New Delhi: Planning Commission.

Government of West Bengal (1999a), *Ninth Five-Year Plan 1997-2002*, Kolkata: Development & Planning Department.

Government of West Bengal (1999b), *Statistical Abstract 1997-98*, Kolkata: Bureau of Applied Economics and Statistics.

Government of West Bengal (2001), *A Review of the Industrial Scene in West Bengal, Annual Report 2000-01*, Kolkata: Commerce & Industries Department.

Johnston, B.F and J.W. Mellor (1961), 'The Role of Agriculture in Economic Development', *American Economic Review*, **51** September, 566-93.

Mukherjee, Amitava (1994), *Structural Adjustment Programme and Food Security*, Aldershot: Avebury.

Raikhy, P. S. & Paramjit Nanda (2001), 'India's Agricultural Exports in the Post-Liberalisation Period: Problems and Prospects', *84th Conference Volume of the Indian Economic Association*, Vellore: Indian Economic Association.

Rao, C.H. Hanumantha (2001), 'WTO and Viability of Indian Agriculture', *Economic & Political Weekly*, **8**, September, 3453-7.

Sen, Raj Kumar, and Suvranshu Pan (2003), 'Globalisation, Trade and FDI in Food Items in West Bengal', in Raj Kumar Sen (ed.) *Economic Reforms and Development*, New Delhi: Deep & Deep Publications, pp.313-26.

Vyas, V. S. (1998), 'Agricultural Trade Policy and Export Strategy', *Economic & Political Weekly*, **34**(13), March 27-April 12, A27-A34.

World Bank (2000), *World Development Report*, Oxford University Press, New York.

# 9. The Global Economy and Institutional Change in Rural Nigeria: A Case Study of Two Villages

**John Gowdy, Raluca Iorgulescu and Steve Onyeiwu**

## 9.1 INTRODUCTION

Development economists increasingly recognise that institutions play a critical role in economic change. But much of what passes for 'institutional' economics is yet another sterile exercise in the mathematics of constrained optimisation. In the view of the new institutional economics, institutions are commodities just like any other and act only as constraints on human behaviour. According to North (1990, p. 5), institutions are 'the constraints that human beings impose on themselves'. A more realistic view is that institutions can both constrain and expand the scope of human opportunities and should be perceived as repositories of myriad incentives, rules, routines, and conventions that constrain and also enhance the ability of agents to act in specific ways. Although institutions do foster and underlie particular behaviours and habits, they can also be influenced and shaped by human action (Hodgson 1998, p. 180).

Using the example of economic change in Igboland, Nigeria, we argue below that traditional development polices have failed to improve the lives of the world's poorest. We argue further that the design of successful development policies depends critically on understanding the institutions of both the poor and non-poor. In this regard, the relationship between globalisation and institutions is critical to the development process. Globalisation has not only weakened traditional institutions but has also fostered institutions that make it difficult for the poor to reap the advantages of the global market economy. It is not enough to focus on why the poor 'refuse to be developed'. We must also understand the relationship between the poor and wealthy countries and the relationship between the poor and wealthy *within* the poor countries. In Bromley's (2001, p. 21) words:

> . . . if we wish to understand why people are – and remain – poor, we must first understand why a large group of others are – and remain – non-poor. Who, if not the non-poor, stand in a legal and economic position to influence the fields of action, the choice domain, for the poor.

Srinivasan and Bhagwati, quoted in Wei (2002, p. 26), argue that cross-country regressions are inadequate for deciphering the complex relationship between globalisation, growth, poverty and inequality, and contend that more compelling evidence must come from case studies. In the pages that follow, we examine the impact of globalisation and institutional change in two Igbo villages in south-east Nigeria. The globalisation process resulted in the implementation of structural adjustment policies in Nigeria. These neoliberal, market-based policies rationalised the withdrawal of state support for social programmes such as spending on health, education and basic infrastructure. Using data from the traditional rural village of Umuluwe and a recently established satellite village (Obigbo) nearer to oil industry jobs, we look at the impact of the changing economy on gender roles, age structure, income distribution and traditional institutions. We collected data from Umuluwe and Obigbo separately, but these two villages should not be considered in isolation. Globalisation reinforced migration to Obigbo, as large numbers of Umuluwe residents left the impoverished village for better living conditions in Obigbo. Understanding the interdependence between them is central to understanding the impact of globalisation and markets on Igboland.

## 9.2 GLOBALISATION, POVERTY AND DEVELOPMENT

Globalisation has different, sometimes ambivalent, connotations. For some, it means increased flow of capital around the world; removal of barriers to trade; increased diffusion of technology (particularly new information technology), and the internationalisation of the production process. Globalisation has also been perceived as a means to institutionalising the market as the overarching mechanism for resource allocation. Two major trends, however, characterise the current globalisation process: the phenomenal growth in cross-border investment and international trade, coupled with the dramatic growth in global communications and technology (Sutherland 2002, p. 20). The flow of foreign direct investment, which amounted to $160 billion in 1991, jumped to $1.1 trillion in 2000. The volume of international trade has increased 16-fold over the past 50 years, with trade in components growing faster than trade in final products (Sutherland 2002, p. 20). Beyond these impressive statistics, however, is the question of the extent to which globalisation has impacted on poverty and living conditions in rural communities of Africa. Some analysts argue that the poor have been made worse off by globalisation, or that the benefits have accrued disproportionately to the more affluent members of society (Wei 2002, p. 26).

World Bank and IMF globalisation policies have ushered in a new global political economy in which developing countries are cajoled and coerced to implement market-based economic reforms – deregulating their economies, liberalising trade policies, and reducing budget deficits – as a precondition for receiving debt rescheduling from creditor nations. For developing countries, the Structural Adjustment Programmes (SAP) have strengthened conservative demand management policies, including cuts in government expenditures on social programmes such as health, education and infrastructure, as well as freezing wages and public sector employment. While these reforms have improved the macroeconomic performance of some developing countries, they have had deleterious effects on many rural communities in developing countries (Onyeiwu 1997).

After more than fifty years experience it is clear that the hope that 'underdeveloped' countries would follow the 'progressive' (Western) path toward prosperity is an illusion. The grim picture of world poverty is now familiar to everyone. As measured by the Human Poverty Index, more than one-fourth of the population of the developing world lives in abject poverty.

Nigeria ranks 136 out of 162 in the Human Development Index (HDI) of the United Nations Development Programme (UNDP 2001). Nigeria, like many other African countries, has experienced economic crises during the past twenty years. The negative effects of national economic downturns have been particularly pronounced in the rural areas. The daily wage of an unskilled worker is now equivalent to the price of a loaf of bread. The average monthly wage is equivalent to what an American can earn in four hours. Rising prices have decreased consumption at an annual rate of 7 per cent during the past decade and material standards of living are now lower than they were in the 1950s. Seventy per cent of Nigeria's population lives below the poverty line. In 1999 the country ranked 187 in terms of Gross National Income per capita (World Bank 2001).

Globalisation offers opportunities for developing countries, and Nigeria in particular would seem to have a large role to play in the growth of the global economy. The country is blessed with large reserves of petroleum, natural gas, respect for education (especially in Igboland), and a world-renowned literary tradition. But Nigeria has been hard-hit by fluctuating primary resource prices. Real commodity prices in the 1990s were 45 per cent lower than in the 1980s. Nigeria also suffers from a lack of supporting institutions and infrastructure that would enable the country's poor to take advantage of its abundant natural resources and human capital.

For the most part, Nigeria's various post-colonial governments have followed a neoliberal approach to development. Convinced that industrialisation and economic rationalisation is the best way to achieve rapid economic growth, the post-colonial leadership relied on foreign direct investment for the implementation of an import substitution strategy. A range of incentives, from tariff protection, tax breaks and duty exemptions on imported raw materials, were offered to foreign investors to encourage investment in the Nigerian economy (Hakam 1966). Infrastructure such as roads, water and telecommunication services were provided within industrial zones established by the government. This policy of rapid industrialisation led to some success in raising Nigeria's GDP but it also created a variety of problems. First, it shifted attention away from agriculture and rural development, resulting in rapid urbanisation and the emergence of a sub-culture that replicated the values, life-styles and attitudes of developed industrial societies. This emerging Western sub-culture, reinforced by the flow of money to the major cities from the oil boom of the 1970s, was instrumental in weakening some of the cooperative values and institutions of rural communities in south-eastern Nigeria (Onyeiwu and Jones 2003). Second, import substitution policies led to a dependence on massive imports of raw materials and intermediate inputs to the manufacturing sector. Subsidies to foreign manufacturers were financed in the 1970s and early 1980s by the proceeds from the oil boom. But with the end of the boom in the 1980s, the government was forced to support its industrial policy with foreign loans, plunging Nigeria into huge debt accompanied by a crushing debt-service burden. Nigeria's long-term public and publicly guaranteed debt rose from just \$480 million in 1970 to \$4.4 billion in 1980, and jumped to over \$11.8 billion in 1984 (World Bank 1989, p. 47) Currently, Nigeria's foreign debt is over \$30 billion and its debt service burden is about 35 per cent of GNP (World Bank 2001).

Rather than using its oil wealth to aid rural areas and local enterprises in ways that would help the average citizen, various Nigerian governments have followed a modernisation programme largely benefiting foreign investors and local elites. The effects of these policies can be seen at the local level in the breakdown of traditional institutions, a changing family structure, and the establishment of new institutions facilitating the transfer of people and wealth between isolated rural communities and rapidly growing suburban villages.

## 9.3 THE VILLAGES OF UMULUWE AND OBIGBO, NIGERIA

The village of Umuluwe is situated within the predominantly Christian south-east region of Nigeria, and is about 20 miles west of the regional capital of

Owerri. Like most communities in Igboland, the Umuluwe people live in a close-knit, nucleated village of about 2000 people. Several small villages sharing the same cultural, social and religious practices surround Umuluwe. The village is a rallying point for Umuluwe descendants, and every individual considers the village as more important than the nation state. Except for interaction (through marriages, the church, and trade) with other neighbouring villages, Umuluwe residents have limited contact with the outside world. For instance, the first contact with Caucasians for most of the villagers was when two of the authors of this paper (Gowdy and Iorgulescu) visited the village in Spring 2001.

Umuluwe is representative of rural Nigerian villages with difficult access from outside areas. The roads are quite a challenge for regular cars that, due to the pervasive poverty, are a luxury only very few can afford. There is no bus line and people walk daily for hours back and forth to reach the nearby villages and the markets where their products are sold. As a consequence of inadequate infrastructure, people cannot commute for work outside the village. Electricity was introduced only in the last two years, due to the concerted effort of the community, but due to undersupply and transmission problems, a chronic problem in Nigeria, power is on intermittently. There is no running water; the only water source is a small spring about one mile away from the centre of the village. The soil has a low fertility and the absence of livestock makes agriculture unsustainable in a poor community unable to afford chemical fertilisers.

The village's main sources of income are cash crops (palm trees and fruit), water and paving stone. Farming is mainly for subsistence, although surpluses are sometimes produced and sold at the weekly markets in neighbouring villages. Proceeds from such surpluses are used to purchase items such as meat, milk, sugar and bread. The villagers also use the proceeds to pay community dues, school fees for their children and health care.

The Umuluwe community has social and political institutions specific to West Africa (Gowdy et al. 2003; Onyeiwu 1997). Almost every adult member of the community belongs to at least one community-based association. The village associations focus on the execution of village development projects such as education, roads, bridges and electricity. Given the lack of government support, these associations play a pivotal role in the economic development of the village. There is no formal, centralised political authority in the community. Nor is there an overall political leader or a traditional ruler in the village. A loose coalition of elders, charismatic members of the village and the village associations govern the village informally. Each extended family also regulates the behaviour of members of the family, and has the authority to impose penalties on deviant members. Although the British colonial rulers established English-style courts in

Igboland (Orji 1987, p. 108), the Umuluwe people rarely used them, mediating conflicts within the community through the traditional institutions (the elders, the extended families, and the village associations).

Igbos migrating to jobs in the oil rich coastal areas of southeast Nigeria founded the village of Obigbo; a name which means 'the heart of the Igbos'. The relationship between Umuluwe and Obigbo is much more than a simple case of rural-urban migration. There is a complex pattern of age and gender-based migration back and forth between the two villages, and an intricate economic relationship. Obigbo is about 20 miles from Port Harcourt, and it increasingly serves as a residential area for workers in Port Harcourt. Unlike Umuluwe, Obigbo has infrastructure facilities such as piped water, electricity, telephone lines and tarred roads, even though these facilities may not function all the time. Out of 10,000 people – the population of Obigbo – originating from different parts of Igboland, about 30 per cent are from Umuluwe. According to residents of both villages, nearly half of Umuluwe villagers have migrated to Obigbo. Thus, to some extent the two villages can be seen as a natural experiment to test the effects of globalisation and urbanisation. Umuluwe is still representative of the older village life while Obigbo represents the newer way of life linked to salaried jobs and the global economy.

In May 2001, the authors conducted a socio-economic survey in the villages of Umuluwe and Obigbo helped by local assistants; 236 questionnaires were completed in Umuluwe and 84 questionnaires in Obigbo. Because of incomplete information, 20 questionnaires were eliminated from the Umuluwe sample and 19 from the Obigbo sample, so that the final total sample size was 216 for Umuluwe and 65 for Obigbo. The survey yielded an abundance of information about the effects of globalisation and economic change on traditional institutions, new institutional arrangements created in response to rapid economic change, and institutions hindering development. Our research group lived in Umuluwe for one week, interacting closely with the people, but we visited Obigbo only once.

Characteristic of Igbo culture before the British colonial age (1900-1960) was membership, sometimes compulsory, in village-level, gender-based associations. Even the poorest people contributed through levies to their community groups. These community institutions are still the focal point of economic activity in the two villages. Our survey results showed that Umuluwe had 17 male associations with most of the people in the village participating in at least four of them and 15 women's associations with most women participating in six of them. For Obigbo, a larger community, men participated in 24 associations and women in 10. Compared to Umuluwe, we found in Obigbo a much clearer delineation of each association's purpose including extended family associations, youth associations, professional associations and branches of the Umuluwe associations. It appears that village associations are stronger in Umuluwe than in Obigbo. Obvious reasons for this include the pressure on people's time in Obigbo, particularly on those with professional jobs, and the fact that Obigbo residents come from a number of other villages. Umuluwe is a much more closely-knit community. While visiting Umuluwe, we were impressed by the frequency with which villagers participated in community associations and by the democratic nature of these institutions.

## 9.4 SOCIOECONOMIC CHARACTERISTICS OF UMULUWE AND OBIGBO

### Income in Umuluwe and Obigbo

The surveys revealed striking income differences between the two villages. In Umuluwe, 56 per cent of the respondents earned less than 10,000 Naira per year (100 Naira = US$1), while in Obigbo only 6 per cent fell into this category. Only 6 per cent of Umuluwe residents earned more than 50,000 Naira, while in Obigbo the corresponding figure was 26 per cent.

*Table 9.1 Comparison of annual incomes by gender in Umuluwe and Obigbo (percentage of total sample)*

| Income group (Naira/year) | Umuluwe | | | Obigbo | | |
|---|---|---|---|---|---|---|
| | Total sample | Males of total sample | Females of total sample | Total sample | Males of total sample | Females of total sample |
| Over 50,000 | 6 | 5 | 1 | 26 | 21 | 5 |
| 20,000-49,999 | 7 | 4 | 3 | 18 | 15 | 3 |
| 10,000-19,999 | 16 | 11 | 5 | 14 | 12 | 1-2 |
| 1-9,999 | 56 | 19 | 37 | 6 | 5 | 1-2 |
| No income | 15 | 2 | 13 | 36 | 25 | 11 |
| Total | 100 | 41 | 59 | 100 | 78 | 22 |

Table 9.1 shows the striking gender differences between the two villages. In Obigbo, 78 per cent of the population is male, while in Umuluwe only 41 per cent are male. Second, we can also say something about the income of males and females since men and women, even when they are married, have independent budgets. The large difference between the percentages of women

and men in higher income categories is evidence of gender inequality of opportunity.

## Gender and Age Structure in Umuluwe and Obigbo

An Umuluwe 'missing generation' of males aged 20 to 40 is 'recovered' as present in Obigbo. We can also 'trace' the people who return at an older age, over 60, from Obigbo to the their ancestral village of Umuluwe, and many of the survey respondents plan to return to Umuluwe when they retire.

*Table 9.2 Age distribution in Umuluwe and Obigbo (percentage of total sample)*

| Age group (years) | Umuluwe | | | Obigbo | | |
|---|---|---|---|---|---|---|
| | Total sample | Males of total sample | Females of total sample | Total sample | Males of total sample | Females of total sample |
| 20-29 | 9 | 2 | 7 | 20 | 17 | 3 |
| 30-39 | 14 | 6 | 8 | 26 | 25 | 1-2 |
| 40-49 | 25 | 9 | 16 | 26 | 20 | 6 |
| 50-59 | 22 | 8 | 14 | 15 | 9 | 6 |
| 60-69 | 20 | 9 | 11 | 5 | 1 | 2 |
| 70-79 | 7 | 4 | 3 | 5 | 3 | 1-2 |
| Over 80 | 3 | 3 | 0 | 3 | 3 | 0 |
| Total | 100 | 41 | 59 | 100 | 78 | 22 |

Table 9.2 shows that males between ages 20 and 40 represent 42 per cent of the population of Obigbo but only 8 per cent of the population of Umuluwe. Males over age 60 represent 16 per cent of the population of Umuluwe, and only 7 per cent of the population of Obigbo. The ratio of males to females in Obigbo is 4:1 while in Umuluwe it is 2:3. The death rate is higher for men than for women in both villages.

For Umuluwe village the average was 5 children per family compared to Obigbo where the average was only 3 children per family. The difference is explained by the high number, for Obigbo, of single people or couples without children (even at an older age, in their forties). The reduced family size is one aspect of 'modernity' introduced by globalisation.

## Education in Umuluwe and Obigbo

The Igbo people are known for their high esteem for education. The survey of the two villages substantiates this assertion. We discuss the educational process undergone by villagers referring to school levels (primary grade 1 to 6, junior secondary grade 7 to 9, senior secondary grade 10 to 11/12, and tertiary undergraduate level).

*Table 9.3 Comparison of education levels between the two villages (percentage of total sample)*

| Education group (education level) | Umuluwe | | | Obigbo | | |
|---|---|---|---|---|---|---|
| | Total sample | Males of total sample | Females of total sample | Total sample | Males of total sample | Females of total sample |
| Tertiary | 3 | 1 | 2 | 11 | 8 | 3 |
| Senior secondary | 13 | 7 | 6 | 31 | 29 | 1-2 |
| Junior secondary | 3 | 1 | 2 | – | – | – |
| Primary | 37 | 19 | 18 | 43 | 34 | 9 |
| No education | 44 | 13 | 31 | 15 | 7 | 8 |
| Total | 100 | 41 | 59 | 100 | 78 | 22 |

Educational levels vary dramatically between Umuluwe and Obigbo (Table 9.3). Forty-four per cent of Umuluwe's residents report no education while the corresponding figure in Obigbo is only 7 per cent. Eighty-one per cent of Umuluwe residents have only a primary education or no education at all, while the corresponding figure in Obigbo is 58 per cent. Only 16 per cent of the residents of Umuluwe report an educational level of 'senior secondary' or higher, while in Obigbo the figure is 42 per cent. The average level of education is higher in Obigbo because a basic education is required to obtain a job in the oil industry. Moreover, educated residents of Umuluwe prefer to live in Obigbo and other sub-urban areas in order to have access to a wider range of infrastructure facilities.

## Income Flows from Obigbo to Umuluwe

As mentioned above about one-half of the villagers from Umuluwe have migrated to Obigbo because of better employment opportunities and higher wages. Per capita annual income in Umuluwe is about 9900 Naira yearly (about US$98) while in Obigbo the figure is about 32,700 Naira (about US$320).

Table 9.4 shows income flows by age, income and education. Not surprisingly, the Obigbo age group 30-39 sends almost 60 per cent of the total amount of remittances sent to Umuluwe. The average annual amount sent per person from this age group is 3,273 Naira. Most of the money sent from Obigbo comes from those with incomes over 50,000 Naira per year

(71.6 per cent) and from those with a senior secondary education (60 per cent). The average amount sent per capita is 1,282 Naira or about US$12 per year.

*Table 9.4 Income flows from Obigbo to Umuluwe*

| **Age group** | **20-29 years** | **30-39 years** | **40-49 years** | **50-59 years** | **60-69 years** | **70-79 years** | **Over 80 years** | **Total** |
|---|---|---|---|---|---|---|---|---|
| Total amount (%) | 6.5 | 58.5 | 13.5 | 21.5 | 0 | 0 | 0 | 100 |
| Naira/ year per capita | 500 | 3,273 | 594 | 1,467 | 0 | 0 | 0 | 1,282 |

| **Income group** | **Over 50,000 Naira/ year** | **20,000-49,999 Naira/ year** | **10,000-19,999 Naira/ year** | **1-9,999 Naira/ year** | **No income** | **Total** |
|---|---|---|---|---|---|---|
| Total amount (%) | 71.6 | 14.6 | 8.6 | 5.2 | 0 | 100 |
| Naira/ year per capita | 4,000 | 1,000 | 760 | 800 | 0 | 1,282 |

| **Education group** | **Tertiary education** | **Senior secondary education** | **Primary education** | **No education** | **Total** |
|---|---|---|---|---|---|
| Total amount (%) | 10.6 | 60 | 29 | 0.4 | 100 |
| Naira/year per capita | 2,167 | 2,846 | 743 | 25 | 1,282 |

## 9.5 GLOBALISATION AND INSTITUTIONS IN IGBOLAND

While globalisation is said to offer 'new and exciting opportunities for raising living standards worldwide' (Sutherland 2002, p. 20), the contrary has been the case for the Umuluwe community. In the village of Umuluwe, structural adjustment has impacted local institutions by destroying social capital and social cohesion, by destroying the capacity for local economic development, by diminishing the capabilities of the village, by reinforcing the asymmetric relationship between the village and the state, and by weakening village institutions.

**Destruction of Social Capital and Social Cohesion**

Stiglitz (2000, p. 63) defines social capital as 'institutions and relations that mediate transactions and reduce disputes'. Social capital encompasses social-structural resources embodied in institutions, civic communities, families and the larger society (Tomer 1999, p. 1950). Economic reform based on modernisation has disrupted the symbiosis between social capital and the rural economy of Umuluwe by increasing poverty and income inequality. The incidence of poverty has been exacerbated by the escalation in the cost of living engendered by economic liberalisation, as well as the removal of subsidies on basic necessities such as health, education and fuel. With little or no significant additional income, Umuluwe dwellers became subject to harsh economic conditions. Many were forced to leave the village in search of better economic opportunities, a process that led to the depopulation of the village and the weakening of community life. More than half the population now lives outside the village. Since the stock of social capital is a function of the close interactions between friends and family within the village, when the social structure of the village is broken up the value of social capital is weakened.

**Destruction of the Capacity for Local Economic Development**

The lack of government investment in social programmes has resulted in villages such as Umuluwe taking responsibilities for the financing of the village primary school, the provision of electricity and water supply. Umuluwe has had to impose huge levies on villagers in order to raise money to finance social programmes hitherto provided by the state. Village norms require that everyone pays village levies, regardless of one's ability to pay. Those with low incomes have had to borrow money from the more affluent villagers in order to meet their village obligations. Some of the indigent villagers have mortgaged their land and other tangible assets in order to pay their levies. For the village as a whole, total taxes actually exceed total income. The ratio of total reported taxes to total reported income is 1.6:1. Taxes exceed income for 96 per cent of the Umuluwe villagers. In fact, payment of these levies has resulted in some villagers having a negative net worth, as their obligations to the village now exceed their income and wealth. The imposition of levies has diverted resources that could have been used for the purchase of inputs necessary for the production of agricultural and other village products. Thus, structural adjustment has undermined the production capacity of the villagers

During the course of our field research, many of the villagers complained that their output of staple crops such as yam and cassava has declined, generating a vicious cycle of low income, low savings and low investment, thereby exacerbating poverty. Survey data not only indicate a high incidence of poverty, the evidence also points to an increasing feminisation of poverty in the village. Economic hardship has shortened the life expectancy of the men in the village from about 55 years during the pre-globalisation era to about 45 years, leaving many young women widowed. Poverty is also increasingly feminised because Umuluwe culture expects women to be responsible for feeding the household.

## Diminishing Capabilities of the Village

Sen (1999) points out that development cannot proceed and be sustained unless the capabilities of individuals within the community are developed. Capabilities are developed and nourished when individuals are healthy, well-fed and live in decent houses. Individuals with well-endowed capabilities are often imbued with self-confidence and the ability to pursue their own goals. A village community that is well-endowed with capabilities is also able to harness its natural, human and mental resources for the development of the local community. By reducing the ability of Umuluwe to provide the basic needs of life, globalisation (via structural adjustment) has undermined the social capital of the community. Umuluwe has witnessed an inexorable erosion of the capabilities of its members. This erosion has been fuelled by the lack of access to the most rudimentary health care, as well as diminished access to quality education due primarily to the discontinuation of state support. Not a single health facility exists in Umuluwe and villagers have to travel at least 10 miles to the nearest hospital. During interviews, villagers were unanimous in identifying education, health and the welfare of their children as their main concerns. They also lamented the increasing inability to achieve these goals, pointing to the neglect of the village by the government. The globalisation process, through its underlying philosophical foundation of 'smaller governments', 'getting the prices right', 'responsibility and accountability', has encouraged state neglect of impoverished and powerless villages at a time when state support is critical.

## Reinforcement of the Asymmetric Relationship between the Village and the State

While the three tiers of government in Nigeria (local, state and federal)

require the villagers to pay taxes, little or no social services are provided for the villagers in return. None of the 236 villagers interviewed acknowledged receiving any form of government assistance during the past decade. Although they expressed displeasure for paying taxes without getting anything in return, they also lamented their inability to change the status quo. The proceeds from the tax revenues are used to support the urban ruling class and to develop projects that benefit only urban dwellers.

**Weakening of Village Institutions**

The cumulative effect of structural adjustment has been to induce many of the villagers to leave the village for other sub-urban areas (such as Obigbo) and cities. The exodus of people from the village undermines village institutions and unwittingly leads to ineffective enforcement of village norms and values. Greater mobility out of the village also implies that deviant villagers can easily avoid village-imposed sanctions. In a study of the Igbo community as a whole, Onyeiwu and Jones (2003) argue that structural adjustment policies have undermined Igbo cultural values and instilled a spirit of 'survival of the fittest'.

One of the dramatic changes in the moral values of the Igbo relates to the institution of chieftaincy. Chieftaincy titles in Igboland were typically awarded to people who served their communities in novel ways, and who upheld the moral and ethical ideals of the community. Titleholders were regarded as role models for youth, and they were perceived as persons of exemplary character. Today, given harsh economic conditions in the local communities, the tendency is to award the title of chief to those who donate money to the community and the local chiefs, regardless of the source of the money. Indeed, well-known criminals now receive chieftaincy titles from their communities – a practice that has now compromised the high moral and ethical values of the Igbo. This has increased conflict in the Igbo community, particularly with regard to land disputes. Most of these disputes are now resolved by the courts, rather than by the elders of the community. The community no longer trusts the ability of the elders to adjudicate in a neutral manner.

## 9.6 CONCLUSION

The situation in Igboland shows that the effects of globalisation are complex and may impact traditional societies negatively. One aspect of the globalisation process that has impacted severely on the two villages is the implementation of market-based economic reforms and programmes.

Structural adjustment has meant deep cuts in government expenditures on social programmes such as education, health and infrastructure. It has also involved drastic reductions in the role of the public sector, resulting in cuts in public sector employment. The effects of the cash economy can be seen in Umuluwe and Obigbo in increasing debt and rising prices for necessities. Subtler are the negative effects on traditional values and social cohesion in village life as indicated by the segregation of Igbo society by gender and age in the two villages.

The march toward globalisation seems unstoppable. Free trade is the one doctrine of contemporary economics that goes almost unchallenged in mainstream discourse. As Tisdell (2001) points out, however, globalisation policies of the World Bank and WTO are based on the 'weak' version of sustainability. Positive social and environmental outcomes are assumed to be natural products of unrestricted markets. We argue above that such a one-sided view of development is over-simplified and misguided. By considering the importance of complex institutions in the development process, a more balanced picture emerges of the positive and negative effects of globalisation.

## REFERENCES

Bromley, D. (2001), 'Institutions, Poverty, and Sustainability: Lessons from the Development Experience', paper presented, 17 September at the Lund School of Economics and Management, Sweden: Lund University.

Gowdy, J.M., R. Iorgulescu and S. Onyeiwu (2003), 'Fairness and Retaliation in a Rural Nigerian Village', *Journal of Economic Behavior and Organization* (forthcoming).

Hakam, A.N. (1966), 'The Motivation to Invest and the Locational Pattern of Foreign Private Industrial Investments in Nigeria', *Nigerian Journal of Economic and Social* Studies, **15** (2), 30-46.

Hodgson, G.M. (1998), 'The Approach of Institutional Economics', *Journal of Economic Literature,* **36** (1), 166-92.

North, D. (1990), *Institutions, Institutional Change and Economic Performance*, Cambridge: Cambridge University Press.

Onyeiwu, S. (1997), 'Altruism and Economic Development: The Case of the Igbo of South-Eastern Nigeria', *Journal of Socio-Economics,* **26**, 407-20.

Onyeiwu, S. and R. Jones (2003), 'An Institutionalist Perception of Cooperative Behavior', *Journal of Socio-Economics* **32** (3), 233-48.

Orji. I. E. (1987), 'Law in Nigerian Society', in J.U. Obot (ed), *Nigeria: The People and their Heritage*, Calabar: Wusen Press, pp. 103-19.

Sen, A. (1999), *Development as Freedom*, New York: Anchor Books.

Stiglitz, J. (2000), 'What I Learned at the World Economic Crisis', *The New Republic Online*, April 17.

Sutherland, P.D. (2002), 'Why We Should Embrace Globalization', *Finance & Development*, **39** (3), 20-1.

Tisdell, C. (2001), 'Globalisation and Sustainability: environmental Kuznet's Curve and the WTO', *Ecological Economics*, **39**, 185-96.

Tomer, J. (1999), 'Social and Organizational Capital', in P. O'Hara (ed.), *Encyclopedia of Political Economy*, **2**, London: Routledge, pp. 1949-51.

United Nations Development Programme (UNDP) (2001), *Human Development Report 2001*, New York: Oxford University Press.

Wei, S. (2002), 'Is Globalisation Good for the Poor in China?', *Finance and Development*, **39** (3), 26-9.

World Bank (1989), *World Development Report, 1988/1989*, New York: Oxford University Press.

World Bank (2001), *World Development Report, 2000/2001*, New York: Oxford University Press.

# 10. Trade Liberalisation, Agricultural Subsidies and Poverty

**Kristin M. Jakobsson and Andrew K. Dragun**

## 10.1 INTRODUCTION

With trade barriers removed, the invisible hand of comparative advantage should lead to widespread gains from trade and the maximisation of global welfare – a win-win game.

Trade liberalisation should mean that poor countries have increased access to export markets, leading to increased income and growth, helping to break the poverty cycle. But can poor countries take advantage of trade liberalisation and thus deal with poverty? And what, precisely, is meant by trade liberalisation?

The necessity to feed the world has been a strong argument for the subsidisation of agriculture in Western countries. But it is a basic principle of economics that public subsidisation of anything, in normal circumstances, will create an over supply and a decline in prices.

This is the case with agriculture. Rich Western countries subsidise their agriculture and – with trade liberalisation – cause a general reduction of world agricultural prices. Cheap food in poor countries may benefit some people in the short run, but many people in such countries are poor farmers who now cannot sell their produce in local markets because Western subsidised agriculture or even food aid destroys the local economy. Thus poverty, in some cases, may be a direct effect of market distortion rather than a technical inability to grow food.

Thus, trade liberalisation without the removal of Western agricultural subsidies is unlikely to reduce, and may even worsen, poverty in poor countries.

## 10.2 TRADE LIBERALISATION, AGRICULTURAL SUBSIDIES AND POVERTY: THE PROBLEM

Free trade is often put forward as a solution to poverty in poor countries.

The extent and nature of poverty in poor countries is a well-documented issue

*Figure 10.1 Cartoon by Nicholson of* The Australian*: http://www.nicholsoncartoons.com.au*

*Figure 10.2 Cartoon by Nicholson of* The Australian*: http://www.nicholsoncartoons.com.au*

(Dasgupta 1993; Oxfam 2002; UNDP *passim*). It is not the intention in this chapter to consider or review this literature in great depth. The insight of the literature on poverty is that the issue of poverty is often seen to be complex and that there are many facets to the policy solutions.

It is argued here that some of the more prominent policy solutions to poverty – particularly in the trade liberalisation setting – could actually exacerbate the poverty problem in poor countries.

Thus, instead of implementing a trade liberalisation policy perspective to reduce poverty in poor countries, it may in contrast be necessary to develop more restrictive measures on trade policy in poor countries if poverty alleviation is of concern.

The insight here is that the failure of the trade liberalisation policy model for poor countries is not an inherent fault of their economic systems or political environment, but rather is a function of policy failure and obstruction in rich countries.

The theme developed in this chapter is that trade liberalisation is not *automatically* a solution to poverty in poor countries. The conclusion of gains from free trade depends on a range of assumptions. If these assumptions do not hold then it may not be possible to make the claim linking trade liberalisation and poverty amelioration. Thus trade liberalisation with policy/market failure and obstructions may actually make the poverty situation in poor countries worse.

The possibility then might be recognised that poor countries might be better off espousing restrictive trade policies in some areas to improve the welfare of their poor people, for example, protecting domestic agricultural production from import competition, or forming regional trade blocs to improve market power and competitiveness (for example, Mercusor in South America).

## 10.3 TRADE LIBERALISATION AND POVERTY AMELIORATION

That trade liberalisation will reduce poverty is a weak argument in orthodox economic theory. In fact, there is no direct causality implied whereby effective trade liberalisation will reduce poverty. Thus, the 'theory' works by osmosis or the 'trickle down effect' – which could hardly be seen as a strong or robust rationale for improvement or change.

The orthodox interpretation of increased trade liberalisation tends to focus on the gains through comparative advantage within an organised Western system of property and law. In this setting, trade liberalisation from the current international standards seems to mean a win-win game, where all countries and citizens gain. This perspective is seen as especially important for the poor countries, who by trade liberalisation and access to the markets of the rich countries, should be able to pull themselves out of the current poverty trap in which they are enmeshed (Kaempfer and Marks 1993).

The international problem of poverty is often interpreted to be that too many small countries are producing too diverse an array of products at too high a price. Accordingly, specialisation into fewer products, where the particular countries have some *relative* advantage, should mean an overall cost saving which could benefit everyone (Anderson and Blackhurst 1992; Bhagwati 1993, 1995).

According to the principles of comparative advantage, best associated with David Ricardo, producers with a comparative advantage in the production of certain goods will specialise and expand their production of that good, according to such factors as specialised skills, improved economies of scale or geographical location. Thus, if a country concentrates on the production of goods in which they have a comparative advantage, and trades with another country to obtain goods in which they do not have a comparative advantage, both countries will achieve a higher level of wealth than if they each tried to produce all the goods themselves. This result holds even if one country has an absolute advantage, that is, it could produce all goods more efficiently.

The conclusion from this analysis is that with free trade, consumers everywhere will be able to purchase the same things cheaper, meaning that a surplus may be generated to yield yet more consumption, production, income, wealth, growth and welfare (Anderson and Blackhurst 1992; Low 1992; Pearce and Warford 1993).

However, the theoretical rationalisation that increased trade leads to reduced poverty is not immediately clear. As a function of the theory of comparative advantage, there does not appear to be any implicit mechanism which links poverty amelioration with increased trade in any free sense.

For Bhagwati, one of the strongest proponents of the position that *free trade will not lead to increased poverty*, the engine of poverty amelioration comes from increased income as a function of the gains from trade (Bhagwati 1993). In these terms poverty amelioration emerges indirectly as a trickle down impact of the efficiency of trade liberalisation.

In the orthodox setting described by Bhagwati, increased international trade and the process of comparative advantage leads to efficiency of production and lower prices for traded goods. Clearly, lower prices for traded goods if they are input factors can lead to lower prices for other goods produced in an economy (for non-traded goods if they still exist!) as well as providing the basis of cost savings for consumers, which then generate higher incomes.

These gains from trade, which should be manifest as increased savings, should then provide the basis of increased investment, which then enables an increase in growth (Bhagwati 1993, 1995; Ghatak et al. 1995). In the orthodox setting, this new engine of growth is anticipated to have several classes of effects. Firstly, increased growth internationally which benefits the poor countries should begin to reduce the disparity between rich and poor countries thus addressing concerns of international equity. This strategy has much to do with the current approaches of such organisations as the IMF and the World Bank (Donaldson 1989; Low 1992).

Secondly, the mechanism of savings, income and growth is anticipated to be continual so that increased growth will yield more income and more saving. Where income levels were originally low, the increase in income levels is anticipated to lead to a general growth in economic performance and thus national welfare.

Another factor, identified by Bhagwati, is that the gains from trade which increase growth and income, also provide the basis for increased government revenue and thus for increased governmental spending on improving economic performance. A categorical contrast of the rich countries of the north and the poor countries of the south is that the countries in the north spend significantly on economic improvement while the countries in the south spend almost nothing at all in this direction.

In conclusion it seems to be the case that there is no *explicit* economic mechanism which links the 'lower price' gains from trade liberalisation to poverty amelioration, but then again there are not too many *explicit mechanisms* which would lead us to think that economic welfare would actually diminish either.

## 10.4 THE STRUCTURE OF THE TRADE LIBERALISATION MODEL

Fundamentally, the trade liberalisation model is driven at the global level by the assumptions that the world economy is competitive, with no market distortions, barriers to entry, externalities and so on.

With real trade liberalisation it would be expected that:

- All countries specialise and produce primarily where they have comparative advantage.
- All goods are produced most efficiently at lowest cost.
- All producers maximise profits.
- All consumers maximise utility.
- Maximum social welfare is generated.
- Maximum income is generated.

For poor countries it could be expected that:

- Trade liberalisation offers an opportunity to build a productive economy specialising in what they are good at.
- Building trade means maximising income and welfare and creating new growth.
- New growth means creating new income and thus building wealth.
- New income and wealth means breaking the poverty cycle.
- New income will also provide a foundation for environmental improvement and an improvement of the quality of life.

It is clear that while comparative advantage means that increased income and growth might be derived in certain sectors where the comparative advantage actually exists, there is no direct effect on other sectors of the economies of poor countries. Thus, the driver for poverty alleviation in a poor economy with certain specific comparative advantage in some or one sectors is a 'trickle down effect' or otherwise 'osmosis'.

Thus, even where the comparative advantage effect might work in a poor country, there is not necessarily a positive effect on all other sectors of the economy and hence the impact on poverty is little more than optimistic speculation.

## 10.5 WORLD MARKETS AND TRADE LIBERALISATION: THE ASSUMPTIONS OF THE MODEL

The gains of trade liberalisation are conditional on the existence of a competitive economy where:

- All markets are competitive. Thus, price is the only determinant of transactions and all prices are determined in free markets.
- There are no market distortions. No monopoly or other price aberration exist which might distort the final market price or quantity of a product produced.
- No policy failure exists. There is no government policy affecting the price or quantity of given products or associated factors of production in any direct or indirect way.
- There are no externalities. Production of all goods and services does not generate negative or positive externalities in relation to any product.
- Market price information is freely available to all participants.

The equilibrium trade model is quite clear in that when these assumptions prevail (there are some other technical assumptions also), it is possible to draw the conclusion that comparative advantage should lead to a maximisation of social welfare.

However, if one or a number of these assumptions do not prevail, then the contention that trade liberalisation and comparative advantage lead to social welfare maximisation is completely ambiguous – as demonstrated in terms of the second-best issue.

Thus, in practice if some part of the world's economy is not competitive, if there are market distortions, if policy failure exists and if externalities are generated, it would not be reasonable to expect that trade liberalisation would lead to social welfare maximisation.

Optimistically, it might be contended that even where *slight* market imperfections, *small* market distortions, *minor* policy failure *or few* externalities existed, it might be preferable to pursue a trade liberalisation approach in preference to any other approach.

However, the global evidence is that many of the assumptions are breached simultaneously and they all fail by very large degrees.

## 10.6 THE REALITIES OF THE GLOBAL MARKET

As suggested above, if most of the competitive assumptions held and, where an aberration occurred, it was restricted to maybe one assumption and was only minor, an optimistic stance might be appreciated. An optimist might suggest that the minor aberration could be identified and remedied so that the principle of comparative advantage and social welfare maximisation could prevail.

Thus, it might be contended that specific remedial policy instruments might need to be implemented simultaneously to resolve a particular problem with one assumption while a trade liberalisation regime was introduced. In practice a Pigovian tax might be applied to a certain factor of production, a monopoly distortion regulated, or a government policy refined so that the essence of the competitive economy is established.

In reality however, the world market economy is characterised with *gross* failure in many of the assumptions simultaneously. And, rather than there being some remediation in any of the particular areas, there is substantial evidence to suggest that the distortions and failures are becoming worse (Oxfam 2002). Thus global environmental problems appear to becoming worse at an increasing rate, while governmental policy failures increase and market distortions accelerate. Some examples of the failures in the assumptions are discussed below, focusing on trade and agriculture.

Trade in agricultural products is particularly important in the consideration of poverty reduction as more than two-thirds of the poor in developing countries live in rural areas (Oxfam 2002) and rely on farming and food processing for their livelihoods. However, developing country farmers face huge obstacles to trade through the subsidisation of agriculture and the imposition of trade barriers by rich northern countries. Developing countries also impose high tariffs on each other. Developing countries' tariffs on agricultural exports from other developing countries are higher than those imposed by rich countries (Oxfam 2002). However, protectionism by the rich countries is more damaging as the potentially most lucrative export markets are in the rich countries.

## Agricultural Subsidies

Subsidisation of agriculture by rich northern countries through direct price support, trade barriers and other measures is on a massive scale, costing billions of dollars annually. The World Bank (2001) contends that total annual agricultural subsidisation emanating from the US, the EU, Canada and Japan is equivalent to the total GDP of the whole African continent. Total OECD agricultural subsidisation is more than the total income of 1.2 billion people living below the poverty line (Oxfam 2002).

Despite much rhetoric about reducing subsidies, the EU and USA were spending more on producer support measures at the end of the 1990s than at the end of the 1980s (Oxfam 2002), with average annual per farmer subsidies of $21000 in the USA and $16000 in the EU (compared with a total annual income of less than $400 for many farmers in developing countries). However, not all rich country farmers do well out of the system – most of the subsidies in the USA (about two-thirds) go to around 10 per cent of the largest farmers and agribusiness companies (EWG 2002; Oxfam 2002; *Wall Street Journal* 2002) and the smaller 'family farmers' are gradually going out of business.

It is also the case that as a result of WTO agreements on agriculture, some aspects of domestic support are being reduced, but some categories of support are exempt from reduction or consideration. In the setting of what has become known as 'green box' measures, a range of public service programmes including, research, pest and disease control, agricultural training services, inspection services, marketing and promotion services and infrastructure services are WTO exempt. In most situations, this yields a significant advantage to the rich countries in terms of an obvious capacity to pay (WTO 2001).

### Excess production and dumping

The gross subsidisation of domestic agriculture by the largest economies of the north, is a function of massive policy failure in each case which results in global agricultural markets having barely a remote link to competitiveness, with prices and outputs fundamentally distorted. While empirical analysis of the price and output impact of agricultural subsidisation is surprisingly scanty, the theoretical expectations of such gross subsidisation would be that equilibrium output would be much higher than expected while equilibrium prices would be much lower.

According to Oxfam (2002) agricultural subsidies account for a quarter of farm output in the USA, 40 per cent in the EU and 60 per cent in Japan.

Much of this subsidised production is then sold at less than the cost of production on world markets, forcing down world prices, and disrupting the domestic markets that many poor, smallholder farmers rely on. For example, the EU is the world's largest exporter of white sugar, which is sold at times for a price equal to one quarter of production costs (Oxfam 2002), making it almost impossible for even the most efficient developing country producers to compete.

Domestic markets are also disrupted as developing countries open their markets through import liberalisation to cheap, subsidised food imports, which local farmers cannot easily compete with. Cheap imports are attractive in the short run as food prices can be reduced, and also trade liberalisation is encouraged by institutions such as the World Bank and IMF, but in the longer run such imports are damaging to domestic farmers' livelihoods and ability to build up production over time, for example in the domestic markets of Haiti, Mexico and Jamaica (Oxfam 2002). It is estimated that in total developing countries have welfare losses of around $20 billion a year as a result of agricultural subsidisation policies (World Bank 2001).

**Externalities**

The agricultural subsidisation policy failure is accompanied by a massive environmental externality as a consequence of agricultural output, which is far in excess of that expected in a competitive equilibrium. It is a feature of agricultural production over the world that where attempts are made to ameliorate the substantial negative environmental impacts, they tend to be based on soft standards – regulatory and subsidy approaches, which might actually increase the quantum of agricultural pollution. Thus, often under the rubric of preserving the 'family farm', farmers are most often compensated or subsidised the cost of pollution remediation. In this way, farmers are maintained in farming and they may actually be able to increase the scale and intensity of their operation and their output. Of course, increased agricultural output then leads to an increase in pollution. As subsidies favour large-scale farmers and agribusiness, intensive industrial agricultural systems are encouraged, which may also exacerbate pollution problems. Since this externality is not accounted, agricultural products produced in a less polluting manner are disadvantaged and less will be produced than is optimal.

## Market Barriers

In addition to facing artificially low prices for agricultural products, there are a number of other market barriers developing countries must deal with in attempting to trade with rich countries.

**Tariffs**

Developing countries exporting agricultural products and labour intensive manufactured goods to rich countries face tariff barriers four times higher than those encountered by rich countries exporting manufactured goods to each other (Oxfam 2002). This is estimated to cost developing countries around $100bn a year.

Average agricultural tariffs are around 10 per cent in the USA and more than 20 per cent in the EU and Japan (Oxfam 2002). Many tariffs (notably in the processed food sector) escalate with the level of processing undergone (for example, peanut butter exported to the USA faces a tariff of 132 per cent), thus discouraging investment in local value adding (Oxfam 2002).

**Non-tariff barriers**

Non-tariff barriers include obstacles such as import quotas or seasonal restrictions, as well as various product standards for health and safety. Although it is necessary to have health and safety standards for food products, they may be applied in a way that blocks trade from developing countries (Oxfam 2002). Product standards cover many issues such as packaging, hygiene and processing standards, additives and levels of pesticide residues. It can be difficult for developing countries to comply, because to meet the required standards, significant investment is required in developing and enforcing regulatory processes, buying analytical and monitoring equipment, and developing the skills required for monitoring, analysis and enforcement of standards. Poor countries may lack the expertise and capital required.

Some countries face significant costs with the risk of being locked out of markets when they are unable to meet pesticide residue or other health standards. For example, rules introduced in July 2001 on horticultural products entering the EU market from the developing world could harm many Kenyan (and other) farmers. The EU has ruled that from July 2001, all horticultural products to its markets must contain no trace of pesticide residue, even if they are non-edible exports like flowers (*The Nation* 2000). Although many large-scale Kenyan producers already meet the standards, smaller-scale farmers have difficulty meeting a zero residue level.

Unequal bargaining power between rich and poor countries may also disadvantage the poor countries where access to markets may be restricted as a function of bargains struck outside of WTO guidelines. Here rich countries may use threats of WTO action to force concessions from poor countries such as on Chinese negotiations with the US on soybean imports.

## Distortions in Input Markets

The market for agricultural inputs is far from competitive, and developing nations also face an uneven playing field with respect to agricultural inputs. Sales of the agricultural inputs of fertiliser, pesticides and other agricultural chemicals and seeds are dominated by a few, rich-country based, transnational companies. For example, a group of eight (Agrow 2001) top companies (merged from 10 in 1998) controls around 80 per cent of global pesticide sales (Dinham 1996). Recent trade rules and patent agreements, Trade-Related Aspects of Intellectual Property Rights (TRIPS), will result in developing countries paying about $40 billion a year to northern countries (Oxfam 2002). In addition, under plant patent laws, poor farmers may have to pay to save and use the seeds and plant material that have been used in their society for generations.

The trade in pesticides presents many problems for developing countries. Although pesticide use can have many benefits in increasing food production and quality, it also imposes high costs. Pesticide use is currently considerably less in developing countries than in developed ones, but it is increasing, particularly as agriculture intensifies (Thapinta and Hudak 2000). The market in developed countries for pesticides has stabilised or is declining, and developing countries have become the target of aggressive (and sometimes illegal) selling practices.

The trade in pesticides includes considerable trade in chemicals that are banned or strictly regulated in industrialised countries, with both Europe and the US exporting significant amounts of these chemicals (Boukhari 1998; *Global Pesticide Campaigner* 1999). It is estimated that around 30 per cent of pesticides marketed in developing countries do not meet internationally accepted quality standards (WHO 2001).

Both the legal and illegal pesticide trade impose huge costs on developing countries, in terms of export produce that may be rejected because of pesticide residues, a disproportionate share of the health costs of pesticides and disposal of accumulated stocks of obsolete pesticides, which present serious health and environmental hazards. The FAO (2001) estimates there are more than 100,000 tonnes of obsolete pesticides requiring disposal in developing countries, with around 45,000 tonnes in Africa. Costs of disposing of obsolete pesticides in Africa alone are estimated at well over $100 million (FAO 2001).

Although developed countries use 80 per cent of pesticides, more than 50 per cent of the pesticide poisonings and deaths occur in developing countries where there are inadequate safety standards, little enforcement, poor labelling (in the wrong language and lacking information), illiteracy, inadequate protective clothing and washing facilities and lack of training and information (Pimental et al. 1992; *UNESCO Courier* 1997). Chronic health problems include cancer, reproductive dysfunction, psychological effects and suicide, and intellectual impairment and learning disabilities, which are also likely to disproportionately affect farmers in developing countries, reducing their ability to work and grow food.

### Implications of Gross Distortions

The gross subsidisation of agriculture, as well as market distortions, externalities and trade barriers, results in the rich countries of the north producing far too much agricultural output with the result that the scale of agriculture in the south is too low.

World prices for agriculture are too low as a consequence of subsidisation in the north (paid for by consumers and taxpayers in the north) as well as the failure to account externalities of agricultural production.

Consumers in the south (those who can afford it) benefit from lower agricultural prices, but producers in the south (mostly poor people) lose producer surplus as a result of lower prices, severely limiting their ability to get themselves out of poverty. In many places, for example, Peru, Haiti, parts of Mexico and sub-Saharan Africa, the poor are actually becoming poorer, and inequalities are increasing within and between countries (Oxfam 2002). It is also the case that, as a function of very high rates of unemployment, capital investment and the need for a learning period, in the poorer countries the possibilities of structural adjustment and industry switching are very much more difficult than in the rich countries.

The impacts of trade liberalisation amongst the countries, which have followed this path, have not been particularly positive. Those developing (and one or two developed) countries that have liberalised their economies the most do not seem to have gained the benefits anticipated by the theory. In many cases, economic performance has deteriorated and poverty increased, for example, several South American countries and New Zealand (Kelsey 1995; OECD 1993). Conversely, countries where economic performance is improving and poverty is being reduced such as China, Vietnam and Thailand, have not opened up their import markets rapidly and freely (Oxfam 2002).

## 10.7 CONCLUSIONS

It has been shown that the assumptions underlying the free trade model do not hold, so it cannot be said that the free trade model leads to best results for poor countries under existing trade rules.

While the trade liberalisation model offers much, any possibility of it functioning properly is sabotaged by the gross subsidisation of traded goods, particularly in the agricultural area. International trade markets are not a level playing field and the major players in the West are the most negligent in terms of subsidising and protecting their agricultural sectors. The large countries of the West are also the big players in the successful trade blocs, such as the EU, NAFTA, FTAA and the like. In this distorted trade environment poor regions, such as the African continent, become a dumping ground for Western subsidised surpluses, particularly in agriculture.

In this setting, to deal with poverty poor countries might wish to adopt a closed market approach to their economies, just like the successful rich countries in the West. A relevant application might include an African trade zone, where nations on the African continent could close their markets to the distortions emanating from the gross agricultural subsidisation coming from the US, the EU and Japan, and trade within the continent. In this way, the nations of Africa might gain benefit from comparative advantage within the African region and poor farmers might be in a position to earn a sustainable income.

## REFERENCES

Agrow (2001), *Agrow: World Crop Protection News*, No. 371, 2 March, p. 16.

Anderson, K. and R. Blackhurst (1992), *The Greening of World Trade Issues*, New York: Harvester Wheatsheaf.

Bhagwati, J. (1993), 'The case for free trade', *Scientific American*, **269**, November, 42-9.

Bhagwati, J. (1995), 'Trade liberalisation and "fair trade" demands: addressing the environmental and labour standards issues', *World Economy*, **18** (6), November, 745-59.

Boukhari, S. (1998), 'Poison of the earth', *UNESCO Courier*, Jul/Aug, **51** (7/8), 15-17.

Dasgupta, P. (1993), *An Inquiry into Well-Being and Destitution*, Oxford: Clarendon Press.

Dinham, B. (ed.) (1996), *The Pesticide Hazard. A Global Health and Environmental Audit*, London: Zed Books.

Donaldson, A.R. (1989), 'The World Bank on trade liberalisation', *South African Journal of Economics*, **57** (1), March, 79-87.

EWG (2002), *Environmental Working Group Farm Subsidy Database*, Washington, DC: Environmental Working Group, http://www.ewg.org.

FAO (2001), *Prevention and Disposal of Obsolete and Unwanted Pesticide Stocks in Africa and the Near East*, Rome: FAO. Various websites: http://www.fao.org/; http://www.fao.org/AG/AGP/AGPP/Pesticid/Disposal/PR96-20.htm; http://www.fao.org/AG/AGP/AGPP/Pesticid/Disposal/PR98-15.htm; http://www.fao.org/NEWS/1999/990504-e.htm; http://www.fao.org/NEWS/1999/990607-e.htm.

Ghatak, S., C. Milner and U. Utkulu (1995), 'Trade liberalisation and endogenous growth: some evidence for Turkey', *Economics of Planning*, **28** (2-3), 147-67.

*Global Pesticide Campaigner* (1999), 'Beyond POPs: persistent pesticides exported from US Ports', December-February 4, 2000, San Francisco: Pesticide Action Network North America. http://www.panna.org/panna/resources/panups/panup_20000204.dv.html.

Kaempfer, W.H. and Marks, S.V. (1993), 'The expected effects of trade liberalisation: evidence from US Congressional action on fast-track authority', *World Economy*, **16** (6), November, 725-40.

Kelsey, J. (1995), *The New Zealand Experiment: A World Model for Structural Adjustment?* Auckland: Auckland University Press, Bridget Williams Books.

Low, P. (ed) (1992), 'International trade and the environment', *World Bank Discussion Papers 159*, Washington DC: World Bank.

*The Nation* (2000), 'EU Rules to Hurt Local Farmers', 2 August, Nairobi: Africa News Service.

OECD (1993), *New Zealand Country Report 1993*, Paris: OECD.

Oxfam (2002), *Rigged Rules and Double Standards. Trade, Globalisation and the Fight against Poverty*, Oxford: Oxfam. www.maketradefair.com.

Pearce, D. and J. Warford (1993), 'World markets and natural resource degradation', in Pearce, D. and J. Warford (eds), *World Without End, Economics and Sustainable Development*, New York: World Bank, Oxford University Press.

Pimental, D., H. Acquay, M. Biltonen, P. Rice, M. Silva, J. Nelson, V. Lipner, S. Giordano, A. Horowitz and M. D'Amore (1992), 'Environmental and economic costs of pesticide use', *BioScience,* **42** (10), November, 750-61.

Thapinta, A. and P.F. Hudak (2000), 'Pesticide use and residual occurrence in Thailand', *Environmental Monitoring and Assessment,* **60** (1), January, 103-14.

United Nations Development Programme (1995), (and annually) *Human Development Report*, New York: United Nations Development Program.

*UNESCO Courier* (1997), 'Thailand's pesticide problems', **50** (2), February, p. 49.

*Wall Street Journal* (2002), 'The farm state pig-out', Editorial, 2 May.

World Bank (2001) (and annually), *World Development Report 2000/2001*, New York: Oxford University Press.

WHO (2001), 'High Quantities of Poor-Quality Pesticides Sold in Developing Countries', 9 March 2001, WHO press release, 1 February.

WTO (2001), Module 2: FAQs (2). http://www.wto.org/english/thewto_e/whatis_e/eole/wto02/.

# PART III

# LABOUR ISSUES AND DISTRIBUTIONAL CONFLICTS

# 11. Effects of Globalisation on Employment and Poverty in Dualistic Economies: The Case of India

**Dilip Dutta**

## 11.1 INTRODUCTION

Although various aspects of *globalisation* are intentional and reflexive, many globalising forces are impersonal and beyond the control and intentions of any individual or group of individuals (Waters 1995, p. 2). In response to the contemporary globalisation process,[1] economic liberalisation has been taking place in India – a labour surplus dualistic economy – over the past two decades. In this chapter, the author explores changes in the degree of socio-economic dualism in India following its adoption of comprehensive economic reforms in July 1991. Many argue that Indian liberalisation policy has been, in many ways, erratic, hasty and unplanned. According to the critics, it has eroded the role of the planning process and aggravated the social problems of unemployment and poverty, and has also increased India's external vulnerability. In order to test validity or otherwise of these arguments, let us first mention that India has a *structural dualism* at the very aggregate level. This means that India has two different socio-economic-technological environments – the *organised* (or modern) segment (predominantly *capitalistic*) and the *unorganised* (or traditional) segment (predominantly *pre-capitalistic*). The *organised* segment includes all establishments in the public sector irrespective of their size and non-agricultural establishments in the private sector employing 10 or more persons. The *unorganised* (or traditional) segment is usually defined to be the segment that is not recorded under any factory legislation. This segment is mostly comprised of self-employed households and casual labourers with no steady employment and, therefore, no secure or sustainable incomes, and above all with no access to the benefits of social security.[2] Although the share of the organised segment in Net Domestic Product (NDP) (at factor cost) has increased from 30 per cent during 1980-81 to 39.1 per cent during 1998-99

*Table 11.1 Share of organised and unorganised segments in India's net domestic product (at factor cost) (percent)*

| Year | Organised | Unorganised |
|---|---|---|
| 1980-81 | 30.0 | 70.0 |
| 1985-86 | 35.2 | 64.8 |
| 1989-90 | 36.3 | 63.7 |
| 1990-91 | 36.2 | 63.8 |
| 1991-92 | 36.7 | 63.3 |
| 1992-93 | 36.5 | 63.5 |
| 1993-94 | 36.9 | 63.1 |
| 1994-95 | 37.5 | 62.5 |
| 1995-96 | 39.6 | 60.4 |
| 1996-97 | 38.7 | 61.3 |
| 1997-98 | 39.4 | 60.6 |
| 1998-99 | 39.1 | 60.9 |

*Source*: *National Accounts Statistics*, Govt of India, 1993 (pp. 203-4), 1998 (pp. 198-9), 2000 (p. 180) and 2001 (p. 192).

*Table 11.2 Estimates of employment in organised and unorganised segments in India (in millions)*

| Year | Organised[a] | Unorganised[b] | Total labour force[c] | Share of organised segment employment |
|---|---|---|---|---|
| 1981 | 22.90 | 282.83 | 305.73 | 7.49 |
| 1985 | 24.58 | 304.43 | 329.01 | 7.47 |
| 1990 | 26.35 | 334.69 | 361.04 | 7.30 |
| 1991 | 26.73 | 342.41 | 369.14 | 7.24 |
| 1992 | 27.06 | 350.56 | 377.62 | 7.17 |
| 1993 | 27.18 | 358.15 | 385.33 | 7.05 |
| 1994 | 27.38 | 366.38 | 393.76 | 6.95 |
| 1995 | 27.53 | 374.88 | 402.41 | 6.84 |
| 1996 | 27.94 | 383.40 | 411.34 | 6.79 |
| 1997 | 28.25 | 392.31 | 420.56 | 6.72 |
| 1998 | 28.17 | 401.91 | 430.08 | 6.55 |
| 1999 | 28.11 | 412.79 | 440.90 | 6.38 |

*Notes*:

[a] Estimates of employment in organised public and private sectors (in million persons as on March 31) obtained from various issues of *Economic Survey*, Govt. of India.

[b] Employment in unorganised segment is derived as total labour force minus employment in organised segment (Parthasarathy, 1996, p. 1860).

[c] Data on total labour force are taken from *World Development Indicator 2001*, World Bank.

(Table 11.1), its share in employment has declined from 7.49 per cent of total workers in 1981 to only 6.38 per cent in 1999 (Table 11.2). As a result, the unorganised segment continues to contain over 93 per cent of India's labour force, in spite of the decline in its share in net domestic product from 70.0 per cent in 1980-81 to 60.9 per cent in 1998-99 (Table 11.3).

*Table 11.3 Share of unorganised segment in India's net domestic product by economic activity (old series, at current prices) (percent)*

| **Sectors** | **80-81** | **89-90** | **90-91** | **91-92** | **92-93** | **93-94** | **94-95** | **95-96** | **96-97** | **97-98** | **98-99** |
|---|---|---|---|---|---|---|---|---|---|---|---|
| Agri, forestry & fishing | 95.2 | 95.7 | 96.2 | 96.4 | 96.5 | 96.5 | 96.6 | 96.0 | 96.4 | 96.5 | 97.0 |
| Mining & quarrying | 9.6 | 7.2 | 7.7 | 9.4 | 9.2 | 7.3 | 6.9 | 8.2 | 7.2 | 7.4 | 7.0 |
| Manufact-uring | 46.3 | 38.5 | 39.1 | 38.3 | 39.8 | 36.6 | 34.9 | 35.1 | 34.5 | 37.8 | 38.9 |
| Electricity, gas & water supply | 6.0 | 4.7 | 3.6 | 3.4 | 2.8 | 7.2 | 5.9 | 5.6 | 6.4 | 5.8 | 5.2 |
| Construction | 48.0 | 54.8 | 55.5 | 53.4 | 55.2 | 51.1 | 52.2 | 50.0 | 51.9 | 56.0 | 57.4 |
| Trade, hotels & restaurants | 89.6 | 93.1 | 91.9 | 89.7 | 88.4 | 88.8 | 87.6 | 85.8 | 85.1 | 83.4 | 82.2 |
| Trans, storage & communic. | 45.2 | 49.1 | 52.3 | 54.8 | 54.5 | 42.7 | 44.4 | 43.2 | 46.3 | 47.4 | 49.1 |
| Fin, insu, real est & bus serv | 65.0 | 43.0 | 40.6 | 35.1 | 36.7 | 50.7 | 48.7 | 44.1 | 44.1 | 42.5 | 42.2 |
| Comm, soc & personal servs | 25.9 | 19.6 | 19.4 | 20.0 | 20.3 | 19.0 | 19.4 | 19.1 | 19.2 | 18.0 | 17.3 |
| **Total** (at factor cost) | **70.0** | **63.7** | **63.8** | **63.3** | **63.5** | **63.1** | **62.5** | **60.4** | **61.3** | **60.6** | **60.9** |

*Source*: *National Accounts Statistics*, Govt of India, 1997 (pp. 250-51), 1998 (pp. 198-9), 2000 (pp. 180-81) and 2001 (p. 192).

The *Report of the National Commission on Labour* (Government of India, 1969, p. 417) provides a list of major unorganised sectors employing large numbers of workers, most of whom are *under*- and *un*-employed. These categories include contract labour such as construction workers; labour employed in small-scale industry; hand-loom/power-loom workers; bidi and cigar workers; employees in shops and commercial establishments; sweepers and scavengers; workers in tanneries; tribal labour; casual and other unprotected labour and so on. Although it is more than 30 years since the publication of this report, the characteristics of the *unorganised* segment remain virtually the same. This segment is usually characterised by low capital-labour ratios, low levels of formal schooling, low-paying jobs, poor working condition, little job security, inferior social status, and, above all, lack of governmental support. India's poverty syndrome is directly associated with the very state and nature of its vast *unorganised* segment, although it is functionally related to its *organised* segment.

For analytical purposes, India's experiences with economic liberalisation and its effects on economic development will be divided into two phases (discussed in Sections 11.2 and 11.3 respectively):

*Phase I*: Policy changes towards liberalisation (1980-90); and
*Phase II*: Comprehensive liberalisation (1991 and onwards).

Section 11.4 focuses on the general impacts of liberalisation and privatisation along with the overall globalisation process on the Indian economy during 1980s and 1990s, and Section 11.5 considers specific implications of these changes for its *unorganised* labour segment. Concluding comments[3] follow in Section 11.6.

## 11.2 POLICY CHANGES TOWARDS LIBERALISATION IN INDIA (1980-90)

Although the Sixth Five-Year Plan (1980-85) was originally scheduled by the Janata Government[4] for the period of 1978-83, it was actually launched after Indira Gandhi came back into power as the Prime Minister in January 1980. 'New Industrial Growth with Direct Measures for Poverty Eradication' was the main focus of this plan.[5] Just before the Sixth Five-Year Plan document was published, a new Industrial Policy Statement was issued by Gandhi's government in July 1980. In fact, this statement involved a special effort to stimulate and accelerate industrial growth against the background of India's slow growth/stagnation in the industrial sphere during the late 1960s and the 1970s. The statement emphasised the necessity of 'a set of pragmatic policies which will remove the lingering constraints to industrial production and, at the same time, act as catalyst for faster growth in coming decades'.[6] Although no special designation was given to the 'directional changes' envisaged, in retrospect the shift was in favour of 'liberalisation' and 'export-promotion' – two thrusts of the industrial policy which came to be explicitly emphasised afterwards by the government of Rajiv Gandhi in the second half of the 1980s.[7]

During the regime of Rajiv Gandhi, several steps were taken to reform the overall Indian industrial policy to promote competition, modernisation and cost efficiency. The reform measures had three basic objectives, namely, to facilitate capacity creation, to facilitate output expansion, and to remove procedural impediments (*Economic Survey* 1988-89, pp. 46-8). Support for these policy reforms is also reflected in the underlying development strategy of the Seventh Five-Year Plan (1985-90) – 'Industrial Growth and Liberalisation'.

Major industrial policy changes fostered by the new industrial policy initiatives were: delicensing of a wide range of industries, expansion of asset ceiling of the big monopoly houses and the regulation of monopoly restrictive trade practices (MRTP) companies,[8] liberalisation of depreciation provisions, reduction of both corporate and personal tax rates, drastic import liberalisation, extension of *broad-banding*[9] to a larger number of industries, and elimination of many of the existing government controls, on industry. The main objective of the industrial policy under the Rajiv government was thus to encourage economic growth led by the private sector, with the public sector playing increasingly a subordinate role. In fact, the modernisation programme stressing technological rationalisation and increased managerial competence was a drastic one involving little consideration of social cost. As the Rajiv government had complete faith in the 'trickle down' approach of economic growth and development, the direct programmes for poverty eradication of the previous plan were no longer an important specific preoccupation of his regime.

According to *Economic Survey* — the official annual report of the Government of India, industrial production during 1980-87 grew at a compound annual rate of 7.6 per cent and during 1987-88 grew at 7.5 per cent as against that of 4.2 per cent per annum during 1971-80. There had been a number of infrastructural developments in the Indian capital market during the second half of the 1980s.[10] In spite of the various positive developments on the industrial front, the regime started experiencing some disturbing events commencing in 1987-88. Besides the monsoon failures, there was a substantial decline in the number of industrial licences, especially for the backward areas, virtual stagnation of employment growth in the *organised* segment, an increasing incidence of low or negative business returns and increasing foreign debt. There had been evidence of a marked slowing down of the rate of growth of industrial production starting in the first quarter of the year of 1989-90. During the short period of about eighteen months from December 1989 to June 1991, when two non-Congress governments were in power, the liberalisation process was also slowed down.

## 11.3 COMPREHENSIVE LIBERALISATION (SINCE 1991)

After the assassination of Rajiv Gandhi on 21 May 1991, a minority Congress government of the Prime Minister P.V. Narasimha Rao came to power in June 1991. Because India was in a state of near bankruptcy because its foreign exchange reserves were extraordinarily low, the Rao government hastily introduced the New Economic Policy (NEP) in early July 1991.

More than a decade of comprehensive liberalisation followed and the Indian economy underwent substantial change. Almost all areas of the economy have been gradually opened to both domestic and foreign private investment, import licensing restrictions on intermediates and capital goods have been virtually eliminated, tariffs have been significantly reduced, and full convertibility of foreign exchange earnings has been established for current account transactions. Financial markets have been liberalised to a greater extent and international standards of regulation have been introduced in the financial sector. As a result of the general election in April 1996, the Congress government of Narasimha Rao was replaced by non-Congress governments, but the reform process went on, although at a slower pace. After the government of Atal Behari Vajpayee's Hindu nationalist *Bharatiya Janata Party* (BJP) was voted into power on 19 March 1998, economic reforms continued. The EXIM Policy announced in March 2001 completed the process of removal of Quantitative Restrictions (QRs) on Balance-of-Payment (BOP) grounds by dismantling restrictions on the remaining 715 items. More recently, a host of measures were adopted to further liberalise the FDI regime.

State-owned public sector enterprises (PSEs), initially established to enable the economy to achieve 'commanding heights', have been affected by the recent liberalisation programmes. In order to offer more functional autonomy to PSEs and remove government interference in their management at the micro-level, 696 guidelines, issued for PSEs in the last three decades of the twentieth century, have been withdrawn. Although legal obstacles in the process of disinvestment have been resolved with the Supreme Court decision in the Bharat Aluminium Company Limited (BALCO) case in December 2001,[11] political obstacles to the disinvestment programme of PSEs have recently resurfaced in relation to privatisation of Hindustan Petroleum Corp. Ltd (HPCL) and Bharat Petroleum Corp. Ltd (BPCL), and disinvestment through public offerings of 10-25 per cent in Indian Oil Corporation (IOC), Oil and Natural Gas Corporation (ONGC), Gas Authority of India Ltd (GAIL), Bharat Sanchar Nigam Ltd (BSNL) and National

Thermal Power Corp. Ltd (NTPC). The Cabinet Committee on Disinvestment (CCD) therefore put aside all decisions on privatisation and disinvestment until December 2002.[12]

With delicensing of the consumer electronics industry – the fastest growing sub-sector of the Indian industry[13] liberalisation in foreign investment and export-import policies, many global companies have either established production facilities in India or are present in the market through technical/financial collaborations. More importantly, the software industry recorded not only a CAGR (compound annual growth rate) exceeding 50 per cent in production during the last five years (1995-96 to 1999-2000) of the twentieth century, but also had a turnover of US$6 billion and exports of US$4 billion during 1999-2000 (Economic Survey 2000-2001, p. 142).

As expected, the role of the Planning Commission has largely diminished with the programme of comprehensive economic liberalisation. In order to keep pace with the liberalisation policy, the Eighth Five-Year Plan (1992-97) therefore redefined the role of the Planning Commission as an instrument for *indicative* planning. However, it duly recognises 'human development' as the core of all developmental effort, and it realises the essential need to involve people in the process of development. Similarly, the Ninth Five-Year Plan (1997-2002) recognises the integral link between rapid economic growth and the quality of life of the masses. It also recognises the need to combine high growth policies with the pursuit of the ultimate objective of improving policies that are pro-poor and are aimed at the correction of historical inequalities. Thus, the focus of the Ninth Plan is: 'Growth with Social Justice and Equity'. The development strategy of the Ninth Plan is oriented to enabling India's broad-based and varied private sector to reach its full potential for raising production, creating jobs and raising income levels in society. A vigorous private sector, operating under the discipline of competition and free markets, is expected to encourage efficient use of scarce resources and ensure rapid growth at least cost. The government's role is, according to the Ninth Plan document, to design government policies that must create an environment encouraging this outcome.

## 11.4 EVALUATION OF INDIA'S ECONOMIC DEVELOPMENT FROM 1980-81 TO 2000-2001

During the 50 years of planned development after the independence, average annual growth rates of India's national income and per capita national income (both at 1993-94 prices) was at moderate rates of 4.3 per cent and 2.2 per cent respectively (Table 11.4), as against the population growth rate of 2.09 per cent per annum (Table 11.5).[14] Only during the 1980s and 1990s (except in

1991-92) were India's annual average growth rates (by both the measures) consistently above the average, and they were even higher in the 1990s (except in 1997-98)[15] compared to those in the 1980s. While India's industrial base became more diversified during the pre-reform period, many of its industries were reported to be inefficient by international standards. Although the import substitution strategy of the earlier decades had been successful to a certain extent, many industries had failed to maintain an appropriate technological standard and, as a result, they required the importation of technology all over again. While India's emphasis on public sector growth might have helped contain the expansion of some large private monopolies, many inefficient public monopolies reduced its economic growth rate.

*Table 11.4 India's annual average growth rate*

| **Plan period** | | **GNP at factor cost** | | **NNP at factor cost** | | **Per capita NNP at factor cost** | |
|---|---|---|---|---|---|---|---|
| | | **At current prices** | **At 1993-94 prices** | **At current prices** | **At 1993-94 prices** | **At current prices** | **At 1993-94 prices** |
| First Plan | 1951-56 | 1.8 | 3.7 | 1.5 | 3.6 | -0.3 | 1.8 |
| Second Plan | 1956-61 | 9.5 | 4.2 | 9.4 | 4.1 | 7.3 | 2.0 |
| Third Plan | 1961-66 | 9.6 | 2.8 | 9.5 | 2.5 | 7.1 | 0.2 |
| Annual Plan | 1966-69 | 12.2 | 3.9 | 12.2 | 3.8 | 9.8 | 1.5 |
| Fourth Plan | 1969-74 | 11.1 | 3.4 | 11.0 | 3.3 | 8.5 | 1.0 |
| Fifth Plan | 1974-79 | 10.7 | 5.0 | 10.4 | 5.0 | 7.9 | 2.7 |
| Annual Plan | 1979-80 | 9.4 | -5.0 | 8.3 | -6.0 | 5.7 | -8.3 |
| Sixth Plan | 1980-85 | 15.2 | 5.5 | 15.1 | 5.4 | 12.7 | 3.2 |
| Seventh Plan | 1985-90 | 14.4 | 5.8 | 14.2 | 5.8 | 11.8 | 3.6 |
| Annual Plan | 1990-91 | 16.5 | 5.5 | 16.7 | 5.4 | 14.3 | 3.3 |
| Annual Plan | 1991-92 | 15.0 | 1.1 | 14.3 | 0.5 | 12.0 | -1.5 |
| Eighth Plan | 1992-97 | 16.3 | 6.8 | 16.3 | 6.7 | 14.1 | 4.6 |
| | 1997-98 | 11.9 | 4.8 | 12.0 | 4.5 | 10.1 | 2.8 |
| | 1998-99 | 16.3 | 6.5 | 17.1 | 6.5 | 15.2 | 4.8 |
| | 1999-2000 | 10.6 | 6.5 | 10.9 | 6.6 | 9.1 | 4.8 |
| Average | 1951-2000 | 11.4 | 4.4 | 11.3 | 4.3 | 9.0 | 2.2 |

*Source*: *National Accounts Statistics* 2001, CSO, Government of India, Table 16(a).

In spite of having more than self-sufficiency in food-grain production and considerable increase in industrial production, about 26.1 per cent of India's population was, even according to the official source, still below the poverty level during 1999-2000 (Table 11.6).[16] Although the poverty ratio has steadily declined over time, it is to be noted that the number of poor remained stable at around 320 million for more than two decades (1973-1994). The latest estimate for 1999-2000, however, shows a significant reduction to about 260 million. One must not, however, ignore the fact that rural-urban and inter-state disparities in terms of poverty ratio are visible.[17]

*Table 11.5 India's population growth (1951-2001)*

| Census years | Population (in millions) | Decadal growth (per cent) | Average annual growth (per cent) | Density (per sq. km) | Sex ratio (females per 1000 males) |
|---|---|---|---|---|---|
| 1951 | 361.09 | 13.31 | 1.25 | 117 | 946 |
| 1961 | 439.23 | 21.64 | 1.96 | 142 | 941 |
| 1971 | 548.16 | 24.80 | 2.20 | 177 | 930 |
| 1981 | 683.33 | 24.66 | 2.22 | 216 | 934 |
| 1991 | 846.39 | 23.86 | 2.14 | 267 | 927 |
| 2001 | 1027.02 | 21.34 | 1.93 | 324 | 933 |

*Source*: *Economic Survey* 2001-2002, Government of India, Table 10.14.

*Table 11.6 Estimates of poverty in India*

| Year | All India number (million) | Poverty ratio (%) | Rural number (million) | Poverty ratio (%) | Urban number (million) | Poverty ratio (%) |
|---|---|---|---|---|---|---|
| 1973-74 | 321 | 54.9 | 261 | 56.4 | 60 | 49.0 |
| 1977-78 | 329 | 51.3 | 264 | 53.1 | 65 | 45.2 |
| 1983 | 323 | 44.5 | 252 | 45.7 | 71 | 40.8 |
| 1987-88 | 307 | 38.9 | 232 | 39.1 | 75 | 38.2 |
| 1993-94 | 320 | 36.0 | 244 | 37.3 | 76 | 32.4 |
| 1999-2000 | 260* | 26.1 | 193 | 27.1 | 67 | 23.6 |

*Note*: * Because the methodology used for the poverty estimate in 1999-2000 is different from that used in the earlier estimates, they are not strictly comparable (*Economic Survey* 2000-2001, Government of India, p. 194).

*Source*: *Economic Survey* 2001-2002, Government of India, Table 10.4.

One can now look at the trend of two important macro-variables namely, investment and employment, in order to have a better picture of the post-reform period. On the basis of disaggregated data published in different issues of *National Accounts Statistics*, one could find that real investment in the 1990s expanded slowly in agriculture and its allied sub-sectors, but that investment in the non-agricultural sector was unstable, more so during the post-1995 years. There has been an overall steep decline in the growth rate of total investment from 5.48 per cent per annum during 1983/1993-94 to 3.9 per cent per annum during 1993-94/1999-2000, or equally seriously, from 5.97 per cent to 3.9 per cent in the case of the non-agricultural sector (Chadha and Sahu 2002, pp. 2020-22).

In order to have a better picture of the post-reform period's impact on poverty, let us now look at the trend in employment – a very important macro-variable related to the incidence of poverty. Firstly, annual average growth rate of overall employment (in both the organised and unorganised segments) was 2.73 per cent per annum during the period from 1972-73 to 1977-78, which declined to 1.54 per cent per annum over the period from 1983 to 1987-88 (Table 11.7). Although the growth rate of overall employment increased to 2.43 per cent per annum during 1987-88 to 1993-94, it dropped below 1 per cent per annum in the subsequent period from 1993-94 to 1999-2000. Growth in organised sector employment has been slowing down as can be seen from Table 11.8. This is mainly due

*Table 11.7 Rate of growth of population, labour force and employment in India, % per annum*

| Period | Rate of growth of population | Rate of growth of labour force (UPSS)* | Rate of growth of employment (UPSS)* (organised & unorganised) |
|---|---|---|---|
| 1972-73 to 1977-78 | 2.27 | 2.94 | 2.73 |
| 1977-78 to 1983 | 2.19 | 2.04 | 2.17 |
| 1983 to 1987-88 | 2.14 | 1.74 | 1.54 |
| 1987-88 to 1993-94 | 2.10 | 2.29 | 2.43 |
| 1993-94 to 1999-2000 | 1.93 | 1.03 | 0.98 |

*Note*: * Usual Principal and Subsidiary Status.

*Source*: *Economic Survey* 2001-2002, Government of India, Table 10.6.

to employment in the public sector falling from an average increase of 1.52 per cent per annum during 1983-94 to a decline of -0.03 per cent per annum during 1994-2000. In the post-reform phase, a natural attrition of excess labour is occurring as industry restructures. While the private sector has dismissed workers because of increased competition, the public sector seems to be relying more on voluntary retirement schemes (Venu 2000). The sector-wise employment trends (Table 11.9) indicate that the deceleration of overall employment growth rates during the period from 1983-1994 to 1994-2000 has been primarily due to slower growth in agricultural employment, with the absolute number of persons employed in agriculture showing a decline for the first time. On the contrary, employment in some of the service related sectors (such as trade, construction, financial services, transport, storage, communication as well as manufacturing) has grown faster than the average; also, share of these sectors in total employment has also increased. These trends reflect explicit structural changes in product markets in the post-reform (comprehensive) period (*Economic Survey* 2000-2001, Government of India, Section 10.11).

*Table 11.8 Total employment and organised sector employment in India*

| **Sector** | **Employment (million)** | | | | **Growth rate (% per annum)** | |
|---|---|---|---|---|---|---|
| | 1983 | 1988 | 1994 | 1999-2000 | 1983-1994 | 1994-2000 |
| Total pop. | 718.21 | 790.00 | 895.05 | 1004.10 | 2.12 | 1.93 |
| Total labour force | 308.64 | 333.49 | 381.94 | 406.05 | 2.05 | 1.03 |
| Total employ. | 302.75 | 324.29 | 374.45 | 397.00 | 2.04 | 0.98 |
| Org. sector employment | 24.01 | 25.71 | 27.37 | 28.11 | 1.20 | 0.53 |
| Public sector | 16.46 | 18.32 | 19.44 | 19.41 | 1.52 | -0.03 |
| Private sector | 7.55 | 7.39 | 7.93 | 8.70 | 0.45 | 1.87 |

*Notes*:

[a] The total employment figures are on Usual Principal and Subsidiary Status (UPSS) basis.

[b] The organised sector employment figures are as reported in the Employment Market Information System of Ministry of Labour and pertain to 1st March of 1983, 1988, 1994, 1999.

[c] The rate of growth of total employment and organised sector employment are compound rates of growth.

*Source*: *Economic Survey* 2001-2002, Government of India, Table 10.7.

*Table 11.9 Growth of employment by sectors (UPSS) in India*

| Industry | Employed workers* (millions) | | | Annual growth rate (per cent) | |
|---|---|---|---|---|---|
| | 1983 | 1993-94 | 1999-2000 | 1983-94 | 1994-2000 |
| Agriculture | 207.23 | 242.46 | 237.56 | 1.51 | -0.34 |
| Mining & Quarrying | 1.76 | 2.70 | 2.27 | 4.16 | -2.85 |
| Manufacturing | 34.03 | 42.50 | 48.01 | 2.14 | 2.05 |
| Electricity, Gas & WS | 0.85 | 1.35 | 1.28 | 4.50 | -0.88 |
| Construction | 6.78 | 11.68 | 17.62 | 5.32 | 7.09 |
| Trade | 19.22 | 27.78 | 37.32 | 3.57 | 5.04 |
| Transport, Storage & Comm. | 7.39 | 10.33 | 14.69 | 3.24 | 6.04 |
| Financial Services | 1.70 | 3.52 | 5.05 | 7.18 | 6.20 |
| Community, Social & Pers. Services | 23.80 | 35.13 | 33.20 | 2.90 | 0.55 |
| Total Employment | 302.76 | 374.45 | 397 | 2.04 | 0.98 |

*Note*: * The NSS gives the percentage distribution across industries of each of the four categories of workers. This distribution is applied to the absolute numbers of workers of each category for each year and the four categories in each industry are added up to derive estimates of total workers in each industry.

*Source*: *Economic Survey* 2001-2002, Government of India, Table 10.9.

In some of the years of the post-reform (comprehensive) period, the real investment (that is, real gross capital formation as a percentage of real GDP at market prices) has moved in an opposite direction to that of the movement in real GDP growth (Reserve Bank of India 1999). Both these trends suggest that productivity increase may have played an important role in the growth process during the post-reform period.[18] What is, however, apparent is a strong structural shift in the composition of the GDP in favour of the services sector since the 1980s. According to the Reserve Bank of India's 1998-99 *Report on Currency and Finance*, the services sector's contribution has been more pronounced in recent years – its share grew from 42.2 per cent of GDP in the 1980s to 46.6 per cent in the 1990s (Anon. 1999a). The report adds that it was the growth in the services sector that helped GDP growth, for example, in 1998-99 despite industrial sluggishness, also particularly important was the contribution of services to India's software exports (Anon. 1999b).

Notwithstanding structural improvements, all the governments of recent years have been aware of the importance of urgently addressing the remaining structural constraints to higher growth. Chief among them are (World Bank Country Study 1996, p. vii): reducing the country's chronically high fiscal deficits;[19] removing the remaining investment and trade restrictions, particularly in agriculture; averting a crisis in the supply of infrastructure; and strengthening the country's human capital base.

## 11.5 IMPLICATIONS OF ECONOMIC LIBERALISATION FOR INDIA'S UNORGANISED SEGMENT

Although it is too early to evaluate the long-run social implications of the policy of economic liberalisation adopted most strongly since the middle of 1991, there is concern that some of India's stabilisation and structural reforms might have led to the erosion of living standards of the poor;[20] increased its regional disparities in terms of industrial benefits;[21] reduced employment generation; and created greater casualisation, feminisation and de-skilling of the work-force (Kurien 1996, p. 67).

It is, therefore, difficult to speculate what kind of ripple effect all these factors have on the *unorganised* segment of the Indian economy. On the one hand, the share of total labour force in the *unorganised* segment has been steadily increasing (Table 11.2), on the other hand, that of net domestic product in the same segment is moving in the opposite direction. Table 11.3 shows that the *unorganised* segment's share of net domestic product in agriculture has remained virtually unchanged since the early 1980s. However, the overall declining trend in its share of net domestic product attributed to unorganised labour is mainly due to its reduction in the manufacturing sector and in a few categories (such as finance, insurance, real estate, business) of the services sector during the 1990s (Table 11.3).

> Indian economists are concerned that the economy is experiencing a distorted development process – the service sector has bypassed the industry sector in the order. What is significant is that the distortion in the development process is not because the industry sector lagged behind, but because the service sector grew at a higher rate. There is a positive side though – a buoyant service sector will add to industry's growth potential. However, if industry fails to grow at the required rate, not only will the growth of the service sector suffer, but it will drag down the GDP growth too. (Mahanti 2000)

In a recent study on the manufacturing sector of urban India for the decade between 1983 and 1993-94, Pais (2002, p. 651) finds there has been a significant decline in casualisation, specifically in manufacturing industries based on agricultural inputs, while the incidence of casual labour in construction and agriculture has increased. In fact, casual labour, according to this study, dominates the construction industry. It is noteworthy that only two sectors in India's unorganised segment – construction and transportation –

have an increasing trend in their share of net domestic product; but this upward trend in the construction sector has been relatively much higher (Table 11.3). Deaton and Dréze (2002) have noted several other recent adverse trends such as impoverishment among specific regions or social groups, and growing uncertainty and hidden hardships associated with recent patterns of economic changes, particularly for impoverished segments of India's unorganised segment.[22]

As the Ninth Five-Year Plan (1997-2002) document agues, the government recognises that high growth of incomes is by itself not enough to improve the quality of life of the poor which is organically related to India's unorganised segment. It goes on, adding

> If the growth is sourced upon those sectors of the economy or those activities which have a natural tendency to involve the poor in their expansion, such growth helps poverty eradication. Therefore, it is important to source a large part of economic growth in agriculture, in rural non-agricultural activities and in productive expansion of the informal sector which all have high employment elasticities, as well as in an export strategy based on labour intensive exports.[23]

On the basis of several recent studies across different states in India, social scientists do not seem to be very optimistic about the possibility for implementing an appropriate strategy of any credible food or employment security for the poor in the near future. For example, Rao (1998, p. 1954) argues that given the ruling elite groups formulating and implementing the strategy for the poorer stratum among the poor, the policies shaped by them lack responsiveness to the aspirations and needs of the large *unorganised* masses including the poor. Perhaps, the former president's 'safe pedestrian crossings for the unempowered of India across the three-way fast-lane of liberalisation, privatisation and globalisation' hopefully partly lie in the poor people's direct involvement in the recently revamped Panchayati Raj Institutions (PRI).[24] Unfortunately, instead of evolving as 'institutions of self-government', the PRI has been, as Aiyer (2002, p. 3296) argues, 'reduced to functional impotence and the corruption which arises out of chairpersons [pradhans] exercising their authority without the involvement and sanction of the members of the panchayat at all levels and of the gram sabha at the village level'.

## 11.6 CONCLUSION

If one looks at the political economy of the Indian nation, one could easily identify the three contending dominant classes such as the industrial capital class, the capitalist farmers and the rentier class including state bureaucrats, politicians and professionals. At the outset of the nation building, an attempt was made to move India towards a 'socialistic pattern of society' based on the ideology of Fabian socialism. From the mid-1960s and onwards, the country gradually relaxed various kinds of control mechanisms, especially in the case of industrial licensing and import policies. In the 1980s, India was pushed towards a stage of transitional capitalism. In spite of being a mixed economy with a very strong public sector, the Indian state had been fundamentally capitalist because of its separation of the immediate producers from the means of production, whatever may be its juridical forms of property ('private' or 'public'). While it may be true that the Indian state enjoys some degree of relative autonomy from any single major dominant class, it would, however, be naive to believe that the Indian state could effectively function in the interest of 'society as a whole' or, more specifically, in the real interest of the vast majority of the poor.

The bureaucracy of the civil administrative apparatus, inherited from the British regime, had grown at a phenomenal rate (about 6 per cent of the total workforce), and pocketed a substantial proportion of national cake in the form of unproductive rent. Another source of unproductive leakage from the national exchequer had been a huge amount of subsidies to the rich capitalist farmers. Generally speaking, the economically deprived class of the Indian society had been all along left at the mercy of a 'trickle down' effect of whatever moderate growth had taken place. Over time, the rhetoric of pro-poor promises by the state had been intensified in terms of several laws and programmes such as land reform laws, anti-monopoly laws, labour laws, progressive tax laws, anti-poverty programmes and so on. The consequences of these measures had done very little to benefit the poor. 'It is,' as Krishna (1988, p. 15) noted, 'a significant novelty of India's political revolution that the relative balance of class forces does not operate at the stage of legislation, planning and pronouncements to prevent a progressive stance, but it effectively blocks and perverts their redistributive effects at the implementation stage'. The case of functional impotence of the recently revamped Panchayati Raj Institutions (PRI) is another example of such institutional failure.

The fact that the unorganised segment continues to contain over 93 per cent of India's labour force, in spite of the continual decline in its share in net domestic product, tends to support the view that economic reforms are, by and large, all about the organised segment and its benefit at the cost of the unorganised segment. The Panchayati Raj Institutions had been expected to rescue the people closely linked to rural India's unorganised segments, from their never ending sufferings at all levels of the Indian society. But, alas, corruption in the panchayats at all levels has become rampant in many states of India (Aiyer 2002, p. 3296). Very recently, the Government of India has been attempting to integrate a comprehensive district-level development programme into the Tenth Five-Year Plan (2002-07) development strategy, with a view to involve backward districts into overall growth process (Anon. 2002b). Unless the central and state governments together take all necessary steps to ensure genuine participation of the panchayats at the village and intermediate levels in the district planning committees, the above attempt is certainly going to be ineffective. From the above evidence, it can be seen that increased economic liberalisation in India and its deepening involvement in processes of economic globalisation have been associated with growing income inequality and with economic effects that appear to have disadvantaged the unorganised (marginalised) segment of the Indian economy. Furthermore, there appears to have been little economic trickle down of the benefits of economic growth to the rural poor and those in impoverished regions of India. The lack of widespread economic gains in rural areas may be due to institutional failures in India, such as political failures associated with local government institutions, in particular Panchayati Raj Institutions.

## NOTES

1. Two phases of globalisation are often compared in continued until the beginning of the First World War and the second one is during the last quarter of the twentieth century. For details, one can see Hoogvelt (1997) and Nayyar (1997).
2. The concept of *social security* in the context of developing countries (especially, with huge *unorganised* segment) needs to be broader than the one applied to the developed countries. Many rightly argue that economic security and social security are intimately connected in these societies. 'There is,' as Jhabvala (1998, p. L8) puts forward, 'a general recognition that social security must be expanded to include not only new elements such as food provision, housing and sanitation; but also income and employment.'
3. The main thrust of the conclusion is based on Dutta (1998).
4. The declaration of a State of Emergency by Mrs Gandhi on 26 June 1975 and later on its lifting for elections in March 1977 are believed to have paved the way for the Janata government – the first non-Congress government at the centre.
5. Of the 'Direct Measures for Poverty Eradication', the major programmes that had been launched during the Sixth Plan are the Integrated Rural Development Programme (IRDP), National Rural Employment Programme (NREP), and Rural Landless Employment Guarantee Programme (RLEGP).
6. Quoted from the Statement on Industrial Policy made in the Parliament by the Minister of State for Industry on 23 July 1980.
7. After the assassination of Mrs Gandhi on 31 October 1984, Rajiv Gandhi assumed power as Prime Minister in December 1984 and ruled until almost the end of 1989.
8. The MRTP companies had to face, following the Monopolies Restrictive Trade Practices Act of 1969, some additional control measures that could curtail the concentration of economic power in the large industrial houses on the one hand, and could generate economic growth on the other hand.
9. The facility of *broad-banding* is presumed to enable manufacturing enterprises to adjust their product mix in line with changing market conditions and also to facilitate better capacity utilisation.

10. The major examples of such developments include institutions such as the Stock Holding Corporation of India, Credit Rating Information Services of India Ltd., Securities and Exchange Board of India, new mutual funds subsidiaries of nationalised banks, new venture capital companies, venture capital funds and so on.
11. As a result of the disinvestment decision of 51 per cent of government-held equity in BALCO on 2 March, 2001 in favour of Sterlite Industries (India) Limited for Rs551.50 crore, three writ petitions were filed against this decision in the Delhi & Chattisgarh High Courts. These petitions were subsequently transferred to the Supreme Court, which in its order dated 10 December, 2001, validated BALCO disinvestment and dismissed the petitions.
12. Anon. (2002a).
13. India's electronic industry achieved a growth of 20 per cent in production during 1997-98, while it was expected to register a growth of 40 per cent per annum during the Ninth Plan period (1997-2002) (*Economic Survey* 1998-99, p. 109).
14. The average annual population growth rate during 1951-2001 is calculated as a simple average of the five average annual growth rates in 1961, 1971, 1981, 1991 and 2001 obtained from Table 11.5.
15. According to the new series of GDP (at 1993-94 prices) released by the Central Statistical Organisation (CSO), there was a significant deceleration of GDP growth to 5.0 per cent in 1997-98 compared to 7.8 per cent in 1996-97.
16. Poverty at the national level is estimated as the weighted average of state-wise poverty levels. The latest poverty ratio, on a 30 day recall basis, has been estimated from the state-specific poverty lines and the distribution of persons by expenditure groups obtained from the latest large sample 55th Round Survey (July 1999-June 2000) conducted by the National Sample Survey Organisation (NSSO).
17. See Table 10.5 in *Economic Survey:* 2000-2001, Government of India.
18. A recent analysis of India's registered manufacturing sector by Chaudhuri (2002, p. 160) suggests that labour productivity increased steadily between 1990-91 and 1995-96, but has stagnated since then. Capital productivity increased marginally until 1995-96 followed by a decline. He also notes that both labour and capital productivity increased in only 70 product groups, accounting for about 37 per cent of the value added.
19. After the fiscal deficit was reduced from 8.3 per cent of GDP in 1990-91 to 6 per cent in 1991-92, the central government has relaxed its fiscal deficit targets. For example, this figure in recent periods not only had been well above the target of 3 per cent, but also has been increasing.
20. Release of preliminary National Sample Survey (NSS) data for 1993-94 has produced a spate of articles that forcefully argued that the poor had been hurt at least in the initial reform period (Papanek 1996, p. 1). Although it is debatable (see Gupta, 1995), both the official source (*Economic Survey:* 1995-96, p. 13) and the World Bank Country Study on India (1996, p. 28) suggest that economic reforms have begun to help the poor.
21. Although economic liberalisation has accelerated industrial development, but benefits have not been evenly distributed across states. Ghuman (1997, p.13) notes that Gujarat, Maharashtra and Tamil Nadu have gained the most from liberalised policy initiatives; other beneficiaries are West Bengal, Karnataka and Orissa; the remaining states have either gained moderately or have suffered losses.
22. Deaton and Dréze (2002, p. 3742) note, for example, of localised impoverishment in the poorer districts of Orissa, deep recession in the powerloom sector, serious crisis in the edible oil industry as a result of slashing import tariffs, periodic waves of bankruptcy among cotton growers, displacement of the traditional fishing sector by commercial shrimp farms, and a number of sectoral crises associated with the abrupt lifting of quantitative restrictions on imports in mid-2001.
23. *Ninth Five-Year Plan* (section 2.1.3).
24. The real spirit of Panchayati Raj Institutions (PRI) is devolution of power from central and state governments to a third tier of self-government at village, intermediate and district levels.

# REFERENCES

Aiyer, M.S. (2002), 'Panchayati Raj: the way forward', *Economic and Political Weekly*, **37** (31), 3293-97.

Anon. (1999a), 'India beats First World in growth of services sector', *The Economic Times*, 31 December: http://www.economictimes.com/today.

Anon. (1999b), 'RBI turns the spotlight on services sector growth', *The Economic Times*, 30 December: http://www.economictimes.com/today.

Anon. (2002a), 'Govt ditches disinvestment, for now', *The Economic Times*, 8 September: http://www.economictimes.com/today.

Anon. (2002b), '10th plan to focus on rural development', *The Economic Times*, 25 September: http://www.economictimes.com/today.

Chadha, G.K. and P.P. Sahu (2002), 'Post-reform setbacks in rural employment: issues that need further scrutiny', *Economic and Political Weekly*, **37** (21), 1998-2026.

Chaudhuri, Sudip (2002), 'Economic reforms and industrial structure in India', *Economic and Political Weekly*, **37** (2), 155-62.

Deaton, Angus and Jean Dréze (2002), 'Poverty and inequality in India: a re-examination', *Economic and Political Weekly*, **37** (36), 3729-48.

Dutta, Dilip (1998), 'Fifty years of economic development in India: rhetoric and reality', in P. K. Basu, N. D. Karunaratne and C. A. Tisdell (eds), *Fifty Years of Indian Development: India in Retrospect, Future Directions and Investment Outlook*, Economics Conference Monograph No. 5, Brisbane, Australia: The University of Queensland.

*Economic Survey*, Delhi: Ministry of Finance, Government of India (various issues).

*Five Year Plan*, Planning Commission, New Delhi: Government of India (various documents).

Ghuman, B.S. (1997), 'Liberalisation and regional patterns of industrialisation: the Indian experience', Paper presented to the International Conference, *South Asian Development in 1997 and Beyond: Its Relevance for Australia*, 12-14 September, University of Sydney.

Gupta, S.P. (1995), 'Economic reform and its impact on the poor', *Economic and Political Weekly*, **30** (22), 1295-1313.

Hoogvelt, A. (1997), *Globalization and the Postcolonial World: The New Political Economy of Development*, Baltimore, Maryland: The Johns Hopkins University Press.

Jhabvala, R. (1998), 'Social security for the unorganised sector', *Economic and Political Weekly*, **33** (22), L7-L11.

Krishna, R. (1988), 'Ideology and economic policy', *Indian Economic Review*, **23** (1), 1-26.

Kurien, C.T. (1996), *Economic Reforms and the People*, Delhi: Madhyam Books.

Mahanti, Tushar (2000), 'Service sector fuelled a higher GDP growth in the nineties', *The Economic Times*, 24 January: http://www.economictimes.com/today.

Nayyar, D. (1997), 'Globalization: the game, the players and the rules', in S.D. Gupta (ed.), *The Political Economy of Globalization*, Norwell, Massachusetts: Kluwer Academic Publishers.

*National Accounts Statistics*, New Delhi: Government of India (various issues).

Pais, Jesim (2002), 'Casualisation of urban labour force: analysis of recent trends in manufacturing', *Economic and Political Weekly*, **37** (7), 631-52.

Papanek, Gustav (1996), *Indian Economic Reforms and the Poor*, Boston, Massachusetts: Boston Institute for Developing Economies (unpublished manuscript).

Parthasarathy, G. (1996), 'Unorganised sector and structural adjustment', *Economic and Political Weekly*, **31** (28), 1859-69.

Rao, V. M. (1998), 'Economic reforms and the poor: emerging scenario', *Economic and Political Weekly*, **33** (29 & 30), 1949-54.

Government of India (1969), *Report of the National Commission on Labour*, India: Ministry of Labour, Employment and Rehabilitation.

Reserve Bank of India (1999), *Annual Report 1998-99*, Appendix Table II.1, 24 August: http://www.rbi.org.in.

Venu, M.K. (2000), 'Productivity wins the day as growth in GDP hits 7.5 percent with employment dip', *The Economic Times*, 4 January. http://www.economictimes.com/today.

Waters, M. (1995), *Globalization*, London & New York: Routledge.

World Bank Country Study (1996), 'India: five years of stabilization and reform and the challenges ahead', Washington, DC: The World Bank.

# 12. Globalisation and the Nature of Unemployment[1]

**Laurence Lasselle, Serge Svizzero and Clem Tisdell**

## 12.1 INTRODUCTION

Since the mid-1970s, two main features have characterised most OECD countries: their growing international economic integration and high and persistent unemployment (Siebert 1997; Nickell 1997). These facts led economists to wonder about possible links between globalisation and unemployment, and eventually about the responsibility of globalisation for unemployment (Haskel and Slaughter 2001; Wood 1994, 1998).

It is well known that globalisation covers a broad range of economic activities, but especially the globalisation of markets for goods and services and for capital is often stressed. However, the labour market seems to be much less globalised than the others (Tisdell et al. 2004). This mainly results from national limitations on immigration of workers to most countries, especially between the north and the south countries. Even though northern countries are usually strong proponents of free trade as far as goods, services, and capital flows are concerned, they remain highly protectionist with respect to labour movements. This latter situation helps support the claim of Rodrik (2000), that 'Contrary to conventional wisdom and much punditry, international economic integration remains remarkably limited'. (Rodrik 2000, p. 178). He also mentions that direct capital investment (and even portfolio investment) is much less mobile than sometimes imagined. National borders demarcate political and legal jurisdictions, and therefore affect the labour market. Indeed, cross-country comparisons of labour markets show differences in unemployment rates, wage determination systems, wage mobility, wage distribution among workers, transaction costs and institutions.

Therefore, even though it is clear that there is no free world labour market, it does not mean that the labour market is only influenced by domestic factors. On the contrary, the labour market has been deeply transformed as a result of economic globalisation for the past three decades, and there is a considerable amount of short-term labour migration, for example, to oil rich nations in the Middle East and Brunei.

After World War II and under the influence of Keynes's contribution to economic theory and policy, most OECD countries[2] were regulated by a Fordist system. Wages were mainly considered as a large part of the total income necessary to support the aggregate demand and then the level of economic activity. Consequently, a significant part of productivity gains was redistributed to wage earners.

Since the mid-1970s and because of a growing economic globalisation, the Fordist system has gradually disappeared. As a result, most economists consider the labour factor to be just like any other commodity. On the one hand, the wage is simply the labour price equalising the demand for labour and the labour supply. Disequilibrium in the labour market – that is, the existence of unemployment – can disappear if the wage is flexible. On the other hand, wages are mainly (sometimes solely) considered as the cost of labour, that is, as a significant part of the total cost incurred by firms. Given this view, wage decrease is the means by which unemployment can be reduced and price competitiveness can be enhanced, thereby leading to economic growth based on export promotion. This is achieved through the deregulation of the labour market and the removal of wage rigidities (Section 12.2).

Such a short-term policy is effective in reducing 'classical' unemployment. However, it appears in the long term that technological change – which is more intense and pervasive as a result of the globalisation process – may lead to capital-labour substitution and then to Ricardian unemployment (Section 12.3). Nevertheless, innovation may compensate, that is, it may also create employment, and then the currently observed unemployment cannot be fully Ricardian. Similarly, existing employment cannot be fully classical since it remains high – especially in Europe – despite the shift towards a more flexible labour market.

With the disappearance of the Fordist system as a result of the globalisation process, a large part of the currently observed unemployment is probably Keynesian in nature, that is, it comes from an insufficient level of aggregate demand (Section 12.4). Indeed, globalisation has reduced the impact of the different components of the demand for goods and services on employment. A general wage cut in developed countries combined with widespread globalisation makes the demand-side policies effective to reduce Keynesian unemployment only if additional conditions to Keynes's original framework – such as an international coordination of economic policies – are met.

## 12.2 PRICE COMPETITIVENESS, DEREGULATION OF THE LABOUR MARKET AND CLASSICAL UNEMPLOYMENT

Some of the most significant features of economic globalisation in the last three decades have been the rapid expansion of foreign direct investment and the liberalisation of trade through regional and multilateral agreements. More open markets and more globalised economic activities have resulted in the emergence of fierce competition, especially in the market for goods and services.

Emphasis on increased international trade has put pressure on countries to base their economic development on export expansion. The example of newly industrialised East Asian countries is obvious. Their main engine of growth (and therefore, job creation) rests on their exporting industries. Their firms secured market shares in economies of more advanced countries throughout the last decades (Odagiri and Goto 1993; Young 1995; Mathews and Cho 2000). Western countries have tried to develop new activities in the search of new markets. They restructured their exporting sectors by reducing their costs, either by making use of plants abroad, or reducing labour inputs at home. In other words, Western firms' response to the phenomenon of globalisation and strong competition has been to increase their international competitiveness by reducing their cost, either the wage level or the number of workers employed. The use of casual labour has increased in order to reduce the cost of social benefits such as pensions and medical insurance. By creating new plants in southern countries, cheaper labour was employed. At home, firms have put pressure on governments to deregulate the labour market, that is, to remove minimum wage regulation and to shift from centralised wage determination systems to bargaining at the workplace level.

For mainstream economists, the above strategy, that is, increasing wage flexibility in order to improve price competitiveness, is a positive strategy since it is also believed to lead to the reduction of unemployment. This belief is reinforced by the existence of a general positive relation between the growth of exports and the growth of employment.

Table 12.1 shows the rate of change of both variables over the period 1985-1995. The relation is clearly positive, with extreme cases for some Asian countries which have relied on export-led growth.

According to mainstream economists, the labour market behaves as any commodity market. Any market disequilibrium can disappear through an adequate adjustment of the price of labour, that is, the real wage.

In this partial equilibrium analysis, *unemployment is classical* because it comes from real wages that are higher than the equilibrium wages. Unemployment is voluntary and persistent since it depends on wage rigidity

*Table 12.1 Changes (%) in employment and exports, 1985-1995*

| | Change in employment | Change in exports |
|---|---|---|
| ASEAN-4 | 32.2 | 145.1 |
| South Korea | 36.1 | 140.9 |
| Japan | 11.2 | 46.9 |
| Australia | 22.9 | 32.4 |
| USA | 16.6 | 54.4 |
| Canada | 15.0 | 28.2 |
| EU-15 | 11.4 | 65.2 |
| Germany | 36.7 | 66.2 |
| UK | 6.8 | 38.3 |
| France | 3.6 | 69.7 |

*Source*: Second European report on S&T indicators, 1997, appendix (European Commission, 1997).

due to the fact that workers and unions do not accept a wage decrease. The policy implications of classical unemployment are straightforward: sticky wages hinder labour market adjustment and rigidities must disappear in order to reduce unemployment.

In the 1980s and the 1990s, this 'old' notion of classical unemployment has been revitalised by two complementary approaches.

On the one hand, many empirical studies have tried to assess the importance of observed labour market rigidities. Among these, unemployment benefits and hiring and firing costs have often been considered as the main distortions. Unemployment benefits discourage job search and induce moral hazard problems. Hiring costs are particularly high for skilled workers when the probationary period is too short. Moreover, firms appear to be very reluctant to hire workers – especially unskilled employees – if they cannot easily get rid of them. Job contracts – that cannot be renewed an indefinite number of times – and restrictions on working time imply that the labour supply is quite rigid while – depending on the level of economic activity – the labour demand is strongly variable over time. Such a mismatch also contributes to higher unemployment rate.

On the other hand, new theoretical approaches – some of them being based on the observations mentioned above – of labour market rigidities have been developed. For some economists, unemployment comes from problems related to the supply-side of the labour market. This includes the cost of job search (Mortensen 1986) and the segmentation of the labour supply between insiders and outsiders (Lindbeck and Snower 1988). For others, the informational asymmetry in the labour market leads to unemployment as a result of firms' behaviour. This is the so-called efficiency-wage theory (Shapiro and Stiglitz 1984). Finally, both sides of the labour market may explain, through the existence of implicit contracts, the occurrence of unemployment (Azariadis and Stiglitz 1983; Rosen 1985).

In the longer run, the existence of classical unemployment should reduce the bargaining power of the workers or their union, leading to a more flexible labour market and a higher level of employment. However, unemployment is persistent at high rates in some Western European countries, France and Italy for example. This stylised fact can be explained through the hysteresis theory (Blanchard and Summers 1987). The current level of unemployment mainly depends on the past history of unemployment. This is particularly the case when a large number of unemployed workers are long-term unemployed. Table 12.2 shows the effect of the incidence of long-term unemployment on total unemployment.

*Table 12.2 Incidence of long-term unemployment (LTU, %)* on total unemployment (TU, %), 1983 and 1996*

| | 1983 | | | 1996 | | |
|---|---|---|---|---|---|---|
| | **TU** | **LTU** | **LTU/TU** | **TU** | **LTU** | **LTU/TU** |
| France | 8.02 | 2.99 | 37.28 | 12.4 | 4.9 | 39.5 |
| Italy | 9.42 | 4.84 | 51.38 | 12.0 | 7.9 | 65.6 |
| Germany | 7.90 | 2.60 | 32.91 | 9.0 | - | - |
| UK | 11.81 | 4.91 | 41.57 | 8.2 | 3.3 | 39.8 |
| Canada | 11.93 | 1.14 | 9.56 | 9.7 | 1.3 | 13.9 |
| USA | 9.61 | 1.28 | 13.32 | 5.4 | 0.5 | 9.5 |
| Japan | 2.67 | 0.29 | 10.86 | 3.4 | 0.7 | 19.9 |
| Australia | 9.80 | 2.45 | 25.00 | 8.6 | 2.4 | 28.4 |

*Note*: * Long-term unemployment rate is the ratio of people being unemployed, at least for one year, over the total labour force.

*Source*: OECD, *Employment Outlook*, relevant issues.

Countries, such as France and Italy, which have historical and current worst employment performances, show a very high incidence of long-term unemployment.

It is quite obvious that long unemployment duration impairs workers' employability since their human capital is gradually eroded, they are discouraged to search for jobs and are often excluded from the labour market. According to this hysteresis theory, short-term as well as long-term unemployment can then be related to labour market rigidities. In other words, wage reduction and the deregulation of the labour market are, for mainstream economists, a panacea for reducing unemployment. However, this conclusion is dubious for several reasons.

Firstly, the deregulation of the labour market may have perverse effects on other economic and social issues. Broadly speaking, it may induce an endless rush to the bottom in labour market regulatory standards. For instance, firms may be willing to fill their vacancies through temporary contracts instead of permanent contracts. This results in a form of inefficiency since temporary contracts hardly evolve into permanent jobs while the vacancy would have been filled anyway. Likewise, for a representative worker, a more flexible market implies shorter unemployment spells and shorter job duration. However, it is not certain, from the social welfare point of view, that such a situation is preferable to longer unemployment periods and higher job stability.

Atkinson (1997) showed that a deregulated labour market is often associated with larger inequality. Since the mid-1970s, inequality has emerged in two different forms, depending on the features of the underlying labour market. When the labour market is quite flexible,[3] its deregulation implies growing wage inequality between workers, especially between the skilled and unskilled. When the labour market is more institutionalised,[4] the distribution of wages among workers remains more stable but inequality also emerges between skilled and unskilled workers in terms of job opportunities and of unemployment rates.

Short-term imperatives associated with the deregulation of the labour market have to be carefully balanced with long-term considerations related to basic labour standards, equity and social cohesion. For instance, labour market deregulation can have positive short-term effects in terms of employment but negative long-term counter-effects in terms of labour productivity and human capital accumulation. Indeed, with shorter job duration and larger mobility, employees and employers have weaker incentives for a joint investment in training and human capital than would have been possible given a long-term commitment between them.

Secondly, the labour market cannot be considered in a way similar to any other commodity market. As pointed out by Keynesian and post-Keynesian economists, the assumptions underlying the shape of the labour supply and labour demand curves are quite strong and not completely realistic.

Indeed, for mainstream economists, work is presumed to give rise to disutility. Therefore, the curve of labour supply is upward sloping since firms must pay to workers a wage which compensates the leisure they are giving up. However, aside from any income provided by work, work may also be a source of great satisfaction (Eichner 1985, pp. 91-6). Moreover, as first stressed by Keynes, most workers are, in the short term, influenced more by nominal wages than by real wages. Due to 'money illusion', Keynes considered the demand for labour to be the basis on which, through the effective demand principle, the level of employment is determined. For that purpose, Keynes admitted that the curve of labour demand was downward sloping. This is consistent with mainstream economists' view that the use of additional workers to increase production leads to diminishing marginal productivity. Such a relationship seems however to hold only in certain cases, particularly in small enterprises using relatively basic technology (Eichner 1985, pp. 88-91). In modern firms, production is carried out as part of a complex social process. The contribution of any worker is necessarily submerged in the overall group effort. Therefore, adding more labour imposes on the organisation the burden of altering its internal structure. Then, there is no way of determining the incremental contribution of a worker to the organisation. Although the negatively sloped demand curve for labour does not hold generally under modern conditions of production, it is on such a relationship that mainstream economists based their critics of wage increases. Indeed, they consider a typical labour market with a decreasing labour demand and an increasing labour supply. In such a market, any increase of nominal wage leads to a disequilibrium. The adjustment toward the equilibrium necessitates a rise of prices. At the overall level, it appears that nominal wage increases involve inflationary effects.

If, as shown above, assuming that the labour demand function is decreasing is quite controversial in a partial equilibrium analysis, it is even more controversial in a macroeconomic framework. As highlighted by Malinvaud (1994, p. 83), '...an increase in real wage leads to an increase in the aggregate demand for goods, hence to an increase also in the demand for labour by enterprises. This phenomenon runs counter to the supposed downward orientation of the curve; one must then account for it when the aggregate relationship is specified'. In such an approach, wage decrease leads to the reduction of firms' total cost but what is more important is the recessionary effect associated with it. Indeed, aggregate demand will be weaker and Keynesian unemployment will occur (see Section 12.4).

Thirdly, the impact of deregulation in terms of employment performance is quite doubtful from an empirical point of view. After more than ten years of reforms in order to deregulate the labour market, unemployment rates remain high in most European countries such as France and Italy. Even if these rates are lower now than before, there is no clear correlation between their reduction and the shift toward a more flexible labour market. Table 12.3 offers a relationship between, on the one hand the rate of unemployment, and on the other hand an indicator of the 'strictness' of the labour market.

*Table 12.3 'Strictness' of the labour market (1985-1993) and unemployment rate (1993)*

| | **Indicator of the "strictness" of the labour market*** | **Unemployment rate** |
|---|---|---|
| USA | 1 | 6.92 |
| Canada | 3 | 11.24 |
| Australia | 4 | 11 |
| UK | 7 | 10.32 |
| Japan | 8 | 2.54 |
| France | 14 | 11.13 |
| Germany | 15 | 6.20 |
| Italy | 21 | 10.34 |

*Note*: * This overall indicator of rigidity is based on different indicators computed on the period 1985-1993. It takes lower values as much as the labour market is considered as flexible.

*Source*: OECD job study (1994).

From Table 12.3 it is impossible to detect a positive correlation between labour market rigidity and the unemployment level. For mainstream economists, this unpleasant result does not contradict their explanation of unemployment and the remedial policy they recommend. They claim that if unemployment rates remain high it is because the reform implemented by European countries is insufficiently drastic, compared to the US reform, and is also not fully credible. This latter point is particularly important in a dynamic framework. As long as employers consider that governments are not fully committed in the reform, that is, as long as they expect a possible turning point – resulting for instance from electoral considerations – they are not willing to hire more workers despite lower wages and increasing flexibility on the labour market.

Another explanation of high and persistent unemployment may be found by looking at the 'true' nature of unemployment. Indeed, if unemployment is not classical, the deregulation of the labour market is not an appropriate policy to create jobs. Such a possibility is quite likely when policy based on increased price competitiveness is carefully examined. Indeed, we know that most countries – developing as well as developed – have based, in response to economic globalisation, their economic growth on export promotion. For that purpose, the most usual strategy has been to enhance price or cost competitiveness through wage cuts and deregulation of the labour market. However, such a policy may not be appropriate to reduce unemployment and to create jobs. This is more obvious when the impacts of increasing price competitiveness are considered at the macroeconomic level.

For a given country, cutting domestic wages reduces firms' costs and then may increase exports. However, it also reduces the domestic demand since the income of wage earners has decreased. Depending on circumstances, the aggregate demand may decrease if the reduction of the domestic demand is larger than the increase of exports. Such a possibility is more likely to occur in developed countries since tradable activities – which are concerned with the export promotion policy – mainly belong to manufacturing industry, that is, they constitute only a small and decreasing part of the overall economy. Therefore, the reduction of wages has ambiguous total effects. It implies a wage reduction in the services sector where employment is large and where most activities are non-tradable. It reduces costs in manufacturing but leaves industrial productivity nearly unchanged, the latter being largely dependent on technology rather than on labour cost.

When several countries are considered, the increase of price competitiveness may lead all countries to be worse off. Indeed, increasing price competitiveness through wage cuts is a short-term strategy accessible to any country.[5] If all countries decide to cut their wage by a same amount, this leads to two negative consequences. On the one hand, price competitiveness of each country remains the same. On the other hand, the overall issue is – like in the prisoner's dilemma – Pareto-dominated by the initial situation. Indeed, the wage cut leads to a reduction of the domestic demand in each country and therefore to lower foreign demand from the other countries.

Clearly, economic growth based on export promotion – that is, based on foreign demand – necessitates coordination among countries in order to maintain a sufficiently high level of the demand for goods, and then of employment. Without such coordination, the occurrence of Keynesian unemployment is certain.[6]

## 3.12 STRUCTURAL COMPETITIVENESS, INNOVATION AND RICARDIAN UNEMPLOYMENT

Schumpeter (1943) first pointed out that price competition is a shortsighted strategy and that competition in the long term only depends on innovation. Nowadays, it is commonly acknowledged that non-price competitiveness depends not only on firms' behaviour, but also on government policy. The former must invest in R&D in order to innovate and thereby try to 'guarantee' its development in the future. The latter gives to firms incentives to invest through policy actions such as the enforcement of intellectual property rights, the development of infrastructures which provide positive externalities, the promotion of human capital accumulation via the educational system and so on.

Innovation may increase efficiency in the production of existing goods, and/or create new products. Consequently, new or vastly altered markets may emerge. It can improve the export capacity of a given country. Indeed, as shown by Vernon (1966), when a firm innovates, its technological superiority puts it in a monopoly situation, at least for a certain time. When a country's exporting industries exhibit high productivity and concentration levels based on continuing innovation (but temporarily protected innovation), they are less exposed to competitive pressures, notably to price competition. Therefore, economic policy must promote structural competitiveness and innovation rather than price competitiveness (Davidson and Segerstrom 1998; Segerstrom 2000). Indeed, innovation is assumed to provide long-term competitive advantages such that the unemployment problem might be solved. This view holds since increasing competitiveness through innovation does not lead to a zero-sum game. Innovation, by creating new products and new markets, can sustain employment growth in the long run. However, innovation can also have qualitative and/or quantitative negative effects on the labour market.

Let us consider first the qualitative effects. Over the last twenty years, the structure of labour demand has deeply altered in OECD countries. On the one hand, there is an increasing demand for skilled labour, and on the other hand, there is a decreasing demand for unskilled labour. This change is, to a large extent (Lawrence and Slaughter 1993; Svizzero and Tisdell 2002a), explained by recent technological change biased against unskilled workers. Innovation is therefore not Pareto improving since it favours only one group of workers, while pushing the others out of their jobs.

Studies on the quantitative effects of innovation on employment often claim that technological change is introduced in the production processes at the expense of employment. Innovation increases capital productivity and then reduces the cost of capital relative to labour cost. Technological change leads to capital substitution to labour and then to what is called *Ricardian unemployment*. This substitution evolves at a pace positively related to the speed of the wage variations and the innovation process. Both were high from the mid-1970s to the mid-1980s, that is, during the period when unemployment rates were particularly high in most developed countries.

Following Wicksell (1961), mainstream economists argue that, even if unemployment is not classical but Ricardian, wage cuts still are the appropriate policy. Indeed, when due to innovation a labour-saving technology is introduced some workers are laid off because the cost of labour becomes too high. If wages are reduced sufficiently, one may expect a technical reversal, that is, a shift back to labour-intensive technology since labour has become cheaper.

Once again, this point of view is valid under the restrictive and partly unrealistic assumptions underlying microeconomic theory. A technological reversal is possible if, on the one hand, capital and labour are perfect substitutes, and on the other hand, the introduction of a new technology is not associated with sunk costs. Both conditions are unlikely to be met.

First, the substitution of capital to labour is not automatic. It depends on workers' skills and also on the nature of technological change (Acemoglu 2002, pp. 7-9). During the nineteenth century, most technological advances appear to have replaced skilled workers and expanded tasks performed by the unskilled. However, there is now a broad consensus that since the early twentieth century, capital and skills are intrinsically complementary (Griliches 1969). Such complementarity is stronger for the highest skilled and has been enhanced by the introduction of new technologies in the latest decades (Krusell et al. 2000).

Second, the introduction of a new technology at the firm level follows a cumulative and irreversible process. This process is irreversible since the firm which has invested must change its structure and therefore incurs sunk costs which commit it to the new technology for a long period. Furthermore, the adoption by firms of a new technology is not uniquely determined by cost consideration but is much more influenced by market features, that is, by the strategy of competitors and by the expected pattern of demand.

It is widely agreed that technological change has negative qualitative effects on the labour market. Its bias against unskilled workers has increased inequality over the last twenty years (Lawrence and Slaughter 1993). Its negative quantitative effects on employment are less obvious. Of course, at the firm level or at the sectoral level, employment is reduced after the introduction of a labour-saving technology. However, at the global level, there are some compensations which operate through different channels, that is, innovation may also create jobs.

First, even if the technical reversal is not likely to occur, the labour demand may increase after an innovation. Production-side innovation, which is usually labour-saving, initially enhances unemployment and therefore reduces the cost of labour. Since labour is cheaper, demand for it rises, at least in the industries that are not directly concerned by the innovation.

Second, production-side innovation leads to productivity gains, that is, to a lower total cost incurred by firms. If the underlying market is not too oligopolistic, one may expect a decrease in the price of the produced good and consequently an increase of its demand. In response to this increase, the employment level in the innovative industry could be pushed up. Likewise, the aggregate demand, and thus the employment level, can be positively stimulated by innovation. Indeed, the latter implies productivity gains which – depending on the way the added value is shared among employers and employees – can be partly redistributed to wage earners,[7] leading finally to a larger demand for goods and services.

Third, innovation often involves the introduction of new products and therefore the creation of new markets. Both have a direct positive impact on employment but also an indirect positive impact through the links between the new industry and the pre-existing industries.

Technological change has therefore destructive as well as creative effects on jobs because it is generally labour saving and also because some compensations exist. The overall effect of innovation on employment is then quite complex. As shown by several empirical studies (for example, Bean and Pissarides 1993), there is no clear correlation between unemployment and growth – the latter being derived from innovation – not over time nor in cross-sections over countries. Table 12.4 shows the existence in the long run of a striking difference between European and other countries.

*Table 12.4 Long-run percentage changes of real GDP (ΔGDP) and total working time (ΔWT)**

| | **USA 1976-1996** | **Canada 1976-1996** | **Japan 1976-1994** | **Australia 1978-1996** | **UK 1976-1996** | **Germany 1973-1990** | **France 1976-1996** | **Italy 1970-1985** |
|---|---|---|---|---|---|---|---|---|
| ΔGDP | 69.97 | 66.00 | 69.92 | 70.35 | 51.78 | 45.10 | 47.49 | 53.34 |
| ΔWT | 47.70 | 32.64 | 9.20 | 37.02 | -2.20 | -9.27 | -8.63 | -5.44 |
| ΔWT / ΔGDP | 68.47 | 49.45 | 13.16 | 52.61 | -4.24 | -20.55 | -18.18 | -10.20 |

*Note*: * Total working time is defined as the product of average yearly hours of work and total employment.

*Source*: Based on OECD National Accounts, Data Stream and ILO data.

In non-European countries, there is a correlation between economic growth and the increased need of working time. In European countries, economic growth is associated with employment stagnation and long-run decline in total working time. Therefore, there are in European countries lower technical coefficients, that is, a strong labour-saving bias.

The theoretical literature also concludes that the overall effect on employment is ambiguous. Many models study this question. For that purpose, every model considers a particular way through which innovation is introduced in the economy (for example, Aghion and Howitt 1994; Mortensen and Pissarides 1998). However, all these different models reach the same conclusion: innovation – and then economic growth – has two opposite effects on unemployment. Old jobs are destroyed when new technologies arrive, but these are subsequently replaced by new more productive employment opportunities. It is remarkable to note that, although new jobs are created when old ones are destroyed, it does not necessarily imply that the economy will settle at a higher or even the same level of employment.

Once again, there is no clear conclusion. Several factors have an influence, such as the nature of innovation, the structure of the economy, industrial relations, and also the moment of time when the study is done. Indeed, as pointed out by several famous authors such as Schumpeter (1943), innovations – or more precisely clusters of innovations – are major reasons for business cycles. In other words, the total effect of innovation on employment is very different during each phase of the cycle.

## 12.4 FORDIST REGULATION, AGGREGATE DEMAND AND KEYNESIAN UNEMPLOYMENT

Although we have just concluded that because some compensations exist, the observed unemployment cannot be entirely attributed to technological change, we need now to qualify that claim. Indeed, there exist some compensation mechanisms described in Section 12.3 that are no longer at work under the growing economic integration at the international level. We noted that aggregate demand, and then the employment level, increased after the introduction of a new technology when a large part of productivity gains was redistributed to workers via wage increases (through the collective bargaining system). This mechanism was at work before the early 1970s, when OECD economies were little integrated and were regulated by a Fordist system.

With growing globalisation, the Fordist system has gradually disappeared and wage determination is nowadays regulated by a more competitive labour market. Therefore, one of the main compensation channels no longer exists and hence unemployment can be, at least partially, Ricardian. Furthermore, what is mainly suggested by the end of the Fordist regulation system is that the aggregate demand, no more supported by the 'Fordist social contract', is too weak and consequently that unemployment is, to a large extent, Keynesian in nature.

This claim can be demonstrated as follows. First, recall that partial-type market forces do not operate at the macroeconomic level according to Keynes. They do not contribute to the determination of economic and employment levels that are found through the effective demand principle. The current level of employment depends on the expected level of the demand for goods. The latter level is itself dependent on entrepreneurs' expectations and on the current level of the components of the demand.

Second, when the aggregate demand is too low (because expectations are too pessimistic or because some of its components are too weak) a demand deficiency or *Keynesian unemployment* appears. Third, Keynesian unemployment can be reduced by the use of economic policies which support the effective demand. The effectiveness of these policies, either monetary or fiscal, depends on two features. On the one hand, it depends on the multiplier effect associated with the components of the autonomous demand.[8] As is well known, the multiplier effect is negatively influenced by the level of taxes, the propensity to save and the propensity to import. On the other hand, if unemployment of other types, either classical or Ricardian, coexists with Keynesian unemployment, an extra effective demand alone cannot cure the latter but merely causes inflation. It is for the previous reason – the co-existence of high inflation and structural problems – that most countries have, since the mid-1970s, given up the view that demand-side policy can reduce unemployment.

Our purpose in this section is to show that with growing globalisation since the early 1970s, every component of aggregate demand has been weakened and therefore a large part of unemployment could be Keynesian. Aggregate demand can be separated into four main components, namely exports, private consumption, private investment and government expenditures. Let us consider how each component has evolved with economic globalisation.

First, exports are the element of demand currently occupying centre stage. Indeed, as mentioned above,[9] many governments, encouraged by international organizations such as the World Bank and the IMF, have based their economic growth on exports. This recommendation was suggested by the faster growth of world trade relative to domestic demand. However, as pointed out previously, such a policy has not been successful except in newly industrialised East Asian countries.

Table 12.5 shows the link between economic growth and the structure of demand, in 1980 and 1995. While private investment and private consumption are essential factors for long-term growth, exports play a different role in particular regions. This lack of success in Western economies can be explained by the fact that exports depend on two key elements, competitiveness and foreign income. Price competitiveness has been sought by wage cuts, leading to a lower income available for domestic demand and imports. Encouraging export promotion was sometimes successful in the past, but it would be misleading to pursue such a policy without international coordination. Indeed, this policy had had positive effects, when several countries[10] decided to engage together into free trade, providing new markets to the other countries and sustaining also their exports. Currently, almost all countries, including China, belong to the WTO, that is, are committed into free trade agreements and therefore there should be no more markets or countries that would be still closed and that could be suddenly opened.

*Table 12.5 Average annual growth rate (%) and the distribution of GDP (%)*

| | GDP, average annual growth rate | | Exports of goods & services | | Private consumpt. | | Private invest. | | Govt expend. | |
|---|---|---|---|---|---|---|---|---|---|---|
| | 1980-90 | 1990-95 | 1980 | 1995 | 1980 | 1995 | 1980 | 1995 | 1980 | 1995 |
| Low/middle income countries | 2.8 | 2.1 | 23 | 22 | 57 | 63 | 26 | 27 | 14 | 14 |
| East Asia & Pacific | 7.6 | 10.3 | 16 | 29 | 58 | 51 | 28 | 39 | 12 | 11 |
| South Asia | 5.7 | 4.6 | 8 | 14 | 75 | 69 | 20 | 23 | 9 | 11 |
| Latin Amer. & Caribbean | 1.7 | 3.2 | 16 | 17 | 67 | 67 | 25 | 20 | 11 | 12 |
| High income countries | 3.2 | 2.0 | 22 | 22 | 60 | 63 | 23 | 21 | 17 | 15 |
| World | 3.1 | 2.0 | 22 | 22 | 59 | 63 | 24 | 23 | 16 | 15 |

*Source*: *World Development Report*, 1997.

The second component of aggregate demand is private consumption. With greater competition and lower prices due to globalisation, one may expect that consumption has increased. This is partly true but several factors have impaired consumption.

Restrictive monetary policies implemented in most countries at the beginning of the 1980s have considerably reduced inflation rates and hence increased real interest rates. The cost of credit was then larger and consumers were less willing to borrow (for exmpale, for housing). Since the mid-1990s, real interest rates have been very low (especially in Japan and in the US) but the consumption level has not increased. This shows that consumption also depends on other factors and notably that it has been hindered by the increase of uncertainty linked with growing globalisation. Consumption has also been restrained by, on the one hand, growing income inequalities, and on the other hand, the increasing volatility of income.

It is well known[11] that the marginal and average propensity to consume is a decreasing function of the income level. For instance, poorer people consume, on average, a larger part of their income than the rich. Since the early 1970s, there has been greater income polarisation in most countries. Globalisation and other phenomena[12] have increased between-groups income inequalities (Svizzero and Tisdell 2002a) and also within-group income inequality (Svizzero and Tisdell 2002b). A larger number of workers have now a lower income, the latter remaining constant over time and sometimes being decreased. Likewise, a larger number of highly-skilled workers have now a larger income, the latter following an increasing path over time. Both trends tend to reduce the overall average propensity to consume to which the multiplier effect is positively related.

Higher unemployment rates, part-time jobs, temporary job contracts and other factors leading to casualisation of the labour market have also increased uncertainty and income volatility. Once again, this has led consumers to be more pessimistic, and therefore they have increased their precautionary savings, that is, they have reduced their propensity to consume. As shown in Section 12.2, growing casualisation of the labour market is partly the result of a deregulation policy recommended by mainstream economists in order to adapt the economy to the globalised context. Growing uncertainty in the labour market, and more generally in all economic activities, also comes from globalisation. Greater economic integration has reinforced spillover and contagious effects among countries. Therefore, any crisis – financial or political – in a given country has, through the financial system, direct and immediate effects on the other economies.

The third component of aggregate demand is private investment. As pointed out in Section 12.3, although investment in the initial process of capital creation may at first add to employment, subsequently investment often has direct negative effects on employment. Indeed, it leads to capital substitution for labour, that is, to the introduction of a labour-saving technology and then to the occurrence of Ricardian unemployment. Moreover, even though investment raises labour productivity and thereby economic growth, it does not necessarily entail job creation. Like the other components of aggregate demand, investment has indirect effects on employment via the multiplier.

Two other influences on investment – namely the interest rate and expectations – have had opposite influences during the last two decades.

Interest rates reached very high levels which slowed down investment. Indeed, until the late 1970s, interest rates were often low as monetary policy was used by governments to support aggregate demand, as recommended by Keynesian economists. The controversy about the relevance of the Phillips curve led governments – influenced by monetarists – to adopt a different monetary policy. For monetarists as well as for new classical economists, there is no trade-off between unemployment and inflation. Money is neutral and any attempt to support aggregate demand by means of monetary policy will only result in increased inflation. Therefore, the only goal of monetary policy is to maintain a low level of inflation, an objective which is reached with restrictive monetary policy, that is, by maintaining interest rates at high levels. Such a policy has also been recommended by international organisations. Indeed, one major feature of economic globalisation has been the growing integration of monetary and financial markets across countries. The latter have been encouraged by deregulation of financial markets and the shift – after the collapse of the Bretton Woods system in 1971 – towards a floating exchange rate regime. In order to prevent deep fluctuations of exchange rates, these organisations recommended governments to adopt monetarist policy, that is, to fight inflation despite the perverse effect on employment resulting from high levels of interest rates.

Entrepreneurs' expectations are the second fundamental determining factor of investment. Of course, they are much more difficult to assess than the level of interest rates. From the mid-1970s until now, these expectations have been influenced by the unemployment rate and trade growth. On the one hand, the weak level of domestic demand in most Western countries made entrepreneurs pessimistic. They then feel that they should invest at a level that just maintains their economic activities. On the other hand, the rapid growth of world trade relative to domestic demand urged entrepreneurs to invest massively abroad. The flows of foreign direct investment (FDI) reached unprecedented records year after year. So, for a given country, investment abroad was much more dynamic than investment at home. This action did not lead to the virtuous dynamic highlighted by Keynesian economics and based on the multiplier effect. Indeed, with the development of FDI and multinational companies, goods – either final or intermediary – are often produced in one country and sold in another. In other words, FDI increases the productive capacity in the host country but it does not necessarily increase the income of this country since the Fordist regulation system has disappeared. Moreover, the produced goods resulting from the FDI are sold to countries where the income has not been affected by this investment and can therefore be insufficient to generate effective demand. The multiplier effect works if the additional demand – resulting for instance from an extra investment – generates an additional income sufficient to buy the additional produced good. When production and consumption take place in different countries without regulated connections, the multiplier effect can be positive or negative, depending on circumstances.

The fourth and last component of aggregate demand is government expenditure. These expenditures take various forms such as spending on goods and services, spending on employment in public firms, spending on transfer payments, subsidies, and payment of debt interest. All these expenditures gradually grew after World War II and helped to sustain the rapid economic growth of OECD countries until the mid-1970s. Since the late 1970s and under the influence of globalisation and structural adjustment policies, there has been a shift toward a market economy and consequently each type of expenditure mentioned above has been reduced.

Under the influence of monetarists, a new orthodoxy has been introduced. It consists in the limitation of the budget deficit[13] and it urges governments to balance their budgets and even to reach budget surpluses.[14] The ideas underlying such policy are that government spending is harmful since it tends to favour inflation and higher interest rates and also crowds out private investment, and increases public debt. Moreover, the latter problem puts pressure on interest rates and induces a lack of credibility on monetary policy when the central bank is not completely independent. As a result, several governments' expenditures have been cut, for example, in Australia, New Zealand and the UK, leading to reduced employment because, on the one hand, employment in the public sector has decreased in most western countries, and on the other hand, the multiplier effect has been less effective since the Western countries are more interdependent. In addition, several public firms have been partly or totally privatised. Some others are still publicly owned but now they compete with private firms. Employment in the public sector is now managed by rules similar to those prevailing in the competitive labour market.

As previously stressed, demand-side policies – based for instance on government expenditure – appear to be less effective or even ineffective under globalisation.[15] However, this does not mean that an expansion of the demand supported by public expenditure is necessarily harmful. On the contrary, what is needed now to reduce Keynesian unemployment in the context of globalisation is coordination of aggregate demand expansion – at least at the regional level – in order to prevent imbalances.

The idea of a coordinated action between countries to reduce unemployment and favour growth for everyone is not a new idea. Rosenstein-Rodan (1943)[16] explains why the industrialisation of eastern and south-eastern Europe can be beneficial to Western Europe, and thereby for all Europe. The industrialisation of international depressed areas is vital for everyone. 'It is *the* way of achieving a more equal distribution of income between different areas of the world by raising incomes in depressed areas at a higher rate than in the rich areas' (Rosenstein-Rodan 1943, p. 202). Unemployment is not confined to rich areas, it does exist everywhere and it is an even more problematic issue in some depressed areas. This high unemployment is going to make people move towards richer areas. 'If the principles of international division of labour are to be applied, labour must either be transported towards capital (emigration), or capital must be transported towards labour (industrialisation)' (Rosenstein-Rodan 1943, p. 202).

Emigration was already a sensitive problem at that time and was not a popular policy. Industrialisation was the best solution for everyone, but it had to be monitored. Rosenstein-Rodan strongly rejected a process of industrialisation made by the depressed countries by themselves. He believed it was an 'unnecessary sacrifice'. It will just shift important resources from consumption to industries and thereby increase the economic deprivation for these countries. He advocated an alternative solution to expand investment and to facilitate the emergence of industries in these countries: namely loans from abroad, or foreign direct investment. In both cases, the involuntary unemployed remain in the depressed areas, do not emigrate and participate in the development of their country. In a certain sense, this policy seems to have been applied in the following years, not because of Rosenstein-Rodan's arguments, but because of cheap labour costs in those depressed areas.

A few decades later, the fast growing East Asian economies made some Europeans or North Americans think that work was stolen from them and their standards of living were decreasing. These arguments were partly developed here in Sections 12.2 and 12.3 and qualified. Nevertheless, this view is at variance with that of Krugman (1996) who pointed out that the standard of living of Western countries cannot be decreased by the rise of that of southern countries.

The migration of labour is an important issue. Its overall economic impact is quite complex since it depends on many factors such as the skills of migrants, the structure of the economy, and the level of economic development. When labour movements across countries are allowed, they mainly consist in migration of southern workers toward northern countries where standards of living are better. When these workers are highly skilled, one speaks about the brain drain and the fact that it endangers the development of southern countries. However, such a brain drain can be imposed rather than chosen since skilled workers may have little prospect of contributing in their home country. Indeed, their skills may be in little demand because there is a lack of complementary factors (Tisdell 1990, Chapters 10 and 11).

Moreover, migrant workers from the South – be they skilled or not – can contribute to the economic development of their native country through international remittance.

In the host country, southern highly-skilled workers are going to compete with local workers and may deprive local unskilled workers of the chance to improve their position in the labour market (by training or better education). However, immigration may also have positive effects in the host country. It stimulates aggregate demand because it often requires extra investment, for example, in housing, schools and so on. This could even help unskilled workers native to the host country. When the domestic population is too low, immigration may also be a means of reaching the critical market size consistent with substantial economies of scale.

## 12.5 CONCLUDING COMMENTS

We have shown that three different mechanisms can explain unemployment, which can be either classical, Ricardian or Keynesian. We have demonstrated that the economic forces underlying the globalisation process have reinforced all these mechanisms. In other words, each type of unemployment is more likely to occur in a globalised world. We have also argued that the largest part of the currently observed unemployment is probably Keynesian in nature. This is mainly explained by two factors: the disappearance of the Fordist regulation system since the mid-1970s and the policies implemented in OECD countries. Up to the mid-1970s, the Fordist regulation system used to support aggregate demand. The policies implemented in OECD countries under the influence of dominant mainstream economists led to wage cuts and deregulation of the labour market.

However, it should be noted that the other types of unemployment – classical and Ricardian – are not excluded. As pointed out in the mid-1970s by economists such as Malinvaud (1977) or Benassy (1982), supporters of the 'fix-price' or 'disequilibrium' theory, different theoretical explanations of unemployment are often complementary rather than substitutes. In a given country, and even in a given sector or industry, unemployment can be partly classical and partly Keynesian. Such a possibility has been observed for EU countries (Lubrano et al. 1996). One major consequence is that it is less easy to find, at the country level, an appropriate policy leading to reduced unemployment. On the contrary, this situation necessitates the implementation of economic policy at the sectoral level.

Finally, there is an additional element which can influence the level of employment: immigration. As first pointed out in Section 12.1 (and also in Tisdell et al. 2004), labour markets are among the least globalised markets since countries have strengthened their immigration policy. However, the flows of migrants are important. Some policies with respect to migration have been implemented (through international agreements), but these are usually restrictive for low-skilled people.

Even if data are not available or very incomplete, illegal immigration has probably risen over the past decades (immigration into EU countries and the United States) and has sometimes led to international agreements (NAFTA for example). According to the Stolper-Samuelson theorem, international movements of products have similar consequences to international labour movements. The countries of the European Union have also agreed by the Schengen agreement to free labour movements within the Union.

Immigration laws could imply a new era of partnership between northern and southern countries. Indeed, the decline of the birth rate associated with the growing demand for skilled labour in Western countries make the future growth of Western economies more uncertain. To offset the forecast lack of highly-skilled labour, the European Community has enhanced education and training of the labour force and teenagers in recent years.[17] Some countries already believe that these actions will be effective only in the longer term and need at the present time to be associated with new immigration laws. They are in favour of selective immigration. Recently, Germany passed a law facilitating the immigration of highly-skilled workers. The United Kingdom employs doctors and teachers from the Commonwealth countries. Other European countries will follow soon. Indeed, some politicians forecast a race between countries to attract the best workers. Unfortunately, this policy of selective immigration can be seen as a pillaging of southern highly-skilled workers who are needed for the development of their own countries.

International labour movements have probably partly contributed to the rise and the persistence of high unemployment rates in rich countries, even though the overall impact of immigration on unemployment is quite ambiguous since it depends on several independent factors. They have partly weakened the position of unskilled northern workers. Any attempt to reduce unemployment should take into account the impact of immigration on unemployment in northern countries and on economic development in southern countries. Once again, as we have already pointed out for economic policy, the effectiveness of immigration policy necessitates coordination across countries, including northern as well as southern countries. However, immigration policy does not only need coordination among countries, it also needs not to be treated separately from economic policy. As is illustrated by the NAFTA, immigration can be monitored at a low cost if there is some economic counterpart for the country which the migrants were coming from. In other words, it is through its direct investment that the United States provides work and economic activity in Mexico and therefore limits the incentive to migrate inward.

In addition, it seems appropriate that economists should give more attention to the economic impacts of international labour migration to correct the current imbalance of their concentration in other commodity markets, including capital markets in the globalisation process.

# NOTES

1. Collaboration of Serge Svizzero and Clem Tisdell in contributing to this chapter was assisted by their 2002-2003 award from FEAST-France. They are grateful for this award. The usual caveat applies.
2. See for instance the Australian income policy implemented since the earliest days of Federation (1901) and called 'The price and income Accord' between 1983 to 1996.
3. Like, for instance, in the UK and in the USA.
4. Like in most European countries.
5. Such a policy is currently accessible exactly as currency devaluation was used in order to improve competitiveness under a fixed exchange rate regime.
6. See Section 12.4.
7. Such a redistribution is effective in a Fordist system through the collective bargaining between unions, employers and the government.
8. That is, components that are independent from current income levels.
9. See Sections 12.2 and 12.3.
10. We can distinguish three groups of countries. First, the former communist countries (including China) which have been, since the early 1990s, more or less open to world trade. Second, some countries (for example, India and South Africa) that were highly protectionist or closed and that are now more open to international trade. Third, there are countries (South America, East Asia) that had based their economic development on import substitution and that, after a while, have adopted a policy based on export promotion.
11. As is stressed by Engel's curve.
12. Such as technological change and the deinstitutionalisation of the labour market.
13. The Maastricht Treaty imposes on countries wishing to enter into the EMU an obligation to maintain the budget deficit at under 3 per cent of GDP.
14. The Amsterdam Pact of Stability introduces such incentives for European countries belonging to the EMU.
15. See for instance the negative result experimented in Germany (1978) and in France (1982).
16. Although the paper was written in 1943, it can still give some interesting insights into todays world economy and it finds an advocate in Krugman (1996).
17. See the policy guidelines accepted by European heads of governments at the different summits since 1997.

# REFERENCES

Acemoglu, D. (2002), 'Technical change, inequality and the labour market', *Journal of Economic Literature*, **XL**, March 2002, 7-72.

Aghion, P. and P. Howitt (1994), 'Growth and unemployment', *Review of Economic Studies*, **61**, 477-94.

Atkinson, A. (1997), 'Bringing income distribution in from the cold', *Economic Journal*, **107**, 291-321.

Azariadis, C. and J.E. Stiglitz (1983), 'Implicit contracts and fixed-price equilibria', *Quarterly Journal of Economics*, **98** (supplement), 1-22.

Bean, C. and C. Pissarides (1993), 'Unemployment, consumption and growth', *European Economic Review*, **37**, 837-54.

Benassy, J.-P. (1982), *The Economics of Market Disequilibrium*, New York: Oxford Academic Press.

Blanchard, O. and L.H. Summers (1987), 'Hysteresis in unemployment', *European Economic Review*, **31**, 288-95.

Davidson, C. and P. Segerstrom (1998), 'R&D subsidies and economic growth', *Rand Journal of Economics,* **29**, 548-77.
Eichner, A.S. (1985), *Toward a New Economics. Essays in Post-Keynesian and Institutionalist Theory*, London: Macmillan Press.
Griliches, Z. (1969), 'Capital-skill complementarity', *Review of Economic Statistics,* **51**, 465-68.
Haskel, J. and M.J. Slaughter (2001), 'Trade, technology and the UK wage inequality', *Economic Journal,* **111**, 163-87.
Krugman, P. (1996), *Pop Internationalism*, Cambridge, MA: MIT Press.
Krusell, P., L. Ohanian, V. Rios-Rull and G. Violante (2000), 'Capital skill complementary and inequality: a macroeconomic analysis', *Econometrica,* **68**, 1024-53.
Lawrence, R.Z. and M.J. Slaughter (1993), 'International trade and American wages in the 1980s: giant sucking sound or small hiccup?', *Brookings Papers on Economic Activity, Microeconomics,* **2**, 161-210.
Lindbeck, A. and D.J. Snower (1988), *The Insider-Outsider Theory of Employment and Unemployment*, Cambridge, MA: MIT Press.
Lubrano, M., F. Shadman-Mehta and H.R. Sneessens (1996), 'Real wages, quantity constraints and equilibrium unemployment: Belgium 1955-1988', *Empirical Economics,* **21**, 427-57.
Malinvaud, E. (1977), *The Theory of Unemployment Reconsidered*, Oxford: Blackwell.
Malinvaud, E. (1994), *Diagnosis Unemployment*, Cambridge: Cambridge University Press.
Mathews, J.A. and D.-S. Cho (2000), *Tiger Technology: The Creation of a Semiconductor Industry in East Asia*, Cambridge: Cambridge University Press.
Mortensen, D. (1986), 'Job search and the labour market analysis', in O. Ashenfelter and R. Layard (eds), *Handbook of Labour Economics*, New York: Elsevier Science Publisher, Vol. 3B, Chapter 39.
Mortensen, D.T. and C.A. Pissarides (1998), 'Technological progress, job creation, and job destruction', *Review of Economic Dynamics,* **1**, 733-53.
Nickell, S. (1997), 'Unemployment and labour market rigidities: Europe versus North America', *Journal of Economic Perspectives,* **11** (3), 55-74.
Odagiri, H. and A. Goto (1993), 'The Japanese system of innovation: past, present and future', in R. Nelson (ed.), *National Innovation Systems*, New York: Oxford University Press.
Rodrik, D. (2000), 'How far will international economic integration go?', *Journal of Economic Perspectives,* **14** (1), 177-86.
Rosen, S. (1985), 'Implicit contracts: a survey', *Journal of Economic Literature,* **23**, 1144-75.
Rosenstein-Rodan, P.N. (1943), 'Problems of industrialisation of Eastern and South-Eastern Europe', *Economic Journal,* **53** (210/211), 202-11.
Schumpeter, J. (1943), *Capitalism, Socialism and Democracy*, New York: Harper.
Segerstrom, P. (2000), 'The long-run effects of R&D subsidies', *Journal of Economic Growth,* **5**, 277-305. Shapiro, C. and J.E. Stiglitz (1984), 'Equilibrium unemployment as a discipline device', *American Economic Review,* **74**, 433-44.
Shapiro, C. and J.E. Stiglitz (1984), 'Equilibrium unemployment as a discipline device', *American Economic Review*, **74**, 433-44.
Siebert, H. (1997), 'Labour market rigidities: at the root of unemployment in Europe', *Journal of Economic Perspectives,* **11** (3), 37-54.

Svizzero, S. and C. Tisdell (2002a), 'Reconciling globalisation and technological change: growing income inequalities and remedial policies', *Intereconomics: Review of European Economic Policy*, **3**,162-71.

Svizzero S. and C. Tisdell (2002b), 'Income inequality between skilled individuals', *CERESUR Working Paper*, La Réunion, France: Université de La Réunion.

Tisdell, C. (1990), *Natural Resources, Growth and Development*, New York: Praeger.

Tisdell, C., S. Svizzero and L. Lasselle (2004), 'Unequal economic gains of nations from globalisation', in C. Tisdell and R. K. Sen (eds), *Economic Globalisation: Social Conflicts, Labour and Environmental Issues*, Cheltenham, UK and Northampton, MA, USA: Edward Elgar.

Vernon, R. (1966), 'International investment and international trade in the product cycle', *Quarterly Journal of Economics*, **80**, 190-207.

Wicksell, K. (1961), *Lectures on Political Economy*, London: Routledge & Kegan.

Wood, A. (1994), *North-South Trade, Employment and Inequality. Changing Fortunes in a Skill-Driven World*, Clarendon Press: Oxford.

Wood, A. (1998), 'Globalization and the rise in labour market inequalities', *Economic Journal*, **108**, 1463-82.

Young, A. (1995), 'The tyranny of numbers: confronting the statistical realities of the East Asia growth experience', *Quarterly Journal of Economics*, **110**, 641-80.

# 13. Globalised Capitalist Development and Income Inequalities: What Does the Data from East Asian Economies Tell Us?

**B.N. Ghosh**

## 13.1 INTRODUCTION

During the last forty years or so, income inequalities in the East Asian economies have shown two distinctive trends. Whereas in the earlier period of their industrialisation, there was a marked reduction in income inequalities, the later phase has witnessed a gradual rise in such inequalities along with acceleration in their growth rates. It is in this context that this chapter examines the relevance of the Kuznets' hypothesis. One of the broad conclusions of the present study is that in the case of the East Asian economies, the Kuznets' hypothesis does not seem to be applicable. The plausible contributing factors to downswings and upswings in Asian income inequalities are analysed alongside the issue of reliability and comparability of data which are often used to explain income inequalities in these countries.

It is apparent from the empirical scenario of many countries that as development proceeds, the developing countries reveal glaring economic inequalities. These economic inequalities are manifested in various ways, for example, income inequalities, gender inequalities, rural-urban inequalities, regional inequalities, racial inequalities, and the like. However, all types of inequalities are not equally important and meaningful for economic development of a country, and in a capitalist mode of development, some types of inequalities are often encouraged and perpetuated. But one of the most serious types of inequalities which is likely to impinge on human development is income inequality. It is a reflection of an unequal pattern of income distribution amongst various classes of people in a country. The generation of income inequalities is often regarded as a concomitant problem of economic development. Income inequality as a phenomenon affects different income classes in different degrees, and therefore, it would be more appropriate to use the concept in its plural sense as income inequalities.

Income inequalities, however, do not remain the same or uniform in the course of economic development. In some countries, the degrees of income inequalities may be different in different stages of development. It is interesting to note that some developing countries having the same level of economic achievement may reveal different degrees of income inequalities. In the same way, some of the developing countries may have the same degrees of income inequality although their income levels are different. This is evident in the case of many East Asian countries.

While all the developing countries are concerned with the problem of growing income inequalities, there does not seem to be any foreseeable clear-cut solution to the problem in the near future. Ever since the inception of Development Economics (DE) as a subject in the 1950s, attempts have been made to ameliorate poverty and income inequalities. But even during the 1960s, which is regarded as the golden period of DE, the basic problem of poverty and income inequalities could not be perceptibly reduced in developing countries. In fact, in the 1970s, poverty and income inequalities intensified in most of these economies. In the 1980s, many contradictions became evident in the simplistic economic paradigm of development. There was indeed an apparent failure of conventional theories of development to suggest ways and means to eradicate poverty and income inequalities. The structural adjustment policies followed by many of the developing countries could not also put an appreciable dent in poverty and income inequalities. The welfare state of the Keynesian type no longer brought any hope for solving these pressing problems. Thus, in the 1990s, the entire development process based on state planning and patronage came in for serious criticism, and more reliance was placed on the market as an organising mechanism for global relations (Harcourt 1997, pp. 5-8). But towards the end of the decade, the limitations of the market mechanism came to the surface with the onset of global financial crises.

Nevertheless, the recent interest in human development has created fresh impetus for the study of income inequalities in the perspective of economic development. Is there any relation between economic development and income inequalities? The answer is elusive from the empirical standpoint. Although it is difficult to lay down the relation in stylised clear-cut apple-pie order, nevertheless some general observations in this regard may be pertinent here. Such observations have been made familiar by Simon Kuznets' study which will be delineated in the following section. The burden of the present paper is to examine Kuznets' hypothesis on the relation between income distribution and economic development in the case of the East Asian economies. The analysis of the chapter is organised in the following way: this introduction is followed by a brief explanation of Kuznets' inverted 'U' hypothesis. Section 13.3 examines trends in income inequalities in the East Asian economies in general and Malaysia in particular, and queries the relevance of Kuznets' hypothesis. Explanations of rising income inequalities in the East Asian countries are provided in Section 13.4. The last section discusses the broad conclusions of the paper and analyses some of the problems and limitations of the present analysis.

## 13.2 THE INVERTED 'U' HYPOTHESIS

In his celebrated study, Kuznets (1955) hypothesised an asymmetrical relation between income distribution and economic growth. This is generally known as the inverted 'U' hypothesis. Kuznets' empirical study shows that income inequality widens during the early phase of development, then it relatively stabilises for some time, then narrows in the later phases of economic growth. Kuznets found greater relative income inequality in less developed countries (LDCs) than in the DCs. This result was confirmed for eighteen countries. Kuznets deduced the following empirical results from his study:

> *First,* the shares of the upper income groups in income distribution are distinctly larger in the LDCs than in the DCs.
> *Second,* although the shares of the lowest income groups in some LDCs are lower than in some DCs, the differences are much narrower than for the shares of the upper income groups.
> *Third*, on the assumption that the Lorenz curves do not intersect in the middle, the Gini coefficient of inequality would be greater in LDCs than in the DCs. The Kuznets curve shows that the incomes of the poorest 40 per cent of the population normally grow more slowly than the average until income per person reaches a range of $700 or $900. Beyond this range, the incomes of poorer grow, or tend to grow, faster than the average. Thus, income distribution is typically less unequal in developed countries than in developing countries.

It should be borne in mind that largely the pattern of income inequalities can be changed by proactive or reactive policy responses, as is found to be the case in the East Asian economies. However, Kuznets' hypothesis is formulated independently of policy issues and options for both developed and developing countries. The basic causes of the asymmetric relation between income inequality and economic development *á la* Kuznets can be stated briefly.

The increases in income inequality during the early phase of economic growth can be explained in terms of structural changes associated with economic growth. During the early phase of economic growth, there is a shift in economic activity in favour of the urban sector. This is characterised by high median income and great inequality within the sector. This type of sectoral shift in economic activity intensifies income inequality.

When income is growing at a very slow rate, capital-intensive technology does not generate sufficient employment to absorb the labour force which consists mainly of migrant rural workers. The marginal farmers and tenants on small farms cannot compete with large mechanised farms. Their (the small farmers') real income falls both due to lower product prices and higher monetary costs. The workers in cottage industries are displaced and the wage gains of the employed are largely negated by the inflationary impact of a tariff-based import substitution method of industrialisation. The inelasticity of international and domestic demand for agricultural goods also prevents rural real income from rising. The terms of trade move against the agricultural sector. The secular relation between economic growth and income inequality is reversed during the later stages of economic development.

Once the rate of expansion in the urban sector exceeds the rate of migration of the rural labourers and the urban labour force, it will narrow the inter-sectoral income differentials by reducing population pressure in the rural sector. Wage rates and employment will rise faster than GNP, provided the rate of labour absorption in high-productivity employment exceeds the rate of growth of the urban poor people. The improvements in human resources owing to expanded education will increase with wage share and narrow the wage differentials in the urban sector. The share of the lowest 40 per cent will improve and so along with it, the income elasticity of demand for agricultural goods. However, rural income will increase in spite of the low price elasticity of demand. Once the rate of increase of productive wage employment exceeds the additions to the labour force, the spread effects of growth will swamp out the back-wash effects. As a result of this, the benefits of growth will trickle down. A minimum rate of growth of 5 to 6 per cent may be required to attain the declining phase of income inequality.

## 13.3 INCOME INEQUALITIES IN EAST ASIA

Generally speaking, income inequalities in the East Asian countries show a common trend: in the initial years of economic development, these countries experienced lower degrees of inequality but after some time, as the rate of economic development rose, they experienced higher degrees of inequalities.

Thus, when the degrees of income inequalities are plotted against the rate of economic growth in these countries, one can get a U-shaped curve. This observation is true for Hong Kong, South Korea, Singapore, Taiwan, Indonesia, Malaysia and Philippines (Table 13.1). The relation between income inequalities and economic development in these Southeast Asian countries do not conform to the inverted 'U' hypothesis as proposed by Kuznets (1955). However, the case of Thailand is an exception. Income inequalities had been gradually increasing in Thailand since 1968 until 1992. The data released by the Asian Development Bank (2000) show that inequalities came down in Thailand substantially in 1999. It should be noted that the Gini coefficients for the present study have been collected from different studies and sources and this may be a limitation of the study.

Be that as it may, as Table 13.1 reveals, income inequalities in Hong Kong went on decreasing from 1986 (Gini coefficient 0.49) until 1980 (Gini coefficient 0.37). However, since the 1980s, the inequalities started rising and the Gini coefficient went up in 1996. The same trend is noticeable in South Korea which recorded a slight rise in the values of Gini coefficient (0.40) in 1988. But since at the time of writing data are not available for the later years, it is difficult to say whether the rising trend was sustained or not. For Singapore, as elsewhere, income inequalities reduced with economic development in the initial years with a Gini coefficient of 0.50 in 1966 declining to 0.41 in 1980. In 1989, the value of the Gini coefficient went up to 0.49. The story is similar for Taiwan where income inequalities went down from 1966 until 1980 after which there was a moderate rise in inequalities. In 1997, the value of its Gini coefficient was 0.32 which was slightly higher than that in 1980 (0.31). In terms of the absolute value of income inequalities and the moderation in the degree of their rise with economic development, Taiwan can be regarded as the best performing country in the East Asian group.

Income inequalities in Indonesia showed a gradual decline from 1980 (Gini coefficient 0.34) to 1990 (Gini coefficient 0.32). But since 1990, income inequalities started increasing and the value of its Gini coefficient rose to 0.36 in 1996. The low absolute value of the Gini coefficient in the case of Indonesia is, however, questionable. In the Philippines, income inequalities went on gradually decreasing between 1965 (Gini coefficient 0.49) and 1989 (0.45). Available data reveal that income inequalities went up in the Philippines in 1997 (Gini coefficient 0.49).

For Malaysia, income inequalities, came down perceptibly between 1967 (Gini coefficient 0.50) and 1990 (Gini coefficient 0.44). But after 1990, income inequalities started rising again, and in 1995, the value of its Gini coefficient went up to 0.49.

*Table 13.1* *Trends in income inequalities in East Asian countries indicated by Gini coefficients*

| Year | Hong Kong | South Korea | Singa-pore | Taiwan | Indo-nesia | Malaysia | Philip-pines | Thai-land |
|---|---|---|---|---|---|---|---|---|
| 1964 | | 0.34 | | 0.36 | | | | |
| 1965 | | | | | | | 0.49 | 0.47 |
| 1966 | 0.49 | | 0.50 | | | | | |
| 1968 | | | | | | 0.50 | | 0.43 |
| 1970 | | 0.33 | | 0.30 | 0.35[d] | 0.51 | | |
| 1971 | 0.44 | | | | | | 0.48 | |
| 1973 | | | 0.46 | | | | | |
| 1975 | | | | | | | | 0.45 |
| 1976 | | 0.39 | | 0.31 | 0.34 | 0.53 | | |
| 1979 | | | | | | 0.49 | | |
| 1980 | 0.37 | 0.39 | 0.41 | 0.31 | 0.34 | | | |
| 1981 | | | | | | | | 0.45 |
| 1985 | | | | 0.32 | | | | |
| 1986 | 0.42 | | 0.46 | | | | 0.45 | |
| 1988 | | 0.40 | | | | 0.46 | | 0.48 |
| 1989 | | | 0.49 | | | | 0.45 | |
| 1990 | | | | 0.31 | 0.32 | 0.44[c] | | 0.50 |
| 1991 | 0.45 | | | | | | | |
| 1992 | | | | | | 0.48[b] | | 0.54 |
| 1993 | | | | | 0.34 | | | |
| 1994 | | | | | | | | |
| 1995 | | | | | 0.34[d] | 0.49[b] | | |
| 1996 | 0.52[a] | | | | 0.36[e] | | | |
| 1997 | | | | 0.32[b] | | | 0.49[e] | |
| 1998 | | | | | | | | |
| 1999 | | | | | | | | 0.44[e] |

*Sources*: Medhi (1994, 1996).
[a] Hong Kong Department of Census and Statistics (1996).
[b] Rao (1988, 2001, pp. 34-7).
[c] Government of Malaysia (1996, p. 91).
[d] Ahuja et al. (1997).
[e] Asian Development Bank (2000).

As some data are available, it has been possible to study income inequalities in Malaysia in greater details in terms both of the Atkinson index and of Gini coefficients. It is also possible now to look into the issue of racial income inequalities in Malaysia, which has often remained a perennial source of vitriolic debate among leaders and academicians in Malaysia. Let me first concentrate on the Atkinson index which is a measure through which one can compare two situations with respect to inequality on the basic of social welfare indices.

Atkinson uses the concept of an equally distributed equivalent level of income (Ye) as that amount of income which, if equally distributed, gives the same level of welfare as the original distribution. The Atkinson index (AI) can be expressed as:

$$A_I = 1 - \left(Y_e / \overline{Y}\right) \qquad (13.1)$$

Where $Y_e < \overline{Y}$, this becomes the isoelastic case, and

$$A = 1 - \left[\frac{1}{n}\sum_{i=1}^{n}\left(\frac{Y_i}{\overline{Y}}\right)^{1-e}\right]^{\frac{1}{1-e}} \qquad (13.2)$$

where,

$Y_i$ = mean income of group I

$\overline{Y}$ = mean income of total population

$n$ = size of population

The meaning of this index (13.1) can be understood with the help of a specific example. Supposing $A_I = 0.7$, it implies that if only 30 per cent of the total current income were equally distributed, it would be valued as equivalent to the original situation. This can be known by rearranging the equation (13.1) in the following way:

$$Y_e = \overline{Y}(1 - A_1) \qquad (13.3)$$

The value of $A_I$ can vary from 0 to 1. In the case of the Atkinson measure, the shape of the social welfare function is very much related to the size of the parameter (e) which measures the degree of inequality aversion. The higher the value of e, the greater is the inequality aversion. If the value of the index is zero, it implies that there is an indifference about the changes in income distribution as all incomes are equal. If e = zero, this is a Rawlsian case where income transfer to the lowest income group can increase social welfare. If the value of ($A_I$) falls, the income distribution becomes more equal, and such a policy is needed to achieve more equal social welfare.

Nevertheless, the ethnic income inequalities in Malaysia on the basis of the Atkinson index show that between 1980 and 1990, racial income inequalities in the country substantially decreased but started increasing after 1990 (Table 13.2). As the table shows, with different values of parameter (1 - e), the levels of income inequality become different, and as the values of the parameter go up, the values of the inequality index go down.

*Table 13.2 Atkinson index for ethnic income distribution in Malaysia during 1980-1995*

| Year | 1-e=-1.7 | 1-e=0.1 | 1-e=0.2 | 1-e=0.4 | 1-e=0.5 | 1-e=0.7 | 1-e=0.9 |
|---|---|---|---|---|---|---|---|
| 1995 | 0.2414 | 0.0343 | 0.0307 | 0.0233 | 0.0196 | 0.0119 | 0.0040 |
| 1990 | 0.2027 | 0.0282 | 0.0252 | 0.0191 | 0.0161 | 0.0097 | 0.0033 |
| 1985 | 0.2252 | 0.0308 | 0.0275 | 0.0208 | 0.0174 | 0.0105 | 0.0035 |
| 1980 | 0.3162 | 0.0459 | 0.0410 | 0.0311 | 0.0261 | 0.0158 | 0.0053 |

*Source*: Estimated by the author.

The analysis of ethnic income inequalities in terms of Gini coefficients more or less corroborates this conclusion. In the present analysis, the calculation of income inequalities for the different ethnic groups in Malaysia is based on the following simplistic expression of Gini coefficient: G indicates the area between the Lorenz curve and the diagonal which shows the line of perfect equality. The Gini coefficient (G) can be estimated as:

$$G = 0.5\sum_{i=1}^{n}[Y_{i-1}X_i - X_{i-1}Y_i] \tag{13.4}$$

where,

$n$ = number of groups (ethnic groups in the case of Malaysia)
$X_i$ = proportion of population in group i in the total population
$Y_i$ = proportion of income of group i in the total income

The analysis shows that income inequalities in Malaysia among the ethnic groups consisting of Malays, Chinese, Indians and the rest declined after 1980 but after 1990, the inequalities started increasing (Table 13.3). The trend in racial income inequalities in Malaysia is similar to the trend in general income inequalities among various income classes regardless of ethnic consideration.

*Table 13.3 Income inequalities among the ethnic groups in Malaysia*

| Year | 1980 | 1985 | 1990 | 1995 |
|---|---|---|---|---|
| Value of Gini coefficients | 0.53 | 0.37 | 0.40 | 0.41 |

*Source*: Estimated by the author.

As a matter of fact, Malaysia happens to be the country with the highest income inequalities among the twelve Asian countries (Table 13.4). The UNDP *Human Development Report 1996* indicates that economic growth rate is not negatively correlated with the degree of income inequality. Thus, countries like Bangladesh, Sri Lanka and India whose economic growth rates are much lower than the rate of economic growth of Malaysia have lower income inequalities in the sense that the income shares of thelowest 40 per cent of these households are much higher than those in Malaysia.

*Table 13.4 Income inequalities in Asia according to UNDP (1996)*

| Country | Income share (%) by lowest 40% of households | Ratio of income share of highest 20% to lowest 20% of households |
|---|---|---|
| Hong Kong | 16.2 | 8.7 |
| Republic of Korea | 19.7 | 5.6 |
| Singapore | 15.0 | 9.6 |
| Thailand | 15.5 | 8.3 |
| Malaysia | 12.9 | 11.7 |
| Sri Lanka | 22.0 | 4.4 |
| Philippines | 16.6 | 7.4 |
| Indonesia | 20.8 | 4.9 |
| China | 17.4 | 6.5 |
| Vietnam | 19.2 | 5.6 |
| India | 21.3 | 4.7 |
| Bangladesh | 22.9 | 4.1 |

*Source*: UNDP, *Human Development Report 1996*.

The data presented earlier show that for the eight East Asian countries, excepting Thailand, income inequalities declined with economic development, albeit in some cases nominally at the initial stage; but subsequently, such inequalities started rising as these countries became more mature. The pertinent question that one may ask is: Why did income inequalities initially decline in these East Asian countries? The answer to such a question is provided by the more or less common strategies that these countries adopted to improve the economic conditions of the lower strata of the population using need-based micro-welfare strategies in these countries.

The common strategies to ameliorate the conditions of the poor included, among other things, the creation of more job opportunities for the poor, supplementary income programmes and the introduction of labour-intensive techniques of industrialisation. The spread of basic and adult education and, in some cases, compulsory primary education went a long way to make the workers more productive and more responsive to changing job opportunities.

In Hong Kong, a number of factors were responsible for the improvement in Gini coefficients in the initial phase of industrialisation. Some of these factors included the occupational shift of population from low-paid primary and tertiary occupations to a high-paid export-oriented manufacturing sector. Hong Kong's real wages rose appreciably and at the same time, its labour force participation rate increased perceptibly (Rao 2001, p. 33). The World Bank's (1993) study concluded that from 1973 to 1987, economic growth in Malaysia was accompanied by improved income distribution resulting from (i) rising share of wages in family income, and (ii) a more even distribution of wages with the broad expansion of education and improvement in literacy. Malaysia's New Economic Policy was able to significantly improve the income distribution pattern of society without adversely affecting the tempo of economic growth.

The improvement in the relative income distribution in the past in Malaysia was due to several reasons. *First*, many successful rural development programmes were able to increase the income of the rural households. *Second,* increase in educational attainment among the Malays relative to other ethnic groups ensured more and better employment opportunities and higher income to the Malays. *Third,* there was restructuring of the ownership of assets in favour of the Malays, which reduced the concentration of wealth in the hands of non-Malays. Thus, between 1970 and 1987, there was overall improvement in income distribution in all ethnic classes in Malaysia. This occurred against a background of a falling income share for the top 20 per cent of the population and a rising income share for the bottom 20 per cent of the people. However, urban income distribution was generally more unequal than rural distribution (Medhi 1994).

In both South Korea and Taiwan, land reforms and agrarian restructuring led to the promotion of labour-intensive patterns of development and contributed substantially to the reduction in income inequalities. In both these countries, an occupational shift of the labour force from the low-paid primary to the high-paid secondary sector was an important means to improve the income distribution of the bottom 20 per cent of the population. The tight labour market situation in both countries was responsible for sustainable higher incomes and employment of the working class. In Taiwan, unlike in

South Korea, the predominance of small and medium-scale industries was also helpful in maintaining the low values of Gini coefficients.

In the case of Indonesia, the decrease in income inequality at the initial phase from a Gini coefficient 0.35 in 1970 to that of 0.32 in 1990 was made possible by agrarian restructuring, additional job creation through increased labour intensity in export industries and the like. More or less the same strategy was responsible for reducing income inequalities in the Philippines between 1965 and 1989. A number of policies and strategies were crucial for the reduction in income inequalities between 1996 and 1980 in Singapore. Labour market dynamics had indeed played a significant role in creating new openings and in reducing the rate of unemployment and underemployment. Labour force participation rate, particularly for females, and the government policy to raise wages also went a long way in moderating income inequalities (Rao 2001, p. 36).

In contradistinction to this, in Thailand, the measures to reduce poverty have not been as successful as those for reducing income inequalities. Only in 1999, the value of its Gini coefficient came down to 0.44 after a protracted period of increasing income inequalities since 1975. Obviously, the programmes implemented to boost income and employment of the Thai people in the wake of Thai financial crises have produced some moderating effect on income inequalities.

## 13.4 WHY IS INCOME INEQUALITY RISING IN EAST ASIA?

In all the East Asian countries studied here, except Thailand, income inequalities are found to be rising in the second phase of their industrialisation process. The observation of the World Bank (1993) that these countries had been experiencing growth with equity was valid only in the initial phase of their industrialisation process. However, in the 1990s, income inequalities in most of these countries began to rise conspicuously, following earlier decline. The earlier trend is reversed now. It is indeed intriguing to consider the reasons for such a reversal of the trend in income inequalities. Hence the present section is devoted to identifying and discussing causes of the contemporary phenomenon of rising income inequalities in the East Asian economies.

Many basic common factors and forces in the second phase of industrialisation in the East Asian economies are primarily responsible for their spurt in income inequalities. These common factors are: structural transformation favouring capital- and technology-intensive methods of production, concentration of economic power and growth of monopolies, growth of state capitalism and cronyism and the like.

Inequalities in educational opportunities, as in Malaysia, have led to income inequalities. In the field of education in many East Asian countries, there are both intra-racial and inter-racial inequalities. For instance, in the field of higher education in Malaysia, most of the Bumiputra students are from the richer section and the children from the poor Bumiputra community constitute only a negligible proportion. Even in countries like Singapore where there are officially declared equal opportunities for education, children from the lower income groups do not have the same effective equal opportunities for higher education as children from higher income groups for many reasons of which lower income is predominant. When income levels are very different, effective opportunities and choices cannot be the same. Higher education can be afforded only by rich people in East Asia as a rule. At present, the rich Malays are having a higher share of subsidies at the secondary and tertiary levels of education compared to the poor Malays (Ghosh 2000, p. 92). A higher rate of human investment by the richer class has been largely responsible for the recent widening income inequalities in these fast growing market economies where there are better opportunities and higher income prospects for the more skilled and professional workers.

A paradigm shift in the production process from labour-intensive (lower value added) to capital/technology-intensive (higher value added) modes of production have made unskilled labourers, who are generally from the low-paid working class, feel alienated and rejected in the labour market. This was evident in Malaysia, South Korea and Singapore. The small size of the economy of Singapore could ensure full employment of the labour force although at a relatively low level of income. But higher human capital investment by the elite class has been responsible for the widening gap in wages and salaries there. This was also true for the Malaysian economy where the pay differences between ordinary workers and skilled professional workers are much higher now (almost ten times) than in the 1960s and 1970. Moreover, some countries like South Korea, Singapore and Malaysia imported qualified labour from abroad, and this adversely impacted on the wage and employment of local labour. Various types of structural adjustments needed by these economies to accelerate their economic growth did not favour the poorer class, and these intensified income inequalities. In South Korea, the vertical growth of big industrial conglomerates (*chaebols*) led to the concentration of wealth and growth of monopoly power in a few hands. The returns to assets and land became abnormally high, and income inequalities between the owners and non-owners of assets widened increasingly.

In Hong Kong, politico-economic reasons compelled the movement of labour-intensive manufacturing operations to China. The policy of de-industrialisation reduced labour demand and wages. This structural transformation trivialised the importance of the manufacturing sector in Hong Kong and the workforce had to fall back mostly upon the low-paid services sector. It needs to be appreciated that services occupations in less developed countries, unlike in developed countries, are poverty and low-income induced. As a result of an occupational shift in Hong Kong in favour of low-paid tertiary jobs, its labour force participation rate fell appreciably and its labour income declined. Consequently, income inequalities in Hong Kong rose. However, in Taiwan, the restructuring in the manufacturing sector was not so unfavourable to the interests of the working class as there was more or less a balance between industrial and services employment. But since structural adjustments led to declining manufacturing employment, some labourers lost lucrative jobs, and income inequalities increased, albeit to a moderate degree. The policy of egalitarianism at the back of the development philosophy of Taiwan is perhaps responsible for moderating its upswing in income inequalities.

During their phase of high economic growth, some classes of people in most Asian countries got special favours such as the business class, rich landlords, the bureaucrats and the cronies. They received favours that enabled them to accumulate more money and wealth, and these classes became more dominant in later years. Also, states (governments) in many East Asian countries became capitalists and wanted to extract more surplus to compete with the private sector. When government industries were privatised, the contracts went mostly to the government cronies who benefited substantially from such clandestine deals. Rampant political cronyism has been alleged in the cases of the Philippines, Malaysia and Indonesia (Ng and Toh 1992, p. 64).

In a bid to achieve a high rate of economic growth, many policies started earlier to assist the poor had been abandoned either for political or economic reasons. The New Economic Policy in Malaysia is a case in point. In some cases, the budget for poverty alleviation was reduced in the name of higher economic growth. Both agriculture and the social sector were neglected during the phase of industrial upswing and the fruits of development did not trickle down to the poor. This was true for Thailand, Indonesia, Malaysia and to some extent the Philippines. Serious data problems for Indonesia and Thailand do not allow one to appreciate fully the true nature and extent of overt income inequalities. However, the trend towards higher income inequalities is illustrated.

The changing demographic structure in many developing countries of East Asia is suggested as a factor contributing to increased income inequalities (Islam and Chowdhury 1997). In these countries, the proportion of ageing people is gradually rising. This phenomenon has been responsible for increasing the dependency load on both the society and the family. The burden of this dependency load is much greater on the poor than on the rich families. The differential burden may be a plausible contributing factor for heightened income inequalities in these countries. But, unfortunately, household income survey data do not often consider the family size differences.

From the foregoing analysis of income inequalities in eight Southeast Asian economies, a few generalisations are possible. These are about the nature and typology of their economic structure, and the reliability and comparability of income distribution data in these countries. From Table 13.1, it becomes clear that there are basically three types of East Asian economies with respect to income inequalities. The economies with high degrees of income inequalities (Gini coefficient around 0.50) include Hong Kong, Malaysia and Thailand. The economies with moderate degrees of income inequalities (Gini coefficient around 0.4) include Singapore and the Philippines, and the economies with low degrees of income inequalities (Gini coefficient around 0.30) include Taiwan, South Korea and Indonesia. It should be noted that the natural or normal value of Gini coefficient for a country is a type of epiphenomenon, it is a function of many factors and forces including the structure of the economy and its occupational distribution of population, resources endowment, development philosophy, policy responses and so on. Income inequalities are basically linked with structural inequalities, and structural factors seem to be partly responsible for the difference in the natural degrees of income inequalities.

However, it must be remembered that the estimated Gini coefficients may partly be a reflection of the nature and type of data used. The income data gathered from household surveys may exclude non-agricultural households. Such surveys (Ginneken and Park 1984) also experience under-reporting of income from various sources. There is often an element of embedded inequality in the estimates of household incomes in the sense that many households may have the same level of income but the family size may be different. Different types of household income/expenditure surveys will have different coverage. For instance, in many labour force surveys, all types of income (especially income from assets or wealth) are not included. Hence, there is a bias resulting in under-reporting of income.

Household income can also be gathered from national accounts. But whether the two sources of income data (household surveys and national income accounts) are comparable or not will depend on the degree of comprehensiveness of the income concept used in household surveys. If the income concept is not comprehensive, it cannot be compared with that of national income accounts. Moreover, survey estimates of income may constitute different percentages of GNP over time, and this may affect the accuracy of Gini coefficients estimated from survey incomes. Generally speaking, the higher the value of the survey income estimate as a percentage of GNP, the more comparable and reliable will be the Gini coefficients. But in reality, different survey estimates of income generally do have different ratios with GNP over a long period of time, even for the same country and for the same type of survey. Thus, because of all constraints, Gini coefficients need to be interpreted with caution and circumspection.

## 13.5 CONCLUDING OBSERVATIONS

Although the studies conducted by the World Bank (1993) and Ahuja et al. (1997) on income inequalities in the East Asian countries did not find any conclusive uniform trend, the latter study found an upward trend in the cases of Hong Kong, Taiwan and Thailand. However, the data used by this study for Singapore (1989), Malaysia (1989), Indonesia (1995) and South Korea (1998), were not up to date. Moreover, their study does not take into account the case of the Philippines. The study presented here considers data for a longer period, namely from 1964 to 1999. The present analysis has been able to establish a rising trend in income inequalities in recent years for Hong Kong, Singapore, Taiwan, Indonesia, Malaysia, the Philippines and South Korea. For Thailand, a lower value of its Gini coefficient was achieved after fourteen years. The present study has generated two broad conclusions. First, the data in the present study show that in the early years of economic development, these countries exhibited a gradual reduction in the degree of skewness in their income distribution – a diametrically opposite conclusion to that predicted by the Kuznets' thesis. Secondly, the present study detects an upward trend in income inequalities in East Asian countries that have experienced high and sustained rates of economic growth. This is contrary to what one may expect on the basis of the Kuznets' thesis. It is, thus, reasonable to conclude that the Kuznets' thesis does not basically apply to these newly emerging market economies, except possibly to Thailand. The case of Thailand does accord with the Kuznets' thesis: in the early phase of its development, Thailand witnessed increasing income inequalities but at the late stage when the Thai economy has substantially developed, the Gini ratio started falling. However, the falling trend is not yet well established.

Be that as it may, the present study has a few limitations. First, the generalisation of increasing trend in income inequalities in some cases has been based on the observation of one or two years' rising trend of Gini coefficients. Such a type of observation may not be warranted to establish a secular trend. Second, although the data used here are drawn from published secondary sources, these may not be free from criticism in terms of comparability and reliability. This is particularly true when the income distribution data for the same country have been drawn from different sources. Often, a researcher has no option but to follow this practice of collecting data like a magpie to make the study up to date when a single source of data is inadequate or not at all suitable for the purpose. Third, the rise in income inequalities has been very negligible in some cases and many may not like to call it an upward trend.

In view of all these limitations, it needs to be appreciated that for a study of this genre, problems with data are well recognised and understood by researchers. However, the data problem should not be considered as too formidable to draw some useful conclusions, at least in the short run. Although the present study does not claim to have established a well-entrenched long-term tend of rising income inequalities in the East Asian economies, it does demonstrate a tendency, however transitory it may be, for these economies to have increasingly skewed income distribution patterns. The conclusion per se may provide an important signal to the leaders and policy-makers of the East Asian economies. The study prima facie provides at least a refutable hypothesis.

It should be noted that most of the East Asian economies are integrated into the world capitalist system and these newly industrialising countries are heavily entangled with the process of globalisation. This is evident from their linkage with the international capital inflow, technology, market and financial interdependence. From the perspective of modern world development, the dependence on capital- and technology-intensive methods of development is itself a manifestation of a more intense relation between the developed and the fast developing world of the East Asian economies. This relationship is a reflection of globalisation in terms of reciprocity of both production, distribution and financial networks. The East Asian economies examined in this chapter are part and parcel of the globalisation process. The mutuality of relations for both these types of economies (the developed and the newly emerging market economies) indicates a very high degree of interdependence in a globalised capitalist world.[1]

## NOTE

1. B.N. Ghosh is a Visiting Professor of Economics, Department of Economics, Eastern Mediterranean University, G. Magusa, Mersin: 10, Turkish Republic of North Cyprus (Turkey), and Director (Hon.) Centre for the Study of Human Development at Leeds (England). Professor Ghosh expresses his indebtedness to Dr Pundarik Mukhopadhaya of the National University of Singapore for his valuable comments and useful suggestions on an earlier draft of the paper. He is thankful to Lean Hooi for her superb computational assistance.

## REFERENCES

Ahuja, V., B. Bidani, F. Ferreira and M. Walton (1997), *Everyone's Miracle? Revisiting Poverty and Inequality in East Asia*, Washington DC: World Bank.

Asian Development Bank (2000), *Asian Development Outlook 2000, Update*, Manila: Asian Development Bank.

Ghosh, B.N. (2000), *The Three Dimensional Man*, Kuala Lumpur: Utusan Publications.

Ginneken, W. V. and Jong-goo Park (1984), *Generating Internationally Comparable Income Distribution Estimates*, Geneva: ILO.

Government of Malaysia (1996), *Seventh Malaysia Plan*, Kuala Lumpur: Government Press.

Harcourt, W. (1997), 'The search for social justice', *Development*, **40** (1), 5-11.

Hong Kong Department of Census and Statistics (1996), http://www.info.gov.hk/censtatd/home.html.

Islam, I. and A. Chowdhury (1997), *Asia Pacific Economies: A Survey*, London: Routledge

Kuznets, S. (1955), 'Economic growth and income inequality', *American Economic Review*, May, **45**, 1-28.

Medhi, K. (1994), 'Income distribution in East Asian developing countries: an update', *Asian Pacific Economic Literature*, **8** (2), 58-73.

Medhi, K. (1996), *Changes in Poverty and Income Inequality in Thailand: 1962/6 to 1992*, Working Paper 1/96, Sydney: School of Economics, The University of New South Wales.

Ng, C.Y. and K.W. Toh (1992), 'Privatisation in the Asia-Pacific region', *Asian Pacific Economic Literature*, **5** (3), 42-68.

Rao, V.V. Bhanoji (1988), 'Income distribution in East Asian developing countries', *Asian Pacific Economic Literature,* March, **2** (1), 26-45.

Rao, V.V. Bhanoji (2001), *East Asian Economies: The Miracles, a Crisis and the Future*, Singapore: McGraw Hill.

UNDP (1996), *Human Development Report 1996, Economic Growth and Human Development*, New York: Human Development Report Unit.

World Bank (1993), *East Asian Miracle: Economic Growth and Public Policy*, New York: Oxford University Press.

# 14. Structural Adjustment Programmes in Bangladesh: Their Origin, Implementation and Effects

**M. Zainul Abedin**

## 14.1 INTRODUCTION

Structural Adjustment Programmes (SAP) as a part of the globalisation process, were accepted by the Government of Bangladesh in the mid-1980s but their implementation was hampered by the floods of 1987 and 1988 and the mass movement of 1989-90 against the then autocratic regime. Substantial implementation of the programmes was not actually started until the early 1990s after a new government came to office in 1991. During the last decade, the SAP were partially successful in removing Bangladesh's serious balance of payments problems, keeping its inflation rates at reasonable levels, reducing budget deficits, promoting the growth rates of gross national income, savings and investment, and in raising the growth rates of both exports and imports to over the pre-SAP levels. Effects on the social sector were also positive and encouraging.

But social and political instability and high levels of corruption hampered the implementation of SAPs in Bangladesh. Democratic practices, accountability, good governance, and commitment of the government in power are necessary for the success of SAPs. Future adjustment programmes should address these issues for reasons outlined here.

Bangladesh's economy is characterised by comparatively low levels of per capita income and low effective demand, high rates of population growth and unemployment. Its illiteracy rate is high. The subsistence agriculture sector still constitutes about a quarter of its gross domestic product (GDP) while the modern manufacturing sector contributes only 17 per cent of the same. Its relatively low rate of saving is an obstacle to efforts to increase investment. More than a half of its development expenditure is met from foreign aid and grants. Its unfavourable situation faced a new threat from the changing world conditions after 11 September, 2001 attacks on New York's World Trade

Center and Pentagon Head Office, and the subsequent war in Afghanistan. Those changing conditions posed a threat to the growing export earnings of Bangladesh, especially from the ready-made garments sub-sector.

Besides, during the last four decades, the country experienced 56 major cyclones and floods, including 17 inundations affecting about one-fifth of the terrain. The devastating floods of 1988 were so severe that the cost of reconstruction and rehabilitation was estimated to be about 4.4 per cent of GDP (ESCAP 1990). After only 10 years, another devastating two-month long flood in 1998 heavily damaged houses, offices, factories, cattle population, crops and other resources in 51 out of the 64 districts of Bangladesh. The duration and damage of these floods surpassed all previous records. That reduced GDP growth rate from the projected 6 per cent to around 5 per cent in 1999.

With these and many other problems, Bangladesh, an independent nation for 30 years, is struggling hard to attain a reasonable level of development that can ensure the basic needs for its people. At different stages, the country was variously termed as a bottomless basket, a test case of development, the largest slum of the world, and so on. But in the early 1990s Bangladesh was seen as an emerging tiger of South Asia.

In its development efforts Bangladesh adopted planning as an economic policy and method for eradicating poverty and attaining progress. Ambitious Five-Year Plans (FYP) were prepared but those were only partially implemented due mainly to the lack of available resources to execute them. Early attempts at restructuring the economy in the 1970s through nationalisation of major industries and banks, price control and so on failed, mainly due to lack of proper institutional support, untrained manpower, and absence of firm political commitment. The denationalisation programmes and other open policies undertaken by post-1975 regimes led to many financial and fiscal problems. With a few exceptions, these, reinforced by socio-political unrest, contributed to macroeconomic mismanagement, corruption, and lack of accountability.

Under the circumstances, Bangladesh had to accept the policy package of Structural Adjustment Programme (SAP) prescribed by the IMF and the World Bank in 1986. Bangladesh received a Structural Adjustment Facility (SAF) loan during 1986-89 and an Extended SAF (ESAF) loan during 1990-1993. In 1991, the newly elected government adopted a comprehensive programme of stabilisation and structural adjustment with the help of the IMF and IDA, which aimed at private-sector led growth. This marked the start of Bangladesh's major globalisation process.

Structural Adjustment Programmes (SAP) include demand management or stabilisation policies, supply promotion or structural adjustment policies, and trade liberalisation policies. It was expected that these policies would remove the weaknesses of the Bangladesh economy. The policies 'sought to address fiscal extravagance, monetary laxity, excessive protectionism, lack of export orientation, exchange rate distortions, excessive domestic economic controls and reliance on the public sector' (Sobhan 1991). To overcome these problems, the SAP policy package aimed to achieve stabilisation in the short run and make necessary adjustments in the structure of the economy in the long run for correcting macroeconomic imbalances and promoting the supply side of the economy. The stabilisation policies included (i) budgetary measures, such as cuts in government expenditure and investment, (ii) monetary measures, such as changes in credit and interest rate policies, and (iii) exchange rate policy adjustments. On the other hand, structural adjustment policies consisted of (i) liberalisation of trade and industrial policies, and (ii) reduced government control of private industry and growing privatisation of the public sector. Domestic liberalisation was required to establish 'true' (market) prices in agricultural and non-agricultural sectors. It aimed at reducing subsidies, eliminating public sector monopolies, abolishing price control and credit rationing measures, lowering import duties and eliminating import restrictions. It was argued that the policies would promote better growth prospects in the medium and long term (Sidhu, 1994).

The major objectives of the SAP policy package in Bangladesh were to: (i) increase the growth rate of its GDP, (ii) raise its agricultural output, (iii) raise tax-GDP and revenue-GDP ratios, (iv) promote exports, (v) mobilise and raise savings and investments, (vi) attract foreign private investments, (vii) control the supply of broad money ($M_2$) by controlling the government's borrowings from the banking system and thereby reduce fiscal deficits and the rate of inflation, and (viii) increase foreign currency reserves and improve balance of payment position. This chapter examines how far these goals were achieved by the middle of 2000, analyses the growth trends of the major macroeconomic indicators of the economy, and suggests measures for macroeconomic improvement.

The time-series data were collected from the sources of the Bangladesh government, Asian Development Bank (ADB) and the World Bank. Implicit GDP deflators (1984/85 = 100) were used to convert current values into the real values of different years. The study period covered two decades from 1979-80 to 1999-2000; the first decade is in the pre-SAP period, and the second decade is in the post-SAP period. This clear division of data was necessary for comparison between the two periods.

A study by Rahman (1992) of the Bangladesh Institute of Development Studies (BIDS) analyses Bangladesh's macroeconomic performance in the 1980s. This comprehensive study explains the growth trend of major macro-variables during the decade of 1980s. It could not show the impact of reforms because in that period those reforms had just been initiated. In the early

1990s some studies were also undertaken by the Centre for Policy Dialogue (1997) but these covered a very limited time period and did not compare the post-SAP period with the pre-SAP period. Therefore, they could not adequately compare the differences of the two periods. This study attempts to fill this gap.

## 14.2 REFORMS IMPLEMENTED SO FAR

Though Bangladesh accepted the policy prescriptions of the IMF and the World Bank in 1986, she was unable to make any meaningful progress in their implementation until 1991. The devastating floods of 1987 and 1988 delayed the process of implementation. So, the actual implementation of the SAP-policy package began after the change of government in 1991. The ground was however, prepared in the late 1980s. The new regime liberalised trade, industrial, credit and exchange rate policies. Attempts were made to open the industrial sector to private entry, deregulate private investment, relax exchange controls, make the Taka convertible on current account transactions, reform business laws, and to downsize the state-owned enterprises. Some of the agricultural policy distortions affecting irrigation, fertiliser use and cropping pattern were removed.

Bangladesh reformed its tax system and introduced the value-added tax (VAT) in 1991 for the purpose of expanding its tax base. The maximum import tariff rate was reduced from 250 per cent to only 45 per cent during 1991-96. The average trade-weighted import tariff rate was brought down to about 21 per cent by 1995.

Foreign direct investment could be undertaken either independently or as a joint venture in all industries except in the four reserved sectors, namely, arms, nuclear energy, forestry and railways. One hundred per cent foreign equity was allowed in all investments. No special permission was required to set up an industry with foreign investments.

By mid-1997, the government had identified over 50 industrial units, including textile factories, sugar mills, chemical works and steel plants for privatisation; but only a few of them could be privatised by mid-2001. To attract private investment into the power sector, the government approved a policy to provide incentives for 'build-operate-transfer' schemes and other investments. The private investors were given 15 years exemption from corporate income tax and allowed to import plant and equipment without paying customs duties, VAT and other surcharges.

With the objective of reducing stock-market speculations, the government issued a set of guidelines outlining the conditions under which loans could be made for the purchase of securities in listed companies. For reducing government deficits, a prudent budget management policy was pursued starting in 1991. Adjustments were made in several administered prices, such as fertiliser, petroleum, electricity and gas. Furthermore, additional fiscal reforms broadened the coverage of VAT and increased non-tax revenue sources.

Financial sector reforms included the withdrawal of public administered rates of interest on deposits and advances, amendment of banking company laws, strengthening of the central bank, adoption of strong measures to deal with the problem of huge outstanding, non-performing loans, setting up of the Financial Loan Court Act 1998, imposing restrictions on the rescheduling of overdue loans, strengthening the Securities and Exchange Commission (SEC), and automation of the Stock Exchange. The Bankruptcy Law 1997 was enacted in 1997 to facilitate the recovery of bad loans. The amended Banking Company Act of 1991 was again amended in 1997 to disqualify defaulting directors from the board of a bank. Meanwhile, some progress was made in removing major defaulters from the directorship of the commercial banks. A central depository company was also created to facilitate scripless trading in corporate stocks. Government efforts are in progress for passing legislation for exploring the possibility of investing a portion of the insurance and private provident and pension funds in the stock market so as to increase the supply of funds to the private capital market.

## 14.3 EFFECTS OF REFORMS

The impact of the reforms is measured here by comparing the data on real GDP, per capita GDP and some other macro-indicators of the post-SAP period with the pre-SAP period. The changes are encouraging and indicative of some progress. The following sections deal with these findings. However, it is very difficult to isolate the impact of SAP on macroeconomic indicators. So, keeping all other variables constant, the post-SAP data are compared with pre-SAP data to determine the differences. It is assumed that the differences are largely influenced by SAP.

### Growth of Real GDP and Real Per Capita GDP

Table 14.1 shows the growth trends of real GDP and real per capita GDP during pre-SAP (1980/81-1989/90) and post-SAP (1990/91-1999/2000) periods. In the first period, except for the years 1989/90 and 1983/84, the growth rates of real GDP were either around 4 per cent or below 4 per cent. The lowest growth rate of real GDP was attained in 1981-82 with only a 1.2 per cent increase. This was because of the poor performance of the dominant agricultural sector due to natural calamities. The same sector also performed badly during 1987-89 due to the damage caused by heavy floods.

*Table 14.1 Growth trends in Bangladesh of real GDP and real per capita GDP (at 1984-1985 constant prices) in pre-SAP (1980/81-1989/90) and post-SAP (1990/91-1999/2000) periods (in crores (10 millions) of taka)*

| **Year**<br>**Pre-SAP** | **Real GDP (crores Tk.)** | **Growth rate (%)** | **Per capita GDP (Tk.)** | **Growth rate (%)** |
|---|---|---|---|---|
| 1980/81 | 35288 | 3.4 | 3899 | 1.06 |
| 1981/82 | 35722 | 1.2 | 3899 | 0.00 |
| 1982/83 | 37470 | 4.9 | 4003 | 2.67 |
| 1983/84 | 39493 | 5.4 | 4127 | 3.09 |
| 1984/85 | 40693 | 3.0 | 4161 | 0.82 |
| 1985/86 | 42459 | 4.3 | 4241 | 1.92 |
| 1986/87 | 44234 | 4.2 | 4320 | 1.86 |
| 1987/88 | 45513 | 2.9 | 4355 | 0.81 |
| 1988/89 | 46661 | 2.5 | 4373 | 0.41 |
| 1989/90 | 49753 | 6.6 | 4569 | 4.48 |
| Total Change % | 41.0 | | 18.42 | |
| Annual Average Change % | 4.1 | | 1.84 | |
| Compounded Growth Rate | 3.89 | — | 1.78 | — |
| **Post-SAP** | | | | |
| 1990/91 | 51444 | 3.4 | 4635 | 1.44 |
| 1991/92 | 53619 | 4.2 | 4741 | 2.29 |
| 1992/93 | 56023 | 4.5 | 4850 | 2.30 |
| 1993/94 | 58384 | 4.2 | 4960 | 2.27 |
| 1994/95 | 60979 | 4.4 | 5086 | 2.54 |
| 1995/96 | 64244 | 5.3 | 5262 | 3.46 |
| 1996/97 | 68021 | 5.9 | 5472 | 3.99 |
| 1997/98 | 71867 | 5.7 | 5695 | 4.08 |
| 1998/99 | 75612 | 5.2 | 5903 | 7.57 |
| 1999/2000 | 80171 | 6.0 | 6166 | 4.46 |
| Total Change % | 55.84 | | 34.95 | |
| Annual Average Change % | 5.6 | | 3.49 | |
| Compounded Growth Rate | 5.05 | — | 3.22 | — |

*Note*: Per capita real GDP was calculated by dividing the real GDP by the population of each year.

*Source*: Ministry of Finance, GOB, *Economic Survey of Bangladesh 2000* (Bengali), pp. 184-5.

The highest growth rate of real GDP of 6.6 per cent was achieved in 1989-90 because of the relatively better performance of the agricultural sector in the post-flood year. Bangladesh's total real GDP increased by 41 per cent and its real per capita GDP rose by only 18.42 per cent in the decade of 1980/81-1989/90. The simple annual average growth rates of its real GDP and real per capita GDP were 4.1 per cent and 1.84 per cent respectively. Its compound growth rates of real GDP and per capita real GDP were 3.89 and 1.78 respectively. Since its population growth rate was around 2 per cent per annum during that period, its actual growth rate of real per capita GDP could not keep pace with population growth. In fact, the growth rates of real per capita GDP for most of the years of that decade were below 2 per cent; and even zero per cent in the year 1981-82. So, the overall performance of the economy was unsatisfactory in the pre-SAP period.

In the first half of the post-SAP decade, the growth rates of Bangladesh's real GDP were around 4 per cent and that of real per capita GDP were over 2 per cent, except for the initial year 1990-91. But in the second-half of the post-SAP period, its growth rates of real GDP were over 5 per cent, and those of per capita real GDP were over 3 per cent. In the decade under the reforms, the real GDP increased by about 56 per cent and per capita real GDP rose by around 35 per cent. The simple annual average increases of real GDP and real per capita GDP were 5.6 per cent and 3.49 per cent, respectively, in the post-SAP decade. Its compound growth rates (CGR) of real GDP and per capita real GDP were 5.05 and 3.22 per cent respectively. Both these rates were much higher than those achieved in the pre-SAP decade.

## Growth Performance of Different Sectors of the Economy

Table 14.2 shows that the dominant agricultural sector of the economy had very unstable and low rates of annual growth during the pre-SAP decade. In the manufacturing sector, the situation was similar. Only the utilities sector (water supply, power and energy supply, sanitary and so on) and miscellaneous sector had relatively stable annual growth rates during that period. Though the public administration and defence sector attained negative annual growth rates in 1981/82 and 1983/84, they achieved the highest annual growth rate of 32.6 per cent in 1984/85 due to the introduction of a new pay scale for public servants. The annual growth rates of all other sectors of the economy were low and unstable during the pre-SAP decade.

The performance of the dominant agricultural sector of the economy was relatively better in the post-SAP period. Though the sector had low annual growth rates (even negative in 1994/95) in the first half of that decade due mainly to droughts and mismanagement of fertiliser supply, it achieved relatively higher and stable annual growth rates in the second half of the

*Table 14.2 Annual growth rates of real GDP in different sectors of Bangladesh in pre-SAP and post-SAP periods in %*

| Year: Pre-SAP | Agri. | Mining | Manuf. | Constr. | Utility | Trans. | Trade | Housing | Pub.Ad | Banking | Misc. |
|---|---|---|---|---|---|---|---|---|---|---|---|
| 1980/81 | 4.2 | -69.2 | -3.0 | 19.8 | 11.1 | 2.2 | -2.8 | 3.1 | 7.4 | 13.5 | 5.9 |
| 1981/82 | 0.2 | 100.0 | 0.3 | 3.6 | 18.5 | 3.8 | 0.4 | 3.2 | -10.7 | 0.1 | 6.4 |
| 1982/83 | 4.2 | -62.5 | 1.9 | -3.4 | 53.1 | 7.2 | 7.4 | 3.1 | 22.5 | 0.5 | 6.5 |
| 1983/84 | 3.6 | 33.3 | 7.5 | 20.1 | 7.1 | 4.2 | 9.1 | 3.0 | -6.9 | 14.5 | 6.8 |
| 1984/85 | 0.7 | - | -1.6 | 12.2 | 8.5 | 4.9 | 7.5 | 3.3 | 32.6 | 3.4 | 4.7 |
| 1985/86 | 3.3 | - | 2.6 | 1.7 | 12.5 | 3.2 | 1.5 | 3.1 | 20.6 | 26.3 | 8.0 |
| 1986/87 | 0.4 | - | 7.9 | 6.8 | 21.8 | 11.1 | 2.6 | 3.3 | 7.8 | 5.5 | 6.9 |
| 1987/88 | -0.8 | - | 0.6 | 12.3 | 16.4 | 3.7 | 3.2 | 3.2 | 7.9 | 1.4 | 11.1 |
| 1988/89 | -1.1 | - | 2.8 | 4.9 | 28.8 | 4.3 | 4.8 | 3.3 | 6.9 | 1.1 | 6.2 |
| 1989/90 | 7.7 | - | 7.2 | 3.2 | 15.3 | 4.3 | 3.0 | 3.3 | 2.6 | 1.1 | 6.3 |
| **Post-SAP** | | | | | | | | | | | |
| 1990/91 | 1.6 | 21.2 | 2.4 | 4.5 | 20.6 | 3.1 | 3.9 | 3.4 | 9.7 | 2.4 | 6.2 |
| 1991/92 | 2.2 | 17.5 | 7.3 | 4.5 | 17.5 | 4.1 | 4.0 | 3.4 | 8.3 | 2.5 | 6.4 |
| 1992/93 | 1.8 | 13.8 | 9.1 | 4.8 | 13.4 | 4.8 | 4.3 | 3.8 | 8.5 | 3.0 | 6.8 |
| 1993/94 | 0.3 | 13.1 | 7.8 | 6.0 | 14.0 | 5.5 | 5.2 | 3.8 | 8.6 | 3.5 | 7.3 |
| 1994/95 | -1.0 | 13.5 | 8.6 | 7.0 | 11.3 | 5.9 | 10.1 | 3.8 | 8.7 | 4.0 | 7.3 |
| 1995/96 | 3.7 | 26.7 | 5.3 | 4.0 | 9.9 | 5.0 | 10.1 | 3.8 | 8.3 | 3.5 | 6.7 |
| 1996/97 | 6.4 | 27.6 | 3.5 | 4.9 | 1.7 | 6.5 | 6.6 | 3.9 | 8.4 | 3.8 | 7.0 |
| 1997/98 | 2.9 | 32.0 | 9.5 | 7.0 | 3.0 | 6.8 | 6.7 | 3.9 | 8.6 | 3.7 | 7.0 |
| 1998/99 | 5.1 | 15.7 | 3.0 | 6.4 | 3.5 | 5.8 | 5.5 | 3.5 | 8.0 | 3.7 | 6.3 |
| 1999/2000 | 7.2 | 19.8 | 4.2 | 6.5 | 3.4 | 5.9 | 5.8 | 3.5 | 7.5 | 3.7 | 6.2 |

*Note*: Utility services include electricity, water, sanitary and so on.

*Source*: Ministry of Finance, GOB, *Economic Survey of Bangladesh 2000* (Bengali), pp. 186-7.

decade due mainly to a favourable climate (except the year 1998), crop diversification, increased supply of agricultural credit and better management of the fertiliser distribution system. The manufacturing sector attained relatively high and stable annual growth rates in the first half of the post-SAP decade due mainly to the better management of the economy and the prevailing stable socioeconomic and political conditions. But the annual growth rates of this sector declined (except the year 1997) in the second half of the post-SAP decade due mainly to mismanagement of the economy, the floods of 1998 and socioeconomic and political unrest. Throughout the post-SAP decade, the mining sector showed high and increasing annual growth rates. However, the share of this sector in GDP is very small, though it is believed to have high potential. The utilities sector (water, sanitary, power and so on) had high annual growth rates in the first half of the post-SAP decade, but the growth rate declined sharply in the second half of the period. All other sectors of the economy had stable and relatively higher annual growth rates in the post-SAP decade than those in the pre-SAP decade.

**Growth Trends of Real GDP, Broad Money, Rate of Inflation, Real Rate of Interest and Forex Reserves**

Table 14.3 displays the growth rates of real GDP, broad money ($M_2$), inflation, real interest and actual foreign exchange reserves in million US dollars in the pre-SAP and post-SAP periods. The simple average annual growth rates of real GDP were 4.1 per cent in the pre-SAP and 5.6 in the post-SAP periods, as against the simple average annual growth rates of broad money ($M_2$) of 11.96 per cent and 11.89 per cent in the respective periods. The differences between the two growth rates (of GDP and $M_2$) were due to increases in rates of monetisation and the rates of inflation (see columns 3 and 5 of Table 14.3). But the difference (7.86) in the pre-SAP decade was higher (also reflected by higher average rate of inflation) than that (6.29) in the post-SAP decade. This is also indicated by the budget deficits shown in Table 14.4. The simple average rate of inflation per annum was 10.28 per cent in the pre-SAP period, and 4.65 per cent in post-SAP period. There were gradual declines of the annual rates of inflation, except for a few ups and downs in the post-SAP years.

With the fall of inflation rates in the post-SAP decade, the real interest rates increased significantly (column 6 of Table 14.3). The simple annual average rate of real interest was 2.09 per cent in the pre-SAP decade, against 3.45 per cent in the post-SAP decade. The rise of the real interest rate was 65 per cent in the post-SAP period compared to that in the pre-SAP period.

The reform package also helped the country to raise its foreign exchange reserves from a simple annual average volume of US$519.3 million in the pre-SAP decade to US$1975.8 million in the post-SAP decade. Here, the rise is over 280 per cent. All these inferences indicate that the performance of the economy was better in the post-SAP decade than that in the pre-SAP decade.

*Table 14.3 Growth trends of Bangladesh's real GDP, broad money, rate of inflation, real rate of interest and forex reserves*

| Year: Pre-SAP | Growth of real GDP % | Growth of $M_2$ (%) | Difference | Rate of inflation | Real rate of interest (%) | Forex reserves (million US$) |
|---|---|---|---|---|---|---|
| (1) | (2) | (3) | (4=3-2) | (5) | (6) | (7) |
| 1980/81 | 3.4 | 21.83 | 18.43 | 11.3 | 0.5 | 155 |
| 1981/82 | 1.2 | 2.45 | 1.25 | 15.8 | (-) 3.3 | 207 |
| 1982/83 | 4.9 | 19.80 | 14.90 | 8.0 | 3.1 | 542 |
| 1983/84 | 5.4 | 24.80 | 19.40 | 13.4 | 3.3 | 406 |
| 1984/85 | 3.0 | 17.83 | 14.83 | 13.2 | 2.1 | 349 |
| 1985/86 | 4.3 | 4.48 | 0.18 | 8.0 | 3.2 | 426 |
| 1986/87 | 4.2 | 2.54 | -1.66 | 10.8 | 2.4 | 866 |
| 1987/88 | 2.9 | 6.45 | 3.55 | 7.8 | 1.1 | 1070 |
| 1988/89 | 2.5 | 8.02 | 5.52 | 7.9 | 4.5 | 523 |
| 1989/90 | 6.6 | 11.35 | 4.75 | 6.6 | 4.0 | 649 |
| Annual average change | 4.1 | 11.96 | 7.86 | 10.28 | 2.09 | 519.3 |
| **Post- SAP** | | | | | | |
| 1990/91 | 3.4 | 2.44 | -0.96 | 7.7 | 1.0 | 1299 |
| 1991/92 | 4.2 | 9.35 | 5.15 | 4.4 | 3.9 | 1847 |
| 1992/93 | 4.5 | 11.32 | 6.82 | 1.5 | 5.5 | 2437 |
| 1993/94 | 4.2 | 15.40 | 11.20 | 1.8 | 5.2 | 3166 |
| 1994/95 | 4.4 | 16.00 | 11.60 | 5.2 | 1.8 | 2367 |
| 1995/96 | 5.3 | 8.20 | 2.90 | 4.0 | 3.0 | 2039 |
| 1996/97 | 5.9 | 10.80 | 4.90 | 2.6 | 6.4 | 1719 |
| 1997/98 | 5.7 | 11.40 | 5.70 | 7.0 | 2.0 | 1739 |
| 1998/99 | 5.2 | 15.40 | 10.20 | 8.9 | 0.1 | 1523 |
| 1999/2000 | 6.0 | 18.60 | 12.60 | 3.4 | 5.6 | 1622 |
| Annual average change | 5.6 | 11.89 | 6.29 | 4.65 | 3.45 | 1975.8 |

*Note*: The real rate of interest is computed as the difference between nominal interest rate on one year term deposit and the average inflation rate, both being the estimates of Bangladesh Bank and Asian Development Bank (1996, 1999 and 2000).

*Sources*: Ministry of Finance, GOB, *Economic Survey of Bangladesh 2000*, pp. 184-5. Asian Development Bank (1996, 1999 and 2000), *Key Indicators 2000*, Vol. XXXI (especially for foreign exchange reserves).

**Trends in Resource Mobilisation, Investments, Expenditure, Deficits, Imports and Exports.**

The crux of the macroeconomic management problem of Bangladesh is associated with the existence of a wide savings-investment gap in every financial year. To meet this resource gap, the country begs from one 'Paris Aid Consortium' to another. In the absence of good governance and accountability, the aid resources are misused at times and shared by vested interest groups and rent-seekers. However, the reform package relies on the real rate of interest as the main policy instrument for raising savings.

Higher nominal rate of interest with high inflation rate, and consequently the lower real rates of interest in the pre-SAP decade failed to raise the savings-GDP ratios. This example suggests that income rather than the real interest rates determines the rates of savings in a low-income country like Bangladesh (annual growth rates of real GDP were also lower in the pre-SAP period).

However, with the rise of real interest rates, accompanied by higher growth rates of real GDP in the post-SAP period (Table 14.4), the savings-GDP ratios increased significantly. Table 14.4 illustrates that both the domestic savings-GDP ratios and national savings-GDP ratios were remarkably higher in the post-SAP decade than those in the pre-SAP decade. Similar were the performance of the public investment-GDP ratios, private investment-GDP ratios and total investment-GDP ratios. Improvements were also made in the case of tax-GDP ratios and total revenue-GDP ratios. But the total government expenditure-GDP ratios were relatively more stable in pre-SAP and post-SAP decades. As a result, the budget deficit-GDP ratios were lower in the post-SAP decade than that in the pre-SAP decade.

Both the import-GDP ratios and the export-GDP ratios were higher in the post-SAP decade than in the pre-SAP decade. Again, the performance of the export sector was better in the post-SAP decade than that in the pre-SAP decade.

## 14.4 EFFECTS ON THE SOCIAL SECTOR AND PUBLIC INVESTMENT

Bangladesh's government has been implementing different socioeconomic development programmes (education, health, social security and social welfare) since its independence in 1971. The goal of its socioeconomic development programme is to reduce poverty and illiteracy and increase the capacity of the poor to cope with socioeconomic conditions. With this end in view, the government annually allocates a portion of its revenue and

*Table 14.4 Trends in resource mobilisation, investments, expenditure, deficits, export and import (as % of GDP) in Bangladesh pre- and post-SAP*

| Year<br>Pre-SAP | Savings (domestic) | Savings (national) | Total invt. | Public invt. | Private invt. | Total revenue | Tax | Total govt. expenditure | Budget deficit | Import | Export |
|---|---|---|---|---|---|---|---|---|---|---|---|
| 1980/81 | 3.24 | 5.88 | 10.53 | 6.34 | 4.19 | 7.52 | 5.97 | 16.62 | -9.1 | 15.98 | 4.92 |
| 1981/82 | 1.97 | 2.73 | 10.39 | 5.96 | 4.43 | 9.70 | 7.69 | 18.40 | -8.7 | 14.60 | 4.67 |
| 1982/83 | 3.38 | 4.58 | 10.30 | 6.05 | 4.25 | 9.94 | 8.14 | 21.14 | -11.2 | 15.69 | 6.24 |
| 1983/84 | 2.90 | 4.74 | 11.03 | 6.38 | 4.65 | 6.94 | 6.70 | 16.14 | -9.2 | 14.53 | 5.75 |
| 1984/85 | 2.33 | 4.45 | 12.77 | 5.43 | 7.34 | 8.81 | 8.21 | 16.01 | -7.2 | 16.76 | 6.44 |
| 1985/86 | 3.05 | 5.77 | 12.37 | 6.09 | 6.28 | 8.22 | 6.89 | 15.82 | -7.6 | 13.49 | 5.87 |
| 1986/87 | 3.16 | 6.42 | 12.53 | 7.84 | 4.69 | 8.56 | 6.90 | 16.96 | -8.4 | 12.70 | 6.24 |
| 1987/88 | 2.84 | 6.40 | 12.93 | 5.81 | 7.12 | 9.58 | 7.82 | 17.38 | -7.8 | 17.03 | 7.65 |
| 1988/89 | 1.96 | 6.06 | 11.49 | 4.99 | 6.50 | 9.25 | 7.51 | 16.65 | -7.4 | 14.41 | 6.47 |
| 1989/90 | 2.00 | 9.20 | 12.80 | 6.40 | 6.40 | 9.30 | 7.80 | 17.10 | -7.9 | 16.90 | 6.80 |
| **Post- SAP** | | | | | | | | | | | |
| 1990/91 | 4.1 | 10.9 | 11.5 | 5.7 | 5.80 | 9.6 | 7.8 | 16.8 | -7.2 | 15.0 | 7.3 |
| 1991/92 | 5.8 | 13.0 | 12.1 | 5.5 | 6.60 | 10.9 | 8.8 | 16.8 | -5.9 | 14.8 | 8.4 |
| 1992/93 | 7.0 | 14.4 | 14.3 | 6.4 | 7.80 | 12.0 | 9.6 | 17.9 | -5.9 | 16.8 | 9.8 |
| 1993/94 | 7.5 | 15.0 | 15.4 | 7.6 | 7.80 | 12.2 | 9.3 | 18.2 | -6.0 | 16.2 | 9.8 |
| 1994/95 | 8.2 | 16.0 | 16.6 | 7.2 | 9.40 | 12.1 | 9.6 | 18.9 | -6.8 | 20.2 | 12.0 |
| 1995/96 | 7.5 | 14.2 | 17.0 | 6.3 | 10.70 | 11.9 | 9.2 | 17.2 | -5.3 | 21.6 | 12.2 |
| 1996/97 | 7.5 | 14.8 | 17.3 | 6.5 | 10.80 | 12.2 | 10.0 | 17.3 | -5.1 | 21.8 | 13.5 |
| 1997/98 | 8.6 | 14.8 | 17.8 | 6.6 | 11.20 | 12.1 | 9.9 | 17.5 | -5.4 | 22.1 | 15.2 |
| 1998/99 | 8.7 | 14.5 | 18.2 | 6.8 | 11.40 | 11.3 | 9.1 | 19.1 | -7.8 | 22.1 | 14.7 |
| 1999/2000 | 9.0 | 15.2 | 18.7 | 7.1 | 11.60 | 12.2 | 9.4 | 18.3 | -6.1 | 22.0 | 14.3 |

*Source*: Ministry of Finance, GOB, *Economic Survey of Bangladesh*, various years.

development budget to such programmes (Table 14.5).

Table 14.5 shows that per capita budget allocation to its social sector in relation to its per capita GDP (current prices) increased in the post-SAP period compared to pre-SAP period. The compound growth rates of the per capita allocation in the social sector as a percentage of per capita GDP were 3.79 and 5.87 in the pre-SAP and post-SAP periods respectively. The social sector includes education, health, social security and social welfare services.

*Table 14.5 Bangladesh government budget allocation to the social sector in pre-SAP (1981-1990) and post-SAP (1991-2000) periods*

| Pre-SAP period year | Allocation (M.Tk) | Per capita allocation (Tk) | Per capita GDP: current price | (3) as % of (4)[a] |
|---|---|---|---|---|
| 1 | 2 | 3 | 4 | 5 |
| 1981 | 4612 | 51 | 2543 | 2.01 |
| 1982 | 5632 | 61 | 2815 | 2.17 |
| 1983 | 6299 | 67 | 3113 | 2.15 |
| 1984 | 6410 | 66 | 3679 | 1.79 |
| 1985 | 9783 | 99 | 4125 | 2.40 |
| 1986 | 11327 | 112 | 4626 | 2.42 |
| 1987 | 13971 | 136 | 5237 | 2.60 |
| 1988 | 16771 | 159 | 5677 | 2.80 |
| 1989 | 17666 | 164 | 6138 | 2.67 |
| 1990 | 20754 | 189 | 6717 | 2.81 |
| Average | | | | 2.38 |
| CGR | | | | 3.79 |
| Post-SAP Period | | | | |
| 1991 | 20783 | 185 | 7443 | 2.49 |
| 1992 | 24440 | 214 | 7935 | 2.70 |
| 1993 | 29406 | 253 | 8144 | 3.11 |
| 1994 | 40568 | 342 | 8685 | 3.94 |
| 1995 | 52066 | 431 | 9679 | 4.45 |
| 1996 | 54154 | 439 | 10563 | 4.16 |
| 1997 | 58902 | 469 | 11173 | 4.20 |
| 1998 | 65640 | 513 | 12100 | 4.24 |
| 1999 | 73250 | 571 | 13554 | 4.21 |
| 2000 | 82480 | 633 | 15230 | 4.16 |
| Average | | | | 3.77 |
| CGR | | | | 5.87 |

*Note*: (a) The per capita average value of 3.77 in the post-SAP period is 58.40 per cent higher than that (2.38) in the pre-SAP period. The social sector allocation was divided by the population to derive per capita allocation.

*Sources*: Social sector allocation data were collected from ADB, *Key Indicators*, 1999, pp. 58-9, for the period from 1981 to 1997, while the rest were collected from GOB, *Economic Survey of Bangladesh*, 2000, p. 26 (Bengali). Social sector includes education, health, social security and social welfare services. Data on per capita GDP (at current prices) were calculated from the GDP figures in GOB, *Economic Survey of Bangladesh*, 2000, pp. 182-3 (Bengali).

These development programmes are implemented by the government to reduce poverty and illiteracy and to increase the capacity of the poor and disadvantaged segments of population to cope with socioeconomic constraints.

Table 14.6 indicates that Bangladesh has had some success in the reduction of poverty in the post-SAP period compared to the pre-SAP period. The percentage of the poor population declined from 59 per cent in 1984 to 53 per cent in 1996; while the percentage of the very poor decreased from 41 per cent to 36 per cent during the same period. However, the rate of reduction in poverty was higher in urban areas and lower in rural areas. Tisdell and Alauddin (2003) also observed that a reduction in the incidence of urban poverty has been associated with the introduction of market-oriented reforms but slight, if any, reduction in rural poverty has occurred.

*Table 14.6 Progress in poverty reduction in Bangladesh: 1984-1996 (percentage of population)*

| Year | Poor (head count index) | | | Very poor (head count index) | | |
|---|---|---|---|---|---|---|
| | Rural | Urban | National | Rural | Urban | National |
| 1984 | 60 | 50 | 59 | 43 | 28 | 41 |
| 1996 | 57 | 35 | 53 | 40 | 14 | 36 |

*Source*: Ahmed (2001, Table 1b, p. 3).

Table 14.7 shows that Bangladesh made significant progress in improving selected human development indicators in the post-SAP period compared to the pre-SAP period. There were considerable improvements in life expectancy, access to safe water, adult literacy rates, primary and secondary enrolments and reduction in total fertility rates and infant mortality rates. Higher growth rates of real GDP allowed the government to increase its financial allocation to the social sector.

However, the overall public investment as percentage of real GDP did not show much improvement in the post-SAP period. Table 14.4 shows that the public investment-GDP ratio fell from 6.4 per cent of GDP in 1989/90 (pre-SAP) to 5.5 per cent in 1991/92 (post-SAP), then again rose to 7.2 per cent in 1994/95 and fell to 6.3 per cent in 1995/96. It slowly increased to 6.8 per cent in 1998/99 and to 7.1 per cent in 1999/2000. It is sometimes argued that in a developing economy like Bangladesh, public investment has positive correlation with private investment (Taylor 1988). To boost private investment, an increase in public investment, especially in the development of infrastructure and social sector, seems to be necessary. However, a lack of adequate commitment by the successive governments, and slow implementation process of reforms meant that the set objectives could only partially be achieved.

*Table 14.7 Indicators of progress with human development in Bangladesh: 1985-1997*

| Indicators | Years | |
|---|---|---|
| | 1985-88 | 1995-97 |
| 1. Life expectancy years | 51 | 60 |
| 2. Infant mortality rate (per 1000) | 118 | 60 |
| 3. Total fertility rate (%) | 5.5 | 3.1 |
| 4. Access to safe water (% of population) | 46 | 84 |
| 5. Adult literacy rate (%) | 33 | 51 |
| 6. Primary school enrolment (%) | 59 | 96 |
| 7. Secondary school enrolment | 17 | 29 |

*Source*: Ahmed (2001, p. 4).

In order to attain economic development as quickly as possible, Bangladesh has been experimenting with various development strategies and implementing reforms one after another since independence in 1971. Lack of continuity in policy directions is a problem since directions change if governments change. Poor economic performance, political instability, social unrest, corruption, terrorism, absence of good governance, and an accountable administration made conditions cloudy and gloomy in the recent past. The future of this country will largely depend upon how effectively the political leadership addresses these problems.

## 14.5 POLICY RECOMMENDATIONS AND CONCLUSIONS

Furthermore, Bangladesh needs to make more progress in improving resource utilisation, largely by reducing corruption and rent-seeking. Improvement in the law and order situation by controlling terrorism and rent-seekers is a precondition for promotion of trade, commerce, industry and development. Good governance and ensuring the accountability of public officials is essential to promote economic development.

It should also be noted that the post-SAP period has seen increasing specialisation in Bangladesh's exports by commodity and destination. For example, by 2000, ready-made garments accounted for over 75 per cent of Bangladesh' total export earnings. Economic theory (for example, the law of comparative advantage) suggests that free trade encourages such specialisation. However, in a dynamic world, this may increase the vulnerability of a country to external economic and political change. The desirability and scope to modify SAPs so as to reduce 'excessive' economic specialisation needs more consideration.

Bangladesh also needs, in my view, more investments for promoting its growth and development. Various incentive packages for attracting more foreign direct investment (FDI) may be needed. Inflows of FDI depend on a country's 'growth prospects, market size, profitability, quality of economic management, few trade barriers, freedom from burdensome regulations on ownership ... government attitude towards private entrepreneurs' (United Nations 1997). Bangladesh should formulate its policies accordingly.

The main focus of any economic programme in Bangladesh should be on maintaining price stability, promoting growth and employment to assist in turn with the eradication of poverty and illiteracy. The political regime should face these challenges and adjust the policies accordingly. Reduction in corruption, rent-seeking, terrorism and improvements in good governance and accountability are necessary preconditions for attracting local and foreign investments. Despite these problems, this chapter indicates that, so far, Bangladesh has benefited significantly from its Structural Adjustment Programmes and its involvement in the globalisation process even though further policy reforms are necessary.

## REFERENCES


Abedin, M. Zainul (1995), 'Impact of Monetary and Fiscal Reforms on Macro Economic Performance: Recent Trends in Bangladesh', *Bangladesh Journal of Political Economy*, **13** (2), 48-61.

Ahmed, Sadiq (2001), 'Bangladesh Since Independence: Development Performance, Constraints and Challenges', *Bangladesh Journal of Political Economy*, **15** (1), 1-29.

Asian Development Bank (1996, 1999 & 2000), *Key Indicators of Developing Asian and Pacific Countries,* Manila: Asian Development Bank.

Centre for Policy Dialogue (CPD) (1997), *Crisis in Governance: A Review of Bangladesh's Development*, Dhaka: University Press Limited.

ESCAP (1990), 'Economic Growth and Structural Transformation in the Asian Least Development Countries', *Economic Bulletin for Asia and the Pacific*, December, Bangkok: ESCAP.

Government of Bangladesh (2000), *Economic Survey of Bangladesh 2000*, Dhaka: Ministry of Finance.

Rahman, S. H. (1992), 'Structural Adjustment and Macroeconomic Performance in Bangladesh in the 1980s', *The Bangladesh Development Studies*, **20**, 89-125.

Sidhu, H. S. (1994), 'India under Structural Adjustment Programme: Performance and Prospects', in G.K. Chadha (ed.), *Policy Perspectives in Indian Economic Development,* New Delhi: Har-Annand Publications.

Sobhan, Rehman. ed. (1991), *Structural Adjustment Policies in the Third World: Design and Experience*, Dhaka: University Press Ltd.

Taylor, L. (1988), *Varieties of Stabilization Experience,* Oxford: Clarendon Press.

Tisdell, Clem and Alauddin, Mohammad. (2003), 'Market Oriented Reforms in Bangladesh and their Impact on Poverty?', in K.R. Sharma (ed.), *Trade Policy, Growth and Poverty in Asian Developing Countries*, London: Routledge, pp.189-201.

United Nations (1997), *Economic and Social Survey of Asia and the Pacific*, New York: United Nations.

# 15. Economic Globalisation and the 'New' Labour Migration in Southeast Asia

**Amarjit Kaur**

## 15.1 INTRODUCTION

The cross-border movement of people, associated with the increased integration of economies and ongoing changes in the international division of labour, forms an essential component of the globalisation process. A sharp increase in labour mobility has coincided with official recruitment agencies and private entrepreneurs providing all sorts of services to migrant workers in exchange for fees. Yet while trade and financial flows are welcomed by nations, labour flows raise concerns about possible influxes of both documented and illegal migrants, the potential erosion of national sovereignty; and, since 11 September 2001, fears of terrorism. This has resulted in more stringent immigration policies and border controls by the state. Migration has thus become a major domestic and international political issue, particularly for developed countries. Moreover, the issue continues to be debated mainly in the context of developed countries. Nevertheless, international migration (in response to global economic forces) within developing regions, such as Southeast Asia, is also an important phenomenon, and worthy of attention on its own.

This chapter examines the changing labour demand patterns and labour supply in the context of increasing economic integration in the Southeast Asian region. It focuses on the economic disparities and structural interdependencies between source and destination countries; and the employment of unskilled contract workers, especially in Malaysia and Singapore. The chapter also makes the point that the institutionalisation of the migration process, particularly for unskilled labour, serves to create both a black market in migration and conditions conducive to human trafficking and exploitation.

## 15.2 MIGRATION IN HISTORICAL AND CONTEMPORARY PERSPECTIVE

### Background

Migration and labour mobility in the region are not new. The imperial-led integration of Southeast Asia into the international economy in the second half of the nineteenth century was consistent with an accelerated demand for Southeast Asian products, particularly those associated with industrial processing and manufacturing, and coincided with the rapid expansion of agricultural and mineral production in the region. Indigenous cultivators, together with an influx of foreign migrant workers became involved in the commercial production of rice, sugar, coffee, tobacco, rubber and tin, resulting in major economic transformations in the region.

Just as labour migration from Europe to the New World had an enormous impact on the economies of these regions, so too did labour migration impact on labour relations and wage labour in Southeast Asia. As subsistence production gave way to new forms of production, various forms of the commodification of indigenous labour and new patterns of labour specialisation emerged. With the exception of areas like Java and North Vietnam, the colonial powers had to rely on a paid workforce to carry out the myriad tasks associated with export production. Consequently, the development of a permanent wage labour force was consistent with Southeast Asia's greater integration into the world economy and the international division of labour. This wage labour force comprised migrants principally from China and India. They worked on an indentured contract basis in the mines, on plantations and in urban occupations. The vast majority of these migrants were regarded as guest workers and sojourners and were not expected to remain on completion of their contracts. Moreover, the design of an ethnic division of labour maintained by the use of political and economic mechanisms ensured labour differentiation along ethnic, gender and occupational lines (Kaur 2003, in press).

What is new about the current migration patterns is that the labour mobility associated with the global restructuring of production is consistent with the 'new international division of labour'. Economic migration is also due to demographic differences and differing levels and rates of economic growth between countries in the region. As before, this international migration needs to be placed in the context of transnational economic developments. These are essential to any analysis of the relationship of globalisation to migration, since much of the labour migration does not operate spontaneously, but takes place within networks, both within the source and receiving countries. Chain migration, for example, within families, extended kinship, or close-knit village-based groups, plays a key role in disseminating information about opportunities available in Malaysia and Singapore, the main receiving countries. Moreover, it minimises both financial and removal disruption costs that migrants face. This cost-minimising factor is critical for two reasons. First, unlike the colonial period, ethnicity and social class have become even more pronounced in migration patterns, and there is both overt and covert hostility to migrants by governments and certain segments of the populations in receiving countries. Moreover, the migrants are forced into segmented labour markets, characterised by wage discrimination, which had led to social tensions. Second, and more important, migrants, their families and prospective employers have to bear the bulk of the financial and social costs associated with migration.

## Migration Patterns

Six main features have characterised the new migration patterns. First, poverty may not be the principal determinant of migration. The three main source or sending countries in Southeast Asia are Indonesia, the Philippines and Thailand, all of which recorded strong economic growth in the last three decades of the twentieth century up to 1997. Migrants in these labour-surplus countries acquired the means to move to countries like Malaysia and Singapore, which experienced sustained and robust economic growth and where there were labour shortages and large differences in wage rates for unskilled workers. In the latter countries, migrant workers (principally from Indonesia, the Philippines and Thailand) comprise between 20-25 per cent of the labour force and are predominantly unskilled or semi-skilled workers.

Second, faced with labour shortages, the Singaporean and Malaysian governments themselves formulated regulations for labour intake targets in consultation with large national employer associations, and in cooperation with governments of sending countries. Their policies are aimed at managing foreign labour flows and at the same time facilitating growth by targeting an appropriate skills mix. Nevertheless, owing to the administrative costs involved, and the insertion of quotas, especially for unskilled contract labour intakes, illegal migration constitutes an important part of the migration streams. Policing people-smugglers and illegal migrants thus represents an important element in the complex and multicentred migration processes in these countries.

Third, unlike the labour migration of the colonial period, when migrants were directed towards the plantation and mining sectors, the new migrant workers are concentrated in the tertiary sector in manual and service employment, with little direct foreign capital involvement. They are employed in four main sectors: agriculture and forestry; construction; services, especially domestic work; and manufacturing. This pattern is consistent with the expansion of tourism and the service industries and is associated with rising levels of prosperity and consumerism among the middle classes in Southeast Asia. Migrant workers from India by comparison are mainly skilled workers.

A fourth significant feature is the growing interconnection between traditional cross-border flows and the more recent forms of migration in areas where there are shared land borders. The phenomenon of daily commuting workers has existed on the Singapore-Johor and Malaysia-Thailand borders since the 1950s at least. In recent years, the Malaysian government has sought to restrict movement along the Thai-Malaysian border (a 27 km wall was built in the late 1990s to stop Thai migrants from entering Malaysia without valid documents), and also the movement of illegal Indonesian workers by sea. Notwithstanding this, the dynamics of demography and development between Sarawak and Kalimantan have resulted in the two governments cooperating in the establishment of a number of large projects at the Entikong-Tebedu border post area (Agustiar 2000, p. 235). This development is part of the growth triangle sub-regional economic zone arrangements involving Indonesia, Malaysia and southern Philippines (Mindanao).

Fifth, unlike the first globalisation era, when migrant workers were predominantly young adult males who migrated without dependants, a large percentage of the new migrant workers are women. This feminisation of the new migrant labour may be attributed to three factors. The first is linked to general changes in the labour markets in Southeast Asia and the production niches (mass-customisation products – electronics, textiles, garments) of Southeast Asian states. The 'new international division of labour', which facilitated the increased labour force participation of women in the formal sector, was consistent with modernisation of the agricultural sector and rural-urban migration, principally of women. There was also a trend towards migration abroad since women's employment in the urban labour market was often impermanent, irregular, and insecure. The second factor is related to the maturing of the labour markets in Singapore and Malaysia, coinciding with relatively high labour force participation rates of women, and general labour shortages in these countries. This in turn created an increased demand for housekeeping and childcare services, which has been met by migrant women workers from the lower-income Southeast Asian countries. Thus, the specific labour needs in the receiving countries for domestic workers largely shaped and continue to shape women's migration in Southeast Asia. The third factor is the attitude of the state itself towards female migration. In the Philippines, the export of people has earned a greater volume of foreign exchange than any single commodity and women migrants are seen as the new heroes who bring in much needed foreign exchange through their remittances. Indonesia too relies on international remittance in its national development plan.

Sixth, a key characteristic of the new labour migration is that this migration is short term and contract-bound, not unlike the labour migration of the colonial period. However, the main difference is that this migration is the migration of free persons, whether dependent on networks or organised through intermediaries. All documented workers have to pay hefty fees – agency fees (including a one way air ticket); insurance fees, a bank guarantee – in both countries, but they cannot stay in the receiving countries on completion of their contracts. They are therefore precluded from making the transition from sojourning to settlement under the complex worker recruitment system. Employers pay their return tickets and face heavy fines if workers are not sent back. In Singapore and Malaysia, workers who overstay are often physically punished. It is therefore not surprising that people smugglers are playing an increasingly important role in transporting illegal migrant workers.

## 15.3 FRAMING THE ECONOMIC AND DEMOGRAPHIC DIVIDE IN THE SOUTHEAST ASIAN REGION

### The Economic Record

At the outset, it should be stated that the economic record of the capitalist Southeast Asian countries since the 1970s has been outstanding. These countries' economic growth was based on three interconnected factors. First, all of them had access to the North American markets, particularly that of the United States. This market access provided, and continues to provide, the demand for their products, which enabled them to make the economic advances and sustain growth. Closer ties through strategic and security relationships between them and the United States also helped. Second, the strengthening of regional ties through the Association of Southeast Asian Nations (ASEAN) and growth triangles, or sub-regional economic zones, have also helped the emergence of a regional economy. More important, however, has been the fostering of Asia-Pacific ties through the Asia Pacific Economic Cooperation (APEC) forum, which embraces Australia, New Zealand and other countries like Japan. Third, the capitalist Southeast Asian countries benefited from trade liberalisation policies and direct foreign investment flows, consistent with free trade and the international institutional structure.

Not all have benefited equally, of course. If we look at one obvious consequence of economic growth, that of GDP per capita, the divergence in development is notable. In 1995, Singapore's GDP per capita was US$22,600 and it made the transition to developed country status. The GDP per capita of the other countries was as follows: Malaysia, US$10,400; Thailand, US$8,000; Indonesia, US$3,800; and the Philippines US$2,800, all at 1995 purchasing power parity equivalents.

### The Demographic Factor

Apart from this economic divide, there were major demographic differences. In 1995, the population of the five countries was as follows: Singapore, 3.3 million; Malaysia, 20.1 million; Thailand, 58.2 million; Indonesia, 166.5 million and the Philippines 67.8 million. Singapore and Malaysia experienced significant tightening of their labour markets, that is, availability of labour relative to demand was low.

The demographic differences between the five countries were crucial to labour market change in the region. Indonesia and the Philippines not only had larger populations compared with Singapore, Malaysia and Thailand but also had higher levels of landlessness and rural poverty. Indonesia, moreover, also had low levels of development in terms of specific social indicators such as education. The problems of a high proportion of employment in low-productivity agriculture, rural poverty and land scarcity in both Indonesia and the Philippines therefore led to varying labour market conditions in the region, and labour thus had an incentive to move from Indonesia and the Philippines (and, to a lesser extent, Thailand), to Singapore and Malaysia. Despite Singapore's and Malaysia's attempts to control and constrain migration, labour markets were, and continue to be, integrated with global capital markets. Southeast Asian economies function in a complementary sense arising from inter-country contrasts in population densities; the incidence of labour surplus or shortage; disparities in demand and wages; and worker education and skills, all of which created strong incentives for intra-Southeast Asian migration.

## 15.4 MALAYSIA: LABOUR FLOWS, SOURCE AND EMPLOYMENT SECTOR

### Introduction

Malaysia has been selected as a prime case to explore the various migration issues outlined above since it was estimated to be the 'largest employer of foreign labour in Asia' in 1999 (Jones 2000, p. 3). Labour migration flows to

Malaysia indicate that the migration networks cover a large number of countries in the region; are consistent with both the growing cross-national income inequality between nations in the region and the links between source and receiving countries. This movement also coincides with reduced barriers to trade and investment and emphasises the inequality between groups that can cross international borders (owners of capital, skilled workers) and those that cannot (unskilled and semi-skilled workers). Globalisation has made the demand for the services of unskilled and semi-skilled workers more elastic and workers from other countries can more easily substitute this category of workers.

Official (documented) migration was characterised by two key features. First, the majority of legal (documented) migrants comprised women, and this labour flow was related to the flexibility of the Southeast Asian female workforce. Studies have shown that female labour force participation in the formal sector increased both absolutely and relative to males. Since economic factors played an important role in influencing participation rates, it is not surprising therefore that women comprised a large percentage of the migration flows. Socio-cultural attitudes in Southeast Asia allowed women, most of them young and unmarried, to travel overseas in search of employment. In their adopted countries, they relied on strong social networks and relationships to survive. Second, Asian women workers' migration was characterised by their concentration in a few occupations – domestic service, the entertainment sector, the hotel and restaurant sector and assembly line work in manufacturing. These were very low status jobs, shunned by local Malaysian (and Singaporean) women because they offered low rewards and limited job prospects. Thus the jobs that had become bearers of gender were in turn passed on to migrant women workers as the local women 'graduated' to other gender-bearing jobs. The major labour flows into Malaysia are shown in Figure 15.1.

## Indonesian Migrant Flows

Indonesian migrant workers dominate labour flows to Malaysia (Hugo 1993b). Moreover, following the Malaysian government's attempts to regulate and control labour migration, flows of undocumented workers also increased. While the labour migration was demand driven, nevertheless it operated within informal and formal networks. Migration flows between Indonesia and Malaysia have strong historical precedents. Consequently, informal networks linking Malaysia and Indonesia were already in existence before the 1970s. These historical and cultural linkages played an important role in facilitating migrant flows from Indonesia to Malaysia.

The Peninsular Malaysia migration system draws workers from East Java, Bawean, Aceh, West Sumatra, Central Java, South Sulawesi and West Nusa Tenggara. Lombok is another source. East Malaysia draws workers mainly from South Sulawesi and Flores in East Nusa Tenggara. Turning to illegal migrants, the migration routes are from East Java and north-west Sumatra to Peninsular Malaysia and Flores-South Sulawesi to Sabah. Reliable details are unavailable on the age composition of these migrant workers. According to one study, about 84 per cent of the illegal immigrant contract workforce on the Malaysian Federal Land Development Authority Scheme (land settlement) plantations were aged between 20 and 30 years. The workers were generally unskilled and had limited education (Hugo 1993a, pp. 45-9).

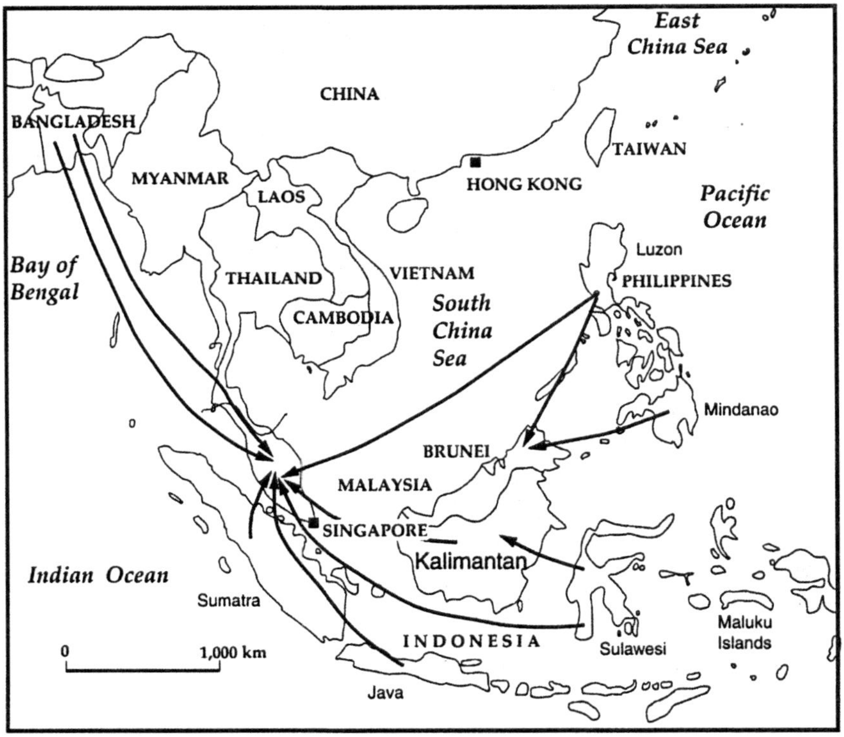


*Figure 15.1 Contemporary migrant labour flows in Southeast Asia*

Indonesian labour outflows coincided with the various development plans in Indonesia instituted since 1969. International labour outflows from Indonesia become large and diverse as can be garnered from Table 15.1. These labour flows were generated from regions where modernisation, mechanisation of agriculture and foreign investment flows encouraged trends towards rural-urban migration and towards migration abroad.

*Table 15.1 Indonesia: destinations of overseas workers in the sixth Five-Year Plan period, 1994-1999*

| Destination | Number | Percentage | Sex ratio (males/ 100 females) |
|---|---|---|---|
| **Asia Pacific** | **848 543** | **58.1** | **79.9** |
| Malaysia | 556 575 | 38.1 | 96.1 |
| Singapore | 146 427 | 10.0 | 22.9 |
| Taiwan | 44 851 | 3.1 | 152.9 |
| South Korea | 37 288 | 2.6 | 524.7 |
| Hong Kong | 35 140 | 2.4 | 1.7 |
| Brunei | 14 040 | 1.0 | 28.3 |
| Japan | 12 274 | 0.8 | 4620.7 |
| Other Asia | 1 943 | 0.1 | 16 091.7 |
| **America** | **12 833** | **0.9** | **40 003.1** |
| **Europe** | **5 204** | **0.4** | **7 667.1** |
| **Middle East/Africa** | **594 656** | **40.6** | **8.3** |
| Saudi Arabia | 550 218 | 37.7 | 8.5 |
| Arab Emirates | 41 768 | 2.9 | 2.6 |
| Other Middle East/Africa | 2 670 | 0.2 | 74.2 |
| **Total** | **1 461 236** | **100.0** | **43.1** |

*Source*: Indonesian Department of Labour (DEPNAKER) cited in Graeme Hugo, 'Women's International Labour Migration', paper presented at Indonesia Update 2001: Gender, Equity and Development in Indonesia's Reform Period, Australian National University, Canberra, September 2001, p. 3.

Concurrently, demand for unskilled labour in Malaysia emerged after 1979 arising from labour shortages in the plantation sector, government land settlement schemes and the construction sector (Kaur 2000a). Subsequently, following repeated calls from the Malaysian Agricultural Producers Association (plantation sector), the construction industry (associated with the property boom) and some state governments (notably Johor) for foreign labour recruitment, the Malaysian government allowed the entry of foreign labour into the country. This step was taken despite strong opposition from the Malaysian Trades Unions Congress (MTUC), which stated that migrant worker recruitment would contribute to depressed wage levels in these sectors. In 1993, the manufacturing sector was also allowed to recruit skilled workers from abroad and to hire unskilled workers from the pool of foreign workers already in the country. At the same time, labour demand in the tertiary sector, comprising the entertainment, hotel and restaurant sector and domestic service also increased rapidly, consistent with the rising affluence in the country. The demand for domestic workers corresponded with increased female labour force participation rates in the formal sector, including that of married women.

The proportion of female to male migrants in the Indonesian emigration flows for the period 1994-99 is shown in Table 15.1 above.

These women were concentrated in the service sector while men were recruited primarily for the plantation and construction sectors. From 1993, women were also recruited as unskilled workers for the manufacturing sector. The documented labour intakes were augmented by illegal labour flows for reasons outlined above. The high costs involved in migration and the existence of networks facilitated this flow. A recent study estimates that Indonesia provided about 70 per cent of the migrant labour in Malaysia in 2000 (Manning 2002, Table 2).

**Filipino Migrant Flows**

Filipinos formed the second largest group of migrant workers in Malaysia. Like Indonesia, there were close historical links between the east Malaysian state of Sabah and Mindanao and Jolo. Filipinos migrated to Peninsular Malaysia and Sabah from 1985 and Filipino migrant workers accounted for almost 1.5 per cent of the total migrant worker population in Peninsular Malaysia in 1994. The majority of Filipinos in Peninsular Malaysia were recruited as domestic workers, while others were employed as musicians and entertainers at holiday resorts, restaurants and petrol stations. In Sabah, most Filipinos were employed either in the plantation or forestry sectors. There were (and are) a large number of illegal migrants as well and in 1990, an official Sabah government estimate put the number of undocumented workers (principally Filipino) at 700,000 against a total state population of 1.7 million (National Report 1994, pp. 16-17).

The typical Filipino worker was a woman, employed in the service sector, mostly in domestic service. These workers were mainly from the Luzon area (80 per cent). Most of them were educated, and were under 30 years. In 1995, the Malaysian government decreed that Filipino women between the ages of 35 to 50 only would be allowed to work in Malaysia. Their security deposits were also raised (*Philippine Daily Enquirer*, 16 September 1995).

**Thai Migrant Flows**

The third largest group of migrant workers comprised Thais from southern Thailand, and their seasonal migration to the northern states of Peninsular

Malaysia coincided with the rice cultivation cycle. Close cultural links between south (Muslim) Thailand and the northern states on Peninsular Malaysia have existed for centuries. The Muslim provinces are relatively poor, and during the agricultural slack period, the Thais migrated to Malaysia to work on a temporary basis. The shared border between the two countries, which was a colonial creation, facilitated this labour flow. The Thais were employed predominantly as agricultural workers (on padi farms, rubber and oil palm plantations), as construction labourers and domestic workers (Taneerananon 1997, p. 2).

## South Asian Migrant Flows

Apart from the above three countries, the Indian sub-continent re-emerged as a major labour exporter to Malaysia in the 1990s. Most of the workers were from Bangladesh, which is one of the least developed countries in the world. The Bangladeshi government followed development strategies similar to those of the Southeast Asian NICs – modernisation of agriculture and a shift to export-oriented industrialisation. Bangladesh became a major exporter of ready-made garments, and of the 1 to 1.2 million workers employed in the textile and apparel industries, 80-90 per cent were women (Wright 2000, p. 236). However, as more women moved into the formal sector, which was consistent with the country's production niche, there was high unemployment among men. These men thus migrated abroad in search of employment. Undocumented migration was also common, particularly via Bangkok and on through southern Thailand. The Bangladeshis were mainly employed in the plantation and construction sectors and in the service sector in urban areas.

The distribution of documented foreign labour by country of origin and job sector in Malaysia from 1992-97 is shown in Table 15.2.

As shown in the table, the official figure for documented migrant workers was under 700,000 in 1997. These figures do not include the undocumented or illegal workers. One of the key features of the migration inflows into Malaysia, and elsewhere, is that the Indonesian migrants were predominantly concentrated in lower skill groups.

The percentages of the total migrant labour supplied by source countries for each of the sectors are shown in Table 15.3.

As noted in Table 15.2, Indonesia, Bangladesh, the Philippines and Thailand represent the major source countries. Their relative positions as source countries can be seen from the last column of Table 15.2. Table 15.3 shows for the major source countries for Malaysia their distribution by sector in Malaysia. Some sectoral specialisation is evident between source countries.

*Table 15.2 Malaysia: distribution of documented foreign workers by country of origin and sector, July 1992 - January 1997. Numbers and percentage (in parentheses) distribution by sectors. Countries of origin arranged by descending number of foreign workers*

| Sector | Domestic help | Agriculture | Construction | Services | Manufacturing | Others | Total |
|---|---|---|---|---|---|---|---|
| Indonesia | 100,324 (67) | 139,701 (72) | 124,777 (67) | 4,154 (29) | 30,773 (28) | 1,047 (32) | 400,776 (61) |
| Bangladesh | 56 (0) | 32,271 (17) | 44,603 (24) | 6,719 (46) | 76,326 (69) | 316 (10) | 160,291 (24) |
| Philippines | 44,539 (30) | 49 (0) | 1,160 (1) | 828 (6) | 1,401 (1) | 568 (17) | 48,545 (7) |
| Thailand | 3,881 (3) | 22,536 (12) | 12,080 (6) | 1,534 (11) | 298 (0) | 748 (23) | 41,077 (6) |
| Pakistan | 53 (0) | 183 (0) | 1,356 (1) | 435 (3) | 1,694 (2) | 3 (0) | 3,724 (1) |
| India | 54 (0) | 306 (0) | 1,347 (1) | 446 (3) | 198 (0) | 27 (1) | 2,378 (0) |
| Myanmar | 17 (0) | 125 (0) | 675 (0) | 282 (2) | 125 (0) | 16 (1) | 1,240 (0) |
| Nepal | n.a. (n.a.) | 25 (0) | 17 (0) | 97 (1) | 262 (0) | n.a. (n.a.) | 401 (0) |
| Sri Lanka | 5 (0) | 4 (0) | 43 (0) | 39 (0) | 28 (0) | 0 (0) | 119 (0) |
| Nigeria | n.a. (n.a.) | n.a. (n.a.) | n.a. (n.a.) | n.a. (n.a.) | n.a. (n.a.) | 5 (0) | 5 (0) |
| Others | 7 (0) | n.a. (n.a.) | 137 (0) | 11 (0) | 54 (0) | 518 (16) | 727 (0) |
| **Total** | **148,936 (100)** | **195,200 (100)** | **186,195 (100)** | **14,545 (100)** | **111,159 (100)** | **3,248** | **659,283 (100)** |

*Notes*: n.a. – not available. Percentages are to nearest whole number – may not add to 100 per cent because of rounding.

*Source*: Based on *The Immigration Department (unpublished data)*, Division of Record and Information System, Ministry of Home Affairs, Kuala Lumpur, Malaysia, cited in Karim et al. (1999, p.45).

*Table 15.3 The distribution of migrants to Malaysia by sectors according to source countries in percentages*

| | **Indonesia** | **Bangladesh** | **Philippines** | **Thailand** | **All others** |
|---|---|---|---|---|---|
| Domestic help | 100,324 (25) | 56 (0) | 44,539 (92) | 3,881 (9) | 136 (2) |
| Agriculture | 139,701 (35) | 32,271 (20) | 49 (0) | 22,536 (55) | 643 (7) |
| Construction | 124,777 (31) | 44,603 (28) | 1,160 (2) | 12,080 (29) | 3,570 (42) |
| Services | 4,154 (1) | 6,719 (4) | 828 (2) | 1,534 (4) | 1,310 (15) |
| Manufacturing | 30,773 (8) | 76,326 (48) | 1,401 (3) | 298 (1) | 2,361 (27) |
| Others | 1,047 (0) | 316 (0) | 568 (1) | 748 (2) | 569 (7) |
| **Total** | **400,776 (100)** | **160,291 (100)** | **48,545 (100)** | **41,077 (100)** | **8,589 (100)** |

*Note*: Percentages may not add up to 100 per cent due to rounding.

*Source*: Based on data in Table 15.2.

One final point needs to be made. The inflow of migrant labour must be viewed in the broader context of the outflow of migration from Malaysia. Generally, the outflow of skilled and semi-skilled Malaysian workers was initially confined within the region, principally to Singapore. In 1991, for example, an estimated 100,000 Malaysians, including professionals, were employed in Singapore. About 24,000 of them commuted daily across the causeway linking the two countries (The Star, 13 February 1991). Again, historical, geographical and economic factors have largely determined this migration flow. Since the mid-1970s, the Malaysian government's affirmative action policy in favour of the Malays, coinciding with the implementation of the New Economic Policy (1971), has resulted in a continuous outward migration of mainly Chinese Malaysians to areas outside the ASEAN countries. This migration, comprising skilled and semi-skilled workers, has been largely to the United States, Canada, Australia, New Zealand, Japan and Taiwan.

## 15.5 INSTITUTIONALISATION OF MIGRATION AND REGULATION OF THE FOREIGN LABOUR MARKET

A major feature of the global mobility of labour (and the perpetuation of migration) since the 1980s has been its dominance by informal micro-level decisions made by individuals, families and kinship groups, and personal networks of cooperation. Nevertheless, as the economics of migration reasserted itself in the 1980s, the cost of travel fell but other related costs (documentation, health check-ups and loan agreements) entered the picture. These costs were associated with the institutionalisation of migration in both source and receiving countries. Additionally, receiving countries like Malaysia and Singapore imposed a variety of restrictions on migrant labour, including exit visas, work permits, bonds, contracts, and age limits.

The specific roles of three main groups – governments of source and receiving countries, intermediaries (labour recruitment agencies/labour brokers, lawyers, people smugglers), and the migrants themselves – are crucial to an understanding of the migration industry that shaped and continues to shape the migration process.

### Governments of Receiving and Sending Countries

Labour issues in the individual countries come under the purview of ministries of labour or manpower or labour and social welfare. Governments in the source countries also established lead agencies to encourage labour exports and to supervise migration flows. These included the Centre for

Overseas Employment (AKAN) of the Department of Manpower in Indonesia; the Philippines Overseas Employment Administration (POEA); the Thai Overseas Employment Administration Office; the Sri Lanka Bureau of Manpower Employment and Training; and the Bangladesh Bureau of Manpower Employment and Training. The Philippines, Thailand and Indonesia moreover established overseas labour offices in the receiving countries to supervise the welfare of their workers. All source countries relied on their embassies or high commissions in receiving countries to intervene in cases of flagrant labour abuse that had raised an outcry in the national press or internationally.

In the receiving countries, the Singapore and Malaysian governments amended legislation to provide for higher penalties and stricter control of labour brokers and recruitment firms and people smugglers. These governments also signed agreements with the specific bureaucratic institutions mentioned earlier. For example, in May 1984, the Malaysian and Indonesian governments signed the Medan Agreement to regulate the recruitment of Indonesian workers for the Malaysian plantation sector. Following this, in 1985, the Filipino and Malaysian governments signed a memorandum of understanding for the importation of domestic helpers. In 1986 employers in the plantation and construction industries in Malaysia were permitted to recruit labour from Bangladesh and Thailand for the plantation and construction sectors, following agreements between Malaysia and Bangladesh and Thailand respectively (Kaur 2000b).

In Malaysia all foreign labour recruitment has to be registered with the Ministry of Labour. The government banned private labour recruitment (excepting firms hiring domestic workers), and initially set up a one-stop task force. This has since been disbanded. Its opposite number in Indonesia is Bijak, a labour agency owned by the Ministry of Manpower. Bijak either supplied workers or farmed out the business to registered labour brokers. Numbers recruited through official recruitment channels are small, and the bulk of workers are recruited through agents/intermediaries in Malaysia, working in concert with their opposite numbers in Indonesia.

Turning now to the legislation affecting foreign workers in Malaysia and Singapore, Malaysia ratified the International Labour Organisation's (ILO) *Convention 1997* by which all foreigners employed in Malaysia are in principle accorded the same rights as Malaysian workers. The Employee's Provident Fund Act 1951, Workmen's Compensation Act 1952, and the Employees Social Security Act 1969 therefore cover migrant workers in Malaysia. These laws, however, do not cover domestic workers. In 1987, following an earlier ban on the recruitment of Filipino domestic workers in Malaysia, the Malaysian and Philippines governments signed a standard employment agreement for the recruitment of Filipino domestic workers.

This employment agreement, like the written indentured labour contract of the early twentieth century, has served as a legal document to protect Filipino domestic workers. Workers were subsequently hired on two-year contracts on a minimum monthly salary of RM540 (US$200 in 1987). The domestic workers' working day was limited to 10 hours and workers were to be given at least a continuous period of eight hours of sleep. They were also granted two rest days per month, a free return airfare, free medical services, and free board and lodging (Raj-Hashim 1994, pp. 126-7).

While Singapore is a member of the ILO, it has not ratified any convention that pertains directly to foreign workers. Notwithstanding this, Singapore does not discriminate against foreign workers and accords them equal rights as Singaporean workers under the Employment Act. However, foreign domestic workers do not qualify for certain labour rights, including unemployment insurance and education of their children (Chew and Chew 1998, pp. 72-3). Both Malaysia and Singapore have very strict restrictions on migrant workers contracting unions with locals. This is especially the case with domestic workers who are barred from marrying nationals; they are not allowed to become pregnant; and they are required to undergo pregnancy tests every six months. Employers of foreign domestic maids in Singapore also have to provide security bonds of S$5000 for their maids. This is higher than the bond (S$2000) for other categories of foreign workers (Lim and Oishi 1996).

In Malaysia, recruitment agencies were bound to the following conditions: a bank guarantee of RM100,000 and a security bond; they were to be licensed with the Department of Manpower; and they had to inform the Department if the maid's service was terminated. Employers also had to meet prescribed conditions. These included earning an average monthly income of RM4000 per month; adherence to a standard employment contract and the provision of a bank guarantee of RM1000 to the Immigration Department. Only legally married couples with children were allowed to hire domestic workers (Raj-Hashim 1994, p. 126). These regulations resulted in greater control by employers over domestic workers.

## Intermediaries

The role of intermediaries in the migration industry is crucial to an understanding of the magnitudes of workers involved. Intermediaries may be categorised into two main groups: official and private.

### Official agencies

Official agencies have not been very successful in the recruitment business. For example, in Indonesia, AKAN set up the Manpower Supplier Companies

(PPTKI) to handle the recruitment of all contract workers. The PPTKI had to adhere to fairly rigid selection procedures, was understaffed and was unable to compete with private agencies. Moreover, most workers preferred to use private agencies since they did not have to pay money to bribe officials to approve their suitability for jobs. Also, PPTKI's official relationship with the labour importing countries proved detrimental to workers in the long run (Dias 1994, pp. 139-40). The Malaysian government's one-stop task force was also disbanded.

**Private agencies**

Although intermediaries have been involved since the 1980s in transporting workers from their rural locations to their ultimate destinations, it was the failure of state-sponsored initiatives that spawned a proliferation of private recruitment agents, brokers and middlemen in both labour exporting and labour importing countries. These private agencies, which currently function as the most effective mechanisms of labour recruitment, provide a multiplicity of services: recruiter, agent, money changer, travel agent and moneylender. Undoubtedly, without their involvement, the trade in migrant workers would not have reached the proportions it has today. These agencies also carry out the promotional aspects of migration – for example, they produce videos for their opposite number/partner agencies in the labour importing countries, which are then used by the latter to 'sell' the workers to prospective employers in Singapore or Malaysia.

Some of these agencies offer free return air tickets, free medical examinations and free renewal of work permits. Some agencies even offer free training on 'Singapore's rules and regulations and home safety to protect the employer's S$5000 bond' (*Sunday Times*, 9 December 2001). Private agencies are required by the state in the source countries to be licensed, which allows them to recruit and place workers. These agencies work with their counterparts in the receiving countries, who could be either individual entrepreneurs or agencies. Some of the agencies in Malaysia and Singapore send representatives to visit their counterpart's opposite numbers in the source countries in order to obtain and provide information on work procedures.

Turning now to the fees charged by the recruitment agencies, most studies show that these fees were very high and exceeded the legally sanctioned amounts. Thus migrant workers often went into long-term debt by borrowing from moneylenders, or mortgaged their houses to pay for their trip. (This is discussed below under the role of the migrants themselves.) Migrant workers were also placed in a dependent relationship in both the source and receiving countries. The agents were the only access to employment opportunities overseas and agencies sometimes withheld the migrants' passports.

Apart from the registered agencies, there were a host of unregistered/unlicensed agencies in both the source and receiving countries. These agencies served the poorer prospective migrants but also put them at risk by providing them with faked documents, dubious employment offers, and often left them stranded at exit/entry points. There are also shadowy syndicates involved in transporting migrants to Malaysia and Singapore. For example, until 1991, Bangladeshi women were barred from leaving Bangladesh. Nevertheless, many still found a way to enter these countries and joined the illegal immigrant labour force.

**Migrants**

The important role played by the migrants themselves in the migration process must also be taken into account. Most migrants are willing to enter into long-term debt by borrowing money from moneylenders or mortgaging their houses. Migrant workers also financed their trips through salary deductions. In Malaysia, for example, documented foreign domestic workers have to pay agencies' introduction fees, training fees, food and lodging costs incurred during the trip and prior to placement, and the cost of the departure ticket. Employers have to pay agencies an introduction fee, a recruitment fee, a training fee and insurance and medical examination fees. They also have to post a bond and levy and pay for the return ticket. Turning to the salary deductions, Filipinos have to forgo six months salary to cover their recruitment, placement and travel costs. Indonesian maids forgo four months salary to cover these costs. Current recruitment costs (March 2002) of documented Indonesian maids in Malaysia are as follows: RM1480 (equivalent to four months salary at RM370 per month). The employer pays the agency RM1870. Of this amount, the Malaysian agency pays the Indonesian agent/intermediary RM800. The levy paid amounts to RM300. Currently, the employment contract is for two years and it can be extended for another year. In practice, extensions are unlimited (author – personal interviews).

Ethnicity is an important consideration in domestic worker placement in Malaysia. Muslims are generally disallowed from hiring Catholic Filipino maids because non-Muslims cannot care for Muslim children. Most Chinese prefer not to hire Muslims and are discouraged from doing so owing to food and religious taboos. Some employers hire only Sri Lankan maids, while Filipino maids, though regarded as 'expensive', are the preferred choice for urban professionals. It is a fairly simple process to hire illegal domestic workers through private arrangements or recruitment agencies. However, it is difficult to tie down these workers who are often circulated every three months by labour recruiters to make money off these migrants.

**Illegal labour flows**

The high migration costs involved, especially for poorer migrants, and the existence of networks has facilitated the presence of a growing number of illegal migrants in Malaysia. According to one Southeast Asian newspaper correspondent, the percentage of illegal Indonesian migrants rose from an estimated 51 per cent in 1994 to more than 70 per cent by 2000 (Greenlees 2001). Consider the costs. While the official Indonesian labour agency, Bijak, charged workers about US$520 (in 1996) to go to Malaysia, illegal labour brokers/people smugglers known as *tekong* charged migrants US$123 for the trip from Riau to Peninsular Malaysia across the Straits of Melaka. Another port of departure is Dumai on Sumatra's east coast. The prospective migrants are held in safe houses prior to departure. The opposite number of the *tekong* is the Malaysian crew boss, known as the *tauke*, who calls in orders for workers. He receives the workers and transports them to their destinations in Malaysia. Some *tauke* rotate workers to get the most from their investment. According to Human Rights Watch/Asia, in the 1990s hundreds of Indonesians died trying to make the crossing to Malaysia (*Far Eastern Economic Review*, 23 May 1996).

Although Malaysia has well-managed migrant labour policies, uncontrolled, illegal migration has thus become a feature of the labour market and often policy has been made on the run to deal with the actions of illegal migrants. The government has also established several detention camps for illegal migrants. There have been a number of complaints about the treatment of the illegal migrants, and in a much publicised case in December 2001, some illegal migrant workers in the state of Johor set fire to their detention camp (*The Star*, 5 December 2001). Subsequently, in February 2002, Indonesian migrant workers burned down the factory they had been working in, prompting the Malaysian Prime Minister, Dr Mahathir Mohamad, publicly to announce that in future migrant workers could only be hired for plantation or manual work (construction), or as domestic workers. These stories testify to the exploitative conditions faced by both documented and illegal workers. The non-governmental organisation, Tenaganita, which works with the Legal Aid Centre in Malaysia, provides legal advice and support services (counselling, crisis intervention, and shelter to migrant workers). On average, Tenaganita receives about 40 cases a day from migrant workers. These range from unlawful dismissal, wage deductions, alleged police brutality and extortion to withholding of passports and other documentation by employers. Tenaganita volunteers also visit migrants detained in detention camps (Tenaganita 1995).

## 15.6 LABOUR MIGRATION: EVERYTHING CHANGES AND NOTHING CHANGES

How did the economic crisis impact on international labour migration in Southeast Asia? Unemployment rates tended to rise among migrant workers, and the labour importing countries made attempts to cut back on migrant labour intakes. In Malaysia attempts were also made to stem the flow of illegal migrants by offering voluntary repatriation during an amnesty period to this group. Subsequently, as conditions improved, labour market conditions also improved and efforts were made to register migrant workers. By the end of 1999, a 'majority of some one million migrants (in Peninsular Malaysia) were formally on contracts recognised by the government' (Manning 2002, p. 375). Foreign worker recruitment has continued in response to the economic growth and structural change in the region, reflecting the increased integration of labour markets in Southeast Asia. Thus, rising absolute differences in wages and levels of living and wage costs between more and less developed economies, coinciding with falling transport costs and the role of networks in the perpetuation of migration, continue to play a key role in supporting international labour migration in the region.

How have Malaysians responded to foreign labour migration? Malaysian workers complain about depressed wages (especially in the plantation sector) due to competition from migrant workers. The Malaysian government is also wary of encouraging too much reliance on foreign labour since migrant workers are identified with rising crime levels in the country. Rising costs (agency fees, bonds, placement fees and registration) also push poorer migrants into illegal immigration, exposing them to lower wages, personal danger and greater indebtedness to unlicensed recruiting agents who smuggle these workers to Malaysia. Migrant workers are concentrated in particular branches of low-skilled work or low-level jobs that have also been identified as difficult, unpleasant and low paid, with no promotional prospects. These jobs include not only plantation work and other outdoor jobs, such as construction, but also urban and industrial occupations, especially assembly-line manufacturing, domestic service, restaurant services and a miscellany of manual and service occupations. For many of these low-level jobs, employers claim that local workers are not available. Furthermore, the projections for these kinds of labour show growth in these low-level occupations principally because of the demographics of Malaysia and Singapore and the wage disparities in these countries compared to the neighbouring countries.

Are labour shortages in these occupations therefore the principal reason for hiring migrant workers? Could industrial investment and reorganisation eliminate certain jobs and upgrade the remaining jobs to make them attractive for local workers, especially women? This argument presupposes an inelastic supply of local workers for the jobs at current wages. Japan has often been quoted as an example of a country that managed to get along without foreign workers. But this is no longer the case. Despite increased mechanisation and more do-it-yourself household activity (that is, new and improved appliances), Japan now relies on migrant workers for a variety of low-paying jobs. Consequently, the hiring of foreign workers via a foreign worker policy governed by labour-market criteria seems to be the only feasible policy to overcome labour shortages.

What are the consequences of unskilled migrant labour for Malaysia and Singapore's future? It is well known that the figures for the employment of migrant labour have been understated, and consequently labour productivity in these two countries may also be overstated. By lowering the price of unskilled labour, it discourages a move towards the structural upgrading of the economy. This means that it will take much longer for Malaysia to achieve increased labour productivity. For both Malaysia and Singapore, where foreign labour accounts for between 20-25 per cent of the total labour force, the net structural effect of this labour is detrimental to both governments' stated aim of achieving a strategic shift to high value-added, high-skill-intensive inelasticities (*ASEAN Economic Bulletin* 1995, pp. 119, 126). Additionally, since migrant labour depresses the wages of the poorer unskilled households in both countries, there is a likelihood that income inequalities will increase.

Another argument that has been put forward is that the employment of foreign labour may lead to harmful political effects since both Malaysia and Singapore have had to preserve their delicate ethnic balance and the choice of migrant workers and policies on settlement are all tied in with pre-existing ethnic divisions. Thus, while changes have taken place in the labour market for skilled workers in both Malaysia and Singapore, the labour market for unskilled cheap workers remains unchanged.

Despite the bad publicity faced by both source and receiving countries, the effects of emigration are not all bad. Migrant workers abroad are regarded as valuable assets by their home countries for at least two reasons: first, as migration has increased, so has the money sent back home. The Philippines government regards its migrant workers as the most valuable source of foreign exchange. Indeed, in 1983, government legislation made it mandatory for overseas workers to remit home 50 to 70 per cent of their earnings. These earnings were converted to pesos at the official rates. Penalties were also introduced to enforce compliance when the ruling led to an amendment of the customs and tariff tax to allow migrants to bring in more gifts (Raj-Hashim 1994, p. 127). According to the World Bank, remittances to the Philippines totalled over US$10.7 billion in the period 1992-95, five times higher than the period 1971-80. In 2000, Filipino migrant workers remitted US$6 billion, and the overseas contract workers (OCWs) were one of the biggest sources of foreign exchange (*Economist*, 22 December 2001).

Indonesian migrant workers also remit home large amounts of money. In 1994, Bank Simpanan Nasional (National Savings Bank) in Malaysia reported that Indonesian workers remitted US$8 million per month to Indonesia (Hugo 1995, p. 288). The true figures may be much higher since cash is often sent via informal routes. Each dollar sent home also translates into three or four times its worth as it works through the local economy. In the Philippines and Indonesia, there are several housing developers who build low-cost housing that is brought by returning migrant workers (*Far Eastern Economic Review*, 8 November 2001).

Second, the outflow of workers has reduced the excess supply of labour in source countries. As noted earlier in this chapter, Indonesia and the Philippines are two of the poorer capitalist countries in Southeast Asia. It is no wonder that both are taking steps to legalise more of the labour flows. Through ASEAN and the sub-regional growth triangles or economic zones, Malaysia and Indonesia, for example, are discussing ways to make it easier for Indonesians to work in Sarawak. Moreover, since migrants send less money home the longer they stay away, or become integrated in the host country, the continuing flow of remittances depends partly on fresh emigration. Thus the labour exporting countries are making the most of their migrant workers.

## REFERENCES


Augustiar, M. (2000), 'Indonesian workers in Sarawak: the direction of the daily commuting workers via the Entikong-Tebedu Border Post', in M. Leigh (ed.), *Borneo 2000 Language, Management and Tourism*, Kuching: Universiti Malaysia Sarawak, pp. 235-44.

Chew, S.-B. and R. Chew (1998), 'Rules and regulations relating to migration: the case of Singapore', in P. Brownlee (ed.), *Migration and Citizenship in the Asia Pacific: Legal Issues*, Asia Pacific Migration Research Network, Working Paper No. 5 (Wollongong: University of Wollongong/(MOST) UNESCO), pp. 71-7.

Dias, M. (1994), 'Overview of mechanisms of migration', in N. Heyzer, G. Lycklama á Nijeholt and N. Weerakoon (eds), *The Trade in Domestic Workers. Causes, Mechanisms and Consequences of International Migration*, Kuala Lumpur: Asian and Pacific Development Centre, pp. 135-50.

Greenlees, D. (2001), 'No refuge for the world's human tide in camps of shame', *The Australian*, 6 September.

Hugo, G. (1993a), 'Indonesian labour migration to Malaysia: trends and policy implications', *Southeast Asian Journal of Social Science*, **27** (1), pp. 36-70.

Hugo, G. (1993b), 'International labour migration', in C. Manning and J. Hardjono (eds), *Indonesia Assessment 1993 – Labour: Sharing in the Benefits of Growth?*, Political and Social Change Monograph, Canberra: RSPAS, pp. 108-26.
Hugo, G. (1995) 'Labour export from Indonesia: an overview', *ASEAN Economic Bulletin*, **12** (2), 275-298.
Hugo, G. (2001), 'Women's international labour migration', paper presented at Indonesia Update 2001: Gender, Equity and Development in Indonesia's Reform Period, Australian National University, Canberra, September.
Jones, S. (2000), *Making Money off Migrants*, Hong Kong: Capstrans.
Karim, A.Z., M.A. Abdullah and M.I. Haji Bakar (1999), *Foreign Workers in Malaysia: Issues and Implications*, Kuala Lumpur: Utusan Publications.
Kaur, A. (2003), *Wage Labour in Southeast Asia Since 1840*, Basingstoke: Palgrave Macmillan, in press.
Kaur, A. (2000a), 'Changing labour relations in Malaysia, 1970s-1990s', *Journal of the Malaysian Branch, Royal Asiatic Society*, 73 (1), June, 1-16.
Kaur, A. (2000b), 'Cogs on the global assembly line: women workers in industrialising Malaysia', in A. Kaur and R. Saptari (eds), *Women Workers in Asia*, Special Issue, *Asian Studies Review*, **24** (2), June, 213-30.
Lim, L.L. and N. Oishi, (1996), 'International labor migration of Asian women: distinctive characteristics and policy concern', *Asian and Pacific Migration Journal*, **5** (1), 85-116.
Manning, C. (2002), 'Structural change, economic crisis and international labour migration in East Asia', *The World Economy*, **25** (1), March, 359-85.
National Report (1994), 'Filipino migrant workers in Malaysia', *Asian Migrant*, **7** (1), January-March.
Raj-Hashim, R. (1994), 'A review of migration and labour policies in Asia', in N. Heyzer et al. (eds), *The Trade in Domestic Workers. Causes, Mechanisms and Consequences of International Migration*, Kuala Lumpur: APDC, pp. 119-33.
Taneerananon, S. (1997), 'Cross border migration from Southern Thailand to Malaysia'. Paper presented at the second Asia Pacific Conference of Sociology, Kuala Lumpur: 18-20 September.
Tenaganita (1995), 'Memorandum on abuse, torture and dehumanized treatment of migrant workers at detention camps', Kuala Lumpur: Tenaganita (typescript).
Wright, D. (2000), 'Industrialisation and the changing role of women in Bangladesh', in A. Kaur and R. Saptari (eds), *Women Workers in Asia*, Special Issue, *Asian Studies Review*, **24** (2), June, 231-42.

# PART IV

# ENVIRONMENTAL ISSUES AND IMPACTS

# 16. Biodiversity Conservation and Globalisation: Global Economic Failures with Implications for Developing Countries

**Clem Tisdell**

## 16.1 INTRODUCTION

The process of globalisation enhances the demand for biodiversity conservation but also actually threatens its conservation. For instance, the combination of economic liberalisation and globalisation (the currently dominant strategy for achieving worldwide economic growth) is based on the belief that the conversion of natural and environmental resources to man-made capital is an effective means to achieve sustainable economic growth or development. But such weak conditions on the conservation of natural resources and environments deprives wildlife of resources and reduces biodiversity. In addition, neo-Malthusian economists argue that economic growth is not sustainable under such conditions because economic production/welfare cannot be maintained if there is 'excess' conversion of natural/environmental capital into man-made capital. While the neo-Malthusian economic position, like the traditional one, is man-centred, it is more acceptable to those with ecocentric values than the traditional economic view. In any case, the dynamics of global economic growth pose an increasing threat to biodiversity conservation, particularly in developing countries.

In addition, important economic spillovers occur between nations from nature conservation and these magnify as globalisation proceeds. They are a source of economic failure and it is suggested in this chapter that they call for a net subsidy to developing countries to support their conservation of biodiversity. The granting to nations of global property rights in their endemic genetic materials and the development of ecotourism are not the complete answers to rectifying these failures. This is because these latter policies rely for their effectiveness on the marketing of use values, whereas much of the economic value of conserving wildlife involves non-use values that cannot be marketed. Market mechanisms are incapable of supplying all economic commodities efficiently, particularly the conservation of nature. As globalisation proceeds, direct government and international intervention to support nature conservation needs to be increased.

The Earth has effectively become a much smaller place for human beings in recent decades because of rapid innovation in communications and transport. This has increased global awareness about threats to nature and biodiversity in developing countries, and has raised concerns of conservation groups in more developed countries about such threats. At the same time, human factors have magnified these environmental threats. These include in most countries rising levels of human populations and/or further economic growth involving greater exploitation of natural resources.[1] These alter the availability of resources to nature, usually depriving nature of needed resources, thereby sealing the fate of many wildlife species (Swanson 1994; 1995). Growth of the global economy adds to pressures on natural resources and on biodiversity.

The desirability of global economic growth (such as has occurred in recent times) is premised, as a rule, on the assumption that weak conditions only are needed for *sustainable* economic growth and that strong conditions are not required (Tisdell 1999b). In other words, it is based on the view that man-made capital is a suitable substitute for natural resource capital and that this substitution can make for a secure/sustainable economic future (Hartwick 1977). This seems to be the guiding policy principle of bodies such as the World Bank, IMF and WTO (Tisdell 2001a). However, some neo-Malthusian economists argue that conversion of natural or environmental resources to man-made commodities is a risky development strategy because it can result in economic growth that may not last because of depletion of natural and environmental resources (Georgescu-Roegen 1971). Thus, even if the liberalisation-globalisation strategy stimulates global economic growth initially, it may not provide lasting economic benefits, especially if it erodes the 'core' stock of natural and environmental resources (Pearce et al. 1989). In fact, the faster the rate of economic growth, the speedier tends to be the depletion of the stock of natural resources and the shorter is the economic growth phase likely to be.

Dominant Western views about *economic* development (for example, whether strong or weak conditions are necessary for the sustainability of economic growth) are based entirely on the objective of promoting human welfare. They are man-centred or homocentric. For example, no value is placed on biodiversity conservation per se. Nature conservation is supported only to the extent that it is instrumental in adding to human welfare.

Nevertheless, strong conditions for economic growth can be expected incidentally to be more favourable to biodiversity conservation than weak ones. Therefore, those with ecocentric values are likely to favour the strong rather than a weak approach to economic development.

Those with an ecocentric bent place more value on biodiversity conservation than economists favouring strong conditions for economic development because they believe that nature conservation has merit in itself. They, therefore, consider biodiversity conservation to be a merit good. Arguably, this seems to be common view amongst those following Hindu and Buddhist beliefs. For example, this may help explain why there is considerable support for the conservation of the elephant in Sri Lanka despite the amount of agricultural damage caused by it (Bandara and Tisdell 2003; forthcoming). However, it may be that this attitude arises from the Buddhist view that no individual animal be harmed rather than from direct support for conserving biodiversity as such (Moyle and Senanayake 1982).

Although some developing countries, such as India and Sri Lanka, have made a substantial contribution to nature conservation (Moyle and Senanayake 1982), the extent of nature conservation in developing countries seems to be inadequate from a global economic viewpoint. The theoretical likelihood of this is explored in this chapter. The results suggest that high-income countries should subsidise nature conservation in developing countries. Problems involved in doing so are also outlined.

In theory, greater appropriation of global economic benefits from biodiversity conservation by individual nations should encourage nations to support biodiversity conservation. Global commercial rights for nations in their genetic material, such as allowed for under the Convention on Biological Diversity, provide one possible mechanism for such appropriation. Ecotourism (nature-based tourism) provides another possible economic appropriation mechanism. These methods are discussed. It is found that although global property rights in biodiversity and ecotourism can provide some positive support for biodiversity conservation, they cannot be relied on to conserve biodiversity to the extent desired globally. This is because they only allow appropriation of economic use values, and then probably do this only partially.

## 16.2 GLOBAL SPILLOVERS AND BIODIVERSITY CONSERVATION

Partly as a result of the efforts of David Pearce (Pearce et al., 1989; Pearce, 1993), the concept of total economic value (TEV) has gained prominence in environmental economics. Although a homocentric concept, it has the advantage of emphasising that nature conservation can have both economic use value (EUV) as well as economic non-use value (ENUV). Use value can involve both consumptive use of nature, such as consumption of wild animals and plants for food and recreational hunting, as well as indirect or non-consumptive use value, such as the use of nature for ecotourism. Mostly use values are obtained on-site in the case of protected areas, but not always. Tangible use values can also be sometimes obtained off-site due to spillovers. For example, a tangible benefit off-site may be cleaner and steadier water flows or a longer duration in the flow of streams originating in a protected area compared to an unprotected one.

Non-use economic values tend to be intangible and are typically obtained off-site. These values include existence value (some individuals are willing to pay purely to know that various wild species continue to exist) and bequest value (the desire to make wild species available for the enjoyment of future generations). Option value is also often included as an NUV. It reflects the value to individuals of keeping open options for themselves but can include an altruistic element because the individual may wish to keep options open for others as well as themselves. A useful discussion of this set of values can be found in Jakobsson and Dragun (1996, Ch. 5).

While spillovers in use values of nature exist between nations, as in the case of birds and other animals migrating internationally, the main international spillovers from nature conservation may derive from spillovers in relation to non-use values. The latter spillovers may occur even in the case of species that do not migrate internationally.[2]

In principle, we can divide the economic benefits obtained globally from nature or biodiversity conservation within a country into two components:

1. that obtained within the country itself and
2. that obtained by the rest of the world.

Thus in Figure 16.1, curve ABC might represent the marginal economic benefits (marginal economic evaluation) to a country of biodiversity or nature conservation within the country and curve DEF might represent marginal economic benefits globally. The vertical difference between curves ABC and DEF represents the marginal spillover benefits to the rest of the world of nature conservation in the focal country, for example, Sri Lanka. For illustrative purposes, let line KBF represent the marginal cost of conserving biodiversity or nature in the focal nation. This cost might be measured in some cases by the net value of market economic opportunities forgone as a result of engaging in nature conservation.

If the focal nation takes full account of its own economic interest, it will conserve $x_1$ of biodiversity. Whether or not it actually does this depends on

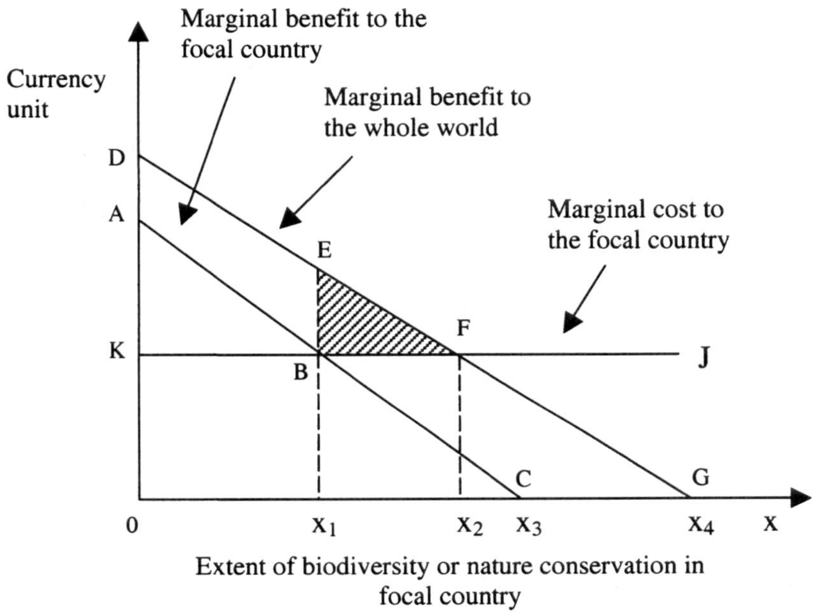


*Figure 16.1 Illustration of global economic failure in biodiversity conservation*

its political will and ability to carry out such a policy. Nevertheless, even if the focal nation acts in its total economic interest, its degree of conservation will be less than is economically ideal for a global perspective. The focal nation should conserve $x_2$ of biodiversity from a global point of view. Therefore, if the focal nation follows only its own total self-interest, a global deadweight social loss equivalent to the area of triangle BFE is experienced. Global economic welfare is less than it could be with more biodiversity conservation in the focal country.

Unless the rest of the world subsidises nature conservation in the focal country, the extent of its biodiversity conservation will be inadequate on a global scale. The minimum subsidy that the rest of the world would need to pay to the focal nation for conservation is as follows: no subsidy on conservation up to $x_1$, then on conservation of $x_1$ or more, an increasing rate of subsidy equivalent to the difference between line BC and EF up to $x_2$. However, the focal country may argue that this is unfair because, to some extent, the rest of the world is free-riding on the focal country. For example, the rest of the world benefits from the conservation of $x_1$ of nature but contributes nothing towards it. This model leads to the possibility of bilateral bargaining between stakeholder nations (Tisdell 1990, Ch. 4).

If higher-income countries are the main beneficiaries of global spillovers from biodiversity conservation, as seems possible because the demand for biodiversity could be a normal good, then (on the principle that 'beneficiaries should pay') high-income nations might be regarded as the main source for subsidising nature conservation in developing countries. In addition, they have the greatest 'ability to pay'. Nevertheless, they appear not to be generous in their support for biodiversity conservation in developing countries.

Reasons for this lack of generosity may include the following. First, they may want to try to make sure that any aid for nature conservation is not merely replacing support which a developing country would provide anyway for conservation. Secondly, they may try to free-ride on one another if a collective approach is not adopted.

In any case, given the situation shown in Figure 16.1, many developing countries may feel that they are saddled with an inequitable burden in relation to nature conservation. If the rest of the world (principally higher-income countries) does not contribute to nature conservation in a developing focal country (one, for example, facing the situation illustrated in Figure 16.1), the net economic benefit to the developing country of its own optimal conservation effort is equivalent to the area of triangle KAB but the economic benefits to the rest of the world are equivalent to the area of quadrilateral ABED. The economic benefits to the rest of the world (mainly higher-income countries) can be greater in this case than are the benefits to the developing country from its conservation efforts. This, plus the fact that higher-income countries do not contribute to conservation in the developing country, makes the situation appear 'doubly' inequitable from the developing country's perspective.

At the same time, concerned residents of higher-income countries may feel that even considerable conservation efforts in developing countries are very inadequate. Residents of higher-income countries have a positive marginal evaluation for a supply of biodiversity greater than $x_1$. Since they do not contribute to the cost of conserving biodiversity in a developing country, they favour increasing the extent of its biodiversity conservation until their marginal economic evaluation of biodiversity conservation in the developing country falls to zero. However, such a desire is based on the mistaken belief that nature conservation is costless in economic terms.

Of course, conservation efforts in *both* higher-income and developing countries have global spillover effects. But it seems likely that these spillovers are much greater for developing countries than for higher-income countries. This is not only because developing countries are mostly in areas where considerable biodiversity is present but it may also occur for economic reasons. Demand for environmental conservation as a result of the income effect may be higher in more developed than less developed countries. Higher-income countries may therefore invest more in nature conservation at home than developing nations, and also have a greater demand for nature conservation abroad. While due to global spillovers all nations may invest less in nature conservation than would be justified on a global scale, the shortfall in conservation efforts can be expected to be comparatively largest in developing countries. Addressing this problem seems to require a net subsidy from higher-income countries to developing countries for conservation purposes. Apart from this 'beneficiary pays' perspective, 'ability to pay' lends further support to such transfers.

While there are some international schemes for such transfers, they are, on the whole, ad hoc and of minute proportions. The Global Environmental Fund (GEF) administered by the World Bank provides some aid to developing countries for nature conservation. Furthermore, some bilateral aid from governments of higher-income countries is provided, but it is a small amount. In addition, private conservation bodies (non-governmental organisations – NGOs) located in higher income countries, such as the Nature Conservancy based in the United States, support specific nature conservation projects in developing countries. However, there is no large-scale international aid project for this purpose. Economic support for nature conservation in developing countries remains inadequate on a global scale.[3]

## 16.3 PROPERTY RIGHTS IN NATURE AND CONSERVATION

Some writers are of the view that if nations can be guaranteed property rights in their endemic genetic materials that this will be a powerful force for nature conservation. The UN Convention on Biological Diversity opens the way for global recognition of such rights. Under this umbrella, China, Brazil and India have signed the Cancun Declaration to fight against alleged 'biopiracy' by wealthy nations. Wealthy nations are accused of prospecting for species in developing nations in order to patent or sell products based on their genetic material without offering economic benefits or concessions to local people (Stevenson 2002).

However, this property rights mechanism (apart from practical problems in its application and unresolved equity issues) is unlikely to be fully effective in conserving nature efficiently from an economic point of view. This is mainly because property rights do not enable non-use values to be appropriated. Furthermore, to the extent that this mechanism is effective, it will favour the conservation of areas and species that have the highest expected (potential) use values. Consequently, those species and natural environments with considerable global spillovers and high non-use values may be lost. Property rights in genetic materials are far from a complete answer to deficiencies in global biodiversity conservation.

In addition to the above, there are difficulties about who should be assigned the property rights, and the rationale for the assignment needs to be considered. To what extent, for example, should the earlier settlers of a nation (indigenous people) benefit compared to later settlers. To what extent should, for example, the original tribes of India or minorities of China benefit compared to later Aryan invaders and Han expansionists from indigenous biodiversity? In the United States, to what extent should American Indians benefit compared to later settlers from such biodiversity? Is the income to be earnt from such biodiversity to be merely seen as a justified pure rent or is it intended as a reward for protecting biodiversity? How is genetic material to be treated that has already been transferred internationally without payment? For example, the rest of the world benefited greatly from transfer of genetic material from the Americas. Even developing countries would have to pay large sums to other nations if they were to pay for all the genetic material they have obtained from elsewhere in recent centuries without payment for genetic rights.

Where a country has a monopoly in some natural genetic material, the restricted use of that material in order to earn monopoly profits can have adverse effects on human welfare. So the question arises of whether these rights should be for a limited period of time, as in the case of patents. In any case, it is by no means clear that all developing countries would have a net gain in income as a result of a widespread and thorough-going system of property rights in endemic genetic material. In fact, some inequitable situations could arise and pure rental income is difficult to justify on moral grounds.

Nevertheless, a situation in which a private company obtains patent rights for the use of genetic material from a developing country can give rise to inequity if this restricts possible future use of the genetic material by the developing country concerned. More consideration of the equity and efficiency issues involved is needed. At the same time, it should not be forgotten that this private property rights mechanism will be ineffective for the conservation of species that have little use value but high non-use value; not to mention species that have little economic value (use or non-use) but which some individuals believe should be conserved for ecocentric reasons.

## 16.4 ECOTOURISM AS A MECHANISM FOR APPROPRIATING ECONOMIC GAINS FROM BIODIVERSITY CONSERVATION

Ecotourism development (discussed further, for example, in Tisdell 2001b) can sometimes provide a way of appropriating some economic benefits from overseas visitors, and from nationals, from biodiversity conservation. Ecotourism is frequently regarded as nature-based tourism that is considerate of nature conservation and which, desirably, includes an education component (compare Wight 1993). It usually involves fees or payments for making use of nature for tourism purposes. However, it is not a perfect mechanism for doing so because it is not always profitable. Furthermore, it can only be used to appropriate economic benefits from actual visits to a protected area. No economic appropriation can be obtained at an ecotourism site from spillovers and non-use economic values arising from nature conservation. This limits its use as an economic-based nature conservation mechanism.

Furthermore, heavy reliance on this mechanism can result in 'biases' in the nature of biodiversity conserved. It can lead to the conservation only of biodiversity and natural landscapes that are profitable from the point of view of tourism and over-concentration on the protection of 'icon' species that attract overseas tourists (Tisdell 1999a, Ch. 8; 1999c). Once again, species with high economic use value tend to be favoured in comparison to those with high non-use economic value but little use value.

While ecotourism can be an effective economic mechanism to support biodiversity conservation, it is inadequate as an exclusive mechanism. It needs to be supplemented by other means including direct government (and global) support for nature conservation.

## 16.5 CONCLUSIONS

Despite global policy initiatives in recent decades to encourage biodiversity conservation, significant global economic failures in biodiversity conservation continue to exist. The economic support of high-income countries for nature conservation in developing countries remains low. Without greater economic support, the conservation efforts of developing countries will remain less than is optimal from a global economic point of view taking into account global spillovers and non-use values. Direct financial subsidisation of the conservation efforts of development countries by those in higher income countries is required.

It seems that the granting of property rights in natural genetic materials is unable to bring about an optimal economic pattern of biodiversity conservation. This is mainly because the property rights mechanism depends on the ability of the owner(s) of genetic material to appropriate a substantial portion of its economic use value. However non-use economic values and spillover values cannot be appropriated by this mechanism. Ecotourism suffers from a similar limitation as a means to conserve biodiversity. Thus there are important limits to the extent to which market mechanisms can be used to ensure a globally optimal pattern of biodiversity conservation. For this reason, non-market mechanisms still have a very important role to play in supporting nature conservation. Furthermore, with increasing globalisation, the need for non-market methods to support biodiversity conservation probably increases rather than decreases.[4]

## ACKNOWLEDGEMENT

This is a revised version of a paper presented at seminars given in Colombo University and Peradeniya University, Sri Lanka in February 2003. I wish to thank participants for their useful comments.

## NOTES

1. Daily and Ehrlich (1992) suggest that the human drain on the world's natural resources depends basically on the level of the world's human population, their level of consumption per capita and the state of technology used in economic activity.
2. This analysis is easily adapted so that it applies to transboundary migratory species where the spillover benefit to a nation mainly arises from the presence of a species in a host country after it has migrated.
3. Further discussion of these matters can be found in Tisdell (1990, Ch. 4; 1999a, Ch. 6).
4. Note that even in cases where only use values are relevant, economic globalisation can result in market failures in the conservation of biodiversity due to path dependence (lock-in effects) and other consequences as discussed in Tisdell (2003).

## REFERENCES

Bandara, R. and Tisdell, C. (2003), 'The Economic Value of Conserving the Asian Elephant: Contingent Valuation Estimates for Sri Lanka', *GAJAH – Journal of Asian Elephant Specialists Group*, **22**, 22-29.

Bandara, R. and Tisdell, C. (forthcoming), 'The Net Benefit of Saving the Asian Elephant: A Policy and Contingent Valuation Study', *Ecological Economics*.

Daily, G.C. and Ehrlich, P.R. (1992), 'Population, Sustainability and the Earth's Carrying Capacity', *Bioscience*, **4**(10), 761-71.

Georgescu-Roegen, N. (1971), *The Economic Law and the Entropy Process*, Cambridge, MA: Harvard University Press.
Hartwick, J. (1977), 'Intergenerational Equity and the Investing of Assets from Exhaustible Resources', *American Economic Review*, **66**, 972-4.
Jakobsson, K.M. and Dragun, A.K. (1996), *Contingent Valuation of Endangered Species*, Cheltenham, UK and Brookfield, US: Edward Elgar.
Moyle, P. R. and F. R. Senanayake, (1982), 'Wildlife Conservation in Sri Lanka: A Buddhist Dilemma', *Tigerpaper*, **9**(4), 1-4.
Pearce, D. (1993), *Blueprint 3: Measuring Sustainable Development*, London: Earthscan.
Pearce, D., A. Markandya and E. G. Barbier (1989), *Blueprint for a Green Economy*, London: Earthscan Publications.
Stevenson, M. (2002), 'China, Brazil, India, 9 other Nations Form Alliance against Biopiracy', Associated Press, 19 February, http://www.enn.com/news/wire-stories/2002/02/02192002/ap_46427.asp.
Swanson, T. M. (1994), *The International Regulation of Extinction*, New York: New York University Press.
Swanson, T. M. (1995), *The Economics and Ecology of Biodiversity Decline: The Forces Driving Global Change*, Cambridge: Cambridge University Press.
Tisdell, C. A. (1990), *Natural Resources, Growth and Development*, New York: Praeger.
Tisdell, C. A. (1999a), *Biodiversity Conservation and Sustainable Development*, Cheltenham, UK and Northampton, MA, US: Edward Elgar.
Tisdell, C. A. (1999b), 'Conditions for Sustainable Development: Weak and Strong', in A. K. Dragun and C. A. Tisdell (eds), *Sustainable Agriculture and Environment*, Cheltenham, UK and Northampton, MA, US: Edward Elgar, pp. 23-36.
Tisdell, C. A. (1999c), 'Investment in Ecotourism: Assessing its Economics', *Tourism Economics*, **1**(4), 375-87.
Tisdell, C. A. (2001a), 'Globalisation and Sustainability: Environmental Kuznets Curve and the WTO', *Ecological Economics*, **39**, 185-96.
Tisdell, C. A. (2001b), *Tourism Economics, the Environment and Development: Analysis and Policy*, Cheltenham, UK and Northampton, MA, US: Edward Elgar.
Tisdell, C. A. (2003), 'Socioeconomic Causes of Loss of Animal Genetic Diversity: Analysis and Assessment', *Ecological Economics*, **45**, 365-376.
Wight, P. (1993), 'Sustainable Ecotourism: Balancing Economics, Environmental and Social Goals within an Ethical Framework', *Journal of Tourism Studies*, **4**(2), 54-66.

# 17. Economic Liberalisation, Environmental Policy in India, and Globalisation

**U. Sankar**

## 17.1 INTRODUCTION

The Government of India began its structural adjustment reforms in June 1991. These reforms envisaged liberalisation and globalisation of the Indian economy in a phased manner. Both internal and external factors were responsible for these reforms. It was realised that India's pursuit of a mixed economy model with a dominant role for the public sector and regulation of the private sector, and stress on self-reliance and import substitution strategies stifled the motivations of both private and public managers to achieve cost minimisation. India could achieve a compound annual growth rate (CAGR) in GDP of only 3.5 per cent during 1950-80, compared with the target of 5.0 per cent. During the 1980s, with a few policy reforms, its CAGR increased to 5.0 per cent. External factors such as rapid developments in transport, communications and information technologies, the demise of communism in the former Soviet Union and Eastern Europe, and the rapid growth in incomes achieved by many East Asian countries by pursuing outward-oriented economic policies, convinced Indian reformers that by opening up the Indian economy for foreign trade and foreign direct investment the Indian economy could achieve a higher growth path. In fact, the CAGR in GDP during the 1990s was 6.0 per cent.

The Tenth Five-Year Plan, which began on 1 April 2002 contemplates a CAGR in GDP of 8.0 per cent, an increase in the share of India's exports in world exports from 0.67 per cent to 1.0 per cent by end of the plan (accompanied by a CAGR of 11.9 per cent) and an increase in the annual flow of foreign direct investment from the level of US$3.0 billion in 2001 to US$10.0 billion by the end of the plan. Is it possible to achieve a sustainable CAGR in GDP of 8 per cent? If so, what kind of environmental policy reform is needed in India? The publication, *Economic Survey* 1998-99 (Government of India 1999), identifies major environmental concerns about land and soil degradation, deforestation, biodiversity, atmospheric pollution, water pollution, solid wastes and coastal and marine pollution, and reports the estimated cost of environmental degradation in 1992 at US$10-13.8 billion or 4-5 per cent of GDP. Both economic theory and empirical evidence suggest that higher GDP growth and trade liberalisation can accentuate environmental degradation in the absence of sound environmental policy.

The present environmental policy regime in India is a command and control (CAC) regime, as is explained fully in Sankar (1999). This policy regime is not consistent with the new economic policy regime. The enforcement of regulations under this regime is also poor. India needs an environmental policy regime for internalisation of environmental externalities in a cost-effective manner and also to cope with the challenges of globalisation, particularly in the areas of foreign trade and foreign direct investment.

While there is a case for government reducing its role in most economic activities, in the area of environmental policy-making it must play a catalytic and facilitating role for the following reasons. First, market failures resulting from externalities, the public goods nature of some environmental goods and uncertainties regarding future use of some environmental resources necessitate government intervention. The government must define and enforce property rights for environmental goods and, wherever feasible, create markets or institutions to mimic competitive market outcomes for internalisation of externalities and make environmental information accessible to public. Second, there are policy-induced distortions in the markets for natural resources. Unless these distortions are corrected, markets cannot signal the social scarcity values of economic goods to decision-makers. Third, with about one-fourth of India's population living below the poverty line and with the poor depending heavily on environmental resources for their livelihood, intragenerational equity cannot be ignored. The government in formulating public policies must make a conscious assessment of the trade-off between environmental quality and the stock of natural resources, and development. Fourth, as a developing country, India must develop the capacity to articulate its environmental concerns in international conventions and protocols dealing with multilateral environmental and other agreements and also evolve an appropriate policy framework to cope with the challenges of globalisation.

The aim of this chapter is to suggest an environmental policy regime for India keeping in view the present state of the environment, the growth target of 8 per cent for GDP, and also bearing in mind India's current domestic and international concerns. Consequently, Section 17.2 deals with features of the existing domestic environmental policy regime and its weakness and judicial intervention in the enforcement of environmental laws, and stresses the need for a mix of regulatory and economic instruments for prevention and control of pollution and natural resource management. Section 17.3 addresses international issues such as trade liberalisation, differences in environmental standards, flow of foreign investment and India's role in multilateral environmental agreements. Section 17.4 contains concluding remarks.

## 17.2 DOMESTIC ENVIRONMENTAL ISSUES

The ancient Indian literature, for example, vedas, upanishads, smiritis and dharmas preached a worshipful attitude towards earth, sky, air, water, trees and animals and enshrined respect for nature, environmental harmony and conservation. The Indian Penal Code of 1860 contained a chapter on offences affecting public health, safety, convenience, decency and morals. Some of the Acts passed before India's independence contained provisions to deal with pollution. Common law-based tort rules operate under Article 372 of the Indian Constitution. However, environmental considerations did not play a major role in policy-making until the early 1970s.

The UN Conference on Human Environment held at Stockholm in 1972 exerted major influence on environmental policy making. The 42nd Constitution Amendment Act 1976 inserted specific provisions for environmental protection in the form of Directive Principles of State Policy and Fundamental Duties. Article 41A enunciates that 'the state shall endeavour to protect and improve the environment and to safeguard the forests and wildlife of the country', Article 51A(g) specifies that the state has the duty 'to protect and improve the natural environment including forests, lakes, rivers, wildlife and to have compassion for living creatures'.

The major laws dealing with environmental protection are:

The Wild Life (Protection) Act 1972
The Water (Prevention and Control of Pollution) Act 1974
The Forest (Conservation) Act, 1980
The Air (Prevention and Control of Pollution) Act 1981
The Environment (Protection) Act 1986
The Public Liability Insurance Act 1991
The National Environmental Tribunal Act 1995

### Pollution Control Policy

The Water Act 1974 created the Central Pollution Control Board (CPCB) and the State Pollution Control Boards (SPCBs) for implementation of The Water

Act. The CPCB and SPCBs are also responsible for implementation of The Air Act, The Environment (Protection) Act 1986 and the rules and regulations issued under the provisions of the Acts. These Acts enable the CPCB and SPCBs to exercise the following powers:

1. Set standards for the quality of different environments.
2. Determine standards for emission or discharge of environmental pollutants from various sources.
3. Restrict areas (locations) in which industries can operate or perform certain processes.
4. Specify procedures and safeguards for the prevention of accidents liable to cause environmental pollution and notify remedial measures to be adopted in the event of such accidents
5. Inspect any premises, plant, equipment, machinery, manufacturing or other processes, materials or substances and, if required, order relevant authorities, officers or persons to take steps for the prevention, control and abatement of industrial pollution.

A detailed discussion of the provision of these Acts may be found in Divan and Rosencranz (2000).

The CPCB has laid down ambient standards for air and water and these are being monitored by a network of institutions in collaboration with the SPCBs. The CPCB has also laid down source-specific standards for industrial units. For water pollution, there are three types of standards. The general standards for discharge of effluents cover more than 40 parameters and the permissible limits vary depending on where the effluents are discharged. These standards are based on concentrations of pollutants per unit of effluent. Wastewater generation standards specify wastewater generation per unit of output/input and are applicable to 11 industries. Load-based standards are prescribed in the form of quantum of pollutant per unit of output. Emission standards are also of three types: concentration-based, equipment-based and load-based. The SPCBs can prescribe tighter standards taking into consideration the assimilative capacity of the local environments.

Penalties for failure to comply with environmental standards include fines, imprisonment of officials, stoppage of water and power supply, and closure of the units involved. Environmental Impact Assessment (EIA) was made mandatory in January 1994 for 29 categories of developmental activities, including industrial projects, thermal power plants, mining projects, river valley hydroelectric schemes and infrastructure projects. The procedure for EIA has been standardised. An EIA manual has been developed and public hearings as a part of assessment procedures were made mandatory in April 1997. Units causing pollution are required to get consent certificates for starting new units and for continuation of production. These units are also required to submit environmental audit statements and annual reports to their SPCBs annually.

Because monitoring of pollution from non-point sources is very difficult, indirect measures of pollution prevention and control are adopted. These include upgrading of automobile technology, improvements in fuel quality, higher emission standards and periodic inspection of vehicles. Liquefied (compressed) natural gas is being increasingly used in Mumbai, Delhi, Baroda and Surat because of its low air pollution intensity.

## Weakness of Pollution Control Regime

There are many problems with the present pollution control regime. First, there is no link between ambient standards and source-specific and other standards. Thus, even when all the units comply with their standards, the ambient air and water quality can deteriorate because of economic growth. Second, the standards are fixed by the CPCB for the whole country. Even though the Acts provide for regional variations based on the carrying capacities of the regions, in practice there are no regional variations in the standards. These standards are the same regardless of the firm size. Third, cost-benefit analysis plays no role in the determination of the standards or other regulations. At present EIA is the only management tool to ensure that development options are environmentally and socially based. Fourth, the technology-based standards and source-specific effluent standards/emission norms for each vent/chimney provide little scope to entrepreneurs to use their private information in finding cost effective solutions for pollution prevention and control. Fifth, there is no incentive for over-compliance. Sixth, the penalties for non-compliance are unrelated to the costs of compliance. The penalties do not depend on the extent of violations. Further, the fines specified at the time of the passage of an Act are not revised periodically. Hence, the fines in real terms fall over time. Seventh, enforcement of the laws and regulations is also poor. The poor performance is partly due to lack of adequate staff, testing facilities and adequate budget provisions in the SPCBs and partly due to lack of political will on the part of the political authorities. Considerations such as fear of loss in output and employment, increases in prices because of the compliance costs, rent-seeking opportunities, and political myopia are responsible for the poor enforcement. The *Annual Report 2000-2001* of the Ministry of Environment and Forests (Government of India 2001) states that of the 1551 large and medium sized industries in 17 categories of highly polluting industries, 1326 had adequate facilities to comply with the standards, 172 were closed and 53 were defaulters. Even units with adequate facilities do not meet the standards.

Non-compliance is pervasive in small-scale industries.

**Judicial Activism**

The judiciary has been playing a proactive role in recent years in the enforcement of the environmental regulations. The Supreme Court expanded the boundaries of the fundamental right to life and personal liberty guaranteed in Article 21 of the Constitution to include environmental protection. In *Virinder Gaur v. State of Haryana* (1995) the court observed that 'enjoyment of life . . . including the right to live with human dignity encompasses within its ambit, the protection and preservation of environment, ecological balance free from pollution of air and water, sanitation without which life cannot be enjoyed. Any contra acts or actions would cause environmental pollution. Environmental, ecological, air, water pollution etc. should be regarded as amounting to violation of Article 21.' It also provided a remedy to any citizen to go to court under the banner of public interest litigation for enforcement of the right to clean air and water (a wholesome environment).

The highly toxic methyl isocynate (MIC) gas leak on 3 December 1984 from the Union Carbide plant at Bhopal resulted in the death of more than 2500 persons and injury of about 200,000 persons. In the *Shriram Gas Leak* case, 1986, the court replaced the doctrine of strict liability, which is subject to a number of exceptions such as natural disasters and sabotage, by absolute liability. The court observed that 'where an enterprise is engaged in a hazardous or inherently dangerous activity and harm results to anyone on account of an accident in the operation of such hazardous or inherently dangerous activity resulting, for example, in the escape of toxic gas the enterprise is strictly and absolutely liable to compensate all those who are affected by the accident and such liability is not subject to any of the exceptions which operate vis-à-vis the tortious principle of strict liability under the rule in *Ryland v. Fletcher*'. Absolute liability is a compensation principle for victims affected by leakage of MIC gas, oleum or other hazardous substances.

In its various judgements, the Supreme Court has endorsed the 'polluter-pays-principle', the precautionary principle, inter-generational equity and the role of the state as a trustee of all natural resources. In cases dealing with tannery pollution, it directed tannery units to install treatment plants or face closure or relocation, and bear the remedial cost as well as paying compensation to the victims of pollution. In cases dealing with vehicular pollution in Delhi, the court directed the government to facilitate a switch from diesel to compressed natural gas for buses, cars and autorickshaws in Delhi within a specified period.[1] In *B.L. Wadhera v Union of India, 1996*

(Delhi garbage case) it said that municipalities should not use non-availability of funds, inadequacy of staff or other insufficiencies to justify the non-performance of the obligations under environmental laws. The Court also gave directions to central and state governments to ensure compliance with the laws, to create new authorities for implementing court decisions, and offered advice on environmental protection.

While the court decisions have been helpful in raising public awareness about environmental problems and in pressurising the governmental agencies to enforce the environmental regulations, it raised questions about the relative roles of executive, legislature and judiciary in a democracy. Difficulties arose in enforcing the court decisions, particularly in determining the extent of compensation to be paid to the victims of pollution. The impact of the decisions on firms' costs, outputs and employment is yet to be assessed.

**Reforms in Pollution Control Policy**

Agenda 21 of the Rio Conference (held in 1992) stressed the need for integrating environment and development considerations in policy-making. It advocated the polluter-pays-principle and suggested a greater role for market forces in internalising environmental externalities. It also advocated the precautionary principle. The Policy Statement on Abatement of Pollution issued by the Ministry of Environment and Forests in 1992 endorsed both these principles and recommended a mix of regulatory and market-based instruments for pollution prevention and control.

Command-and-control policies for environmental management, such as bans on activities, restrictions on locations and input-output usages, and technology standards should, in the author's view, be applied only in those cases where the following occur: irreversibilities, great uncertainties regarding use and non-use values of a resource, or where pollution in a region reaches a threshold warranting application of the precautionary principle. Also, in some cases, for example, controlling pollution from non-point sources, high transaction costs of implementing a market-based instrument may justify use of command-and-control type policy. Otherwise, use of economic instruments should be preferred. Economic instruments offer greater choice to polluters to search for least-cost options for pollution prevention and control. There is a case for location-specific standards in a large country like India where carrying capacities of the regions/threshold limits for certain pollutants in regions differ. The 73rd and 74th Constitutional amendments of 1992 devolve powers to local bodies to act as institutions of self-government. These institutions are assigned some environmental functions, and thus can function as institutions of governance for solving local environmental problems.

Currently there is little prospect of introducing pollutant permit trades as environmental instruments in India. Indian law provides only usufruct right for use of a natural resource while implementation of the tradable permit system requires that the rights are exchangeable. Furthermore, the design and operation of a tradable permit system requires a good information base on the types of and concentrations of pollutants in emissions from different sources, geographical dispersions of pollutants and pollution loads, and administrative capacity to design suitable permit trading systems, certification of credits, monitoring of permits trading and so on. However, it is worth exploring the feasibility of introducing intra-industry permit trading for a few major industries like thermal power, iron and steel and cement.

There is scope for introducing pollution charges or taxes in India. Ideally, the charge system should consist of a charge based on the volume of effluent or emission and charge for each pollutant based on the difference between its concentration in the effluent and the specified standard. Econometric studies of abatement cost functions can provide the information for such an exercise.[2] However, in view of the data and measurement problems, it becomes difficult to get robust estimates of marginal abatement costs corresponding to the required standards. Partly as a result and partly as a matter of political expediency, most countries have designed and implemented the charge system on considerations of revenue requirements for achieving certain environmental goals, or consensus among different stakeholders (compare Anderson and Karlin 1999; O'Connor 1999; World Bank 2000). Pilot studies are being planned in India for a few environmental hotspots to evolve charge systems.

There is ample scope in India for introducing taxes on outputs/inputs that cause negative externalities. The advantage of this approach is that the existing tax administration, for example, excise tax department is familiar with commodity taxes; there is also no legal obstacle to ecotaxes. If pollution occurs at production stage, then a tax rebate may be needed for a firm complying with the environmental standards. This type of tax can not only reduce pollution but also generate revenue for government. At present the charges for sanitation and sewerage, and garbage collection services by local bodies are unrelated to the volumes or types of service. Design and implementation of user charges for such services is an urgent need in India.

Fiscal concessions, for example, accelerated depreciation allowances, rebates on customs and excise duties on pollution control equipments, and concessional credit are means used to encourage polluting units to setup and operate effluent treatment plants and adopt cleaner technologies. It is desirable to provide such concessions to large and medium units only when the treatment or control devices enable the firms to recycle or reuse materials from their emissions, effluents and solid wastes. The objective is to make the net operating cost, that is, operating cost less value of materials recovered or recycled, negative so that the firms have an incentive to operate the devices on their own.

Liability schemes can be devised to internalise environmental externalities when the damages are expected to occur in a random manner in the future, for example, accidents in plants using hazardous chemicals or the cost of clean-up after the mines are closed. The two options available for achieving this goal are performance bond and liability insurance. A performance bond is desirable when the expected damage is smaller than the firm's net worth. Public insurance is desirable in other cases. In India, the aim of the Public Liability Insurance Act 1991 is to provide immediate relief to the victims of an accident involving a hazardous substance. This no-fault insurance limits the compensation for injury or death to Rs25,000 (US$520) and limits compensation in respect of damage to private property to Rs6000 (US$125). Victims have a right to claim additional relief under any other law. The amount of compensation is small. This Act does not provide enough incentive to internalise fully the externality to the polluter. It is worth considering the idea of performance bonds for large mines and large industries using hazardous chemicals.

The Indian Ministry of Environment and Forests has recently launched an eco labelling scheme. It has also sponsored pilot studies on green rating and public disclosures. A World Bank report (2000) documents how public disclosures, ratings and community and market pressures can alter the behaviour of polluting firms. The ministry also assists in setting up waste exchanges, adoption of environmentally sustainable technologies and financial and technical support for the establishment of common effluent treatment plants for small polluting units in industrial clusters. It has launched an environmental information system (ENVIS) with about 100 nodes distributed all over the country.

## Natural Resource Management

Three issues are being addressed in India's management of natural resources. These are: (a) provision of information systems; (b) appropriate institutional arrangements for resource use; and (c) pricing.

As for the information systems, considerable progress has been achieved. The Botanical Survey of India is responsible for documentation of flora. It has set up a database relating to medicinal plants and launched a programme for conservation and sustainable use of the plants. The Zoological Survey of India is responsible for faunal surveys and taxonomic studies. The Forest Survey of India provides state of forest reports every two years. It uses satellite images to assess forest cover. It also provides vegetation mapping.

Twelve biosphere reserves have been set up to protect representative ecosystems. There are also programmes for conservation of wetlands, mangroves and coral reefs. A National River Conservation Authority has been set up for conservation of major rivers.[3]

As for the institutional arrangement for management of natural resources, attempts are being made to involve the affected people, particularly indigenous people in forests via joint forest management, tree-grower associations in common property areas, and water users association in agriculture. However, the focus appears to be more on technical and administrative aspects than on devising incentive and penalty structures for optimum resource use. The poor depend on these resources for their livelihood. The dependence of the poor on the environmental natural resources base has, for example, been documented by Dasgupta (1993). Furthermore, some indigenous people living in mountains and tribal areas have a better understanding than outsiders of local ecology and it could be desirable to endow these people with the rights to manage and use the resources.

As for natural resource pricing, major reforms are needed. At present, irrigation water and drinking water are heavily subsidised. Irrigation charges in most part of India are independent of the season and the crop cultivated. As a result, cropping patterns are also distorted. Electricity for agricultural pumpsets is heavily subsidised all over India, and in some states, it is provided free. As a result, there is an alarming extraction of ground water. Water is becoming a very scarce resource and already serious conflicts over access to and sharing of water have emerged.[4] The prices of coal, chemical fertilisers, kerosene and many other products are below their real social costs. The markets for these goods (mostly because of government intervention) fail to signal the social scarcity values of the goods to producers and consumers. What is needed is the political will to undertake the price reforms, at least in a phased manner with subsidies restricted to deserving target groups.[5]

## 17.3 INTERNATIONAL ISSUES

Two different views exist in India about the opening up of the Indian economy for free trade and free capital flows. One view is that globalisation will have an adverse social effect on its economy. The fear is that the pattern of production will be influenced by world demand rather than domestic needs. It is alleged that a shift in favour of value added production in agriculture would affect the basic foodgrains needs of the poor and thus endanger food security and affect the livelihoods of many farmers. Furthermore, it is argued that because property rights to most natural resources are undefined or ill-defined in India and these resources are under-priced, export of primary goods would amount to export of natural capital. Because the Indian capital market is not well developed, capital flows, particularly short-term capital flows, can create volatility in India's capital markets, and something like the Asian financial crisis might occur. Also with a highly skewed distribution of income and wide variations in resource endowments and market opportunities, globalisation would benefit only those individuals who can seize market opportunities to their advantage. Hence, at least in the short-run, inequalities in income distribution will increase in India.

The opposite view is that globalisation, by enlarging market opportunities for trade, and access to modern technologies and foreign capital, can enhance productivity and efficiency. It is argued that India's export pessimism and fear of adverse effects is based on its victim mentality because of centuries of colonial rule and pursuit of restrictive policies towards foreign trade and foreign capital during the first four decades of planning, that is 1951-1991. It is contended that pursuits of closed economy policies such as import substitution and restrictions on foreign direct investment in the past made India a high-cost economy and denied the opportunity to achieve a high rate of growth.

The author's view is that globalisation offers both opportunities and challenges. It is not possible for India to remain an isolated economy in an age of globalisation. India's vast natural resources, tropical climate and large skilled labour force offer comparative advantage in the export of many goods and services, but to realise these advantages, India must liberalise and globalise. India needs large amounts of foreign direct investment to develop its infrastructures, manufacturing industry and other sectors. The risk of financial crisis is now less in India than it used to be because at present India has only current account convertibility, and capital account convertibility will be achieved only in a phased manner over a period of time, after certain pre-conditions are met.

Now let us focus on links between globalisation and environment. The main focus is on trade-related issues such as: (i) the effect of trade liberalisation on the environment when environmental damage occurs only in the production stage of economic activity and is only a local public bad, (ii) environmental damage arising at the consumption stage in importing countries, (iii) problems arising because of differences in environmental standards between countries, (iv) capacity building, and (v) consequences of foreign investment. Discussion of these aspects is followed by a brief consideration of worldwide environmental issues raised by economic globalisation.

## Local Public Bads and Trade Liberalisation

It is well known that, in the absence of a sound environmental policy, rapid growth in production and exports of pollution-intensive commodities can cause environmental degradation. Consider, for example, exports of leather goods. The compound annual growth rate of India's leather exports increased from 5.5 per cent in the period 1951-52 to 1971-72 to 15.0 per cent during 1971-72 to 1981-82 and further to 19.0 per cent during 1981-82 to 1991-92. This rapid export-led growth along with poor enforcement of environmental regulations caused serious environmental damages in the tannery towns, culminating in public interest litigation and Supreme Court directives for compliance with the regulations (Sankar 2001). Now, the growth prospects for India's leather exports are threatened because of the environmental compliance costs, competition from China and other Asian countries and use of non-tariff barriers by other countries. In this case, environmental damage is a classic example of local public bad. It is also an instance where the environment-development trade-off is most visible because the tannery units are small, decentralised, labour-intensive and benefit mostly minority communities and deprived sections of society. Government responses in India to this challenge are incentives for erection of common effluent treatment plants in industrial clusters of tanneries, creation of new industrial estates for tanneries and efforts to encourage adoption of cleaner technologies by tanneries. According to Sankar (2001), ample scope exists for prevention and control of pollution by adoption of an incentive-based cost-sharing scheme among members of common effluent treatment plants.

## Damage in Importing Countries

Export of a good may result in environmental harm in an importing country. In the case of agricultural products, Articles 3.1 and 3.2 of sanitary and phyto-sanitary standards under WTO Agreements on Agriculture require members to base their sanitary and phyto-sanitary measures on international standards, guidelines and recommendations to protect humans, animals or health. For food products, the Codex Alimentarius Commission (CAC) established by the WHO and FAO have almost become mandatory. The food processing companies are expected to follow a food quality management system called Hazard Analysis and Critical Control Points (HACCP). The European Commission banned imports of fish from companies in Gujarat that did not adopt HACCP. During 1997-98, Indian exports of herbal products worth Rs1 billion (about US$24 million) to the USA were affected because the US planned to impose a ban on the imports for violating HACCP. There are also threats to India's exports of food products in cases where the chemical content exceeds certain norms (Deodhar 2001).

India can respond to these quality problems in the following ways. First, exports of such products may be permitted and certified only if they meet the quality standards of the importing countries. The government should create an information exchange and make it accessible to the exporters and the certification scheme should be transparent, quick and simple. As production of most food products is carried out by small units, centralised marketing agencies at national or regional levels are needed to standardise the products and to ensure the quality standards for export purpose. The Indian corporate sector can also be involved in marketing. Second, access to environmentally friendly food processing technologies and access to foreign markets will be easier if the government encourages joint ventures between firms in developed countries and Indian firms. Third, the government should ensure adequate investment in post-harvest technologies, processing technologies and facilities for storage and transport. Fourth, cumbersome procedures in India's ports must be simplified and cargo handling operations in ports ought to be made efficient and fast.

**Differences in Environmental Standards**

In general, the level of environmental protection a country aims at depends on the quantity and quality of environmental endowments, environmental pressures, stage of development and preferences for environmental quality. The environmental Kuznets curve indicates a 'U'-shaped relationship between per capita income and environmental quality.

UNCED Agenda 21 (1992) advocates the following principles: (i) seek to avoid the use of trade restrictions or distortions as a means to offset differences in cost arising from differences in environmental distortions and increase protectionist tendencies; (ii) ensure that environment-related regulations or standards, including those related to health and safety standards, do not constitute a means of arbitrary or unjustifiable discrimination or a disguised restriction on trade; and (iii) ensure that special factors affecting environment and trade policies in the developing countries are borne in mind in the application of environmental standards, as well as in the use of any trade measures. It is worth noting that standards that are valid in the most advanced countries may be inappropriate and of unwarranted social cost for the developing countries (UNCED 1992, p. 8)

Some developed countries want to be able to discriminate in industrial trade against imports from other countries that do not in their view adopt socially or environmentally acceptable methods in production of their exported commodities. They, therefore, favour the addition of social clauses, for example, relating to the use of child labour and environmental standards to be added to WTO agreements. Such additions would provide a legal basis for discriminating against imports from developing countries that fail to meet such standards. This move is being resisted by many developing countries including India.

Bhagwati (2000) argues that incorporation of such a linkage through a social clause or any attempt at harmonisation of environmental standards should be resisted in WTO negotiations. He claims that the appropriate forum for considering these issues is not the WTO but special inter-governmental organisations such as UNEP set up to address these issues.

In the dolphin-tuna case and the shrimp-turtle case, the USA denied market access of tuna and shrimp unilaterally to Mexico and Malaysia respectively on the ground that they violated US laws. The issue in both cases is related to objections to the WTO rule about production and process methods (ppm). However, on appeal, the Appellate Body Report in the Shrimp Turtle II case legitimised the use of unilateral trade measures to realise environmental protection goals provided the involved parties negotiated such an agreement in 'good faith'. Chimni (2002, p. 133) contends that this report not only tramples upon the sovereign rights of states to have their own environmental protection regimes, but also goes a long way in legitimising green protection.

Harmonisation of environmental standards raises many questions. First, whether the harmonisation refers to ambient standards or emission standards or performance standards. Second, given differences in natural endowments, environmental pressures and stage of development among countries, the trade-off between environment and development varies from country to country. Third, harmonisation of standards corresponding to the levels prevailing in developed countries would raise the costs of most exportables in developing countries and, hence, the very purpose of trade liberalisation is defeated. If developed countries prefer higher environmental standards for developing countries, they must address the root causes of environmental degradation in the developing countries, namely, poverty, unemployment and lack of access to environmentally sustainable technologies.

## Capacity Building

India must also develop its capacity to patent its unique resources, rare medicinal plants and certain natural products of Indian origin. Products such as basmati rice, Darjeeling tea, alfonso mango and neem are 'brand' names, but they are not protected legally. There is a danger that many ayurvedic products and herbal plants available in India may be pirated and used by foreign companies to manufacture and sell products differing only in name.

Furthermore, international trade in transgenic crops remains a contentious issue. Batie and Ervin (2001) advocate three reasons for careful public scrutiny regarding the adoption of transgenic crops. They argue that: (i) the technology is shaped by private firms and is not induced by growing scarcity in key natural resource inputs nor by consumer demand for such products; (ii) missing markets and incomplete regulatory frameworks hinder this technology from reaching its potential for social good; and (iii) it is doubtful that transgenic crops are necessary to protect wildlife habitat and wilderness, and to feed the world's population. The supply of transgenic crops seems to be supplier-led rather than consumer-led. Thus, consumer sovereignty does not seem to play a decisive role in such developments. In the case of India, the impact of transgenic crops on the traditional varieties and on high-yielding varieties developed by government agencies, both of which are in the public rather than private domain, need to be studied.

The Ministry of Environment and Forests is now preparing the National Biodiversity Strategy and Action Plan. A Biodiversity Bill was passed in December 2002.

**Foreign Investment**

The 'pollution havens' hypothesis suggests polluting industries will leave the highly regulated and environmentally sensitive industrialised economies for the relatively unregulated and poorer developing countries. The empirical evidence in support of the hypothesis is weak. Mani and Wheeler (1997) found from cross-country analysis a pattern of evidence which does seem consistent with this hypothesis. But their evidence also showed that pollution haven effects have not had major significance, for a number of reasons. Among the most important is evidence that environmental regulation increases continuously with income. According to them, any tendency toward formation of a pollution haven is self-limiting, because economic growth brings countervailing pressure to bear on polluters through increased regulation.

The flow of foreign direct investment in India increased from US$280 million in 1992-93 to a peak of US$2956 million in 1997-98; the figure for 2000-2001 was US$1910. As for the sectoral distribution of foreign direct investment, the share of chemicals and allied products fell from 17 per cent in 1992-93 to 7 per cent in 2000-2001, engineering from 25 per cent to 14 per cent, and food and dairy products from 10 per cent to 4 per cent, while the shares of services increased from 1 per cent to 12 per cent and of computers from 3 per cent to 16 per cent. The sectoral composition of foreign direct investment is changing in favour of clean industries.

There is some anectodal evidence in favour of the pollution haven hypothesis. Environmental activists argue that lead, ash, battery cell scrap, asbestos and poly-chlorinated bipheryles are dumped at Indian ports. Alang in Gujarat has the world's largest ship-breaking yard. There are about 5000 scrap recycling plants employing more than 500,000 persons.

India ratified the Basel Convention on the Control of Transboundary Movements of Hazardous Wastes and their Disposal on 24 June 1992, but on 4 August 1997, the Supreme Court noted that, despite the lapse of several years, the authorities had not taken effective steps for implementing the Hazardous Waste Rules. It is hoped that the judicial activism and public protest by environmental activists will result in better enforcement of the rules.

**Global Bads**

There is consensus that for global environmental externalities collective decisions at the global level are necessary. The Ministry of Environment and Forests is the nodal Indian agency for participating in conventions on international trade in endangered species, wetlands, conservation of wild animals, substances that deplete the ozone layer, biological diversity, climate change, transboundary movement of hazardous substances, combat of desertification and so on. Most global environmental conventions recognise the common but differentiated responsibilities of developing countries. The developing countries' responsibilities, especially in meeting the costs of such agreements, are relatively small partly because their contributions to the problems, for example, accumulations of greenhouse gases and ozone depletion are low, and partly because their ability to pay is low.[6]

As the developing countries account for significant shares in the world's natural capital, for example, tropical forests and wetlands, which are partly public goods, these countries may demand financial transfers from developed countries for conservation and regeneration of the natural capital. Global Environment Facility is one mechanism for such transfer.[7] A major handicap of many developing countries is the lack of an adequate information base and skills to articulate their concerns in international forums during the negotiations stages to seek concessions or aid. *Agenda 21* stresses the responsibilities of the developed countries in this area of capacity building in developed countries. However, each developing country, including India, must develop its own capacity both in terms of documentation of the relevant materials and creation of the necessary expertise to articulate its concern in international forums.

## 17.4 CONCLUDING REMARKS

The existing environmental policy regime in India is not conducive to sustainable development of its economy. The main weaknesses of the regime are (a) heavy reliance on command and control measures which stifle incentives for minimisation of the compliance costs, and (b) poor enforcement partly because the penalties are unrelated to the compliance costs. The prices of many important natural resources do not reflect their true social costs. The annual cost of environmental degradation is estimated at about 5.0 per cent of India's GDP. In this context, the targets of compound annual growth rate in GDP of 8.0 per cent, and increases in the shares of India's share in world exports from 0.7 per cent to 1.0 per cent, and direct foreign investment from less than US$3.0 billion to US$10.0 billion, from 2001-2002 to 2006-2007, will worsen environmental quality.

The domestic environmental policy reforms suggested are (a) use of economic instruments for pollution prevention and control, except in cases where there is justification for application of the precautionary principle, (b) removal of distortions in the prices of natural resources, and (c) state support in creating a legal framework for introduction of economic instruments, providing access to environment-friendly technologies, capacity building on environmental information and management systems, and extending technical and financial assistance to small and medium-sized industries to ensure environmental compliance at affordable costs. The objective should be the creation of an enabling environment for economic agents to internalise environmental costs in a cost-effective manner.

As for the international issues, the government must act as a facilitator in export promotion and in attracting direct foreign investment and as a skilful negotiator on multilateral environmental issues. India's comparative advantage in exports of agricultural commodities, marine products, leather products and textile garments can be realised only if the government provides an enabling environment for the exporters to meet the phyto-sanitary and other environmental standards imposed on these products by the importing countries. The pollution haven problem due to foreign investment can be minimised via a regulatory policy regarding dirty industries and environmental impact assessment. India must articulate its environment-development trade-off in the global forums on multilateral environmental agreements and seek support from developed countries for access to environment-friendly technologies and financial support on the basis of the net incremental cost principle for undertaking activities which confer local and global environmental benefits.

## NOTES

1. It is interesting to note that the Mashelkar Committee on Auto Fuel Policy in its preliminary report in January 2002 has recommended only emission norms and not fuel standards even though the Supreme Court had directed the use of compressed natural gas in Delhi. The Mashelkar Committee recommendation gives greater choice to auto manufacturers, oil refineries and others to search for cost-effective means of achieving the emission norms.
2. See Sankar (2000), Chapter 14 for an assessment of econometric studies on pollution abatement costs in India.
3. See *Annual Report 1999-2000* of the Ministry of Environment and Forests.
4. There are different sources of conflict – local conflicts over access to and use of village tank and canal outlets, disputes and contestations concerning the sharing of water resources of Cauvery, Krishna, and Narmada river basins, and public interest litigations by farmers and NGOs relating to discharge of untreated effluents on land and water bodies by polluting industries and municipalities.
5. Brown (2001) notes that the market does not recognise basic ecological concepts of sustainable yield nor does it respect balances of nature. He argues that by restructuring taxes and subsidies, prices can be made to reflect the true ecological costs. The challenge is how to value the ecological costs of a natural resource.
6. Although the share of India in world greenhouse gas emissions is only 4 per cent now, the share might increase because of its high targeted GDP growth rate of 8 per cent and heavy reliance on coal for power generation.
7. As there are both local and global benefits in environmental programmes such as afforestation, substitution of natural gas for coal in power generation, and non-conventional sources of energy, according to the Global Environment Facility guidelines, developed countries have to bear only the net incremental costs of reduction in global bads.

## REFERENCES


Anderson, R.C. and A. Karlin (1999), *Economic Savings from Using Economic Incentives for Industrial Pollution Control*, Washington DC: Environmental Law Institute.

Batie, S.S. and D.E. Ervin (2001), 'Transgenic crops and the environment: missing markets and public roles', *Environment and Development Economics*, **6** (4), October, 419-34.

Bhagwati, J. (2000), 'On thinking clearly about the linkage between trade and environment', *Environment and Development Economics*, **5** (4), October, 485-96.

Brown, Lester R. (2001), *Eco-Economy: Building an Economy for the Earth*, London: Earthscan.

Chimni, B.S. (2002), 'WTO and environment: legitimisation of unilateral trade sanctions', *Economic and Political Weekly*, **37** (2), January 12, 133-9.

Dasgupta, P. (1993), 'Poverty and environmental resource base', in P. Dasgupta, *An Enquiry into Well-Being and Destitution*, Oxford, UK: Oxford University Press, pp. 269-96

Deodhar, S.Y. (2001), 'WTO pacts and food quality issues', *Economic and Political Weekly*, **36** (30), July 28, 2813-16.

Divan, S and A. Rosencranz (2000), *Environmental Law and Policy in India*, New Delhi: Oxford University Press.

Government of India (Ministry of Finance) (1999), *Economic Survey* 1998-99, February, New Delhi.

Government of India (Ministry of Environment and Forests) (1992), *Policy Statement for Abatement of Pollution*, February, New Delhi.

Government of India (Ministry of Environment and Forests) (2001), *Annual Report 2000-2001*, New Delhi.

Mani, M. and D. Wheeler (1997), 'In search of pollution havens? Dirty industries in the world economy, 1960-1995', http://www.worldbank.org/research/peg/ wps16/ index.htm.

O'Connor, D. (1999), 'Applying economic instruments in developing countries: from theory to implementation', *Environment and Development Economics*, **4** (1), 91-110.

Sankar, U. (1999), 'Laws and institutions relating to environmental protection in India', presented at the Conference on the Role of Law and Legal Institutions in Asian Economic Development, Erasmus University, Rotterdam, November 1-4, *Occasional Paper No. 2*, Madras School of Economics, Chennai.

Sankar, U. (2000), *Environmental Economics*, Reader in Economics, Oxford University Press, Delhi. Also available as Oxford India Paperback, 2002.

Sankar, U. (2001), *Economic Analysis of Environmental Problems in Tanneries and Textile Bleaching and Dyeing Units and Suggestion for Policy Action*, Delhi: Allied Publishers.

United Nations Conference on Environment and Development (1992), *Agenda 21*, Rio de Janeiro.

World Bank (2000), *Greening Industry: New Roles for Communities, Markets, and Governments*, New York: Oxford University Press.

# 18. Globalisation and the Environment: The Chinese Experience[1]

**Joseph C.H. Chai**

## 18.1 INTRODUCTION

The impact of the globalisation of the Chinese economy on the Chinese environment over the last two decades has been mixed. On the one hand, globalisation has made several significant positive contributions to the Chinese environment. It has enabled China to specialise according to its comparative advantages and relocate its resources away from capital, land, and energy-intensive dirty industries to labour-intensive cleaner industries. It has also enabled China to gain access to the world's advanced pollution abatement technology. Finally, and not least, despite its rapid intake of foreign investment the much-publicised race-to-the-bottom effect cannot be confirmed in China. On the other hand, the considerable expansion of Chinese exports generated by trade and foreign investment liberalisation produced a huge negative scale effect on its environment that dwarfs the positive effects of globalisation and has led to increased environmental degradation. To prevent air, water and soil pollution from reaching a critical threshold, environmental regulation needs to be strengthened in China.

China has embraced the globalisation process since 1979 under its ' open-door' policy. Both its foreign trade and foreign investment regime have been significantly liberalised. Trade liberalisation resulted in a significant reduction of its tariff and non-tariff barriers. According to the quantitative assessment of Zhang et al. (1999, pp. viii and 8), by the late 1990s, China's simple average tariff was reduced to 17 per cent. Its weighted average tariff and non-tariff barriers in highly protected sectors in mid-1990s was roughly comparable to those in its Asian neighbours such as Japan and South Korea, which had an income per capita several times of that of China and have long been members of the WTO. Similarly the speed of its foreign investment regime liberalisation is also spectacular. By the late 1990s China had opened up most of its cities and industrial sectors for foreign investment. More recently in anticipation of its re-entry into the WTO, China has even opened up sectors, which have long been considered as vital to its national interest such as banking and infrastructure facilities for foreign investment. Trade and foreign investment liberalisation over the last two decades had significantly increased the rate of globalisation of its economy. The share of exports and imports in China's GDP has shot up from 11 per cent in 1979 to 44 per cent in 2000 (Chai 1998, p. 148; *ZGTJNJ* 2001, p. 34). In recent years, China has become the largest recipient of foreign direct investment among the developing countries (UNCTAD, *World Investment Report* 2001). Trade liberalisation accompanied by liberalisation of its foreign investment regime and economic reform enabled China to achieve a double-digit rate of growth during the last two decades. But what has been the impact on its environment? The rapid environmental degradation in China during the last twenty years has been well documented (see Smil 1993; Tisdell 1997; Vermeer 1998). However, so far there have been very few systematic studies on the relationship between globalisation and China's environment. Xia (1999) and Wheeler (2001) are among the few examples. The former found that trade expansion and an increased inflow of FDI have been detrimental to the Chinese environment as export expansion was accompanied by increased pollutant emission and FDI did transfer pollution-intensive industries into China. On the other hand, the latter found that despite China's rapid intake of foreign investment, its major urban centres have experienced a significant decline in air pollution.

The purpose of this chapter is to fill in this gap. This chapter is structured as follows: following the introduction, section 18.2 surveys both the theoretical and empirical literature on the effects of trade and foreign investment liberalisation on the environment. Sections 18.3 to 18.6 offer some historical evidence on how trade and foreign investment liberalisation have affected China's environment through export and import expansion as well as the increased activities of foreign invested enterprises (FIEs). This study in this chapter is limited in several respects. Firstly, to narrow the analysis to a manageable proportion, it focuses only on the manufacturing sector. Secondly, due to data constraints, only China's domestic pollution problem is considered. No attempt is made to look at the problem in a global context. Finally, it takes into account only the pollution emissions in the production of final products, not those arising from the production of intermediate products used in the final products.

## 18.2 LITERATURE SURVEY

There has been a growing body of literature on the impact of globalisation on a country's environment. For an excellent survey of this literature, see Tisdell

(2001), Beghin and Potier (1997), Ferrantino (1997), Levinson (1996) and Dean (1992). The findings of this literature are mixed. On the one hand, there are strong reasons to suggest that globalisation and the environment are complementary because of its positive composition and technical effects. The composition effect refers to the fact that free trade allows countries to specialise in the manufacturing activities in which they enjoy a comparative advantage. As a result, the output composition of a country's industry will change. This change may have either a positive or negative impact on the environment. The impact is positive if a country has a comparative advantage in the production of less pollution-intensive industries. As a result, its output composition will become cleaner after trade liberalisation. Technical effect refers to the fact that openness to trade enables a country to access cleaner production techniques. In addition, the increased demand for a cleaner environment, which often accompanies rising per capita incomes due to trade liberalisation, will lead to the eventual adoption of these techniques.

On the other hand, there are also various reasons to believe that globalisation is likely to damage the environment. Firstly, trade liberalisation will have a negative impact on the environment if the composition effect is negative. A negative composition effect refers to the fact that trade liberalisation may result in a country specialising in pollution-intensive industries due to its factor endowments. Secondly, the scale effect caused by an expansion in output as a result of trade liberalisation is detrimental to the environment. Thirdly, trade and foreign investment liberalisation are likely to result in a race to the bottom in the setting of environmental standards. This race-to-the-bottom hypothesis refers to the fact that low-income countries will engage in a competitive lowering of environmental standards in order to attract foreign investment that has been driven out of high-income countries because of their stringent environmental regulations. In the process, they transform themselves into 'pollution havens'.

From the above, it is clear that the net effect of globalisation on the environment depends very much on whether its positive composition and technical effects outweigh its negative composition effect, scale effects and the race-to-the bottom effect or not. With regards to the relative size of the composition, technical and scale effects, most empirical studies (see Beghin and Potier 1997; Cole et al. 1998) find that while trade liberalisation may give rise to positive composition and technical effects, these positive effects are dominated by a negative scale effect. Hence, trade liberalisation ultimately results in some degree of environmental damage. With regards to the race-to-the-bottom effect, most studies (see Levinson, 1996; Mani and Wheeler 1998; Neumayer 2000; Wheeler 2001) find that the stringency of environmental regulations is not importantly correlated with the pattern of trade or the location of foreign investment. Hence, there is no empirical evidence to support this hypothesis. The lack of influence of environmental factors on the location of industry can be explained by the fact that pollution abatement costs often comprise only a small share of total production costs, particularly when compared to other costs such as labour.

## 18.3 COMPOSITION EFFECT

Central to any attempt to quantify the composition impact of the globalisation of the Chinese economy is the estimate of the pollution intensity of China's manufacturing sector. Due to data unavailability, most studies of industrial pollution problems of a country rely on a database constructed at the World Bank by Lucas et al. (1992), which is based on US technology and environmental standards of 1987. Since the pollution intensity of manufacturing sectors varies across countries because of their divergence from US technology and environmental standards, studies relying on the US database are necessarily biased. In this study, the database of pollution intensities of China's manufacturing sector collected by China's State Environmental Protection Agency (SEPA) is used. These data are collected from a sample of industrial enterprises, the number of which varies from 68,715 in 1993 to 54,909 in 1997 (*China Environment Yearbook 1994*, p. 420 and *1998*, p. 562). These sample enterprises refer to 'industrial enterprises at or above the county level which cause various pollution'. The main weakness of SEPA's database is its incompleteness in coverage. In particular, it does not cover industrial enterprises below the county level, which include seriously polluting township and village enterprises (TVEs). TVEs have accounted for about half of China's industrial output in recent years (see Vermeer 1998, p. 959 and 983).

Table 18.1 presents the pollution intensities of China's manufacturing sector for 1993. This table also gives the 1987 ranking of pollution intensities of the US manufacturing sectors for comparison. The comparison between the two sets of pollution intensities suggests that it is not justified to apply observed US pollution intensities to China. The rank correlation coefficient between the two sets of pollution intensity is 0.116, which is statistically insignificant. It also reveals that, although the set of pollution-intensive industries is broadly similar between the two countries, their rankings and pollution intensities are different. In the Chinese context, the most pollution-intensive industries are iron and steel, nonferrous metals, pulp and paper, chemicals, non-metallic mineral products, and petroleum and coal. In terms of water pollution, pulp and paper have the highest pollution intensity. Construction materials such as cement and other non-metallic mineral products have the highest pollution intensity of air pollutants, and iron and steel have the highest pollution intensity with respect to solid waste.

*Table 18.1 Pollution intensity of China's manufacturing trade, 1993 (tons per million RMB)*

| Industry | Water pollutants [a] | Air pollutants [b] | Solid waste pollutants [c] | Total emissions | China's rank | US rank |
|---|---|---|---|---|---|---|
| Food, beverage and tobacco | 10.1 | 6.4 | 40.1 | 56.5 | 9 | 18.0 |
| Textile | 2.0 | 3.0 | 23.7 | 28.7 | 13 | 11.0 |
| Leather furs, & down | 4.6 | 2.0 | 15.4 | 21.9 | 14 | 2.0 |
| Pulp and paper | 100.0 | 17.0 | 121.2 | 238.1 | 3 | 7.0 |
| Printing | 0.4 | 1.0 | 8.3 | 9.7 | 18 | 6.0 |
| Petroleum & coal | 1.5 | 5.1 | 102.7 | 109.2 | 7 | 12.0 |
| Chemical | 8.5 | 10.7 | 200.7 | 219.9 | 4 | 1.0 |
| Medicine | 6.8 | 3.4 | 29.9 | 40.1 | 10 | 9.0 |
| Chemical fibre | 6.0 | 4.1 | 55.1 | 65.2 | 8 | 10.0 |
| Rubber products | 0.7 | 2.9 | 25.3 | 28.9 | 12 | 15.0 |
| Plastic products | 0.2 | 1.2 | 9.7 | 11.1 | 17 | 3.0 |
| Nonmetallic mineral products | 1.5 | 62.7 | 82.5 | 146.7 | 6 | 13.5 |
| Among them: Cement | 0.8 | 122.8 | 57.3 | 180.9 | 5 | 13.5 |
| Iron and steel | 5.2 | 14.1 | 563.2 | 582.5 | 1 | 5.0 |
| Non-ferrous metals | 1.6 | 13.8 | 371.1 | 386.5 | 2 | 4.0 |
| Metal product | 1.2 | 2.2 | 15.5 | 18.9 | 15 | 8.0 |
| Machinery, electric & electronic equipment | 0.3 | 1.4 | 14.7 | 16.4 | 16 | 17.0 |
| Other manufactures | 2.1 | 4.0 | 32.5 | 38.6 | 11 | 16.0 |

*Notes*:

[a] Water pollutants: sum of 11 types including HG, Cd, $Cr^{6+}$, Pb, As, volatile phenol, cyanide, petroleum, COD, suspended substance, and sulphide.

[b] Air pollutants: sum of 3 types including sulphur dioxide, industrial soot and dust.

[c] Solid Waste pollutants: sum of 7 types including dangerous wastes, metallurgical slag, coal ash, slag, coal gauges, tailing, and radioactive waste.

*Sources*: *China Environment Yearbook 1994*, pp. 419 and Lucas, Wheeler and Hettige (1992), Table 5.1.

Matching the pollution intensity data from SEPA with manufactured export data from China's customs derives the composition effect of China's manufactured export expansion on the environment. Out of the 18 manufacturing sectors, only 13 sectors were found to have both sets of data. The five sectors for which there was no data were printing, chemical, fibre, plastic products, cement and other manufactures. Hence, these 13 sectors were chosen for this study. These 13 sectors accounted for about 73 per cent of Chinese manufactured trade during 1996 to 1998. The changing shares of these 13 sectors in China's foreign trade are presented in Tables 18.2 and 18.3 for two periods, 1980-1982 and 1996-1998. Table 18.2 reveals that the open-door policy adopted by China since the late 1970s has made the composition of its manufactured net exports cleaner.

*Table 18.2 Pollution intensity of China's manufacturing trade, 1982-1983 (100 million US$)*

| Branches | Value | Share (%) | Pollution intensity (tons/mill. RMB 1993) |
|---|---|---|---|
| **Net Exports** | | | |
| Petroleum and coal | 48.0 | 49.7 | 109.2 |
| Textile and garment | 39.4 | 40.8 | 28.7 |
| Metal products | 4.2 | 4.4 | 18.9 |
| Nonmetallic mineral products | 2.3 | 2.4 | 146.7 |
| Medicine | 2.2 | 2.3 | 40.1 |
| Rubber products | 0.5 | 0.5 | 28.9 |
| Total | 96.6 | 100.0 | 71.4* |
| **Net Imports** | | | |
| Machinery, equip. and instrum. | 36.7 | 49.3 | 16.4 |
| Chemical | 18.2 | 24.5 | 219.9 |
| Iron and steel | 14.5 | 19.5 | 582.5 |
| Nonferrous metals | 2.7 | 3.6 | 386.5 |
| Pulp and paper | 1.7 | 2.3 | 238.1 |
| Food, beverage and tobacco | 0.6 | 0.8 | 56.5 |
| Leather, fur and down | negl. | 0.0 | 21.9 |
| Total | 74.4 | 100.0 | 195.4* |

*Note*: * Weighted average.

*Source*: Table 18.2 and *Zhongguo Shangye Waijing Tongji Ziliao*, 1952-1989, pp. 432-7 and 438-43 and *China's Customs Statistical Yearbook 1998*, pp. 7-8.

*Table 18.3 Pollution intensity of China's manufacturing trade, 1996-1999 (100 million US$)*

| **Branches** | **Value** | **Share (%)** | **Pollution intensity (tons/mill. RMB 1993)** |
|---|---|---|---|
| **Net exports** | | | |
| Textile and garment | 290.3 | 78.8 | 28.7 |
| Metal products | 39.6 | 10.8 | 18.9 |
| Nonmetallic mineral products | 23.8 | 6.5 | 146.7 |
| Food, beverage and tobacco | 7.9 | 2.1 | 56.5 |
| Rubber products | 5.0 | 1.4 | 28.9 |
| Medicine | 1.9 | 0.5 | 40.1 |
| Total | 368.5 | 100.0 | 36.0[1] |
| **Net imports** | | | |
| Machinery, equip. and instrum. | 117.1 | 37.2 | 16.4 |
| Chemical | 105.4 | 33.5 | 219.9 |
| Iron and steel | 30.1 | 9.6 | 582.5 |
| Pulp and paper | 22.3 | 7.1 | 238.1 |
| Leather, fur and down | 16.3 | 5.2 | 21.9 |
| Petroleum and coal | 13.9 | 4.4 | 109.2 |
| Nonferrous metal | 9.5 | 3.0 | 386.5 |
| Total | 314.5 | 100.0 | 170.1* |

*Note*: * Weighted average.

*Source*: as for Table 18.2.

In the early 1980s, pollution-intensive products such as petroleum and coal dominated Chinese manufactured net exports and coal products, which together accounted for almost half of Chinese manufactured net exports. By the late 1990s, China has become net importer of petroleum and coal instead. The only pollution-intensive products remaining in China's net export list are non-metallic mineral products, which accounted for only 6.5 per cent of China's net exports. In contrast, the share of the cleanest industries in Chinese net exports, such as textile and garments, rose from 41 to almost 80 per cent between the two periods. Thus, trade liberalisation has made China's net export composition cleaner. This is evidenced by a drop in the weighted pollution intensity of its net exports by almost 50 per cent from 71.4 to 36 tons per million 1993 RMB between the early 1980s and the late 1990s.

Any discussion of the impact of trade liberalisation on the environment would not be complete without considering the effects of imports. Trade liberalisation enables a country not only to specialise in products in which it holds a comparative advantage in production, but also provides a channel to transfer environmental effects to other countries through imports.

The concept of embodied effluent trade (EET) was first introduced by Lee and Roland-Holst (1997). It captured the idea that traded commodities embodied an environmental service, that is, the amount of pollution emitted when goods are produced domestically. By comparing the pollution content of exports ($E_m$) and imports ($E_x$) one can arrive at a country position in the effluent trade balance. If $E_m/E_x$ is larger than unity, this implies that a country's overall imports are more pollution intensive than their overall exports. If a country's trade is balanced, this also entails that a significant amount of environmental costs are transferred from this country to its trading partners, and vice versa.

Tables 18.2 and 18.3 present estimates of implicit pollution contents of Chinese manufactured net imports for 1980-82 and 1996-98. Chinese manufactured imports are basically dominated by two categories: one is dirty products, which are mainly industrial materials. The other is cleaner products, namely machinery. In the early 1980s, both machinery and industrial materials dominated China's net imports. Compared with its net exports, the weighted pollution intensity of China's net imports was almost three times as intensive. In recent years, China's net imports were still very much dominated by industrial raw materials and fuels. However, due to the increased share of machinery imports, the pollution content of Chinese manufactured net imports has been reduced somewhat. Yet, compared with its net export counterpart, it was almost five times as pollution-intensive. This implies that import trade has had a beneficial effect on China's environment as it enabled China to transfer a significant amount of environmental costs to other countries.

Thus, the Chinese experience with trade liberalisation is consistent with the international experience. Dirty industries are in general found to be relatively intensive in capital, energy and land, whereas the cleanest industries are relatively intensive in labour according to Mani and Wheeler (1998, p. 219).[2] Since China's comparative advantage lies with labour-intensive products, trade liberalisation enables China to reallocate its resources away from capital, land and energy-intensive dirty industries to labour-intensive cleaner industries. Hence, its net exports are cleaner and net imports are relatively dirtier. As a result, the composition effect of trade liberalisation in China is positive.

## 18.4 TECHNICAL EFFECT

The opening up of China to the outside world increased public awareness of industrial pollution problems in China. It also enabled China to gain increased access to the best international practices in environmental control technology. At the same time the government has also stepped up its efforts to control industrial pollution by adopting industrial pollution control measures through SEPA. For an excellent survey of these pollution control efforts and of their limitations, see Xie Jian et al. (1999), and Vemeer (1998). As a result, there has been a significant drop in the pollution intensity of China's manufacturing sector in recent years.

*Table 18.4 Pollution intensity of China's manufacturing trade, 1993 and 1997*

| **Branches** | **Pollution intensity (tons per mill. RMB)** | | **Change (%)** |
|---|---|---|---|
| | **1993** | **1997** | |
| Food, beverage & tobacco | 56.5 | 22.4 | - 60.4 |
| Textile and garment | 28.7 | 17.2 | - 40.1 |
| Leather, fur & down | 21.9 | 8.6 | - 60.7 |
| Pulp and paper | 238.1 | 143.7 | -39.7 |
| Petroleum and coal | 109.2 | 26.3 | - 75.9 |
| Chemical | 219.9 | 97.3 | - 55.8 |
| Medicine | 40.1 | 20.6 | - 48.6 |
| Rubber products | 28.9 | 18.9 | - 34.6 |
| Nonmetallic mineral products | 146.1 | 95.7 | - 34.8 |
| Iron and steel | 582.5 | 364.7 | - 37.4 |
| Non-ferrous metals | 386.5 | 197.1 | - 49.0 |
| Metal products | 18.9 | 11.2 | - 40.7 |
| Machinery, equip. and instrum. | 16.4 | 8.1 | - 50.6 |
| Average | | | -47.7 |

*Sources*: Table 18.1 and *China's Environment Yearbook 1998*, pp. 580-81, 586 and 588.

Table 18.4 compares the annual pollution intensities of China's manufacturing sectors. Since no official pollution intensity statistics are available prior to 1993, the comparison in Table 18.4 is limited to two years, namely 1993 and 1997. Between 1993 and 1997, as Table 18.4 shows, all manufacturing sectors in our study have experienced a decrease in their pollution intensities. The rate of decrease ranges from a low of 35 per cent for rubber products and non-metallic mineral industries to a high of 76 per cent for petroleum and coal. The unweighted average reduction of pollution intensity during these four years alone amounted to 47.7 per cent. In other words, over a four-year period, the average manufactured pollution intensity has been halved because of the technical effect.

## 18.5 RACE-TO-THE-BOTTOM EFFECT

The race-to-the-bottom hypothesis can be tested in the following way. If the hypothesis is correct, it should be expected that after decades of globalisation of the Chinese economy, China should have attracted a significant amount of

*Table 18.5 Gross output of China's domestic manufacturing and FIEs ranked in terms of pollution intensity, 1995 (100 million yuan)*

| **Branches** | **Domestic enterprises** | | **FIEs** | |
|---|---|---|---|---|
| | **Value** | **Share (%)** | **Value** | **Share (%)** |
| Iron and steel | 3430.2 | 8.7 | 230.0 | 2.2 |
| Nonferrous metal | 1198.9 | 3.0 | 173.4 | 1.7 |
| Pulp and paper | 841.9 | 2.1 | 172.6 | 1.7 |
| Chemicals | 3316.3 | 8.4 | 503.5 | 4.9 |
| Nonmetallic mineral products | 2665.9 | 6.8 | 352.5 | 3.4 |
| Petroleum and coal | 1999.2 | 5.1 | 28.9 | 0.3 |
| Chemical fibre | 698.5 | 1.8 | 111.4 | 1.1 |
| Food, beverage & tobacco | 4999.8 | 12.7 | 1200.3 | 11.6 |
| Medicine | 773.0 | 2.0 | 188.3 | 1.8 |
| Other manufactures | 930.7 | 2.4 | 400.4 | 3.9 |
| Rubber products | 464.7 | 1.2 | 155.2 | 1.5 |
| Textile and garment | 4512.9 | 11.5 | 1561.3 | 15.1 |
| Leather, fur and down | 451.8 | 1.2 | 522.6 | 5.1 |
| Metal products | 1211.3 | 3.1 | 439.4 | 4.3 |
| Machinery, equipment and instrument | 10610.3 | 26.9 | 3642.5 | 35.3 |
| Plastic products | 751.4 | 1.9 | 376.3 | 3.7 |
| Printing, record pressing sports goods | 522.6 | 1.3 | 260.1 | 2.5 |
| Total | 39379.4 | 100.0 | 10318.7 | 100.0 |

*Sources*: Table 18.1 and *China's Environment Yearbook 1998*, pp. 580-81, 586 and 588 and *ZGTJNJ*, 1996, pp. 424-5.

polluting foreign-invested enterprises (FIEs) because of its loose environment standards. Other things being equal, it should be expected that the pollution intensity of FIEs in the Chinese manufacturing sector should be significantly higher than that of its domestic enterprises. To test the race-to-the-bottom prediction, Table 18.5 compares the output of FIEs with that of domestic enterprises in terms of pollution intensity. If the race-to-the-bottom model is correct, one would expect to find that FIEs tend to concentrate in China's dirtiest industries. However, Table 18.5 shows that the output of composition of FIEs is broadly similar to that of domestic enterprises and there is no sign of a concentration of FIEs in the dirtiest industries and, hence, no sign of a race to the bottom. In fact, if one focuses on the five dirtiest industries (that is, iron and steel, non-ferrous metals, pulp and paper, chemicals and non-metallic mineral products) and the five cleanest industries (that is, leather, fur and down products, metal products, machinery equipments and instruments, plastic products and printing, record pressing and sports goods) in the table, and calculate the ratio of output share of the five dirtiest industries to that of the five cleanest industries for both types of enterprises, one finds that in 1995 the ratio for FIEs is 27.3 whereas that of domestic enterprises is 84.5. This means that the output composition of the FIEs is significantly cleaner than that of the domestic enterprises.

## 18.6 SCALE EFFECT AND AGGREGATE EFFECT

The scale effect of the globalisation of the Chinese economy on the environment depends very much on the rate of expansion of Chinese manufactured output related to trade and foreign investment liberalisation. For instance, the aggregate pollution caused by China's manufactured export expansion due to trade liberalisation, $Y$, can be described by the following simple equation:

$$Y = \sum_i s_i e_i X \tag{18.1}$$

where $s_i$ is sector $i$'s share in total exports, $e_i$ is the pollution intensity of sector $i$ and $X$ is total exports. The change in aggregate pollution can be described as

$$\dot{Y} = \sum_i \dot{s}_i e_i X + \sum_i s_i \dot{e}_i X + \sum_i s_i e_i \dot{X} \tag{18.2}$$

where a dotted variable represents that variable's time derivative. The first term on the right-hand side is the composition effect. It represents the change in pollution levels due to change in China's export composition. Since the value of $s_i$ is limited from 1 to 0, the scope of change in composition effect is limited. The second term is the technical effect, which indicates the change in pollution levels, caused by a change in China's sectoral pollution intensity. The size of the positive technical effect is limited as it is technically difficult to reduce the value of $e_i$ substantially. The third is the scale effect. It represents what China's growth in pollution levels would have been due to export expansion in the absence of changes in export composition and sectoral pollution intensity. The scope of change of the scale effect is very large as $X$ may assume any value. Hence, the scale effect in most empirical studies tends to outweigh those of the composition and technical effects of trade liberalisation.

Over the last 16 years between 1982 and 1998, based on our sample of 14 manufacturing sectors, China's manufactured exports expanded by 796 per cent. Thus, other things being equal, one should expect that industrial pollution caused by manufactured export expansion must have increased by a similar proportion. This huge negative scale effect dwarfs the modest positive composition and technical effects of the globalisation of the Chinese economy. Thus, the aggregate effect of globalisation on the Chinese environment must have been negative.

However, the above estimate should be regarded as tentative as there are reasons to believe that it may be either underestimated or overestimated. It may be overestimated as many Chinese manufactured exports are based on processing trade arrangements, whereby many pollution-intensive components, parts or materials contained in those exports are not produced in China but imported instead. It may be underestimated due to the limitations of pollution-intensity data provided by SEPA, which, as mentioned earlier, fails to account for the pollution caused by TVEs. These rural enterprises have accounted for an increased share of China's manufactured exports in recent years. It may also be underestimated as it takes into account only the direct negative scale effect and fails to consider the indirect negative scale impact induced by the growth of Chinese GDP as a result of increased manufactured exports.

Last, but not least, the above assessment of the aggregate environmental impact of China's globalisation experience is based on the total weight of different pollutants (air, water and soil) combined. This aggregate weight may be a poor indicator of pollution as different pollutants have different health and environmental effects.

## 18.5 CONCLUSIONS AND IMPLICATIONS

China's experience with globalisation in the last two decades is consistent with international evidence. The Chinese experience shows that trade and foreign investment liberalisation does not necessarily result in a developing country specialising in dirty industries. The study finds that the race-to-the-bottom hypothesis is not confirmed in China. On the contrary, freer trade has made a significant positive contribution to the Chinese environment. It has enabled China to specialise according to its comparative advantage and relocate its resources away from capital, land, and energy-intensive dirty industries to labour-intensive cleaner industries. As a result its current net export composition is about 50 per cent cleaner than two decades ago. It has also enabled China to gain access to and to adopt the best international practice in pollution abatement technology leading to a significant drop in the pollution intensity of its manufacturing industry. Finally, trade liberalisation has also enabled China to transfer a significant amount of environmental costs to other countries by importing dirty industrial products instead of producing these domestically.

Nonetheless, China's experience also shows that the scale effects of trade and foreign investment liberalisation on the environment overwhelmed other sources of pollution change and offset other environmental gains from specialisation and increased access to international best practice in pollution control. As a result, over the last two decades, water, air and soil pollution expanded at a rate not much dissimilar to that of manufactured exports. This suggests that China needs to take the trade-off between the environment and trade liberalisation more seriously. To prevent pollution from reaching a critical threshold (see Tisdell 1997) China needs to tighten up its environmental regulations and adopt a more cost-effective pollution abatement strategy.

## NOTES

1. Sections of this chapter draw heavily from my paper 'Trade and environment: evidence from China's manufacturing sector', in *Sustainable Development*, **10**(1): 25-35, 2002 © John Wiley. This material is reproduced with permission. This study is part of a joint research project on Globalization, Trade, Environment and Sustainable Development: Implications for China and WTO, sponsored by IDP Education Australia and managed by Hassal International Research Associates. The author thanks James Laurenceson for his valuable research assistance.
2. This finding appears to be over-generalised. Some labour-intensive industries such as tanneries and scouring plants are serious water polluters, which have been banned in China.

# REFERENCES


Beghin J. and M. Potier (1997), 'Effects of trade liberalization on the environment in the manufacturing sector', *World Economy*, **20**(4), 435-56.

Chai J.C.H. (1998), *China: Transition to a Market Economy*, Oxford: Clarendon Press.

China Environment Yearbook Editorial Committee (1999), *China Environment Yearbook 1999*, Beijing: China Environment Yearbook Publisher.

Cole M.A., A.J. Rayner and J.M. Bates (1998), 'Trade liberalization and the environment: the case of the Uruguay Round, *World Economy*, **21**(3), 337-47.

Dean J.M. (1992), 'Trade and environment: a survey of literature', in P. Low (ed.), *International Trade and the Environment*, Washington D.C: World Bank, pp. 15-28.

Ferrantino. M.J. (1997), 'International trade, environmental quality and public policy, *World Economy,* **20**(1), 43-72.

Lee H. and D. Roland-Holst (1997), 'The environment and welfare implications of trade and tax policy', *Journal of Development Economics,* **52,** 65-82.

Levinson A. (1996), 'Environmental regulations and industry location: international and domestic evidence', in J. Bhagwati and R. E. Hudic (eds), *Fair Trade and Harmonization: Prerequisites for Free Trade, Vol. 1, Economic Analysis*, Cambridge, MA: MIT Press, pp. 429-57.

Lucas R.E.B., D. Wheeler and H. Hettige (1992), 'Economic development, environmental regulation and the international migration of toxic industrial pollution: 1960-1988', in P. Low (ed.), *International Trade and the Environment*, Washington DC: World Bank, pp. 67-86.

Mani, M. and D. Wheeler (1998), 'In search of pollution havens? Dirty Industry in the World Economy 1960-1996', *Journal of Environment and Development*, **7**(3), 215-33.

Neumayer, E. (2000), 'Trade and environment: a critical assessment and some suggestions for reconciliation', *Journal of Environment and Development*, **9**(2), 138-59.

Smil, V. (1993), *China's Environmental Crisis*, Armonk: M. E. Sharpe.

Tisdell, C.A. (1997), 'China's environmental problems and its economic growth', in C.A. Tisdell and J.C.H. Chai (eds), *China's Economic Growth and Transition: Macroeconomic, Environmental and Social /Regional Dimensions*, Commack, NY: Nova Science Publishers, pp. 295-316.

Tisdell, C. A. (2001), 'Globalization and sustainability: environmental Kuznets curve and the WTO', *Ecological Economics*, **39**, 185-96.

UNCTAD (2001), *World Investment Report*, New York: United Nations.

Vermeer E. B. (1998), 'Industrial pollution in China and remedial policies', *China Quarterly*, December, 156, 952-85.

Wheeler, D. (2001), 'Racing to the Bottom? Foreign Investment and Air Pollution in Developing Countries', Policy Research Working Paper No. 2524, Development Research Group, World Bank.

Xia Youfu (1999), *Lun 21 Shiji Woguo Duiwai Kaifang Yu Ke Chixu Faizhan* (On China's Open Door and Sustainable Development in the 21st Century), Beijing: University of International Business and Economics.

Xie Jian, Wang Jinnan and Ge Chazhong (1999), 'Mian Xiang Shichang di Huanjing yu Ziyuan Baohu Zhengce' (Environmental Protection Policy in a Market Economy), *Huanjing Guancha Yu Pinglun*, **1**(1), 40-51.

Zhang Shuguang, Zhang Yansheng and Wan Zhongxin (1999), *Measuring the Costs of Protection in China*, Washington DC: Institute of International Economics.
ZGTJNJ, *Zhongguo Tongji Nianjian* (China's Statistical Yearbook), various issues.

# 19. Conflicts about Global Trade in GMOs: General Issues and Chinese Case Studies

**Dayuan Xue, Yanmei Lin and Clem Tisdell**

## 19.1 INTRODUCTION: CHALLENGES TO MONOPOLISATION TRENDS OF TNCs ON TRADE IN GMOs

As economic globalisation has become more pervasive, many large transnational companies (TNCs) involved in the biotechnology sector have become interested in the Chinese market. For example, Monsanto, Dupont and Pioneer based in the USA, Sygenta in Switzerland, Zeneca in the UK and KWS of Germany have invested heavily in research into genetically modified organisms (GMOs) and have conducted experiments in China through single ventures or joint ventures. Some foreign biotechnology TNCs have already begun to undertake GMO pilot tests, environmental releases and commercial production in China (Xue and Tisdell 2000, 2002; Xue et al. 2000). Based on its investigation of patent applications to the China Patent Office, Greenpeace found that all the major agrochemical transnationals filed applications to have their genetically engineered (GE) crops patented in China. Bayer, BASF, Dow, DuPont, Monsanto and Sygenta all applied. The Swiss-based Sygenta topped the list of applications filing at least 11 applications. Its subsidiary, Pioneer, has two applications. This means the Sygenta group has a total of 13 applications. It is followed by the US-based Monsanto, with a total of seven applications. Three applications came from Dupont. Bayer, Dow and BASF each have one application.[1]

Besides imports of genetically modified (GM) technology, imports of GM food such as GM soybean, have become a large trade item in China in recent years For example, up to 14 million tons of GM soybean were imported to China in 2001, close to the whole amount of China's domestic soybean production in the same year. Following China's accession to the World Trade Organisation (WTO) in December 2001, the Chinese technological market is expected to become more open, and to be more intensely competitive. This will lead to substantial import of foreign advanced technology and products using such technology, especially biotechnology and its products.

However, trading by TNCs in GMOs faces a lot of challenges. First, they must cope with government restrictions in importing countries. To protect the environment and human health, many governments control some imports, for instance GMOs, by strict legislation, often involving technical barriers to trade. The transboundary movements of GMOs are also restricted by some international conventions, such as the Convention on Biological Diversity, the Cartagena Biosafety Protocol, trade-related aspects of intellectual property rights (TRIPs), Sanitary and Phytosanitary (SPS) Agreement of WTO and others. Furthermore, GMOs and related biotechnologies are often subject to competition from domestic institutions, pressure from public opinion and concerns about actual environmental impacts. This paper outlines and analyses these challenges to the global trade in GMOs taking China as a case study.

## 19.2 GOVERNMENTAL CHALLENGES AND CONFLICTS ON INTERNATIONAL TRADE IN GMOs: THE GM SOYBEAN CASE

Only six weeks after joining the WTO, China faced the threat of a possible dispute over its GMO labelling regulations. The US government threatened to launch a formal complaint to the WTO against China's new regulations on the import of GMO foodstuffs. The US government described the new regulations (designed to protect public health and the environment) as an unfair trade barrier.

The US has a significant history of using WTO complaints to free up trade in GM commodities. In May 2001, the US successfully pressured Sri Lanka to suspend a ban on imports of GM food, even though it will affect only four percent of US agricultural exports to Sri Lanka.[2] However, it might have been a test case. US dissatisfaction also centres on EU Directive 2001/18 and the labelling and traceability proposal COM(2001)425 which would give the public the right to know if their food contains GM material or derivatives.

Shortly after the WTO meeting in Doha, the US Secretary of Agriculture, Ann M. Veneman criticised the EU over its move to strictly regulate GMOs and said that a WTO complaint against EU was 'a big option'.[3] All the above conflicts are linked to great economic benefits lost by the US as a result of restrictions on its international exports of GMOs. For example, the US Trade Representative Office report stated that because of the 1998 EU moratorium on approvals of GM crops, 'over $200 million in US corn exports have been lost each year' since that time. Thus, there is no wonder that Chinese GMO regulations have provoked the anger of the US government because they primarily impact on US soybean exports to China, that total about $1 billion annually.[4]

The US, as the leading developer and producer of agricultural biotech products, has a significant interest in promoting biotech products worldwide, and exports its technical assistance to Asia-Pacific Economic Cooperation (APEC) countries. Also, it seems to want to alter the WTO agreements on SPS, and Technical Barriers to Trade (TBT) to reduce the GMO trade barriers. Taking the dominant role of the US in the WTO into account, reduction in such barriers seems to be inevitable.

Nevertheless, when ratified, the Biosafety Protocol to the United Nations Convention on Biological Diversity (CBD) will provide a regulatory framework for international trade in GMOs, referred to as living modified organisms (LMOs) in the protocol text. The protocol is an environmental agreement aimed at protecting biodiversity and human health. It was adopted by more than 130 countries on 29 January 2000 in Montreal, Canada, and it came into force on 11 September, 2003.

As a result of direct influence by TNCs on the WTO agreements, especially the SPS based on the standards devised by the Codex Alimentarius Commission, these two international forums operate in different directions and create tension and conflict. The Chinese position appears to be that trade in GMOs should primarily meet the requirements of the precautionary principle recognised by the Biosafety Protocol because environmental safety and human health should be given the highest priority.

## China's Food Policies and Control of GMOs

The need for government regulation of GMOs arises not only because of environmental security and food safety issues, that is biodiversity concerns and the protection of public health, but also because of the rights of people to decide whether or not to consume GMO food. Moreover, it is a critical issue for small farmers, including subsistence farmers, whose livelihood is threatened by competition from agribusinesses that plant GMOs and undercut agricultural prices as well as producing surpluses for dumping overseas.

The US-China GMO dispute about soybean imports escalated when the China Ministry of Health issued a regulation that came into force on 1 July 2002 requiring the approval and labelling of processed foods that include GMOs. Implementation of the regulation forms part of a broader policy of Agricultural Genetically Modified Organisms (GMOs) Safety Administration Regulation originally announced by the China State Council in June 2001. According to that regulation, any releases of GMOs to the environment must be approved by the relevant authorities and safety certification provided for imports. The regulation requires the labelling of all GMOs, including seeds, animal feed and food products containing GMOs. Unless GMOs are labelled, their sale will be illegal.

Based on Agricultural GMOs Safety Administration Regulation, China's Ministry of Agriculture (MoA) issued three detailed rules on 7 January 2002 for implementation of the regulation. They are the 'Rule for Safety of Agricultural GMOs Importing', the 'Rule for Agricultural GMOs Labeling' and the 'Rule for Agricultural GMOs Safety Assessment'. The Rule for agri-GMOs Importing provides a series of requirements for import of agri-GMOs used in research, field trials, commercial production, and processing materials as follows:

- Introduction of agri-GMOs for research, field trials, environmental release and production test are subject to application and approval by MoA and shall be accompanied with a series of relevant certifications and documents for risk assessment and risk management.
- Import of GMOs for commercial use. A foreign company is required to apply for permission to export to China genetically modified planting seeds, breeding livestock, poultry and fish fry and micro-organisms, as well as planting seeds, breeding livestock, poultry, fish fry, pesticides, veterinary medicines, fertiliser and additives containing genetically modified animal, plant, or microbial ingredients. Relevant certification and documents must be provided.
- Before beginning field trials, a foreign company should apply for permission to import relevant materials. Only after the approval of the application can those materials can be legally imported to China. Applications are needed for all three development phases, one by one, that is for the field trials, environmental releases and productive tests. After all the phases have met the safety requirements, MoA will issue the company with the Review and Approval Certification

for the agri-GMO. Then the foreign company can apply for the Safety Certification of Agri-GMOs based on the Review and Approval Certification. Safety Certification is needed before export of the GMO is permitted.

- As above, a foreign company should apply for Safety Certification of agri-GMOs when they export these for use in processing,
- When the first application is approved, the further applications will be expedited if it is the same company and the same agri-GMO as in the first case.

## Food Security and the GM Soybean Trade

### Impacts of the soybean trade on farmers' livelihood

President Bush of the USA, during his two visits to China in 2002, has raised concerns about China's GMO regulations which impact significantly on the United States' exports of soybeans to China, valued at US$1 billion. However, China is the place where soybeans were first cultivated some 5000 years ago. Around 30 million Chinese peasants depend on soybean production to make a living, cultivating on average 0.2 ha of soybean. They are now facing stiff competition from subsidised American production of soybeans, much of which is GMO-based. Chinese small farmers have been unable to compete with soybean imports (see Figure 19.1).

Figure 19.1 indicates that the soybean imports to China began in 1995, and that imports have increased year by year with accelerating growth during 1999 to 2001. The incomes of Chinese soybean farmers have decreased greatly since 1995. Based on the field investigation by one of the authors (Dayuan Xue) in Heilongjiang Province, China's main soybean production region, the farmers could get 4000 yuan per ha net income from soybean in 1995, but only about 2000 yuan in 2001. The main reason for the decrease is that the soybean price has fallen as a result of soybean imports. In 1995, the market price of soybean was 2.5 yuan per kg, while the price was down to 1.5 yuan per kg in 2001, a fall of 40 per cent. Now in Northeast China, more and more farmers are abandoning their traditional soybean plantation and switching to rice and other crops. This change requires new capital investment by farmers. Due to the shortage of money for capital investment, many farmers have to continue in the lower-profit soybean industry. WTO entry will only accelerate the trend because of the removal of Chinese import quotas on soybeans under this agreement; the tariff on soybean imports is pegged at the current low level of 3 per cent and that on soybean meal at 5 per cent.[5]

In a country with a large population like China, many feel that it should be self-sufficient in food, especially in soybean *Glycine max* L. supplies. Soybean is now a multi-billion dollar commodity crop internationally, and is particularly important for oil and animal feed. In addition, soybean remains an important vegetable and protein crop for Asians.

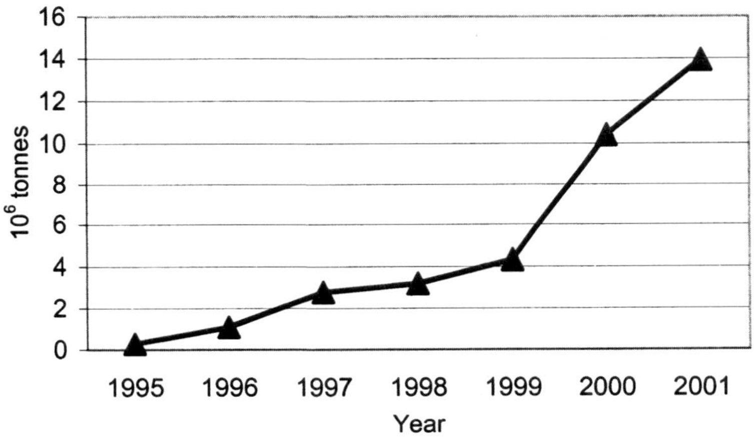


*Source*: Based on data from the Chinese Ministry of Agriculture (2000, Table 1) and personal communication from Ministry of Agriculture (2001).

*Figure 19.1 China's imports of soybeans (in millions of tonnes) for the calendar years 1995 to 2001*

In the newly added chapter on 'food security' in the Law of Agriculture as revised, we can see the consistent follow-up policies launched by the Chinese government, as the draft makes the stipulations: 'food production capacity should be protected and a system for the protection of arable land should be established; The state should grant key support to food-producing regions regarding policy, funding and technology, thus establish stable commodity food bases; Some crop varieties may adopt protective prices.' [6]

**Environmental concerns**

Soybean imported to China is mainly from the USA and Argentina, but the soybean varieties in both countries are mostly from Monsanto's Roundup Ready (RR) soybean. It is a transgenic herbicide-tolerant soybean variety. In

1996, Monsanto's RR soybean was grown commercially for the first time by farmers in the US and Argentina. It was granted market approval (for import and processing into non-viable soybean bean fractions only) in the EU in 1996[7] and in Japan.[8] Since Monsanto's 'safety' assessment of its RR soybean has been approved, it has never ceased to be criticised. In particular, a newly published scientific report on the RR soybean's unknown DNA sequence indicates that there are serious errors in the submission by Monsanto (Windels et al. 2001).

Of great concern to China is the risk of gene flow from GM *Glycine max* L. to related wild plants. Bees can carry pollen to other soybeans and related wild or weed plants. Soybean can cross with other member of the genus *Glycine*, some of which are also found in Australia and Japan. Natural hybridisation is known to occur between cultivated soybean and G. soybean, a common weed in Japan.[9] China is the centre of origin and centre of diversity for soybeans, with more than 6000 wild soybean germ materials, over 90 per cent of the global total, present. There are major risks if the GE soybean is grown in places where related wild species occur. A further risk involves unintended release into the environment, especially in these nations just mentioned. Spillage of RR soybean is inevitable during transport and handling. As one ecologist commented, 'Given that crop seeds travel hundreds of kilometres between seed merchant, farmer and processing factory, spillage in transport is inevitable – and more worrying than pollen spread.'[10]

**GMOs market shift**

China imported 13.94 million metric tons (MMT) of soybeans and 0.1 MMT of soy meal in the marketing year (MY) of 2000/2001, roughly 22.7 per cent of the international soybean exports. Of the trade figure, the Chinese bought 5.2 million metric tons of US soybeans in the year, up from 4.3 million metric tons in 2000, and about one-fifth of annual US soybean exports of 27 million metric tons in 2000/2001. However, it is reported that 63 per cent of USA soybean production in 2000/01 consisted of GMOs and more than 90 per cent of soybean production in Argentina consisted of GMOs (Table 19.1).

China's restrictions on genetically modified (GM) food imports will probably benefit worldwide sales of non-GM soybean as Chinese importers seek to replace bio-engineered soybeans. A Chinese government mission met with leaders of cooperatives from the southern Brazilian state of Rio Grande do Sul in the early of March 2002 to negotiate orders of non-genetically modified soybeans from the 2001-2002 crops.[11] China is the largest soybean market in the world, so producers and traders are likely to adjust to China's requirements.

*Table 19.1 World soybean exports and proportion of production accounted for by GMOs, 2000/2001*

| Country or country group | Soybean exports (MMT) | Soy meal exports (MMT) | Proportion of production accounted for by GMOs (%) |
|---|---|---|---|
| USA | 27.1 | 7.0 | 63% |
| Brazil | 14.0 | 9.9 | little - assume 10% |
| Argentina | 6.7 | 13.7 | more than 90% |
| Paraguay | 2.5 | 0.5 | little - assume 10% |
| India | 0 | 2.2 | none |
| EU | 0 | 1.4 | none |

*Source*: USDA Foreign Agricultural Service (2002, Table 8), Soybeans and products: world trade, http://www.fas.usda.gov/oilseeds/circular/2002/02-09/table8.pdf.

## USA Trade Strategy and Inter-Governmental Negotiations

It is no coincidence that the USA criticised Chinese policies when mandatory labelling of GMOs became a legal requirement in China. President Bush is said to have already raised the issue twice in meetings with Chinese leaders: in October (2001) on the sidelines of an Asia Pacific Economic Cooperation (APEC) forum in Shanghai, and then in Beijing in February (2002). One approach of the USA to lowering barriers to export of GMOs to China is to encourage it to adopt the same management model as the US[12] and another is use of its coercive power, that is, threat of an action in the WTO. One of the basic American criticisms of China's regulations is that 'there is no segregation of GMO and non-GMO soybeans in the US at the moment and such an act is equal to discrimination in China'.

Based on intergovernmental negotiations, the China Ministry of Agriculture said in March 2002 that a compromise deal had been worked out with US trade negotiators and the ministry had agreed to establish a transition period of nine months, until 20 December 2002 after the new rules of safety certification and labelling took effect on 20 March 2002. Due to the time needed for the interim agreement, US soybean exports did not start getting unloaded in China again until mid-June.

**Downward Harmonisation of Standards or Globally Efficient GMOs Management: Review of Cartagena Biosafety Protocol to the Convention on Biological Diversity, and WTO Agreements**

China is both a member state of the WTO and the United Nations Convention on Biological Diversity. Under the WTO agreement, national laws and regulations must be harmonised with international standards. International standards are supposed to be the basis for local regulations, and any excess requirements over these international standards are labelled as disguised unfair trade barriers. Because of the dominant role of the US/Canada/Argentina group in the WTO, private industry has considerable influence on the standard. So there is a reduction of standards in many cases to achieve international harmonisation.

Consequently, there could be inherent conflicts between the provisions of the Biosafety Protocol and the WTO rules. The Cartagena Protocol on Biosafety, commonly known as the Biosafety Protocol – so far the only protocol adopted under the Convention on Biological Diversity – was adopted on the 29 January 2000 after almost six years of painstaking intergovernmental negotiation. The Biosafety Protocol establishes an international regulatory framework. The protocol mainly prescribes minimum standards to control principally the harm arising from the import of GMOs on the conservation and sustainable use of biodiversity and maintenance of human health. The precautionary principle is mandated by the protocol as the basis for decision-making.

Regardless of the shortcomings and loopholes of the protocol, its preamble clearly states that the protocol is not subordinate to the WTO Treaties, which would include the general agreement on trade and tariffs (GATT) and SPS and TBT Treaties. Thus, it would be expected that the Biosafety Protocol, being a specific treaty dealing with GMOs, would prevail over the more general SPS treaty dealing with sanitary and phytosanitary issues.[13]

However, WTO Treaties are now being developed using the standards devised by the Codex Alimentarius Commission as the international standard. An example is the WTO agreement on SPS, a set of rules and obligations about health and hygiene inspection of imports. This commission is heavily influenced by representatives of major food and chemical corporations. US-based agri-food TNCs participate in the meetings of the commission and influence the positions taken by governments. Therefore, it seems likely that global Codex standards for GM food will become very lax and weak, especially since neither farmers nor conventional food producers/retailers have been involved in Codex discussions so far.

**Potential Solution**

The Biosafety Protocol requires that 50 countries ratify it before it can come into effect. As at August 2003, 56 countries have ratified the protocol. Ratification, however, is only a first small step towards ensuring safety in trading in GMOs. China's legislation goes beyond the current protocol text. China, like the European Union (EU), imposed the traceability system. The identification system will be reviewed within two years of the protocol coming into force. Until then, WTO trade rules on GMOs will clear disputes centred around the regulation of trade in GMOs.

Here, the importance of protecting the status of protocol from subordination to the WTO rules is best summed up as follows: 'what is at stake here is the very question of global governance, where the Multilateral Environmental Agreements (MEAs) represent a rare and strategically important space in today's international governance architecture to protect people and the planet. They must be defended and strengthened as a countervailing force to the WTO rules.' [14]

## 19.3 CHALLENGES IN SEED MONOPOLISATION AND ENVIRONMENTAL IMPACTS: *Bt* COTTON CASE IN CHINA

**Monsanto's *Bt* Cotton Strategy and Marketing**

Currently, *Bt* (*Bacillus thuringiensis* Berliner) transgenic cotton is the main GMO crop variety sown commercially in China. It is an insect-resistant cotton variety and contains a toxin designed to control the cotton bollworm, a pest of cotton. Though some test areas were planted in China with Monsanto's *Bt* transgenic cotton in early 1995, the formal permission for commercial production of Monsanto's *Bt* transgenic cotton was granted by the China Ministry of Agriculture in 1997. Since then, the area planted to *Bt* cotton has expanded rapidly. To popularise its *Bt* cotton, Monsanto established two joint venture companies in Hebei and Anhui provinces respectively in 1997 and 1999 and engaged in activities to support agricultural extension and market promotion.

By 2000, *Bt* cotton was grown on 1 million hectares, accounting for 30 per cent of cotton production in China. It is estimated that the area planted to *Bt* cotton increased to 1.5 million hectares in 2001, or 35 per cent of China's total cotton area (Table 19.2). Monsanto's *Bt* cotton accounts for approximately two-thirds of the *Bt* cotton grown, while several domestically developed *Bt* cotton varieties account for the remaining third (Table 19.3).

*Bt* cotton cultivation has become widespread in China and is popular in more than 10 provinces. Currently, *Bt* cotton is mainly planted in the Yellow River Valley of North China, including Shandong, Henan, Shanxi and Hebei provinces. *Bt* cotton acreage is expanding quickly in the Yangtze River Valley of South China, predominantly in Hubei, Hunan, Anhui and Jiangsu provinces. In 2000, about 75 per cent of *Bt* cotton was planted in the Yellow River Valley, 24 per cent in the Yangtze River Valley, and 1 per cent in the Xinjiang Autonomous Region located in Northwest China.

*Table 19.2* Bt *cotton plantation in China (1996-2001)*

| Year | Total *Bt* cotton (ha) | Total cotton area (ha) | *Bt* cotton (%) |
|---|---|---|---|
| 1996 | 16,667 | 4,720,000 | 0.35 |
| 1997 | 34,000 | 4,490,000 | 0.76 |
| 1998 | 228,000 | 3,868,667 | 5.89 |
| 1999 | 578,000 | 3,169,333 | 18.24 |
| 2000 | 1,076,000 | 3,600,000 | 29.89 |
| 2001 | Est. 1.4 – 1.8 m | Est. 4,733,333 | Est. 29.6-38 |

*Source*: Cui, Jinjie (2002), personal communication, Cotton Research Institute, Chinese Academy of Agricultural Sciences.

*Table 19.3 Areas planted with Monsanto* Bt *cotton and with domestic* Bt *cotton in China (1996-2001)*

| Year | Monsanto *Bt* cotton (ha) | Domestic *Bt* cotton (ha) | Total *Bt* cotton (ha) | Monsanto *Bt* cotton (%) |
|---|---|---|---|---|
| 1996 | 0 | 16,667 | 16,667 | 0 |
| 1997 | 12,667 | 21,333 | 34,000 | 37.3 |
| 1998 | 182,667 | 45,333 | 228,000 | 80.1 |
| 1999 | 393,333 | 184,667 | 578,000 | 68.1 |
| 2000 | 709,333 | 366,667 | 1,076,000 | 65.9 |
| 2001 | Est. 1.0-1.3 m | Est. 0.4-0.5 m | Est. 1.4-1.8 m | 71-72 |

*Source*: Cui, Jinjie (2002), personal communication, Cotton Research Institute, Chinese Academy of Agricultural Sciences.

It is reported that the *Bt* cotton planting area has increased to 2 million ha in 2002, accounting for 48.8 per cent of the whole cotton planting area in China in that year (personal communication).

## Market Competition between Monsanto and Chinese Institutional Competition

The cotton seed market in China is large and Chinese domestic companies are competing strongly with Monsanto for sales in the *Bt* cotton seed market. In recent years, more than 30 Chinese research units have focused on the development of *Bt* transgenic cotton, and now many varieties of *Bt* transgenic cotton have been developed and approved for environmental release and commercial production. Therefore, competition has developed between Monsanto and domestic companies.

It was noted that domestically developed *Bt* cotton accounts for one-third of *Bt* cotton seed market and this percentage should increase over the next few years. The main domestic *Bt* cotton varieties include the GK Series (such as GK-2, GK-12) and stacked varieties with *Bt* plus cowpea trypsin inhibitor – CpTI (such as Shiyuan 321) developed by the Biotechnology Centre of the Chinese Academy of Agricultural Sciences (CAAS), the Zhong-Mei Series (such as Zhong-29 and Zhong-30) developed by the Cotton Research Institute of CAAS and others.

*Bt* cotton seed is expensive, partly because of market imperfections. Normally, *Bt* cotton seed sells at 45–150 yuan per kg (1 US$ = 8.26 yuan), but sometimes up to 200 yuan per kg, equivalent to 8 per cent - 25 per cent of a farmer's net income from *Bt* cotton cultivation. However, conventional cotton seed cost only 4–10 yuan per kg, about 5 per cent of that of *Bt* cotton seed. Strong competition between Monsanto and domestic companies in China's *Bt* cotton seed market will continue and probably increase in coming years.

## *Bt* Cotton's Environmental Challenges

On 3 June 2002, a national workshop was held in Beijing to discuss environmental impacts of *Bt* cotton. More than 40 academics participated in the meeting and more than 10 presentations outlined the adverse impacts of *Bt* transgenic cotton on the environment.[15,16] A Summary of Research on the Environmental Impacts of *Bt* Cotton in China[17] was issued in the workshop. This summary is based on the research conducted at four domestic Chinese academic institutions. It was concluded that *Bt* cotton is effective in controlling the primary pest of cotton – bollworm (*Helicoverpa armigera* Hübner), especially in the seedling stage of cotton. However, laboratory experiments and field research have also demonstrated that there are adverse environmental impacts associated with the cultivation of *Bt* cotton. These impacts are summarised below.

- Although in the Chinese studies, no significant impacts were found on predatory natural enemies associated with *Bt* cotton, there are adverse impacts on parasitic natural enemies of cotton bollworm. In *Bt* cotton fields, researchers have shown a decrease in the ratios of parasitisation and eclosion. Consequently, the populations of parasitic natural enemies in *Bt* cotton fields are significantly reduced (Cui and Xia 1998, 1999).
- *Bt* cotton is not effective in controlling many secondary pests, especially sucking pests. Field experiments show that the populations of secondary pests such as cotton aphids, cotton spider mites, thrips, lygus bugs, cotton whitefly, cotton leaf hopper and beet armyworm increased in *Bt* cotton fields after the target pest – bollworm – had been controlled. Some pests replaced bollworm as primary pests and damaged cotton growth (Cui and Xia 1998, 1999; Cui et al. 2001a, 2001b; Zhang 2000; Wu et al. 1999, 2000; Shen 2001).
- The diversity indices of the insect community, the pest sub-community and the pest-natural enemies sub-community, as well as the evenness index of *Bt* cotton fields are all lower than those in conventional cotton fields. However, the pest dominant concentration in *Bt* cotton fields is higher than in the conventional cotton fields. Therefore, the stabilities of insect community, pest sub-community and pest-natural enemies sub-community in *Bt* cotton fields may be less than those in conventional cotton fields, and the possibility of outbreaks of certain pests in *Bt* cotton is much higher (Cui and Xia 2000a, 2000b; Zhang 2000).
- Both laboratory tests and some field monitoring have verified that cotton bollworm can develop resistance to *Bt* cotton. Laboratory tests for selection of *Bt*-resistant bollworm indicated that susceptibility of bollworm to *Bt* cotton fell to 30 per cent after 17 generations under continuous selection with a diet of *Bt* cotton leaves. The resistance index of the bollworm increased 1000 times when the selection was continued to the 40th generation. Based on these results, some scientists concluded that *Bt* cotton would probably lose its resistance to bollworm in fields after the *Bt* cotton

has been planted for 8-10 years continuously (Cui and Xia 1999; Shen et al. 1998; Zhao 1998).

- *Bt* cotton demonstrates excellent resistance to the second generation bollworm and chemical control is not generally needed for the seedling period of *Bt* cotton. However, the resistance of *Bt* cotton to bollworm decreases over time, and control is not complete in the third and fourth generations. In fact, farmers must use chemicals 2-8 times to control bollworm, particularly from mid-July to early September.

**Debate on Environmental Impacts of *Bt* Cotton in China**

This Summary Report, mentioned above, was circulated by Greenpeace worldwide and subsequently led to an international debate through media and the internet (Li 2002).[18,19,20] Both Monsanto and domestic biotech companies denied *Bt* cotton's serious adverse impacts and made representations to the researchers and authors. The China Ministry of Agriculture held two special workshops on *Bt* cotton. They have commonly recognised that some secondary pests have often become the main pests in *Bt* cotton fields and farmers have to use additional pesticides. They also concluded that in medium and later growth phases of cotton, pesticides are needed to control the target pest of the cotton bollworm in *Bt* cotton fields. However, some people consider that the resistance of cotton bollworm to *Bt* cotton is not yet evident in the field and further monitoring is needed.

## 19.4 PUBLIC CONCERNS ABOUT MONOPOLIZATION VIA PATENTS FOR PLANT VARIETIES: THE SOYBEAN PATENT CASE IN CHINA

**Monsanto's Soybean Patent Application**

Monsanto's worldwide patent application (WO/0018963) was published on 6 April 2000, under the title of 'Methods for breeding and for screening of soybean plants with enhanced yields'. As the title indicates, Monsanto aims to use this patent to gain control over whole families of soy.

The specific wild soya that Monsanto describes in the patent application dossier originated from South China, but Monsanto got the germplasm from the US national germ-plasma collection. Some of the molecular markers can be found in other wild soybeans originating in Russia and in five provinces of China and also in some domesticated soya varieties found in Japan. Monsanto aims to identify and select these markers in other wild, 'exotic' or domesticated soya. The objective is to breed these enhanced yield characteristics into cultivated high value/elite soya varieties using the molecular markers to get elite soya plants with enhanced yield characteristics. In addition, the option to introduce these markers into other plants through genetic engineering is also foreseen.

In the patent application, Monsanto requests patent protection for:

- the markers associated with enhanced yield;
- all plants (wild and domesticated) in which these markers occur, including all their progeny;
- the screening methods that allow these markers to be identified;
- the plant breeding methods for the production of an elite *Glycine max* through 'crossing', and 'screening' and 'selecting' for further crossing and selection; and
- the breeding method for the production of enhanced yield *Glycine max* plant and genetically engineered plants where such a marker would be introduced (alfalfa, *Arabidopsis*, thaliana, barley, *Brassica*, broccoli, cabbage, citrus, cotton, garlic, oat, oilseed rape, onion, canola, flax, an ornamental plant, pea, peanut, pepper, potato, rice, rye, soybean, sorghum, strawberry, sugarcane, sugarbeet, tomato, wheat, maize, poplar, pine, fir, eucalyptus, apple, lettuce, lentils, grape, banana, tea, turf grasses, sunflower, oil palm, and Phaseolus).

## Biopiracy: Greenpeace's Accusation

Greenpeace has accused Monsanto of seeking to monopolise soybean. It revealed the patent application at the start of the United Nations (UN) Conference on Biodiversity in Bonn, Germany on 22 October 2001. The patent, however, has not yet been approved. The European Patent Office in Munich has raised doubts about the patent in its initial evaluation. However, both in Europe and in the USA numerous patents, regarded as cases of biopiracy by Greenpeace, have been granted, according to a Greenpeace press release.[21]

**'Planting Chinese soybean, infringing American patent right?': public discussion in China**

The above is the title of an article published in the Chinese newspaper *Southern Weekend* on 25 October 2001. The article points out that Monsanto will wield significant commercial power if its US patent application on high-yield, fast-growing soy DNA is granted. If Chinese farmers were to unwittingly ignore such a Monsanto patent, that 'might make it impossible to export some Chinese soy products and could even result in international trade sanctions'. The state-run newspaper *Southern Weekend* gave a front-page to this story. Afterwards, much public discussion occurred throughout China nationwide. Chang Ruzhen, chairman of the China Soybean Society and an expert on soybean genetic resources, was quoted as saying, 'This could affect genetic research throughout the world. It's not good news for anyone.' [22]

After examining the application, a soya-breeding expert, Professor Junyi Gai of the Chinese Engineering Academy and director of the Soybean Research Institute of Nanjing Agriculture University, questioned whether Monsanto's application is an invention or just a discovery. 'Markers exist in nature. The screening and comparison (by Monsanto) have not altered its state of existence. According to the application, Monsanto has not identified the gene that is alleged to be associated with high-yield. Nor has it separated or cloned that gene sequence.' Professor Gai added that 'claiming the patent to cover all soybean varieties containing these markers is unjust and inappropriate because it is not based on scientific facts'.

Generations of farmers and plant breeders in China and other parts of East Asia, where a huge diversity of soybean varieties exists, have created the high-yielding soybean varieties over a long period. However, the individual peasant households in China are seldom organised, and their voices and rights were mostly ignored.

Such kind of patent claims over genetic resources are generally obtained without the prior informed consent of the government or community where the materials originated. Neither the country nor its people nor farmers or plant breeders would benefit from this patent. Nor will they be able to share in the economic benefits that Monsanto hopes to generate through monopolising the genetic resources. This is in sharp contradiction to the principle of the Convention on Biological Diversity (CBD) which calls for fair access to genetic resources and benefit sharing. Thus the contribution of farmers who have been domesticating, improving and breeding soybean for years is ignored and disregarded. Furthermore, these farmers would be blocked from using these resources unless they pay Monsanto for it, and this has been criticised.

Four months after the Monsanto patent case was exposed, China joined Brazil, India, and nine other biodiverse countries and signed an alliance, the Cancun Declaration, to fight biopiracy and press for rules protecting people's rights to genetic resources originating from their own land. The Cancun Declaration echoed complaints long voiced by indigenes and environmentalists: that wealthy nations are 'prospecting' for species in order to patent or sell them without offering concessions or benefits for local people.[23]

**Review of the Relationship between CBD and TRIPs Agreement and Intellectual Property Rights**

Internationally, the World Trade Organisation and the Convention on Biological Diversity (CBD) are two critical forums determining principles and legal frameworks on the patenting of biological materials and life forms.

The WTO's trade-related intellectual property rights (TRIPs) agreement will have the most decisive influence over national laws. TRIPs, in particular Article 27.3(b), contains vague language that could lead to contradictory interpretations about rights in living organisms. Patenting of micro-organisms is compulsory, plants and animals can be excluded, but effective *sui generis* protection of plant variety rights is required. This clause is, however, under review, and is dealt with under Paragraph 19 of the Doha Declaration, which also instructs the TRIPs Council to examine the relationship between TRIPs and CBD and the protection of traditional knowledge (TK) and folklore. The outcome of the review process will be of crucial importance.

The Convention on Biological Diversity (CBD) was concluded at the 1992 Earth Summit. It recognises 'farmers' rights' to their knowledge over the use of biodiversity. The rights of indigenous people are also likely to be included in the convention's future agenda. The treaty's references to intellectual property rights is finely balanced between recognising the need to implement Intellectual Property Rights (IPRs) and the need to ensure that IPRs do not block the sustainable use of biodiversity. CBD endorses legal access and benefit sharing (ABS) for all parties and protection of the rights of providers of genetic resources.

From a legal perspective, there is no conflict between the CBD and the TRIPs agreement. However, differences could arise in interpretation. Steps need to be taken to ensure compatibility in interpretation.

## 19.5 CONCLUSION

The WTO has achieved a significant reduction in quantitative barriers to international trade and continues its efforts to lower qualitative barriers to such trade. In particular, it wishes to stop countries from using the WTO agreements on Sanitary and Phytosanitary Measures and on Technical Barriers to Trade as mere disguises for economic protection of their home industries. But there are difficult situations where some health, environmental and other safety concerns exist in a country about imports, the restriction of which also affords some economic protection to local industries. A judgement is then required about whether the safety concerns of the country involved outweigh any economic benefits forgone globally, as a result of a restriction on international trade. Such issues are especially important in relation to international trade in GMOs. As illustrated in this article they have been a source of conflict between the United States and China in relation to international trade in GM soybeans.

Continual international diplomacy occurs to try to change international law and the application of different international agreements and practices to the regulation of international trade, especially that involving qualitative restrictions, as in the case of trade in GMOs. Strategic behaviour by the United States in this regard has been highlighted, and this behaviour seems to be directed at ruling out the possibility that the Cartegena Biosafety Protocol of the UN Convention on Biological Diversity will become binding on the WTO. As matters now stand, if the Biosafety Protocol comes into force, the policies of the WTO in relation to international trade in GMOs will need to conform with it. So intense international conflict can arise over the over-arching legal framework in which globalisation proceeds. Economic globalisation does not occur in a legal or institutional vacuum.

Furthermore, economic globalisation is not occurring with a view to establishing an entirely competitive market situation, that is, perfect competition of the type envisaged by neoclassical economists. One reason for this is that there is often a conflict between allocative and 'dynamic' efficiency as far as the commercial creation of new products and knowledge is concerned (see, for example, Svizzero and Tisdell 2001). A temporary monopoly is often needed to enable inventors and innovators to profit from their efforts and so induce them to invest in research and development and innovation. This is recognised in the WTO's trade-related intellectual property rights (TRIPS) agreement. This provides for rights in intellectual property which are capable of facilitating global monopolies in the use of intellectual property.

As illustrated in this article, this has become a concern for several developing countries as far as transgenic organisms are concerned. China, for example, is worried about the possibility that plant or patent rights in relation to GM soybeans could limit its opportunities to obtain intellectual property rights if it undertakes genetic development of its soybeans. In addition, monopoly pricing of the supply of transgenic seed to farmers in developing countries has been criticised because it contributes to monopoly profits of multinational companies involved in the development and sale of transgenic seed. Furthermore, the question is raised of whether or not it is just that such monopoly prices be charged in developing countries given that in many cases, they are the source of the basic organism being modified. This is so in East Asia, especially China, in the case of soybean. These concerns about biopiracy have been raised in the Cancun Declaration, in relation to the Convention on Biological Diversity.

China has been concerned about the possibility of Monsanto obtaining a monopoly on sales of cotton seed in China via its sale of transgenic seeds. In response, China has developed and continues to develop, its own varieties of *Bt* cotton. In this case, globalisation by stimulating competitive research and innovation in China may actually be adding to future environmental problems in China. Several scientists believe that transgenic engineering of crops for pest control will not provide sustained control of the target pest and encourages non-target pests. Therefore, particularly in the long term, this method is unlikely to be economic. Furthermore, the widespread use of transgenic crops can be expected to reduce the number of varieties conserved of a crop. This can have further adverse consequences for the sustainability of agricultural production.

Because the thrust towards free trade encounters environmental and health concerns in some nations as far as international trade in transgenic organisms is concerned, this has become a major area of international conflict. This is further compounded by provision of global rights in intellectual property, as in the TRIPS agreement. This has become especially controversial in relation to plant variety rights and rights in genetic manipulation since these are capable of providing some multinational companies (mostly with headquarters in higher-income countries) with substantial monopsony power. There is a fear that this may be used 'to exploit' farmers, especially in developing countries, and redistribute income in favour of more developed countries. A further criticism is that such rights may limit the scope for developed countries to genetically develop and use their own crops, such as soybeans in China. In effect, this restricts their future development path. Distributional justice seems to be at the core of such global conflict.

# NOTES

1. Based on the Investigation Report for Activities of Agricultural Transnationals in China for Greenpeace, June 2002.
2. 'Sri Lanka defers GM food ban', *Checkbiotech*, 13 June 2001, http://www.checkbiotech.org/root/index.cfm?fuseaction=search&search=sri%20lanka&doc_id=1244&start=1&fullsearch=0.
3. 'US moots GM action', *The Grocer*, 16 February 2002.
4. 'Zoellick Outlines Concerns Raised By Lags in China's WTO Compliance' by Chris Rugaber, *WTO Reporter*, Friday, 1 February 2002, The Bureau of National Affairs Inc., Washington DC. ISSN 1529-4153.
5. 'Millions of Chinese farmers fear the growing impact of global agribusiness as they prepare for entry into the WTO', writes John Gittings, 13 November 2001, http://www.guardian.co.uk/elsewhere/journalist/story/0,7792,592848,00.html.
6. 'Food security, farmers' rights top new ag law', *ChinaOnline*, 25 June 2002, www.chinaonline.com/industry/agriculture/.
7. EU Commission Decision of 3 April 1996 concerning the placing on the market of genetically modified soya beans (*Glycine max L.*) with increased tolerance to the herbicide glyphosate, pursuant to Council Directive 90/220/EEC (96/281/EC). The decision directs the UK government to grant the EU market consent for Monsanto's RR soya.
8. According to the Database of the OECD, RR soya was first approved in the USA for planting and use in 1994, it is approved for planting and use as well in Canada, Argentina and Mexico, for use but not for planting in the EU, Japan and Switzerland. This list may be incomplete.
9. USDA/APHIS (1994) Response to Monsanto petition P93-258-01 for determination of nonregulated status for glyphosate tolerant soybean line 40-3-2. United States Department of Agriculture, Animals and Plant Health Inspection Service, Biotechnology, Biologics and Environmental Protection.
10. Crawley, M. (1996), 'The day of the triffids', *New Scientist*, 6 July, pp. 40-41.
11. Alastair Stewart, FWN, 5511 3071 3990, http://www.txinfinet.com/ban-gef/01/11/11-22.HTML.
12. 'APEC Leaders Endorse US Proposal on Biotechnology', US Department of State, International Information Programs 21 October 2001, http://usinfo.state.gov/topical/global/biotech/01102101.htm.
13. Duncan Currie, LL.B. (Hons.), LL.M., International Law relating to Genetic Modification, submitted to the New Zealand Royal Commission on Genetic Modification on behalf of Greenpeace New Zealand Inc. on 9 March 2001.
14. 'Johannesburg Earth Summit must agree that the World Trade Organisation Rules will respect Multilateral Environmental Agreements', joint statement by Friends of the Earth International, Greenpeace International, WWF International, Third World Network, Northern Alliance for Sustainability (ANPED) and Sierra Club-Press Release, 3 April 2002, www.worldsummit2002.org/download/MEA-WTOstatement.rtf.
15. Dayuan Xue and Sze-ping Lo (editors in chief), *International Biosafety Newsletter*, No 4, 2000.
16. Dayuan Xue and Sze-ping Lo (editors in chief), *International Biosafety Newsletter*, No 5, 2000.
17. Dayuan Xue, 2002, A summary of research on the environmental impacts of *Bt* cotton, published in the *National Workshop on Environmental Safety of GMOs*, held on 3 June 2002 and co-organised by the Chinese Society of Agri-Biotechnology, Nanjing Institute of Environmental Sciences of State EPA and Greenpeace International.
18. Xinhua News Agency, 'GM cotton damages environment: balance in community of insects lost by using transgenic plants', *China Daily*, p. 2, 4 June 2002.
19. Liu Quanyou, 'To control introduction of genetically modified organisms', *People's Daily*, p. 9, 25 June 2002.
20. 'Greenpeace launch attack on *Bt* transgenic cotton', *Southern Weekend*, 27 June 2002,

http://www.nanfangdaily.com.cn/zm/20020627/.
21. 'Greenpeace attacks Monsanto's Biopiracy Plans', Bonn/London, 22 October 2001, press release, www.greenpeace.org/pressreleases/geneng/2001oct22.html.
22. Elaine Kurtenbach, 'Monsanto's attempt to patent soybeans causes alarm in China', Associated Press, 12 December 2001, http://www.mindfully.org/GE/GE3/Monsanto-Alarms-China.htm.
23. Mark Stevenson, 'China, Brazil, India, 9 other nations form alliance against biopiracy', Associated Press, 19 February 2002, http://www.enn.com/news/wire-stories/2002/02/02192002/ap_46427.asp.

## REFERENCES

Cui, Jinjie and Xia Jingyuan (1998), 'Effects of *Bt* transgenic cotton (with early maturity) on population dynamics of main pests and their natural enemies', *Acta Gossypii Sinica*, **10** (5), 255-62.

Cui, Jinjie and Xia Jingyuan (1999), 'Effects of transgenic *Bt* cotton on the population dynamics of natural enemies', *Acta Gossypii Sinica*, **11** (2), 84-91.

Cui, Jinjie and Xia, Jingyuan (2000a), 'Effects of transgenic *Bt* cotton R93-6 on the insect community', *Acta Entomologica Sinica*, **43** (1), 43-51.

Cui, Jinjie and Xia, Jingyuan (2000b), 'Studies on the components of diversity of the community in transgenic *Bt* cotton', *Acta Ecologica Sinica*, **20** (5), 824-829.

Cui, Xuefen, Cui Jinjie and Xia Jingyuan (2001a), 'Selection of a resistant strain of cotton bollworm (Helicoverpa armigera) to *Bt* toxin protein (Cry1Ac)', unpublished report.

Cui, Xuefen, Cui Jinjie, Xia Jingyuan, Wang Chuanyi and Ma Lihua (2001b), 'Study on the biology of resistance variability of cotton bollworm to Bt toxin protein (Cry1Ac)', unpublished report.

Li, Fang (2002), 'Debating on transgenic cotton in China', *China Cotton Prospect*, **7**, 29-30.

Ministry of Agriculture (2000), *China Report for Agricultural Development*, Beijing: Agricultural Publishing House.

Shen, Jinliang, Zhou Weijun, Wu Yidong, Lin Xiangwen and Zhu Xiefei (1998), 'Early resistance of Helicoverpa armigera (Hubner) to Bacillus thuringiensis (*Bt*) and its relation to the effect of transgenic cotton lines expressing *Bt* toxin on the insect', *Acta Entomologica Sinica*, **41**, 8-14.

Shen, Jinliang (2001), Field test report of Bt cotton's impacts on natural enemies and non-target pests, unpublished report.

Svizzero, Serge, and Clem Tisdell (2001), 'Concepts of competition theory and practice', *Revista Internazionale de Scienze Economiche e Commerciali*, **48**, 145-62.

Windels, P., I. Taverners, A. Depicker, E. van Bockstaele and M. De Loose (2001), 'Characterisation of Roundup Ready Soybean insert', *European Food Research Technology*, **213**, 107-12.

Wu, Kongming, Guo Yuyuan and Nan Lu (1999), 'Geographic variation in susceptibility of Helicoverpa armigera (Lepidoptera: Noctuidae) to Bacillus thuringiensis insecticidal protein in China', *Journal of Economic Entomology*, **92** (2), 273-8.

Wu, Kongming, Liang Gemei and Guo Yuyuan (2000), 'Study on risk assessment of cotton bollworm resistance and pest control technologies in Bt cotton fields of North China', unpublished report.

Xue, Dayuan and C. Tisdell (2000), 'Safety and socio-economic issues raised by modern biotechnology', *International Journal of Social Economics*, **27** (7), 699-708.

Xue, Dayuan and C. Tisdell (2002), 'Global trade in GM food and the Cartagena Protocol on Biosafety: consequences for China', *Journal of Agricultural and Environmental Ethics*, **15**, 337-56.

Xue, Dayuan, C. Tisdell and Y. Xia (2000), 'Impacts of Biosafety Protocol on importing trade of genetically modified organisms and potential countermeasures in China', *Rural Eco-Environment*, **16** (4), 45-50.

Zhao Jianzhou (1998), 'The resistance and countermeasures of cotton bollworm to *Bt* cotton', *Agricultural Biotechnology Newsletter*, **2**, 1-2 (internal publication).

Zhang Qingwen (2000), 'Report of Working Conclusion during 1999 to 2000 for the Project of Cotton Production Development Fund', unpublished report.

# 20. Economic Globalisation Impacts on Pacific Island Environments and Aid Implications

**Colin Hunt**

## 20.1 INTRODUCTION

The Pacific Ocean contains many island countries that are vulnerable to the environmental changes wrought by economic globalisation. Their renewable resource base and associated environments are being depreciated or threatened by rates of exploitation for export. Capital and technology inflows exacerbate the depreciating effects of resource exploitation. Regional organisations coordinating marine resources management are considered aid priorities. At the same time, population growth and surges of imports are threatening urban environments, making the continuation of assistance for urban environmental improvement important. Poor implementation of environmental and resource policy characterises the performance of Pacific island governments. Aid targets should therefore be broadened to include governance as well as technical and institutional strengthening.

In this chapter, 'economic globalisation' is used in its narrow context of flows of trade and investment across borders. Trade is comprised of exports and imports. Investment includes foreign direct investment (FDI) (where one country invests directly in another), capital market flows (resulting from borrowers accessing foreign capital markets) and official development assistance (ODA), or aid (under bilateral or multilateral arrangements).

The purpose of this chapter is to show the effects of trade and investment on key Pacific island environments and resources, and identify where aid can ameliorate these effects.

Pacific island independent states are usually categorised as 'developing' and tend to fall into three groups. The resource rich group includes Papua New Guinea, by far the largest island economy, and the Solomon Islands and Vanuatu; the more economically advanced group contains Cook Islands, Fiji Islands, Federated States of Micronesia, Samoa and Tonga; and the resource poor group includes the atoll states of Kiribati, Tuvalu, Nauru and the Marshall Islands.[1]

The Global Conference on the Sustainable Development of Small Island Developing States (United Nations General Assembly 1998) concluded that small island developing states were the most vulnerable to economic and environmental shocks. The relative openness of Pacific island economies (in terms of contribution of trade to the economy) compared with many developing countries in other regions, tends to exacerbate this vulnerability. Figure 20.1 shows, however, that this openness has either tended to change little or to decrease, sometimes markedly, over the last two decades. The cause of this relative fall in the importance of trade is the lacklustre performance of export sectors. This is despite the South Pacific Regional Trade and Economic Cooperation Agreement (SPARTECA) of 1981, under which Australia and New Zealand offer non-reciprocal duty free and unrestricted or concessional access to virtually all products originating from Forum Island countries (FICs).[2]

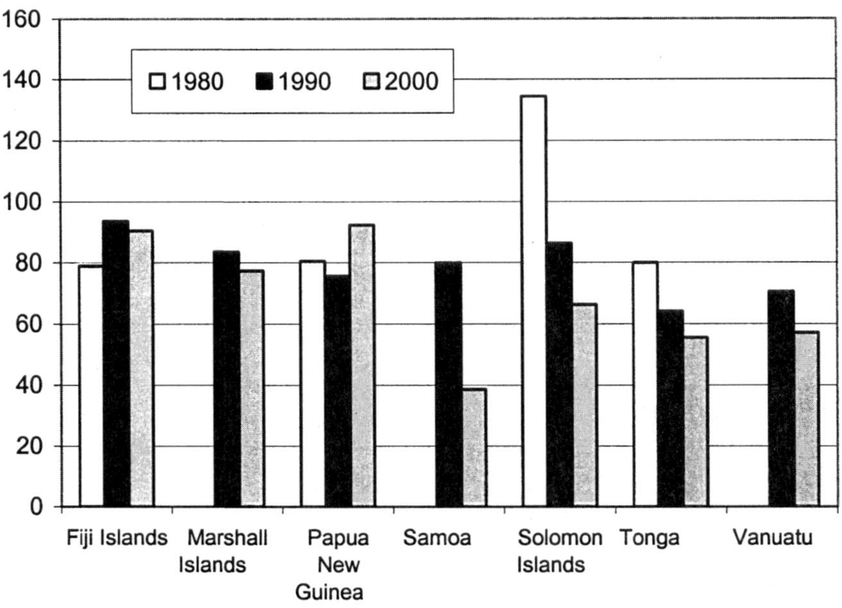


*Source*: ADB (2001, Table 32).

*Figure 20.1 Foreign trade as a percentage of GNP, selected Pacific island countries, 1980/1990/2000*

Apart from the political, social and economic instability in Melanesia, the generally poor comparative economic performance of Pacific island economies is linked to a lack of opportunities for diversification and industrialisation as well as relative isolation from markets. There is also a significant lack of dynamic institutions and progressive policy formulation that could compensate for these disadvantages (Duncan et al. 1999). Figure 20.2 details the recent poor economic performance in three Melanesian countries.

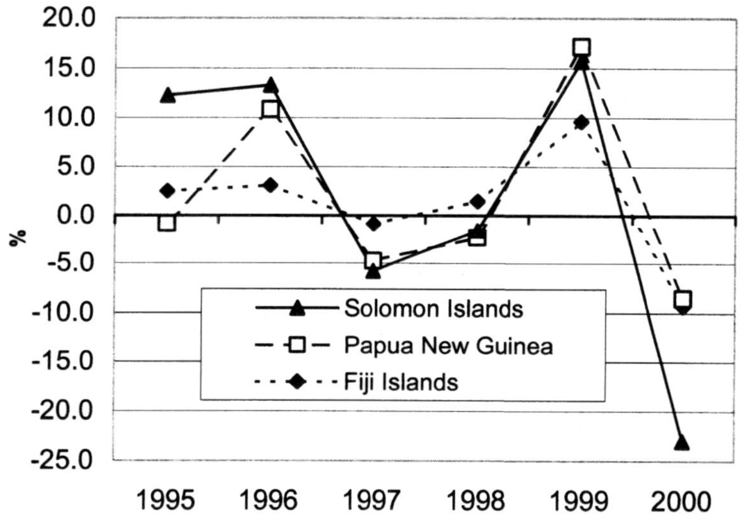


Source: ADB (2001, Table 12).

*Figure 20.2 Gross domestic product growth in three Pacific island countries (constant prices), 1995-2000*

Political, economic, institutional, social and geographic factors together serve to explain the lack of interest on the part of private investors, and the continuing heavy reliance on official aid (ADB 2001, Tables 38, 39). Figure 20.3 shows that while the share of net private capital in total capital flow in the Pacific islands has recovered from a severe downturn (coinciding with the Asian financial crisis), it has remained at less than 50 per cent of the total, with ODA continuing to be very important. The figure shows that, in contrast, developing countries as a whole have enjoyed capital contributions from private sources of around 80 per cent over the last few years.

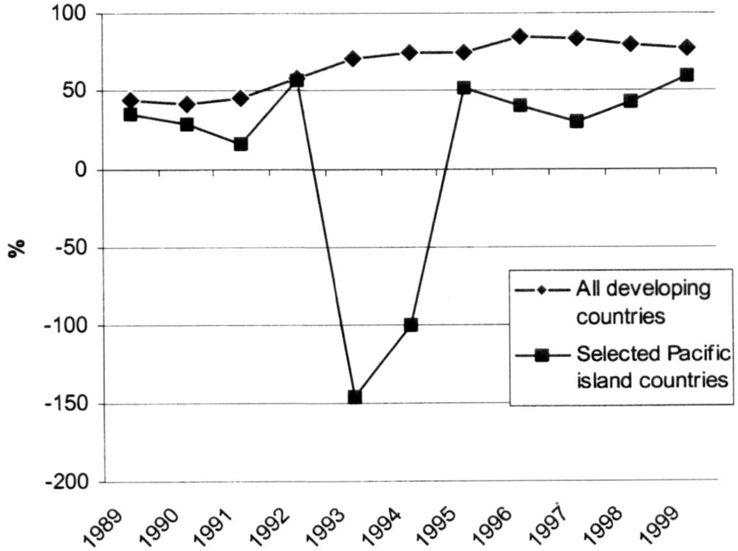


*Source*: ADB (2001, Tables 38, 39).

*Figure 20.3 Share of net private capital in total capital flows, 1989-1999*

## 20.2 THE ENVIRONMENTAL IMPACTS OF GLOBALISATION IN PACIFIC ISLAND COUNTRIES

The modification of the impacts of economic globalisation through public policy has been recognised as important by the Organisation for Economic Cooperation and Development (OECD) (1994) and Panayotou (2000). Policies of Pacific island governments modify the depreciation of renewable natural capital and the generation of externalities by economic globalisation. Likewise, policy in the rest of the world modifies the effects of exogenous globalisation (an increase in trade and capital flows in the rest of the world) on Pacific islands.

In this discussion there are two classes of environment, 'natural capital' and 'urban'. Natural capital is defined as including all the renewable resources of forest, agricultural lands and oceans. Net depreciation of the renewable natural capital stock occurs when depreciation due to extraction exceeds appreciation due to the natural accumulation of new stock; and is a function of the volume of resources extracted for exports and domestic consumption resulting from capital flows. The same criterion applies to the biodiversity harboured in natural capital.

The extracted resources that enter world trade are our interest in this exercise. However, the extraction for export per se of non-renewable minerals is not considered depletion of natural capital. The focus of the chapter is rather on the externalities generated by the extraction of minerals, for example the depreciation of resources caused by river disposal of mine tailings, and damage at the site itself.

While renewable resources of the Pacific islands, principally forest and marine resources, are the basis for major export industries they are also the direct source of subsistence (defined as food and material that does not enter the cash economy but are consumed directly) for large proportions of the population of countries with relatively large rural populations, that is, Papua New Guinea, Solomon Islands and Vanuatu. Table 20.1 shows the extent of urbanisation – and inversely the proportion of non-urban populations – among Pacific island countries.

*Table 20.1 Urban population in Pacific island countries, 1980, 1990, 2000, % of total*

| Pacific island country | 1980 | 1990 | 2000 |
|---|---|---|---|
| Fiji Islands | 37.8 | 41.6 | 42.3 |
| Cook Islands | 54.8 | 57.7 | 63.0 |
| Kiribati | 31.7 | 34.6 | 37.3 |
| Marshall Islands | 58.3 | 65.7 | 71.9 |
| Micronesia, Fed. States of | 25.0 | 26.4 | 29.7 |
| Nauru | 100.0 | 100.0 | 100.0 |
| Papua New Guinea | 13.0 | 15.0 | 17.4 |
| Solomon Islands | 10.5 | 14.6 | 19.7 |
| Tonga | 27.0 | 32.6 | 46.4 |
| Vanuatu | 17.9 | 18.2 | 20.0 |
| Tuvalu | 30.0 | 40.9 | 52.2 |

*Source*: ADB (2001, Table 4).

The other major class of environmental assets considered is urban. These are principally potable water supplies, safe inshore waters and clean air. Water and air quality tend to depreciate because of increasing domestic consumption and imports especially in urban concentrations. Table 20.1 shows that urbanisation is already high and increasing in the small island and atoll states.

## 20.3 THE EFFECT OF EXPORTS ON NATURAL CAPITAL STOCKS

### The Export of Forest Products

The Solomon Islands and Papua New Guinea are blessed with extensive natural forests and the export of logs is a major industry in both countries, contributing about 60 per cent of the total value of merchandise exports in the former and 10 per cent in the latter.

In the Solomon Islands the rate of logging over the last 10 years, at over 0.5 million cubic metres per annum has been unsustainable; that is, extraction far exceeds the forests' recovery rate and at current rates of exploitation all accessible forest will have been logged in 5 year's time (Bouro 2001; Hunt 2002a). The government has encouraged logging, one of the few remaining viable export industries, as a means of ameliorating the economic crisis that grips the country (Hunt 2002a).

In Papua New Guinea the rate of logging relative to its forest resource base has been low compared to the Solomon Islands and has been declining. About one million hectares have been logged over the last 10 years while about 11 million hectares of forest remain suitable for commercial production, that is, about 16 years of production at the current rate. Forest administration in PNG is notoriously corrupt and forestry operations have been badly managed so that the main concern is not so much the national rate of logging compared with the size of national resource base, but the fact that logging has often been carried out in an unregulated manner, precluding forest recovery, and has tended to be concentrated in certain provinces (Hunt 2002b).

In Vanuatu, the other Melanesian country with a large industry based on natural forests, logging escalated to an unsustainable rate in the early 1990s, triggering a log export ban by the government. Exports are now exclusively in the form of sawn timber. Logging for domestic production is nevertheless still resulting in net depreciation (Vanuatu Department of Forests 2000). This situation illustrates that forestry planning and management are the keys to sustainability, rather than log export bans.

### The Export of Marine Resources

The most important source of marine resource exports in the Pacific is the common property tuna stocks. The tuna stocks generate by far the largest flow of receipts from any single source. They also constitute a major or even the main source of government revenues in some small atoll states,[3] pointing to the importance of the maintenance of the renewable tuna stocks for the future economic well being of Pacific island countries.

The bulk of the tuna catch is by foreign fleets operating under licence in the Exclusive Economic Zones (EEZs) of the island countries and on the high seas. The foreign fleets ship their catches to the canneries of Southeast Asia or American Samoa or, in the case of the longline fisheries, directly to the markets of Japan. The following question is addressed: are the common tuna stocks suffering net depreciation because of exports? In addition to the extraction by foreign fleets, there is a relatively small level of export of tuna by the domestic fleets of Pacific island developing countries capitalised by both foreign and domestic sources.

There are in fact four main species that make up the tuna catch. They are skipjack (*Katsuwonus palamis*), yellowfin (*Thunnus albacares*), big eye (*Thunnus obesus*) and albacore (*Thunnus alalunga*). These tunas differ in their biology, habits and value. Skipjack, which comprises the bulk of the catch in the Western Central Pacific Ocean (WCPO), are very fecund and may be able to sustain further increases in exploitation. The other more valuable species are generally slower maturing and therefore tend to be more vulnerable to increasing levels of fishing effort.

The depreciation of big eye stocks, due to over-exploitation, has emerged as a problem in the WCPO (Hampton et al. 2000, p. 17). Further study is required but preliminary results raise a concern of over-fishing and decline in adult biomass. Big eye is the most sought after of the Pacific tuna species in the Japanese fresh fish markets – the depletion of the species will incur a future opportunity cost in terms of export income to Pacific islands.

Fostering appreciation of big eye stocks in the WCPO faces two major hurdles. The first is the need for organisation and action that is multilateral as a consequence of the common property nature of the stock. The second is the difficulty of differentiating between tuna species in the multi-species fishery. On the second, a promulgation of a reduction in the catch of skipjack and yellowfin – the major money earners from canning – in order to conserve big eye stocks, may be unpopular with distant water nations and Pacific island nations alike. Other possible solutions for a reduction in big eye catch include gear configurations and limits on fish aggregate device (FAD) fishing as have already been implemented in other oceans. A newly formed convention on conservation and management of tuna in the WCPO will tackle these issues.

A large proportion of the population in most Pacific island countries – and an overwhelming majority in some – are still in a subsistence economy and reliant on inshore fish stocks (ESCAP 2001; Hunt 1997, 1999). The export of live fish and the aquarium trade are depreciating inshore fish stocks. The regulation of such live fish operations is often non-existent because fishing administrations tend to be weak and underfunded (SPC 2001a). Coastal development may be an even more serious threat to inshore resources (SPC

2001a).

Government policies in the case of oceanic fish stocks are becoming more tied into regional policy that in turn stems from international policy on the management of common fish stocks. The flow of aid to Pacific island countries has been influential in enabling their participation in the international and regional meetings that have formulated the conventions aimed at preventing or minimising the depreciation of tuna stocks. More indirect but just as important has been the financial support of developed countries for the regional organisations, the Secretariat of the Pacific Community (SPC) and the Forum Fisheries Agency.[4] Likewise SPC activity through aid is essential to assist island governments in tackling the many threats to vital inshore resources.

## The Export of Agricultural Products

In most Pacific island countries, a large proportion of the population is in subsistence or in subsistence mixed with small-scale production and trading. Smallholders commonly engage in the export production of crops including coffee, cocoa, vanilla, ginger, oil palm and copra; the cropped area rarely exceeding a few hectares interspersed with other land uses, and the level of inputs of imported agrochemicals is minimal. The environmental impact of small-scale agriculture is consequently generally low.

In Fiji, agriculture is still the most important sector economically despite increasing industrialisation. The past decade has seen increasing land degradation caused by widespread and indiscriminate slash-and-burn cultivation, as well as cultivation on steep land for export sugar production and for the export of ginger and kava. While there is no shortage of legislation requiring good husbandry practices, there has been an almost complete lack of enforcement in Fiji's post-independence era (ESCAP 2001).

Tonga has a small, open economy with a narrow export base in agricultural goods, which contributes 30 per cent to GDP (ADB 2001). Agricultural exports make up two-thirds of total exports with squash (a small pumpkin) export to Japan now the most important. However, the transition from subsistence farming to export cash cropping has necessitated an increase in the use of imported agrochemicals. It is claimed that excessive chemical use has led to ecological damage, and environmental pollution, and has affected public health (Tupou 2000). According to ESCAP (2001) the institutional capacity of the Kingdom of Tonga to deal with environmental issues is weak, moreover a legislative framework is lacking.

The development and implementation of environmental policy is also weak in Samoa. The 1992 National Environmental Management and Development Strategies were accepted by cabinet, yet agreed policies and actions are ignored, as is the case with the national environmental strategies of other countries of the region (ESCAP 2001).

An illustration of the type of environmental impacts expected from the establishment of an export palm oil venture in a forested area of PNG, taken from a foreign direct investment proposal submitted to the PNG government, is in Table 20.2.

Table 20.2 suggests that the removal of rainforest has the largest impact but positive impacts are claimed for oil palm establishment. The existing palm oil exporting companies in PNG are international companies that self-regulate to minimise environmental controversy. They establish cover crops on cleared land and minimise the effect of disposal of processing waste by returning it to the land under palms. The companies justify the inevitable environmental trade-offs by emphasising the size of the social and economic benefits generated. An additional impact to that in Table 20.2 is that of the effluent generated by the concentration of worker housing (200 workers per 1000 hectares of palms).

*Table 20.2 Environmental impacts of oil palm establishment*

| **Environment impacted** | **Activities** | | | |
|---|---|---|---|---|
| | Logging roads constructed | Timber felling, transport, milling | Maintenance of residual flora and afforestation | Planting oil palm |
| Soil and land | -4 | -8 | +4 | +4 |
| Hydrology | -2 | -8 | +2 | +4 |
| Climate | 0 | 0 | +2 | +2 |
| Flora | -6 | -14 | +4 | +4 |
| Fauna | 0 | -2 | +2 | -2 |
| Conservation area | -2 | -4 | +4 | 0 |

*Note*: * Numbers represent level of negative or positive environmental impact.

*Source*: After ARAB (1994, p. 373).

## The Export of Minerals

The export of minerals is important for PNG, New Caledonia and Nauru. In the case of PNG, crude oil, gold and copper dominate. Mineral export taxes generated 14 per cent of total government revenues in 2000 (Bank of Papua New Guinea 2001, Tables 8.1, 8.2). A characteristic of mines in PNG is that tailings dams are not reliable due to unstable geology. Tailings are therefore discharged into river systems. The Jaba River, Bougainville, became unnavigable as a result of tailings disposal from the now closed Panguna copper mine. The Strickland-Fly River system receives tailings and overburden disposal from the Porgera copper/gold mine and the Ok Tedi/ Fly River has received tailings from the Ok Tedi copper/gold mine since 1986.

Environmental depreciation often incurs social costs and the Ok Tedi mining project was subjected to a range of social impact studies. However, the studies were undertaken *after* government approval was given for development (ESCAP 2001). The World Bank's unpublished review of the Ok Tedi mine, cited by Mineral Policy Institute (2002a) concluded that, from an environmental standpoint, the best option was to close the mine immediately.

The gold mines situated on small islands in PNG dispose of tailings into the ocean, as will the proposed coastal Ramu nickel mine. In the case of the latter, neutralised tailings will be discharged at 150 metres depth off the coast – it is claimed well below the surface ocean mixing zone – the tailings then flowing into and becoming buried in a two kilometre deep offshore basin. The proposed technology is 'state of the art' but is similar to that used at the Misima and Lihir mines in PNG (Highland Pacific 2002). Despite the Ramu mine proponent's claims, there is a great deal of controversy over the effect that large quantities of tailings will have on water quality, marine flora and fauna and adjacent reef and coastal ecosystems (Mineral Policy Institute 2002b). Doubts that the environmental affects of the operating Lihir mine are in fact minimal have arisen because some believe that cyanide will remain as a contaminant in tailings; moreover, there is satellite evidence that there is large plume of turbulence in the bay into which tailings are pumped (Mineral Policy Institute 2002c).

ESCAP (2001) highlights the continued failure of the PNG government, through its agencies, to develop a consistent and effective approach to social impact assessments and social monitoring in the minerals sector, as reflected in its inability to decide who should be responsible and who should pay. The approval of the Kutubu petroleum project, for example, did not require the developer to undertake a social monitoring programme.

Strip mining for phosphate has destroyed most of the forest and land of the small island of Nauru. Australia was the last of a succession of colonial rulers to mine the phosphate. Bad management by successive governments has eroded the capital base of the Nauru Phosphate Royalties Trust that could have generated substantial revenues for the government in perpetuity. Nauru has not only suffered an almost complete depletion of its limited land asset, but is now heavily in debt (ADB 2000).

## 20.4 THE EFFECTS OF IMPORTS OF TECHNOLOGY ON NATURAL CAPITAL STOCKS

Capital inflows enable the import of technology for the efficient exploitation of resources for export. In the case of natural forests, imported heavy equipment allows for economically efficient log extraction, as discussed under exports above. There was a discussion above of the impacts of export agriculture, and it was concluded that the imported agrochemical inputs could depreciate both land and inshore waters.

Mining in the Pacific is often characterised by technology that allows the economically efficient extraction of minerals from low-grade ores. However, this requires the removal of vast quantities of overburden and the generation of huge quantities of tailings.

Inshore stocks of fish, an important food source in the Pacific islands, are now more easily depleted because of use of outboard motors and nets replacing traditional methods of fishing (Hunt 1999). Governments face difficulties in devising effective policies that will limit inshore stock depreciation. More emphasis is now being placed on the devolution of fisheries management to local communities, given the high costs of central administration.

## 20.5 URBAN ENVIRONMENTS AND GLOBALISATION

It is promulgated that the impact of globalisation on urban environments (water and air quality) is a function of the volume of domestic production (induced by capital flows) and of imports, as modified by environmental policies.

Table 20.3 suggest that that the potential for urban environmental depreciation per capita has increased as a result of the rate of growth in imports outstripping the rate of population growth in two atoll countries.

*Table 20.3 Estimated growth in population and merchandise imports, Tuvalu and Kiribati, 1990-2000, %*

| Country | Population growth | Merchandise imports growth |
|---|---|---|
| Tuvalu | 21 | 100 |
| Kiribati | 26 | 56 |

*Source*: ADB (2001, Table 1, Table A6).

The waste disposal habits of households on Pacific islands can lead to the dispersal of solid wastes into the environment with attendant health risks. Poor waste collection services encourage the burning of garbage containing a high proportion of plastics, commonly generating air pollution. The 'sanitary landfills' of Pacific island cities and towns that receive unrecycled household and industrial wastes are unlikely to be lined, and the leachates that issue from them are likely to destroy the quality of underground waters, adjacent streams and inshore waters. Recycling in the region can be effective in intercepting materials that are imported or the result of foreign investment in manufacturing, before they impact the environment – such as some plastics, metals and glass (Hunt 1998). However, markets are non-existent for many types of waste that do not have an economic value, such as newspapers.

The import of technology through aid can improve urban environmental quality in the Pacific. Tuvalu is benefiting from an AusAID project that promises to reduce the spread of disease associated with poor waste management and to improve the quality of inshore waters (ADB 2002). This project has the potential to become a model for implementation among Pacific islands.

Advanced reticulated sewage systems can replace septic tanks that leak into underground aquifers and inshore waters. However, the design and implementation of culturally, financially and environmentally sustainable solutions to sewage disposal problems – particularly on atolls – pose a challenge to aid agencies (Hunt 1996). In the case of water supplies, the provision of rainwater tanks under aid projects has been beneficial. JICA (the official development arm of the Japanese government) has funded the rehabilitation of the Port Moresby water supply system. Notwithstanding the importance of aid projects in the reticulated delivery of potable water is the emphasis that should be given to the adoption of appropriate water pricing by local authorities (Hunt 1998).

## 20.6 THE ENVIRONMENTAL IMPACTS ON PACIFIC ISLANDS OF TRADE AND CAPITAL FLOWS IN THE REST OF THE WORLD

The chapter now turns to consider the effects of flows of trade and capital in the rest of the world on Pacific island environments.

An increase in global trade and investment has contributed to global economic growth. The resulting increase in the volume of gaseous emissions, principally carbon dioxide ($CO_2$), has been exceeding the assimilative capacity of the global environment and caused their accumulation in the atmosphere. The global warming that is expected to result poses the greatest long-term threat to atolls and low islands.

The IPCC (2001) projects a sea level rise of 0.09 to 0.88 m for 1990 to 2100, with a central value of 0.48 m. It is important to note that even if greenhouse gas concentration were stabilised, the sea level would continue to rise for hundreds of years.

If the mean sea level rises, present extreme levels will be attained more frequently. The increase in maximum heights will be equal to the change in the mean, which implies a significant increase in the area threatened with inundation. Under such circumstances, even incrementally small elevations in sea level would have severely negative effects on atolls and low islands through inundation and salination, manifested in a reduction in the amount of land available for human habitation as well as for agriculture.

**Policies to Mitigate Effects of Climate Change on Pacific Islands**

The domestic policies of Pacific island countries can be applied at several levels to mitigate the effects of sea level rise – the principal threat resulting from climate change – and can well be integrated with policies governing fishing, agriculture and coastal development. For example, the practice of mining coral for road construction should be discontinued; while policies that limit urban or agricultural runoff, and hence encourage coral growth, should be encouraged. Given the dearth of institutional resources to formulate mitigation and adaptive policies, Pacific island states are benefiting from policies adopted in the rest of the world. Aid to 10 Pacific island countries, aimed at reducing the rate of natural capital depreciation resulting from sea level rise, under the Pacific Islands Climate Change Assistance Programme (PICCAP), is organised by the South Pacific Regional Environment Programme (SPREP) and funded mainly by UNDP (SPREP 2002).

## 20.7 CONCLUSIONS

The volumes of timber exported were found to exceed the rate of forest renewal in the case of the Solomon Islands and Vanuatu, and the manner of exploitation was found environmentally damaging in the Solomons and Papua New Guinea. ODA for forestry administration in the three countries has not been effective in putting forest exports on a sustainable footing.

Export agriculture is implicated in the depreciation of natural capital through erosion and pollution. In the case of mineral exports, private capital flows and imported technology were shown to be responsible for serious and long lasting degradation of downstream environments. If island governments attempt to stimulate economic growth, it is likely to be through increased rates of resource exploitation.

In the case of inshore waters, the depreciation of marine resources is a function of unregulated exports for the live fish trade, together with imported technology enabling an expansion of commercial fishing. Conflict between the need to generate cash from inshore stocks and the maintenance of the same stocks for subsistence is likely to intensify. It was shown that the level of government resources devoted to inshore management is commonly inadequate.

As in areas of resource management and regulation, low levels of economic growth have prevented governments from increasing investment in urban infrastructure and regulation. And although official development assistance has been effective in the provision of potable water supplies, the percentage of the population that can access piped water is still very low in some countries. Fresh water supplies and coastal environments, particularly on atolls and smaller islands, are threatened by a rapid growth in imports per capita that has resulted in the generation of increased volumes of waste.

The world's largest tuna fishery is based on four main species that comprise a valuable common property resource in the WCPO. It was emphasised that an important task now faces Pacific island countries, through regional agencies and conventions, to devise methods that will prevent further depreciation of specific tuna stocks and by-catch species in the multi-species fishery. In this process, aid will not only be crucial to strengthen the work of regional agencies but also vital to assist governments to participate adequately in regional tuna management programmes.

Aid will continue to make up a relatively high proportion of capital inflows in Pacific island countries because of generally poor economic performance. An important aid component will be assistance for environmental and resource management necessary to combat the effects of economic globalisation. However, it is suggested that the focus of aid should broaden. It is clear that an important issue is the weakness of Pacific island governments in formulating, and more so in implementing, environmental and natural resources policy. Unless this weakness is addressed – through assistance for governance – the effects of technical assistance will tend to be nullified. An additional challenge to be met by aid agencies is to ensure that improvements and projects should be able to be maintained after the aid flow has ceased.

In addressing the environmental effects of globalisation in the rest of the world on Pacific island countries – the greenhouse effect – it was concluded that inundation due to rising sea levels could severely reduce the land area available on atolls and small islands over the next 100 years. ODA to support risk analysis, combined with cost-benefit analysis of a range of protection strategies, would appear to be a useful exercise to gain time and provide information for Pacific island governments. In the long run, immigration policy linked to climate change will need be developed in the rest of the world with respect to low islands and atolls in the Pacific and other regions.

## NOTES

1. New Caledonia and French Polynesia are French colonies, while US territories and possessions in the Pacific include Hawaii, Guam, American Samoa, and the Northern Marianas.
2. Signatories to SPARTECA are Cook Islands, the Federated States of Micronesia, Fiji, Kiribati, Marshall Islands, Nauru, Niue, Papua New Guinea, Solomon Islands, Tonga, Tuvalu, Vanuatu and Samoa. The agreement also provides for special treatment and assistance to be extended to the smaller island countries Cook Islands, Kiribati, Nauru, Niue, Tonga, Tuvalu and Samoa.
3. Kiribati and Tuvalu, small economies with large Exclusive Economic Zones (EEZs), usually receive a very high proportion of their total government revenues in the form of licence fees from foreign tuna fleets. In 2001, the Tuvalu government derived US$6.7 million from licences, 50 per cent of total government revenue (ADB 2002, Ch 6). Even in PNG, which has a relatively large and diversified economy, the government is anticipating that the large tuna stocks will be an important contributor to future national income and development.
4. Pacific Community (PC) member countries are American Samoa, Australia, Fiji, France, French Polynesia, Guam, Kiribati, Marshall Islands, FS Micronesia, Nauru, New Caledonia, New Zealand, Northern Mariana Islands, Palau, Papua New Guinea, Samoa, Solomon Islands, Tonga, Tuvalu, USA, Vanuatu.

   FFA member countries are Australia, Cook Islands, Federated States of Micronesia, Fiji, Kiribati, Republic of Marshall Islands, Nauru, New Zealand, Niue, Palau, Papua New Guinea, Samoa, Solomon Islands, Tonga, Tuvalu and Vanuatu.

## REFERENCES


ADB (2000), *Country Highlights*, Manila: ADB: http://www.adb.org/Countries/Highlights/default.asp.

ADB (2001), *Asian Development Outlook 2001: II. Economic Trends and Prospects in Developing Asia*, Manila: ADB: http://www.adb.org/Documents/Books/ADO/2001/default.asp.

ADB (2002), *Tuvalu 2002: The Role of Government in Development*, Manila: ADB.

Agriculture Research and Advisory (SDN) BHD (ARAB) (1994), *Feasibility Study of Vailala Oil Palm Project*, Kajang, Malaysia: ARAB.

Bank of Papua New Guinea (2001), *Quarterly Economic Bulletin*, **29** (3).

Bouro, G. (2001), Commissioner of Forests, Honiara, personal communication.

Duncan, R., S. Cuthbertson and M. Bosworth (1999), *Pursuing Economic Reform in the Pacific*, Manila: ADB.

ESCAP (2001), *Integrating Environmental Considerations into the Economic Decision-making Process*, Bangkok: ESCAP.

Hampton, J, A. Lewis and P. Williams (2000), 'The Western and central Pacific tuna fishery: overview of the fishery and current status of tuna stocks', http://www.spc.org.nc/OceanFish/Docs/wcptf.htm

Highland Pacific (2002), http://www.highpacific.com.au/news&info/factsheet.htm.

Hunt, C. (1996), 'Tackling environmental management problems on Pacific atolls', *Pacific Economic Bulletin*, **11** (2), 58-69.
Hunt, C. (1997), 'Cooperative approaches in marine resource management in the South Pacific', in P. Larmour (ed.), *The Governance of Common Property in the Pacific Region*, Australian National University: Asia Pacific Press, pp. 145-64.
Hunt C. (1998), *Pacific Development Sustained; Policies for Pacific Environments*, Pacific Policy Paper 32, Australian National University, Canberra: Asia-Pacific Press.
Hunt, C. (1999), 'Fiji's fisheries: their contribution to development and their future', *Marine Policy*, **23** (6), 571-85.
Hunt, C. (2002a), 'Efficient and equitable forest rent capture in three Pacific island nations: Opportunities and impediments in forest policy reform', Small-scale Forest Economics, *Management and Policy*, **1** (1), 1-15.
Hunt, C. (ed.) (2002b), *Production, Privatisation and Preservation in Papua New Guinea Forestry*, Institute for Environment and Development, London/Monograph 38, Port Moresby: National Research Institute.
IPCC (2001), *Climate Change 2001: Impacts, Adaptation and Vulnerability*, IPCC Secretariat, c\o World Meteorological Organization, 7bis Avenue de la Paix, C.P. 2300, CH-1211 Geneva 2, Switzerland.
Mineral Policy Institute, (2002a), *The 'Leaked' World Bank Report on Ok Tedi*: http://www.mpi.org.au/oktedi/world_bank_summary.html.
Mineral Policy Institute (2002b), *Recommendations on the Ramu Nickel Project*: http://www.mpi.org.au/std/ramu_fisheries.html.
Mineral Policy Institute (2002c), Satellite Image of Lihir Island and Mine: http://www.mpi.org.au/std/images/overview_small.jpg.
OECD (1994), *The Environmental Effects of Trade*, Paris: OECD.
Panayotou, T. (2000), *Globalization and Environment*, CID Working Paper 53, Center for International Development, Harvard University: http://www.cid.harvard .edu/cidwp/053.htm.
SPC (2001a), *South Pacific Commission Coastal Fisheries Programme*: http://www.spc.org.nc.coastfish/News/Fish-News/89/Gillett.htm.
SPREP (2002), *South Pacific Regional Environment Programme, Projects*: http://www.sidsnet.org/pacific/sprep/Project/default.htm.
Tupou S. (2000), *Cash Cropping: The Case of Squash Pumpkins in Tonga*: http://www.abc.net.au/ra/carvingout/issues/squash.htm.
United Nations General Assembly (1998), *Development of a Vulnerability Index for Small Island Developing States*, a report for the Secretary General on the outcome of the Global Conference on the Sustainable Development of Small Island Developing States, New York: United Nations.
Vanuatu Department of Forests (2000), *Annual report 2000*, Port Vila: Government of Vanuatu.

# Index